AF552788

Exploring India's Medieval Centuries

Exploring India's Medieval Centuries

Essays in History, Society, Culture and Technology

Harbans Mukhia

EXPLORING INDIA'S MEDIEVAL CENTURIES
Harbans Mukhia

First Published, 2010

ISBN 978-93-5002-047-0 (Hb)

Published by
AAKAR BOOKS
28 E Pocket IV, Mayur Vihar Phase I, Delhi-110 091
Phone : 011-2279 5505 Telefax : 011-2279 5641
aakarbooks@gmail.com; www.aakarbooks.com

Printed at
Mudrak, 30 A Patparganj, Delhi-110 091

For Maurice Aymard
in friendship and admiration

Contents

Preface

Time was when, during the nineteenth century and much of the twentieth, History dealt in certitudes. Its highly overstated claims to being a 'science' in the shadow of Positivism and its extension, Marxism, gave it the image of an intellectual endeavour in search of an 'objective truth' lying out there in dusty records in the archives. Since then, over the past few decades, things have come a long way with the realisation that the aesthetic of History rests in it forever being tentative, forever engaged in renewal through self-questioning. Its rationality does not eliminate its ambiguities, its ambivalence and vulnerability; on the contrary. Its methodology — and its language — in some ways stands in contrast to the methodology of natural sciences and this realisation does not quite amount to an admission of inferiority.

In this sense every historiographical exercise is an exploration, a tentative hypothesis, subject to revision or rejection through one's own second glance or the glances of others. It is in this frame that the essays put together in this anthology *explore* some themes and motifs in the vast canvas of India's expansive medieval centuries. Their vintage varies from around three decades to a couple of months even as the most recent ones too have emerged through a long period of incubation. These have all been published in some journal or book or an earlier version of this anthology; their availability in one volume makes for easy access.

The first two essays engage with the notion of time in two different historiographical contexts, though not unrelated to each other. Time is after all one of the two fundamental constituents of the study of history anywhere, the other being space. We are all historians of ancient India or medieval Europe or the modern world etc. Our notion of time therefore forms a critical perspective of our reconstruction of history. Abu'l Fazl, historian par excellence of medieval India, disengages his reconstruction of history from its conventional Islamic moorings by positing an alternative to the *hijri* era; he thus displaces the old Islam-*kufr* dichotomy with a new dichotomy situated between universal religiosity and sectarian religions. The essay appears in *Studies in History,* vol. 25(1), which was due in July-December 2008. 'Time in India's Religions and History' is located against a much wider backdrop of Western construction of Oriental time as cyclical and its own as linear and the gross distortions it introduces in the study of history, both Indian and European. It is a revised version of two earlier drafts published in Sølvi Songer, ed, *Making Sense of Global History,* Oslo, 2001 and *Historical Inquiry* (Taipei), 29, 2002.

Urdu language and its magnificent poetic expression, the *ghazal,* is what I have grown up with but never had the opportunity to study. A chance to review *Urdu and Muslim South Asia* edited by Christopher Shackle for *Book Review* opened the window to follow up on this deficiency; the result was the paper on 'The Celebration of Failure as Dissent in Urdu *Ghazal*'. I was fascinated by the fact that *ghazal,* whether in Persian or Urdu, never celebrated success, but always stood up for failure. The paper seeks the meaning of this celebration and finds in it a form of social dissent. Published in *Modern Asian Studies,* vol. 33 (4), 1999.

'"Medieval India": An Alien Conceptual Hegemony?' appeared in the inaugural issue of *The Medieval History Journal* in 1998; the issue was centred on the theme of the history of the notion of 'medieval' around the world.

The year 1969, centenary year of Mahatma Gandhi's birth, was ironically rocked by a series of communal riots, which, to compound the irony, were especially violent in his home state, Gujarat. The Govt of India was worried and, among other steps, called a meeting of All India Radio officials in New Delhi for a discussion. Romila Thapar, Bipan Chandra and I were asked to address them on the relationship between communalism and history writing. These were meant to be popular lectures. The People's Publishing House (PPH) got to know of these and insisted on publishing them as a booklet. Since then it has gone into almost innumerable reprints. The underlying premise of the booklet was that communalism was virtually the creation of British colonialism and history was the instrument of its wide propagation. I for one began to have serious doubts about this premise as time passed; the result was a reappraisal of that argument and my own paper in the booklet. 'Communalism and the Writing of Medieval Indian History – A Reappraisal' first appeared in *Social Scientist*, 123, 1983.

In the heat of the Babari masjid-Ram Janmabhumi dispute in the late 1980s and early 90s, as an 'aware' citizen I tried to investigate the genesis of the dispute in terms of historical evidence from the medieval sources and a visit to the site. The paper here reproduces that investigation. The conclusion that repeatedly forced itself was that no temple, much less a Ram temple, existed underneath the masjid and that it was not until the late 19th century that the site came to be identified where a temple devoted to Ram had once supposedly stood. First appearance in Lallanji Gopal, ed, *Ayodhya: History, Archaeology and Tradition*, Kashiraj Trust, Varanasi, 1994.

Sometime in the early 1970s, I had undertaken to explore the ideology of the Bhakti movement of the medieval centuries, taking as my entry point the poetry of one of the movement's major figures, Dadu Dayal. Growing as we did in the 1960s and 70s on the staple diet of a veritable class struggle between the Mughal state and the common masses, i.e. the peasantry, what struck me was the ideological continuum, in lieu of contradiction, between, say, the political ideas of Abu'l Fazl at the highest plane and those of Dadu Dayal at the ground level. Its implications worked themselves out much later, when I began to feel the oppressive imposition of a neat class struggle upon a scenario which lent little support to it. First published in D P Chattopadhyay, ed, *History and Society: Essays in Honour of Professor Nihar Ranjan Ray*, K P Bagchi, Calcutta, 1978.

But my interest in Marxism and its methodology of studying history was still strong. The examination of Marx's perceptions of pre-colonial India and the rich insights the methodology yielded even in the midst of his complete misunderstanding of India forms the substance of this exploration. 'Marx on Pre-Colonial India: An Evaluation' was a homage to him on the centenary of his death in 1983. First published in Diptendra Banerjee, ed, *Marxian Theory and the Third World*, Sage Publications, New Delhi, 1985.

Thus far the intellectual and cultural milieu of India's medieval period; or some aspects of these. There was too the vast arena of the period's economy and society. 'Was There Feudalism in Indian History?' was originally the Presidential Address to the Medieval India Section of the Indian History Congress at its 40th session in 1979 in Waltair. For the preceding decade I had been teaching and developing a course on Feudalism for my post-graduate students at JNU; this essentially comprised a theoretical exploration of the concept of feudalism and its contextualisation in a comparison between medieval Europe and medieval India. The notion of an Indian feudalism was then hegemonic in Indian historiography, but my own growing dissatisfaction with it was forcing me to reconsider the terms on which it had been constructed. It was indeed a point by point replica of the Pirennean version of European feudalism, which was premised upon a trade-feudalism dichotomy, itself under severe strain in European historiography then. It led me to expand the terms to encompass the mode of production as a whole which in turn was to be premised upon the nature of ecology in each region, the given and developing technology of agricultural production and the forms of labour organisation. On these terms, 'Indian feudalism' didn't stand a chance. The paper was published in *The Journal of Peasant Studies* in 1981 and became the centre of an international debate resulting, in 1985, in a special double issue of the *JPS* entitled *Feudalism and Non-European Societies*, also published as a book by Frank Cass, London. But the debate did not end with it; it carried on until 1993. Therefore a second book, incorporating a large part of the first and some new contributions, was published as *The Feudalism Debate* by Manohar Publishers in New Delhi in 2000. It was a major debate of my academic life and was a great learning process, especially the familiarisation with enormous diversity of opinions and views among committed Marxist historians around the world even on a single theme. It is with gratitude that I note that as the debate basically centred on Professor R S Sharma's notion of Indian feudalism and my problems with it, one great benefit I received from it all was that Professor Sharma's affection for me grew many folds with the debate. It is rare to come across such overwhelming grace which goes with such immense scholarship.

'Peasant Production and Medieval Indian Society' was my response to the debate.

The summer of 1976 took me to the fabulously rich Rajasthan State Archives, Bikaner, in search of data for the problem of below the legal surface extortions by dominant groups in village society from those with least resources. The *chitthis* (letters) written by the state's Diwan in eastern Rajasthan to various officials and functionaries on receipt of complaints against them instructing them to desist from illegal extortions open a fascinating window to the working of power relations in rural society, invariably to the detriment of the groups at its lower end. It also points to the forms of resistance to such extortions. The paper, 'Illegal Extortions from Peasants, Artisans and Menials in Eighteenth Century Eastern Rajasthan' resulted from that visit. Published in *The Indian Economic and Social History Review*, vol. 14 (2) 1977.

The *Risāla-i Zirā't* (A Treatise on Agriculture) is the only manuscript of its kind, written in 1785 in Bengal and now lodged in the Edinburgh University Library. Although it purports to deal with agriculture, its chief emphasis is on revenue collection and the distortions that had become part of it. Excerpts of it had earlier been translated in two versions, with varying degree of veracity. This is the first complete translation. It had earlier appeared in my *Perspectives on Medieval History*, Vikas Publishing House, New Delhi, 1993.

The last section explores the theme of technology in two

papers: one deals with agricultural technology in medieval north India first published in a badly mauled form in A Roy and S K Bagchi, eds, *Technology in Ancient and Medieval India*, Sundeep Prakashan, New Delhi, 1986; and the other with the problematic of how the superiority of technology is no guarantee of its social acceptance. The argument rested on a case study of the introduction of the filature silk technology in Bengal during the eighteenth century by the East India Co. The paper first appeared in *The Indian Historical Review*, vol. 11 (1-2), 1984-85.

I could perhaps say with some satisfaction that a part of a verse of Faiz Ahmad Faiz – *har haqīqat majāz ho jāyé* (let every established truth become suspect) – has been the guiding light of my endeavours, whatever be their worth.

December 2009.

The Intellectual and Cultural Milieu

1

Time in Abu'l Fazl's Historiography

Time is precious and is irreplaceable.
Abu'l Fazl, *Akbar Nāmā*.[1]

In writing the *Akbar Nāmā* in two huge volumes (and the *Ā'in-i Akbarī* as its companion) Abu'l Fazl was acutely aware of the departure he was making in history writing, one that marked him out not only from a host of fellow historians of his age but also from a very long tradition that had been their shared inheritance. His own innocuous description of history and the historian as 'the events of the world recorded in a chronological order ... and those who are proficient (in recording them) are known as historians'[2] hides an elaborate construction of meaning into his project. 'The general group of writers set down nothing but what they could quickly lay their hands upon.... By commands of my heart, the help of my resolution, and the corpulence of my good fortune, a new palace has been constructed for composition in this auspicious record, and the narration has assumed a new gait.... My jewel has been placed before connoisseurs ...'[3] This was indeed 'the story of stories',[4] an epic of epics. It had received approbation from those who were not 'self-opinionated ones and not immersed in received knowledge'[5] and disapproval from those 'who had staked their money on what was customary.'[6]

It was not in the basic form of a work of history that Abu'l Fazl was being very innovative; indeed, he was building upon the legacy from the preceding generations of professional historians in India itself and, by a long shot, from Iran, inasmuch as the reduction of a 'universal history' to regional, dynastic and in the end an annalistic account of the current ruler had been the predominant practice among them.[7] The departure inhered in constituting an alternative conception of time in history from the almost universally practiced Islamic conception by historians of the Muslim world. Innate to the alternative conception of time was an alternative worldview. Abu'l Fazl sought to constitute a new worldview of the past and the future.

The rise of Islam in seventh century Arabia had, among so many other things, created an idea of history in its cultural zone, where virtually little existed earlier. The Arabic word for history, *tārīkh,* seems to have had no pre-Islamic provenance. It does not occur in the Quran, nor in the old *hadīs*, observes Franz Rosenthal, in his classic work, *A History of Muslim Historiography*. 'But to all appearances, the word *tārīkh* is mentioned in Arabic literature first together with the stories of the introduction of the Muslim era.'[8] A more modern voice reaffirms Rosenthal's perception: 'The Arabs learnt a new history when they acquired a new religion.'[9]

Time in Islamic theology and history did not, expectedly, conform to a single pattern. If in theology it was construed as eternal and therefore without boundaries,[10] it was also on the other hand perceived with a beginning and an end. On one hand it was attributed infinite totality, on the other it was seen as juxtaposition of discontinuous moments, or instants adding up to totality until the Day of Judgment.[11] However, E Goodman's emphasis that discontinuous time is one among several strands of religious thought in Islam seems appropriate.[12] Islam had inherited Christianity's notion of linear time from Creation to the Day of Judgment. This was nevertheless nuanced by the cyclicity of the appearance of prophets until the arrival of Muhammad. The old Arab tradition of genealogy itself reinforces linear time; its extension to dynastic history, on the other hand, implicitly replicates cyclicity as in the work of the landmark historian Ibn Khaldun.[13]

With all its variations and nuances, the institution of the

hijri era marks that sharp departure in the conceptualisation of historical time that remained predominant in the Islamic world. It divided time vertically into two clearly marked units: the age of *jahiliya*, ignorance, savagery, before the rise of Islam and the beginning of history with its rise. Since Muhammad was, for the devout Muslims, the last of all prophets, and the Quran revealed by God through him the ultimate truth, inscribed in this construction was interminable conflict between the Truth and all else that is by definition false, with the eventual victory of the Truth, i.e. Islam, assured throughout the universe before the Day of Judgment. Whether the conflict was to take violent shape or remained dormant, there was to be no shared space between Islam's truth and the rest. In some ways this too was an inheritance from Christianity which also visualised itself as God's own Truth, revealed through Jesus, which would prevail the world over before the Judgment Day arrived. Indeed, claim of monopoly over the ultimate truth and the implicit assumption of universal triumph over all others constitute the driving force of all proselytising ideologies, whether religious, such as Christianity or Islam, or secular, such as Marxism.

This division of historical time before and after the birth of Islam formed the predominant frame of reference for history writing in most of the Islamic world, with the *hijri* calendar as the temporal straitjacket. The histories of different regions compiled in what for us now constitute medieval centuries mostly virtually replicate the *jahiliya*-Islam dichotomy, inasmuch as the historian very seldom shows much interest in the remote histories of those regions; these comprised the age of *jahiliya* in those parts, best ignored.

In India, of the numerous histories written in the Persian language, a historian rarely ventures into the past before Islam had established itself here. Akbar's courtier and unofficial historian, Mullā Abdul Qādir Badāunī, puts it very graphically why he began his 3-volume *Muntakhab al-Tawārīkh* with Subuktgīn, father of Mahmūd of Ghaznī. He could have begun it with the conquest of Sindh by Muhammad bin Qāsim in the early eighth century when Islam made its first incursion into

India; but he chose not to, because Islam could not get a permanent footing then. It was with the conquests of Sultan Mahmūd of Ghaznī, son of Nāsir al-Dīn Subuktgīn, that 'Islam was never (thereafter) eliminated from this land' which prompted Badāunī to begin his narration with him.[14] Badāunī puts the perspective explicitly; others are less explicit. But the perspective is common to most historians, for whom forays into the pre-Muslim age are unnecessary. And the *hijri* era is of course the only time frame employed.

The history of these regions, here India, is then the history of the Muslim rule. The ruler is not only a Muslim by his religious profession, but he rules by legitimacy derived from Islamic theology, idiom and jargon: the reading of the *khutba* by the Imam at the congregation of Muslims for the Friday prayers, the invocation of recognition by the Caliph as the legitimate ruler, frequent use of the phrase 'armies of Islam wiping out *kufr* from the land', seeking theologians' opinions for the legitimacy of rulers' actions—all these and much more place the ruler firmly in the camp of Islam. He rules on behalf the *millat*, the Muslim community. He is above all a *Muslim* ruler.

Most works of history reflect this profile of the ruler, even if most rulers were differentially inclined towards the implementation of its diktats. The format of these works is evocative of the premises underlying them. These open with the praise of Allāh, go on to lavish praise on Muhammad, followed by caliphs, the past sultans, down to the current ruler. The political lineage drawn here is firmly, unambiguously Islamic.

It is here that Abu'l Fazl makes a profound departure. He opens his *Akbar Nāmā* with the praise of Allāh, for sure, and makes no mention of Muhammad and the caliphs. From Allāh he goes on to Adam and states that between Adam and Akbar, 52 generations had elapsed. He knew the history of 26, but not that of the other 26 and goes on to narrate what he portrays as history.[15] With one stroke then he disengages history writing from its Islamic lineage and in projecting Akbar as the 53rd generation descendant of the first human being, he disengages his political lineage from its Islamic moorings. Akbar was the ruler of all humanity, not a *Muslim* ruler. Interestingly, Abu'l Fazl never refers to Muhammad or the caliphs etc. except when he is citing a passage with the prophet's name in it, and this happens just a couple of times in the *Akbar Nāmā*.

More emphatically, Abu'l Fazl refuses to deploy the *hijri* era as the temporal frame for his work and thereby denies any break in the flow of historical time from Adam to the age of Akbar. His teleology begins with the birth of humanity, as it were, to culminate in the person of Akbar, and history, beginning with Adam, to culminate in Akbar's reign. He is somewhat undecided about the beginning of Time handed down by Islam, conventionally as 14000 years, and of the birth of Adam 7000 years ago.[16] He cites Imam Ja'far al-Sādiq and Ibn al 'Arabī to the effect that there were thousands of Adams before Adam and one race of Adam was succeeded by another, with overlap between their last stages.[17] But Abu'l Fazl at one time accepts the date of the birth of Adam and then casts doubt on it, both on the same page.[18] He examines the birth of the universe against the evidence of astronomy, 'reliable ancient books of the Hindus and of Cathay' and successive chronicles of the sages of those regions, and concludes: '...it appears that the beginning of the universe or its inhabitants and the source of the manifestation of God's attributes has not become visible. Either it is eternal, as was held by several sages of yore, or of such antiquity as to merge with eternity.'[19] He recounts several notions of time around the world and therefore the origin of the universe and eclectically observes: 'Traditions and stories like these are current in the vast expanse of God's creation and it is not far fetched that these may [all] be true. There might have been many Adams.'[20] However, in the midst of incertitude, one teleology definitively marks Abu'l Fazl's entire vision: The birth of humanity with Adam is legitimised in its culmination in the birth of Akbar and the beginning of time to find its fulfilment in the reign of Akbar. Time freezes, though it does not end here. Abu'l Fazl inverts the received notion of historical time: for him it has an uncertain beginning but a definite goal—the reign of Akbar, after which there is eternity. In some very interesting ways, Abu'l Fazl seems to be replicating here the Islamic concept of Muhammad being the last prophet. He seems particularly to have borrowed from Ibn al-'Arabī's extremely complex idea of the 'Perfect Man', (*insān-i kāmil*).[21] Muhammad was for Ibn al-'Arabī the *insān-i kāmil*; Akbar was for Abu'l Fazl.[22] Historians have often seen in this construction outright flattery of an imperial patron by his minion[23]; they miss out on a massive alternative perspective of history under construction, a major deviation from the established pattern, which in significant ways also reflected the evolving ideology of the state under Akbar.

The Islam vs *kufr* dichotomy, much as faith vs infidelity dichotomy in Christianity, inescapably implicated subjugation and the ultimate elimination of the latter. Akbar's state abandoned this dichotomy in favour of the ideology of 'harmony' and 'absolute peace' (*sulh kul*) in which no religious denomination would have primacy; for him 'reason inhabited every religion... how was it then that one religion and one community that was relatively young—it had not been around even for a thousand years—should receive affirmation at the expense of others?'[24]

This ideology implicated abrogating the interruption of the flow of time and therefore of the *hijri* era. In a beautiful passage, Abu'l Fazl erases the dividing lines between the past, the present and the future: 'Indeed, today, tomorrow, yesterday, the present and the absent may have the appearance of contrariness. But with the nursling of the divine light (his favourite phrase for Akbar) ...the future and the past are subordinate to the present and the absent is visible like the present before him.'[25] Abu'l Fazl in any case had a rather low opinion of the general tenor of the *hijri* era, which for him 'opens with a day of rejoicing for foes and distress for the dear ones',[26] and one 'that presages disappointment.'[27] He substituted for it the *Ilāhī* (or Divine) era, drafted at Akbar's command in the 28th year of his reign by the multifaceted Iranian intellectual, Fathullah Shirazi, courtier of Akbar, but made effective retrospectively from the inception of his reign.[28] Indeed, a difference of 25 days between the Akbar's accession to the throne and the beginning of the calendar was written off so that the onset of the spring in March, marking the renewal of the earth, and the beginning of the exceptional reign, marking the renewal of time, could coincide with the inauguration of the new era and the new calendar.[29] The notion of what is divine, but not Islamic, permeates several of Akbar's measures, the other very important one being the *Dīn-i Ilāhī*,[30] and constitutes a basic premise of Abu'l Fazl's construction of history, indeed of his entire worldview. This was tantamount to virtual repudiation of Islam. Indeed, he often avoids the use of the term Islam and substitutes for it a rather derogatory phrase, *'Ahmadī kayish'* [sect or religion of Ahmad (Muhammad)].[31] Clearly, by assigning to it the status of one among several sects, Abu'l Fazl is driving a hole into its universalist ambitions and its claims to being the conclusive religion. Very fond of the pre-Islamic Persian language term *farr-i izdi* (divine light) he generally avoids *nūr* because of its Islamic association, for Allah is envisioned in Islam as immense light. *Farr* opens up the space for the inclusion of the notion of light from a number of sources from various cultural zones. *Nūr* is included in it of course; but also fire, sacred to both Hindūs and Pārsīs, the Sun, extremely important to the Hindūs and the pre-Islamic Egyptians, and the notion of Enlightenment, a fundamental premise of Sūfī doctrine. Inclusiveness, in lieu of subjugation and conquest, was the new ideology.[32]

This worldview is deeply premised upon a universal God and a universal religiosity in opposition to a sectarian God and a denominational religion. Clearly his chief target of opposition was Islam, which envisages Allāh in its own sectarian vision, although Abu'l Fazl expresses his disinclination towards all sectarian religious identities. If a religion emanating from a sectarian God, with claims of monopoly over the ultimate truth seeks subjugation of other sects, Abu'l Fazl posits harmony and peace among them all as the alternative. Harmony becomes an ideological construct with him at the opposite end of dispute, conflict and conquest. 'Absolute peace' (*sulh kul*) is for him 'a four-square garden of concord',[33] 'a pleasant abode of peace with all.'[34] The ideology of *sulh kul* was not merely a construct of Abu'l Fazl's mind; this was also the foundation of the new state evolving under Akbar's supremacy. The coincidence between the intellectual architecture of Abu'l Fazl and the operative state policy of Akbar seems complete in this one case. On Abu'l Fazl's testimony, 'the lord of the world (Akbar) rules on the basis of *sulh kul*; every group professes its doctrine without apprehension and everyone worships God in accordance with one's faith.'[35]

Thus in lieu of the Islam vs *kufr* dichotomy, Abu'l Fazl constitutes an alternative dichotomy, that between universal religiosity and sectarian religions. This is his 'rationality', not one akin to post-Enlightenment rationality which counterposes itself to any legacy of the 'dark ages' of superstition, its designated equivalent of religion or religiosity. His 'rationality' is deeply rooted in religiosity. It draws inspiration from India's ground level, as it were, where a massive movement of protest against religious discord was flourishing and a universal God for all was conceptualised in the poetry of such epoch making figures as Kabir, Nanak and a host of leaders of Bhakti.

Abu'l Fazl's own life history, propelled by his ever inquisitive mind, inspired him to question a great part of received wisdom. The period of his intellectual pursuits covered much of the second half of the sixteenth century, which witnessed more than the usual anxieties in the Islamic world. As Islam neared the first millennium of its existence, the neat round figure of 1000, implying a vision of completion and signifying a probable closure, had exacerbated the anxieties. Its history was teeming with movements of protest, especially at the loss of its upheaval-creating egalitarian ideology and its awe-inspiring energy to the creation of huge empires and powerful states. With these came enormously privileged groups, both secular and ecclesiastical, in turn creating avenues for protests in the guise of a yearning for the imagined pristine purity of the days of Muhammad and the first four 'pious' caliphs, unmindful that three of these four had been assassinated by fellow Muslims. Sufism had long been a form of dissent against these distortions, albeit taking a passive stance of refusing contact with the state, although even this was not uniformly the conduct of all Sūfī orders. Ambivalence in relationship with the state was integral to many of them.

There was, however, a more strident assertion of protest within the fold of Islam. This was the Mahdawī movement.[36] The concept of a Mahdī, one who would revive puritanical Islam, does not occur in the Quran but is traceable to some of the *hadīses*.[37] As the millennium drew to a close, a powerful Mahdawī movement began around the middle of the sixteenth century, in the years when Sher Shah's descendants were ruling over a declining empire, with deteriorating authority. The leader of the movement was Syed Muhammad of Jaunpur, very erudite and incorruptible—always a threat to Authority, religious or other. The movement grew and along with it grew the nervousness of the 'ulamā—its chief targets—and the rulers, the 'ulamā's protectors. The counterattack launched by their combined forces left no one, with the slightest predilection for dissent, untouched. Any dissent, or suspicion of it, would now be branded Mahdawī, and persecution would follow. In its wake would come penury and privation.

Shaikh Mubārak, father of Abu'l Fazl, was an extremely learned Islamist scholar, with a very wide range of knowledge, who had taught himself and his sons to interrogate received wisdom. After Syed Muhammad of Jaunpur, he ideally fitted the target of the 'ulamā's persecution. Abandoned by old friends, unable to find new ones, the Mubārak family experienced extremes of penury and privation. This experience and his own upbringing in the haunted family turned Abu'l Fazl into some sort of an intellectual rebel. In a longish note, at the end of vol. 2 of the *Akbar Nāmā*, comprising a sort of intellectual autobiography, Abu'l Fazl repeatedly emphasises his quest for intellectual freedom, 'the result of right purpose'.[38] He immersed himself not only in the study of Islam but several other religions and civilisations. All this reinforced his questioning spirit, unwilling to accept anything merely because it had prevalence or had been so received. He was forever seeking his own answers.[39] From here it was a short distance to questioning the legitimacy of the all encompassing tensions within the Muslim community and between Islam and other religions and to construct the alternative ideology of harmony. The same spirit had led his patron Akbar to ground the working of his state on the principle of harmony in lieu of conflict between religions.

If Abu'l Fazl stands out and virtually stands alone among medieval Indian historians to have disengaged history writing from the axis of Islam, he had nevertheless a fellow traveller in the neighbouring Iran. Azar Kayvān, a near contemporary of Abu'l Fazl, had similarly undertaken to establish continuity of Iran's historical links and its imperial destiny with an imagined pre-Adam Adam whom he designates Mahābad, a name that Abu'l Fazl also invokes as the first Pārsī. Kayvān too was seeking to break the link between Iran's history and its Islamic roots, taking this long way back.[40] But it is worth remembering that Azar Kayvān was a Pārsī by birth and religious persuasion and Abu'l Fazl a Muslim by birth and intellectual training. Indeed, he was reported by some near contemporary and later writers to have been a devout Muslim in his personal life.[41] It was probably much tougher for him to break out of the straitjacket that had bound his fellow professionals before and after him, not to mention his own times.

Abu'l Fazl's extreme, sometimes ridiculous obsession with the accuracy of temporal calculation is also a marked departure from the current, rather vague practice among historians. He had acquired an expert's training in mathematics, astronomy, and in the study of different calendars: Hindu, Jain, Greek, Hebrew, and Islamic.[42] Bābur in his *Memoirs* also frequently refers to time. He notes that while back home 'in our countries' *kīchagūndūz* (day and night) 'is divided into 24 parts, each called '*sā'at*' which is in turn divided into 60 parts, each called a *daqīqā* 'so that a day and night consist of 1440' *daqīqās*; on the other hand, 'the people of Hind divide the night-and-day into 60 parts, each called a *gharī*. They also divide the night into four and day into four, calling each part a *pahr*.'[43] Bābur, like almost everyone else among the Mughal writers, begins to use the

Hindi terms *pahr* and *gharī*. His daughter, Gulbadan, almost always uses these Hindi words in an account written in otherwise chaste Persian.[44] But for most of his record, Bābur has the Islamic prayers (*namāz*) as the reference point. He would record an occurrence with the preface 'Near the Afternoon Prayer....', 'Somewhere between the two Prayers of the day....', '...between the Afternoon and Evening Prayers....' etc.[45] However, vague as these references to time are, it is hard to excel the delights of vagueness in his reference to Mewat, which 'Hasan Khān Mīwātī and his ancestors one after another had ruled with absolute sway for a hundred years or two.'[46]

Not for Abu'l Fazl any of this vagueness. His calculation must include the exact number of millennia, centuries, years, months and days. Thus 191 rulers ruled over Kashmir for 4109 years, 11 months and 9 days.[47] Akbar spent precisely 3 months and 29 days in Kashmir.[48] As his chronicle of the reign of Akbar proceeds along annalistic lines, he notes the hour and the minute when each regnal year commenced. Thus the seventh year began at 3 hours and 49 minutes (past midnight) on 15 March, 1562.[49] The ninth year opened at 3 hours and 27 minutes after the night of 11 March, 1564.[50]

In the midst of his search for exact temporal measurements and dates, Abu'l Fazl at times mixes up mythological and historical figures. He calculates the age of the Hindu epic, *Mahābhārat* at 4831 counting down in reverse from the 40th regnal year of Akbar, towards the close of the *dwāpar yuga,* 135 years before commencement of the *kali yuga*.[51] Or, he records: 'it is said that 2,355 years, 5 months and 27 days prior to the 40th year of the Divine Era, an ascetic named Mahābah kindled [the flame] in a fire temple and worshipped God.'[52] In the same *ā'in* on *sūbah* Malwa, enumerating the duration of the reigns of the past rulers of the region amounting in all to 1062 years, 11 months and 17 days, sometimes he records the exact number of years, months and days of a reign, at others he gives round figures like 100 years, 80 years and so forth.[53] At any rate, he does not follow a uniform pattern while enumerating the rulers and their reigns in all the regions; sometimes he gives detailed accounts of years, months and days (and that in select cases) and at others just years. The exercise had clearly exhausted even such a painstaking scholar like him.

Abu'l Fazl's monumental journey along a new historiographical trajectory found many admirers but few takers down the subsequent centuries.

NOTES

1. Abu'l Fazl, *Akbar Nāmā* (Persian text), vol. 2, ed. Maulavi Abd al-Rahim, Calcutta, 1871, p. 136: *auqāt-i girāmī ke badal nadārad.*
2. Abu'l Fazl, *Ā'in-i Akbarī* (Persian text), vol. I, ed. H Blochmann, Calcutta, 1872, p. 280: *sawānih-i rūzgār ke pāye bund-i sāl meh shudah dar aurāq jāi gīrad 'ilm-i tārīkh bar shumārand wa dānindah rā maurikh guyand.*
   This definition in fact inherits characteristics of history writing from its Arab-Islamic moorings. On one hand, the notion of Islam as the universe-encompassing religion implicated the history of any region as part of world history; on the other, insistence on very minute chronological location of any event was reinforced by the ascription of numerical value to each letter of the Arabic alphabet, inherited from Hebrew, enabling historians to reinforce the numerically recorded dates with a series of words or a verse.
3. Abu'l Fazl, *Akbar Nāmā,* vol. 2, p. 381: *girūhā girūh-i 'āmmah ghair az sukhnān-i dast zadah-i zūd fahm nanawisand.... Bafarmāish-i dil wa yāwari-i himmat wa tanūmandī-i bakht-i bīdār dar īn humayūn nāmā sukhnān sarāī rā kākh-i dīgar bar afrākht... wa gauhar-khud rā basirfiyān dīdahwar rasīdah.*
4. Ibid. p. 384 *dāstān-i dāstān*
5. Ibid., p. 381: *rah zadah-i pindār wa ghāratkardah-i taqlīd.*
6. Ibid. The editor seems to have made a mess of this passage, *ke naqd-i khwīsh bagarugānī-i kānchah mālūf dādah und*, and the translator, Beveridge, has made it worse: 'the faction which had staked its money in the old petty shops'; see H. Beveridge, Eng. Tr. of *The Akbar Nāmā,* vol. 2, Delhi repnt. 1989, p. 555. A long discussion with my Persian language Ustad, Dr Yunus Jaffrey, has led us to believe that the text should have read: *naqd-i khwīsh bagarugānī ke āncheh mālūf būd dādah und.* As always, I am very grateful to him for the insight.
7. See Harbans Mukhia, *Historians and Historiography During the Reign of Akbar*, New Delhi, 1976.

8. F Rosenthal, *A History of Muslim Historiography*, Leiden, 1952, p. 13.
9. Tarif Khalidi, *Arabic Historical Thought in the Classical Period*, Cambridge, 1994, p. 7. See also Aziz Al-Azmeh, 'Chronophagous Discourse: A Study of Clerico-Legal Appropriation of the World in an Islamic Tradition' in Frank E Reynolds and David Tracy, eds, *Religious and Practical Reason*, Albany, 1994, pp. 166, 167.
10. Paul E Walker, 'Eternal Cosmos and the Womb of History: Time in Early Ismaili Thought', *International Journal of Middle Eastern Studies*, vol. 9, 1978, p. 357; E Goodman, 'Time in Islam' in Anindita Niyogi Balslev and J N Mohanty, eds, *Religion and Time*, Leiden, 1993, pp. 138-62.
11. Louis Massignon, 'Time in Islamic Thought', *Man and Time*, Bollingen series, vol. 30, no. 3, 1957, pp. 108-09.
12. Goodman, 'Time in Islam'.
13. Aziz Al-Azmeh, *Ibn Khaldun: An Essay in Reinterpretation*, Budapest, 2003.
14. Badāunī, *Muntakhab*, vol. I, ed., Maulavi Ahmad Ali, Calcutta, 1868, pp. 7-8.
15. Abu'l Fazl, *Akbar Nāmā*, vol. I, pp. 52 ff.
16. Tarif Khalidi, *Arabic Historical Thought*, pp. 8, 120.
17. Abu'l Fazl, *Akbar Nāmā*, vol. I, p. 52: *pīshtar az ādam... hazār hazār ādam būdah und.*
18. Abu'l Fazl, *Ā'in*, vol. I, p. 273.
19. Abu'l Fazl, *Akbar Nāmā*, vol. I, pp. 49-50: *...īn ālam wa ālamiyānrā ibtadāi wa īn mazāhir-i isāmī safātī rā mabadāyi padīd nīst. Yā ba ma'nī-i qadm chunānke aksaré hukmāi mutaqaddamīn bar āyand. Yā bā ma'nī-i kamāl-i tūl imtadād ke pahlū baqadam mīzanand.*
20. Ibid., p. 52. ... *imsāl īn riwāyāt wa hikāyāt-i gunāgūn dar wussat-i ābād-i qudrat-i ilāhī dūr nīst ke sūrat-i sihhaté dāshta bāshand wa ādam-i bisyār ba zahūr āmdah bāshad.*
21. S A A Rizvi, *Religious and Intellectual History of the Muslims in the Reign of Akbar*, New Delhi, 1975, pp. 356-57.
22. For a fuller discussion see Harbans Mukhia, 'Time, Chronology and History: the Indian Case' in Sølvi Sogner, ed, *Making Sense of Global History*, Oslo, 2001, pp. 247-53; 'Time, Religion and History in India', *Historical Inquiry*, vol. 29, Taipei, 2002, pp. 169-80; and *The Mughals of India*, Oxford, 2004, pp. 42-44. The notion of *insān-i kāmil* raised Akbar above the denominational identity marks of being a Muslim or a Hindū.
23. V A Smith calls Abu'l Fazl a 'shameless flatterer of Akbar' and Ahmad Bashir more recently endorses the observation. Smith,

Akbar the Great Mogul, 1542-1605, Oxford, 1917, Preface; Bashir, *Akbar the Great Mughul: His New Policy and His New Religion*, New Delhi, 2009, Preface.

24. Badāunī, *Muntakhab*, vol. 2, p. 256: *'aqlā dar har hamah adyān maujūd wa muhayyā und... pus inhisār ān dar yak dīn wa yak millat ke nau paidā shudah wa hazār sāl barū naguzashtah bāshad cheh lāzim wa asbāt yaké wa nafi dīgré.*
25. Abu'l Fazl, *Akbar Nāmā*, vol. 2, p. 43: *Ārey, imruz wa fardā wa dī wa hāzir wa ghāyab pīsh-i ākhshījiyān zāhir bāshad. Ammā pish-i nūr parvardān īzdi ....āyindah chūn guzashtā dar khidmat-i hāl ast. Wa ghāyab chūn hāzir dar sharf-i huzūr.*
26. Ibid., p.12: *chūn tārīkh-i hijrī ke āghāz-i ān az ruz-i shamātat-i 'aida wa kulfat-i ahabbāst.*
27. Abu'l Fazl, *Ā'in*, vol. I, p. 277: *...tārīkh-i hijrī ke az nākāmī āgahī bakhshad.*
28. Abu'l Fazl, *Akbar Nāmā*, vol. 2, pp. 9-13.
29. Ibid., pp. 9, 18; *Ā'in*, vol. I, pp. 277-78.
30. For the use of this term, see Badāunī, *Muntakhab*, vol. 2, p. 304: *Dīn-i Ilāhī Akbarshāhī.*
31. Abu'l Fazl, Ā'in, vol. 2, p. 235.
32. For further discussion of the theme, see Harbans Mukhia, *The Mughals of India*, pp. 46-47.
33. Abu'l Fazl, *Akbar Nāmā*, vol. 3, ed. Maulavi Abd al-Rahim, Calcutta, 1886, p. 293: *chār chaman-i āshtī*. The beauty and tranquillity of the garden encompasses the four corners of the universe.
34. Ibid., vol. 2, p. 390: *nuzhatgāh-i sulh kul.*
35. Ibid. vol. 3, p. 527: *kishwar khudā bafarāz-i sulh kul jahānbānī kunad har giruhe qarārdād-i khwīsh rā bé andesha basarāyad wa har yaké ba 'āin-i khwīsh īzad parastī numāyad.*
36. S A A Rizvi, *Muslim Revivalist Movements in Northern India in the Sixteenth and Seventeenth Centuries*, Agra, 1965, chs. 2 and 3; Qamaruddin, *The Mahdawi Movement in India*, Delhi, 1985.
37. I H Queshi in his characteristic dogmatic assertiveness denies any space for the Mahdi in the whole of Islam: '...belief in the appearance of a Mahdi is not a part of Islam', *Ulema in Politics*, 2nd edn., Karachi, 1974, p. 40.
38. Abu'l Fazl, *Akbar Nāmā*, vol. 2, 389: *khair basījī dānistah*
39. See Harbans Mukhia, *Historians and Historiography During the Reign of Akbar*, ch. 2.
40. Mohamad Tavakoli-Targhi, 'Contested Memories of Pre-Islamic Iran', *The Medieval History Journal*, vol. 2 (2), July-December 1999, pp. 245-75.

41. Mu'atmid Khan, *Iqbālnāmā-i Jahāngīrī*, Lucknow, 1870, vol. 2, pp. 457-58; Sujān Rāi Bhandārī, *Khulāsāt al-Tawārīkh*, ed. Zafar Hasan, Delhi, 1918, p. 435; Shaikh Farid Bhakkari, *Zakhīrat al-Khawānīn*, ed. Syed Moinul Haq, Karachi, 1961, p. 72; Shah Nawaz Khan, *Ma'āsir al-Umarā*, eds, M Abd al-Rahim and Ashraf Ali, 3 vols. Calcutta, 1888-91, here vol. 2, p. 610.
42. On occasions he gives us an insight into these calendars in different contexts. At one go he discusses the eras and temporal calculations of several civilisations; see Abu'l Fazl, *Ā'in*, vol. I, pp. 265-70.
43. *Bābur Nāma*, Eng. Tr. A S Beveridge, Delhi repnt., 1970, p. 516.
44. Gulbadan Begum, *Humayūn Nāmā*, ed. A S Beveridge, London, 1902, Delhi repnt., 1996, pp. 10, 37, 38, 76 and passim.
45. Ibid., pp. 99, 116, 150 and passim.
46. Ibid., p. 577.
47. Abu'l Fazl, *Ā'in*, vol. 1, p. 578. There is of course a long, though inconstitent history of such precise measurement. Megasthenes in the fourth century BC records that from Dionysus to Sandracottus (Chandragupta [Maurya]) 153 kings ruled over India for 6042 years. See Thomas R Trautmann, *The Clash of Chronologies. Ancient India in the Modern World*, New Delhi, 2009, Chapter 2: 'Indian Time, Europen Time', p. 33.
48. Abu'l Fazl, *Akbar Nāmā*, vol. 3, p. 733.
49. Abu'l Fazl, *Akbar Nāmā*, vol. 2, p. 158: *b'ad az guzashtan-i sih sā'at wa chahal wa neh daqīqā...*
50. Ibid., p. 203.
51. Abu'l Fazl, *Ā'in*, vol. 1, p. 516.
52. Ibid., p. 469: *gūyand pīshtar az chahal sāl-i ilāhī ba du hazār wa sīsad wa punjāh wa punj sāl wa punj māh wa bīst wa haft rūz mahābāh nām riyāzat garé ātishgāh afrokhtah izdī purastish kard.*
53. Ibid., pp. 467-68.

REFERENCES

Abu'l Fazl, *Akbar Nāmā* (Persian text), edited in 3 vols. by Maulavi Abd al-Rahim, Asiatic Society of Bengal, Calcutta, 1871-1886.

Abu'l Fazl, *Ā'in-i-Akbarī*, (Persian text) edited in 2 vols by H. Blochmann, Asiatic Society of Bengal, Calcutta, 1872-1877.

Abu'l Fazl, *Akbar Nāmā*, vol. 2, Eng. Tr. By H.Beveridge, Delhi reprint, 1989.

Aziz Al-Azmeh, 'Chronophagous Discourse: A Study of Clerico-Legal Appropriation of the World in an Islamic Tradition' in Frank E Reynolds and David Tracy, eds, *Religious and Practical Reason*, Albany, 1994.

Aziz Al-Azmeh, *Ibn Khaldun: An Essay in Reinterpretation*, Budapest, 2003.

Zaheer al-Din Muhammad Bābur, *Bābur Nāmā*, Eng. Tr. A S Beveridge, Delhi repnt, 1970.

Mullā Abd-al Qādir Badāunī, *Muntakhab al-Tawārīkh*, (Persian text), 3 vols., eds. Maulavi Ahmad Ali and W N Lees, Calcutta, 1865-69.

Ahmad Bashir, *Akbar the Great Mughul: His New Policy and His New Religion*, New Delhi, 2009.

Shaikh Farīd Bhakkarī, *Zakhīrat al-Khawānīn*, ed. Syed Moinul Haq, Karachi, 1961.

Sujān Rāi Bhandārī, *Khulāsāt al-Tawārīkh*, ed. Zafar Hasan, Delhi, 1918.

E Goodman, 'Time in Islam' in Anindita Niyogi Balslev and J N Mohanty, eds, *Religion and Time*, Leiden, 1993.

Gulbadan Begum, *Humayūn Nāmā*, ed. A S Beveridge, London, 1902, Delhi repnt., 1996.

Tarif Khalidi, *Arabic Historical Thought in the Classical Period*, Cambridge, 1994.

Louis Massignon, 'Time in Islamic Thought', *Man and Time*, Bollingen series, vol. 30, no. 3, 1957.

Mu'atmid Khan, *Iqbālnāmā-i Jahāngīrī*, vol. 2, Lucknow, 1870.

Harbans Mukhia, 'Time, Chronology and History: the Indian Case' in Sølvi Sogner, ed, *Making Sense of Global History*, Oslo, 2001.

Harbans Mukhia 'Time, Religion and History in India', *Historical Inquiry*, vol. 29, Taipei, 2002.

Harbans Mukhia, *The Mughals of India*, Oxford, 2004.

Qamaruddin, *The Mahdawi Movement in India*, Delhi, 1985.

I H Queshi, *Ulema in Politics*, 2nd edn., Karachi, 1974.

S A A Rizvi, *Muslim Revivalist Movements in Northern India in the Sixteenth and Seventeenth Centuries*, Agra, 1965.

S A A Rizvi, *Religious and Intellectual History of the Muslims in the Reign of Akbar*, New Delhi, 1975.

F Rosenthal, *A History of Muslim Historiography*, Leiden, 1952.

Shāh Nawāz Khān, *Ma'āsir al-'Umarā*, eds, M Abd al-Rahīm and Ashraf Alī, 3 vols. Calcutta, 1888-91.

V A Smith, *Akbar the Great Mogul, 1542-1605*, Oxford, 1917.

Mohamad Tavakoli-Targhi, 'Contested Memories of Pre-Islamic Iran', *The Medieval History Journal*, vol. 2 (2), July-December 1999.

Thomas R Trautmann, *The Clash of Chronologies. Ancient India in the Modern World*, New Delhi, 2009.

Paul E Walker, 'Eternal Cosmos and the Womb of History: Time in Early Ismail Thought', *International Journal of Middle Eastern Studies*, vol. 9, 1978.

2

Time in India's Religions and History

'What we think of as real time is in reality only imaginary time.' —Stephen Hawking in *A Brief History of Time*

Even as the Positivist notion of historical time as linear, premised upon irreversible universal human progress through the instrumentality of scientific reasoning and technological means of realising it, has dominated the generation of historical knowledge around the world over the past two centuries, its inevitable consequence has been the subjugation of diverse conceptions of history. The linear concept of time becoming the reference point has also meant deriding all other notions of time, displacing them from the very process of accretion of universal knowledge. That this displacement has coincided with the relationship of hegemony and subjugation of vast regions of the world's economies and civilizations by Western Europe, home of the origin of Positivism, is clearly no accident.

One of the simplest and most prevalent distinctions between the Western and the Indian notions of time was the characterisation of the former as linear and the latter as cyclical. The linearity of one ensured the society's triumphal onward march, mediated through constant and irreversible change, often occurring as transformation —'revolution' was the favoured term —, and the cyclicity of the other equally ensured endless repetition, changelessness and stagnation to infinity. Cyclical time in other words amounted to a denial of history.

James Mill, author of the very influential The *History of British India* (first published in 1817), contemptuously describes this notion as 'a boastful and turgid vanity [which] distinguishes remarkably the oriental nations'; these are indeed 'rude' nations.[1] The Asiatic social system, for him, was 'one in which all progress had ceased thousands of years ago.'[2] Montesquieu was among the earliest of modern thinkers to underline the denial of history in the Orient: 'The laws, customs and manners of the Orient—even the most trivial, such as mode of dress—remain the same as they were a thousand years ago.'[3] The image of an unchanging East remained pervasive in European thought. For Hegel, 'the Hindoos have no History in the form of annals *[Historia]* . . . they have no History in the form of transactions *[Regestrae];* that is no growth expanding into a veritable political condition.'[4] Therefore, when Karl Marx announced in 1853 that 'Indian society has no history at all, at least no known history. What we call its history is but the history of successive intruders who founded their empires on the passive basis of that unresisting and unchanging society'[5], he was merely reiterating the well-established European cliché about the East. Nor was the cliché reconsidered even into the waning decades of the twentieth century. Arnold Toynbee considers the Hindu philosophical notion of *kalpa* and cannot conceal his contempt for it, calling it 'an everlasting cosmic practical joke ... a certain meaningless measure of time [which] cannot fail to stultify all our human exertions by reproducing the same situation again and again *ad infinitum*.'[6] Toynbee is here referring to a version of *kalpa,* envisioned as a mountain from which every one hundred years a silk handkerchief wipes away one particle of dust, and the time it takes for the disappearance of the whole mountain would amount to a *kalpa*. Clearly, in treating it as an empirical statement, Professor Toynbee missed out on what was meant to be a metaphor signifying the immensity of time.

In modem Western perception then a single, undifferentiated notion of cyclical time characterised Indian civilisation and taken entirely as an empirical description, divorced from its religio-philosophical context, it signified singular absence of any change in social, political and civilisational, i.e. material history. It drew very sharp demarcating lines between mythology and history. It defined the West and its other.

Returned to the contexts of Indian religio-philosophical systems, the notion of cyclical time emerges at best as one among several notions and even as cyclical time, it does not implicate closure of social change. Indeed, one commentator has put his suspicion of the single notion of cyclical time rather forcefully:[7]

> It appears that the description of the Hindu notion of time as cyclical is so lopsided as to be misleading. It overlooks the fact the *sruti* is almost free of such a notion and it further overlooks the fact that *smriti* provides striking exceptions and limitations to this cyclical notion of time. The Hindu notion of time is not a monochrome but a mosaic; it is too complex to be described as merely cyclical.

This questioning finds favour in another scholar's observation: '[A]lthough the appearance of "cyclic time" features so often in the Western encounter with the Indian tradition, the idea can hardly be identified as the view of any particular school of Brahmanical philosophy or even as an issue for debate in polemical literature.' This scholar too emphasises the existence of 'great diversity of views' within the fold of Hindu philosophical traditions and pleads that 'To ignore this variety of views and to reduce them under the single caption of "cyclic time" is to distort the image of a complex and a major tradition of world-religions.'[8]

The perception of cyclical time in Hinduism derives strength chiefly from the notion of for *yugas* (ages) which move in several concentric cycles. Truth, reflection, long human life, plenitude of material comforts, absence of greed etc., mark the first, *krta yuga*. It lasts anywhere between 4800 years and 4000x360, i.e. 1,440,000 years according to different sources. The next, *treta yuga*, witnesses some decline compared to the first and is also shorter, and so on, to the *dwapar yuga* until the last, the *kali yuga*, the one of the present time. Human beings in this age will live up to a maximum of 100 years and this would be marked by a general decline of truth and rectitude. According to the *Visnu Purana*,[9] in this *yuga*, property alone would confer social rank, wealth would become the sole criterion of virtue, passion and lewdness the sole bonds between mates, falsehood the condition of success in life, sexuality the sole means of enjoyment and an outward, purely ritualistic religion would get confounded with spirituality.

The declining duration of each *yuga* corresponds to the declining ethical and moral standards, construed as *dharma* (code of moral behaviour). Incidentally, the names of the *yugas* are derived from the throws of dice.[10] The throw here does not suggest chance, but degrees of perfection: figure 4 is construed in Hinduism as signifying perfection, completeness; 3 is thus slightly less perfect and so forth.[11] The *yugas* move in a cycle, one complete cycle comprising a *maha-yuga*, a 'grand age'.

The link between the rarefied conceptualisation of time in the Brahmanic tradition, with Vedic texts as its primary source,[12] and popular traditions too has been the subject of scrutiny. The notion of the Absolute Time (*kalavada*) is not only 'a very ancient concept ... but above all, it is a widely held popular view, belonging probably to the less Brahmanic stratum of Indian tradition.'[13] Indeed, Mircea Eliade in a celebrated essay spatially and temporally expands the scope of the evolution of what is largely accepted as the specifically Hindu view and forcefully argues that 'The myth of cyclical Time—of the cosmic cycles that repeat themselves *ad infinitum* —is not an innovation of Indian speculation.'[14] As he has shown in his *The Myth of Eternal Return*, 'traditional societies conceive of man's temporal existence not only as an infinite repetition of certain archetypes and exemplary gestures but also as an eternal renewal. In symbols and rituals, the world is renewed periodically.'[15] Richard Lannoy too points to the tribal origins of the ideal of the *krta yuga*: 'Hindu society was probably aware that the time sense of the surrounding tribal societies was even more consistently non-linear than their own.'[16]

The hegemonic Western view has perceived in cyclical time in Hindu thought the implication of inescapable destiny and therefore a disincentive to human intervention to seek to alter it. We have seen above the derisive references to the Orient's comfort in changelessness; there are too many others in the same genre to bear repetition. A second intuitive implication derived from inevitable destiny is one of the denial of the existence of reality, everything—life, world, time, wealth—being an illusion, *maya*. This prevailing perception has of course no space for any change, no evolution whatever. Timelessness of the object of analysis thus gets embedded in the subjective perception itself. This should have worried the commentators, for there are indeed numerous qualifications to this rather simplistic construction.

In one important strand of Hindu philosophy, time itself is defined not in its own terms but in terms of action. Even as time for the philosopher Bhartihari is absolute in as much as there is no division of it into the past, the present and the future in its own terms, it is because of difference in action (*krya bhed*) that differentiation and division occur and time gets crystallised in relation to an action which suggests a before and an after, speed or tardiness. The *Mahahharata* already speaks of change (*parinama*) in beings that forces us to accept the reality of time.[17] Indeed the term for destiny, *gati,* also means motion.

If the metaphor of the wheel for time, a constant feature in Hinduism, Jainism and Buddhism, has been understood to mean infinity and unbreakability of time, this meaning is restricted to a two dimensional phenomenon; this by itself is suggestive of the opposite context of multidimensionality of reality and the invitation to break free of the circumference of time. If time encloses, it also provides escape routes through the attainment of *jnan* (contemplation), *yoga* (union) and *karma* (action). *Moksha,* freedom from the binding of time is the ultimate aim of human existence. Life or the world as *maya* (illusion, among many other meanings) is not unreal in the sense of not being in existence but being transitory in the context of time's eternity. Any event in history thus becomes illusory in the sense of being transitory over stretches of time, even as the occurrence of the event is a reality.

But then time itself is perceived in some strands of Indian philosophy as eternal and in some others as ephemeral. In the Buddhist philosophy in particular, even as the Buddha himself is the Absolute and timeless, having transcended the aeons, time comprises neither the past nor the future; it is constantly the present and therefore transitory, impermanent.[18] In one school of *yoga*, time has no absolute, objective existence outside of human experience. *Yoga Vasistha* insists that instants and cosmic ages are non-existent as objective realities; depending upon the state of one's mind, an instant might appear as a *kalpa* (aeon), or a *kalpa* might be experienced as a single instant. In short, time *per se* does not exist.[19]

II

The arrival of Islam first to the periphery of India in Sind in early eighth century and later to the heartland of northern India from the beginning of the eleventh century on, brought a new religion, a new conception of time and of history to the ancient land. A legatee to the Judaic-Christian monotheistic tradition, Islam also inherited the concept of linear time, from the Creation to the Day of Judgment. This was its only concept. Yet, the repeated appearance of prophets prior to the appearance of Muhammad to restore humanity to its puritanical state also implicates a cyclical recurrence. There was a strong coincidence of theological and historical time within Islam.

The debates on the notions of time were limited to the date of the creation of the world and the equivalence between human and divine time. Consensually, creation is located 14,000 years ago and the birth of Adam 7,000 years later, though there is divergence of opinion on both. The Quran itself establishes the equivalence of one day of God and 1,000 earthly years. It is on this basis that the historian al-Tabari calculates the age of the universe to be 14,000 earthly years, equally divided between Creation and the birth of Adam and from there to the Coming of the Hour.[20] The age of Adam, however, is subject to different estimates. The great medieval Indian historian, Abu'l Fazl, cites Imam Ja'far al-Sadiq and lbn al-'Arabi to the effect that there were thousands of Adams before Adam and one race of Adam was succeeded by another, some parts of their existence overlapping with one another.[21] On the origins of the universe too, Abu'I Fazl takes account of the evidence of astronomy, 'reliable ancient books of the Hindus and of Cathay and successive chronicles of the sages of those regions,' and observes: '...[l]t appears that the beginning of the universe and its inhabitants and the source of the manifestation of attributes of divinity has not become visible. Either it is eternal or of such antiquity as to merge in eternity.'[22] After enumerating several notions of time and therefore of the origin of the universe, he eclectically remarks: 'Traditions and stories like these are current in the vast expanse of God's creation and it is not impossible that these may [all] be true.'[23]

Islam also brought a new vision of history to India. In the home of its origin, the Arab land, the birth of Islam drew a sharp dividing line in historical time: the age of the world before Islam, characterised by *jahiliya*, ignorance, savagery, and after when ignorance was terminated. History became a narrative of events in actual time, very precisely measured in years, months and days, at times even in hours. Since Muhammad was the last of all prophets and God had revealed the ultimate truth through him in the Quran, this truth would in the end triumph in the entire world. All history is therefore world history, a feature that is an essential element in the Arab-Muslim historiographical tradition.[24] Most of the histories written during India's medieval centuries belong to this genre. They were written by courtiers, mostly Muslim, in the Persian language and in Arab-Muslim and Persio-Mongol tradition.[25]

However, within the Islamic world there were dissenting voices. If Islamic religious and historical scholarship operated with the temporal dividing line drawn around AD 622, the inaugural year of the *hijri* era, there were alternative constructions too which envisioned historical time as an uninterrupted flow either from the beginning of the universe or from the beginning of humanity with the birth of Adam. Abu'l Fazl is the most outstanding of such historians and posits an alternative to the hegemonic Islamic temporal vision, for embedded in that vision was legitimation of strife, conquest and subjugation of one religious sect of humanity by another. To this Abu'l Fazl posits the alternative of a universal religiosity deriving from one universal God in lieu of several religions, each with its own sectarian god and all at war with one another. By eliminating the Islamic dividing line in historical time, Abu'l Fazl is fundamentally questioning all received wisdom from around his intellectual milieu.[26] Interestingly the historian had complete support of the contemporary state in his endeavour. He was a courtier, friend and admirer of the Mughal emperor Akbar (r. 1556-1605) himself keen to distance the functioning of the state from Islamic moorings and seeking to establish a polity where the religious identity of a subject became neither a basis of privilege nor punishment.

Such however was not the fate of another contemporary scholar in neighbouring Iran where Azar Kayvan also sought to erase the Islamic dividing line in his country's political history by linking the lineage of the current rulers to pre-Adamite Adam, Mahabad. Unable to face persecution in his home, he had to seek refuge in Mughal India in the end. But, unlike Abu'l Fazl, Azar Kayvan was merely asserting Iran's pre-Islamic Sasanian identity and displacing the Islamic identity from centre stage; he did not envisage an alternative vision of universal history.[27] We might add that unlike Abu'l Fazl again, who was in his personal life probably a devout Muslim, Azar Kayvan was a Zoroastrian.

Even as time is visualised as linear in Islam, it is perceived as eternal and infinite in some strands[28] and as discontinuous juxtaposition of instants in others, each finite in the context of an infinite totality, until the day of Judgment.[29]

In medieval India then, even as Sanskrit texts expounding the ambivalent old scholarship continued their course, the notion of time and history brought forth by the Muslim tradition became hegemonic, even when the historians themselves were Hindu. The two continued to be practiced as parallel streams.

III

The 'modem' [i.e. Western] notion of time in history came to Indian history in two parallel strands: one of patronising approval of India's ancient wisdom and the other of strident denunciation of it. Either way, the Eastern and the Western were constituted as two ends of the spectrum. Since the idea of irreversible progress inhered in both linear historical time and in the tripartite division of history into Antiquity, Middle (or Dark) Ages and Modem Times, its introduction to India by James Mill in I817 was heavily qualified by the utilitarian assumption that 'progress' was the end result of science and reason which were opposed to religion; hence all of India's pre-British past was one chunk of stasis and rigidity, the characteristic of societies with religion as the guiding force. Indeed the tripartite division was modified as the Hindu, the Muslim and the British periods of Indian history. The asymmetry between the three is quite well thought out and emphatic. In the beginning of the twentieth century, in 1903 to be precise, 'Ancient, Medieval and Modern' were first used again by a British historian, Stanley Lane-Poole.[30]

But the terms hid under them the old basis of division and these continued to remain interchangeable right into the 1960s. The growing influence of Marxism on Indian historiography during the mid-1950s until about three decades later also emphasised linear change and progress, sometimes going contrary to Marx's own evaluation of India's past.[31] With focus shifting to social, economic and technological change where the earlier preoccupation was with the history of ruling dynasties, the boundaries of ancient, medieval and modern got redefined, but the tripartite division remained in tact. It is in the last decade of the twentieth century and the first of the new century that ever newer problematiques of the history of time, space, habitat, cultural morés and interpersonal relations are coming centre stage and the conventional temporal divides are under a strain, for these problematiques defy easy placement within defined temporal boxes.

IV

There is still the persistence of a certain notion of time and history to be considered: the one that appertains to nearly a quarter of India's population, i.e. the tribes. With no literate tradition surviving from the past, their myths—recorded by outsiders—are the only 'facts' available for retrieving their construction of time, with rarely an explicit elaboration. Their notions come nowhere near what is construed as history or time in high culture zones. Their time is independent of virtually any kind of measurement in aeons, millennia, centuries or years; there is no explicit logic, nor an elaborate and cogent construction of an argument; there is no conscious retrieval, nor denial of history as we understand it. Yet, there is a strongly implicit sense of the present and the past in their ever evolving myths. Usually, these myths relate to their origin which implicate their present status vis-a-vis other groups they come into contact with, either caste groups representing social power or others representing state power. In constructing their origin myths, which vary according to each situation, they either visualise a continuous flow of time since their origin, or fractured time, indicating consciousness of their own changed status and power.

If several strands of Hindu thought have drawn upon some of these elements to weave their own conceptual mosaics, the autonomous being of these implicit and scattered notions of time and history, expressed in the medium of myths, still remains a strong presence across the length and breadth of the country and outside of, though related to, the dominant Brahmanic Hindu ethos.[32]

NOTES AND REFERENCES

1. James Mill, *The History of British India,* vol. I, 5th edn. (London: Maden, 1858), p. 107.
2. Marian Sawer, *Marxism and the Question of the Asiatic Mode of Production* (The Hague: Nijhoff, 1977), p. 20.
3. Cited in Perry Anderson, *Lineages of the Absolutist State* (London: N.L.B. 1974), p. 464.
4. W. F. Hegel, *The Philosophy of History* (New York: Willey Book Co., 1944), p. 163.
5. Karl Marx, 'The Future Results of the British Rule in India,' in *The First Indian War of Independence, 1857-1859,* by Karl Marx

and F. Engels (Moscow: Foreign Languages Pub. House, [1960]), pp. 33-44.

6. Arnold Toynbee, *A Study of History*, rev. and abridged in 1 vol. (New York, 1972), p. 487.
7. Arvind Sharma, 'The Notion of Cyclical Time in Hinduism,' in *Time in Indian Philosophy, A Collection of Essays*, ed. Hari Shankar Prasad (Delhi: 1992), p. 210.
8. Anindita N. Balslev, 'Time and the Hindu Experience', in *Religion and Time*, eds, A. Balslev and R. N. Mohanty (Leiden: Brill, 1992), p.177.
9. *Visnu Purana*, IV, p. 24.
10. P V Kane, *History of Dharmasastras* (Poona: Bhandarkar Oriental Research Institute, 1946). vol. 3, pp. 886-90.
11. Mircea Eliade. 'Time and Eternity in Indian Thought.' in *Time in Indian Philosophy*, pp. 101-02.
12. The *Atharva Veda* is the first to encapsulate Time in various aspects, especially as the 'creator of the creator': [Time engendered Heaven above Time (also) engendered the Earths we see Set in motion by Time, which were, Are and shall be assigned their place] See Raimundo Panikkar, 'Time and History in the Tradition of India: Kala and Karma,' in *Time in Indian Philosophy*, p. 23.
13. Ibid.
14. M. Eliade, 'Time and Eternity in Indian Thought,' p. 108.
15. M. Eliade, *The Myth of the Eternal Return* (New York and London: Pantheon Books, 1954).
16. Richard Lannoy, *The Speaking Tree: A Study of Indian Culture and Society* (London: n.p. 1971), p. 288.
17. R. Panikkar, 'Time and History,' pp. 28-29.
18. G. C. Pande, 'Time in Buddhism' in *Time and Religion*, pp. 183-89: M Eliade, 'Time and Eternity' pp. 115-16.
19. R. Panikkar, 'Time and History,' p. 30.
20. Tarif Khalidi, *Arabic Historical Thought in the Classical Period* (Cambridge: Cambridge University Press, 1994). pp. 8, 120.
21. Abu'l Fazl, *Akbar Nama*, vol. I. ed. Maulavi Abd al-Rahim, Asiatic Society of Bengal (Calcutta, 1877), p. 52.
22. Ibid., pp. 49-50.
23. Ibid., p. 52.
24. Tarif Khalidi, *Arabic Historical Thought*, p. 115.
25. See Peter Hardy, *Historians of Medieval India* (London: Luzac, 1960); M. Hasan, ed., *Historians of Medieval India*, (Meerut: Meenakshi Prakashan, 1968); Harbans Mukhia, *Historians and*

Historiography During the Reign of Akbar (New Delhi: Vikas Pub. House, 1976).

26. Harbans Mukhia, *Historians and Historiography*, pp. 72-84; Idem, '"Medieval India": An Alien Conceptual Hegemony?' *The Medieval History Journal*, Vol. 1, no. 1 (1998), pp. 91-105.
27. See for an excellent treatment of the intellectual movement inspired by Azar Kayvan's historical vision, Mohamad Tavakoli-Targhi, 'Contested Memories of Pre-Islamic Iran,' *The Medieval History Journal*, vol. 2, no. 2 (1999), pp. 245-75.
28. Paul E. Walker, 'Eternal Cosmos and the Womb of History: Time in Early lsmaili Thought,' *International Journal of Middle East Studies*, vol. 9 (1978), p. 357; E. Goodman, 'Time in Islam,' in *Time and Religion*, pp. 138-62.
29. Louis Massignon, 'Time in Islamic Thought,' in *Man and Time*, Vol. 3 of Papers from the Eranos Year books, Bollingen Series, no. 30 ([New York]: Pantheon Books, 1957), pp. 108-9; E. Goodman, 'Time in lslam'.
30. Stanley Lane-Poole, *Mediaeval India under Mohammadan Rule: AD. 712-1764* (London: T. Fisher Unwin, 1903).
31. Harbans Mukhia, ' Marx on Pre- Colonial India: An Evaluation,' in *Marxian Theory and the Third World*, ed. Diptendra Banerjee (New Delhi, Sage Publications, 1985). pp. 173-84.
32. See for a very sensitive treatment of the theme of the tribal notions of Time, Prathama Banerjee, *Polilics of Time: 'Primitives' and History-writing in a Colonial Society* (New Delhi, Oxford University Press, 2006).

3

'Medieval India': An Alien Conceptual Hegemony?*

One of the most significant cultural legacies of around a thousand years' stretch in Indian history, between c. seventh or eighth century A.D. and the eighteenth—'medieval India' as it is constituted now—is a large number of histories. Frequently going by the Arabic term *tarikh* (and its plural, *tawarikh*), which originally meant both 'date' and 'era', and was later to acquire the meaning of 'history' around the third century A.H/ninth century A.D.,[1] these works, written in the language of the court, Persian, are at best, court chronicles. Some of these have a grand historical perspective and a world-view, even the deliberate constitution of an ideological intervention; most, however, barely record events centred in and around the court, though the recording itself is not devoid of an implicit perspective.[2]

In terms of its format, all these works fall in the category of 'dynastic' history. Inspired by the ambition to write a 'world history', a tradition that goes back to the ninth century A.D.

---

* Much of the research for this article and most of its writing took place at Leiden, The Netherlands, thanks to a generous three-month fellowship at the International Institute of Asian Studies in 1997. The very congenial academic ambience at the IIAS and its ever accessible Director, Professor Wim Stokhof, and other staff made the stay there memorable. A mere 'Thank You' to all of them remains a very inadequate expression of gratitude.

historian Yaqubi, author of the first surviving work in this genre in Arab historiography,[3] and to Rashid al-Din, the Mongol-Persian historian of the early fourteenth century A.D.,[4] it is, yet, on rare occasions that medieval Indian historians go beyond the spatial boundaries of their region and the temporal boundaries of Muslim ruling dynasties.[5] The dynastic frame of history writing, not unknown to the Arabs[6] was more fully developed in the Persian tradition which comes in for a forceful defence by al-Tabari.[7] The history of the dynasty in medieval India is broken up into regnal units and the account of the current reign is usually broken up further into an annalistic arrangement, a feature that came from Tabari.[8] However, it is the event that constitutes the irreducible unit of narration. Each event turns into an individual, independent entity, unrelated to other events, and each is located in a strict chronological order, again an Arab historiographical invention.[9] Indeed, the Arab historians date an event by the year, the month and the day, not failing to note even the day of the week of its occurrence.[10] Chronological location is further reinforced by the use of chronograms, coining of phrases or verses, the numerical value of whose combination of letters yields the year of the event's occurrence.

Even as the concern for precise chronology becomes obsessive in medieval Indian historiography, it is simultaneously marked by the absence of any conception of historical periodisation, except, of course, for the temporal dividing lines drawn by the rise of Islam. Barring Abul Fazl, sacral time thus becomes the single reference point for historical time for all historical writings, a feature inherited from the Arabs. History then came to be divided into two phases: one of *jahiliya*, the age of ignorance and savagery before the emergence of Islam, and the second after it. The break with the age of *jahiliya* was emphatic not only because Islam constituted its repudiation but also because the *jahiliya* culture was essentially pre-literate, marked by the absence of articulate historical thought. In Tarif Khalidi's words, 'The Arabs learnt a new history when they acquired a new religion.'[11]

Islam permeates, in varying degrees, the writing of the histories in medieval India, with the exception of Abul Fazl who seeks to counterpose to Islam's denominational identity a universalist religious identity emanating from the universal God; he thus begins his account of Akbar's reign with Adam, the first human being.[12] The tradition of tracing the lineage of the current ruler to Adam was not Abul Fazl's original creation; it had been practiced in Iran for long though it was resorted to both for linking as well as counterposing Iran's and Islam's histories.[13] Indeed, a victim of Iranian exile in India, Azar Kayvan (1533?–1618), a contemporary of Abul Fazl, traced the history of Iran to pre-Adamite Mahabad as a strategy for subverting the Islamicate prophetography beginning with Adam and ending with Muhammad, and asserting Iran's pre-Islamic identity,[14] though this happened after Abul Fazl's death. But barring Abul Fazl, all other historians of medieval India begin their account with praises of God, Allah, followed by Muhammad, again showered with encomia; the lineage is then traced through the pious caliphs, their successors, past sultans, down to the current sultan. The ruler's political descent is thus traced exclusively through the denominational lineage of Islam.

Islam permeates, too, in the exclusive use of the hijri calendar of historians. Emperor Akbar (r. 1556-1605) had sought to counterpose to it a new universal calendar marking the beginning of a new era in history, rivalling the era of Islam. This was the Divine era (*Tarikh-i Ilahi*) calibrated upon a solar calendar as opposed to the hijri era which followed a lunar calendar. Drafted by a multifaceted Iranian intellectual, Fathullah Shirazi, a noble of Akbar's court, in A.D. 1584, its operation was effected retroactively since the beginning of Akbar's reign in 1556.[15] Indeed, a difference of 25 days between the accession and the beginning of the calendar were written off so that the onset of spring in March, marking the renewal of the earth, and the beginning of the exceptional reign, marking the renewal of time, could coincide with the inauguration of the new era and the new calendar.[16] The calendar's format had been borrowed from Iran, including the names of the months and its boisterous celebration of the arrival of spring, the New Year festival, *nauruz*, which had survived into Islam, and has survived even Ayatollah Khomeini's puritanical Revolution. Although the Christian calendar too began in March in its first centuries,[17] it seems unlikely that Shirazi was aware or inspired by it, the contact with Jesuit priests in Akbar's court notwithstanding.

Abul Fazl follows the new era in his writings punctiliously and makes scarce reference to the Muslim calendar, even as in his own perception Akbar felt 'perturbed over serious inadequacies of the hijri era', but had refrained from acting accordingly in excluding it from reckoning in view of 'the short-sightedness and lack of comprehension of the multitudes....'[18] The Divine era remained indifferently operative during the reign of Akbar's successor, Jahangir, until his own successor Shah Jahan abolished it altogether in his tenth regnal year, A.D. 1637–38, and restored the lunar hijri calendar in deference to the sentiments of orthodox Muslim theologians.[19] Historians, too, reverted to it without loss of time.

Barring this brief and limited experiment with an alternate historical time, however, the beginning of 'history' with Islam remained hegemonic during India's 'medieval' centuries. The histories that were written began their narratives with the eve of the conquest of India or other neighbouring regions by Muslim rulers and moved on to the narration of the battles, establishment of new regimes, their administration, victories and defeats and so forth. The historians exhibit profound ignorance as well as indifference to the remote histories and societies of these regions long before contact with Islam was established. Here again Abul Fazl made an astounding exception. Counterposing a universalist to Islam's sectarian perspective on history, he goes to great lengths to understand India's ancient mythology, literature, history, astronomy and so forth, and he does so not adversarially but sympathetically.[20] Even his occasional criticism of mythology, etc., is one from a friend.

Such is not the case with the others. Between mildly 'liberal' Muslim historians like Shams Siraj Afif at the end of the fourteenth century, Nizam al-din Ahmad during Akbar's reign and Abdul Hamid Lahori of Shah Jahan's reign (A.D. 1627–1658) and several others on one hand and frenetically orthodox historians like Zia al-Din Barani (writing in A.D. 1357) and, above all, Mulla Abdul Qadir Badauni, Akbar's courtier and Abul Fazl's friend-turned-foe, on the other, variously shaded Islam remains the unshakable dividing line.

Badauni puts the perspective in its extreme and therefore clearest form. He wrote his three-volume *Muntakhab al-Tawarikh* ('Elect among Histories' or 'Selection from Histories') as a counterpoint to Abul Fazl's *Akbar Nama* to put the record straight on behalf of Islam, for Abul Fazl had made a travesty of the truth by maligning the true religion.[21] Since Abul Fazl had Akbar's patronage, and since Badauni needed the salary that his employment as the Imam of Wednesday's prayers at the court and sundry other jobs of translating Hindu mythological texts into Persian brought him, he could give vent to his passion for Islam only in secrecy. The self-imposed secrecy perhaps fuelled the passion further. Fortunately for him, his deed was discovered only after both he and Akbar were dead, though Jahangir did impose a mild punishment on Badauni's children at the discovery.[22]

In the *Muntakhab* Badauni writes the history of India up to his day. After the praise of Allah, Muhammad, the caliphs, etc., the text opens with the statement that the author had elected not to begin his account with Muhammad bin Qasim, the Arab conqueror of Sind in A.D. 712 because his conquest had proved ephemeral; instead, he had chosen to begin it with Subuktgin, whose son Sultan Mahmud of Ghazni had embarked upon the conquest of India from where Islam was never to recede thereafter.[23] Badauni articulates an assumption that the 'Muslim' conquest of India was the dividing line of historical periodisation, an assumption implied in the works of other historians, except Abul Fazl. There is scarce reference to any event or phenomenon prior to that conquest in their works. This was a quiet reiteration of the Arabic *jahiliya*-Islam dichotomy, by now long established as an axiom.

If adherence to chronology was strict and historical priodisation given once and for all, time was yet vague and variable. On one hand, Islam underscores eternity and timelessness;[24] on the other, time for it is discontinuous, a juxtaposition of instants, each finite in the context of an infinite totality, until the moment of Judgement.[25] The Quran itself divides time into the divine and the earthly where one day of the former equals a thousand years of the latter. Tabari follows this division and calculates the age of the world at 14,000 earthly years equally divided between Creation and the birth of Adam, and from Adam to the Coming of the Hour.[26] Even as the age for Adam comes to be consensually accepted as 7,000 years by scholars of Islam, unanimity on this score eludes them. Abul Fazl cites Imam Ja'far al-Sadiq and Ibn al-Arabi to the effect that there were thousands of Adams before Adam and one race of Adam was succeeded by another, their last stages overlapping,[27] but himself remains undecided about the age of the world, of humanity and of Adam. He judges them against the evidence of astronomy, reliable ancient books of the Hindus and of Cathay and successive chronicles of the sages of those regions, and observes: '... it appears that the beginning of the universe and its inhabitants and the source of the manifestation of attributes of divinity has not become visible. Either it is eternal, as was held by many sages of yore, or of such antiquity as to merge in eternity'.[28] After recounting several notions of time and therefore of the origin of the world, he electically remarks: 'Traditons and stories like these are current in the vast expanse of God's creation and it is not impossible that these may [all] be true. There may have been many Adams....'[29] Yet, a while later, on the very same page he unhesitatingly accepts the birth of Adam 7,000 years ago. But doubt returns subsequently and he notes that the origin of Adam has been variously dated.[30]

The first Indian Mughal emperor Babur meticulously records events and observations in his delightful diary, the *Babur Nama* and at one place gives exact details of the hours and minutes in a day and night and various modes of measuring time.[31] Yet, he is deliciously vague about time and period. Of the region of Mewat in modern Rajasthan that he had conquered, he writes: 'Hasan Khan Mewati and his ancestors one after another had ruled it with absolute sway for a hundred years or two.'[32] Usually, however, he makes one or another Prayer time his reference point: A cracked fort-tower 'fell at the Bedtime Prayer'; 'At the Sunset Prayer we reached Fort Marghanian...'; 'It was after the Mid-day Prayer that we rode out...'[33]

Abul Fazl's penchant for exactly measured historical time, on the other hand, besides pointing to his general inclination towards precision, was perhaps reinforced by his interest, indeed practice of astrology. He studies in some detail Brahmin and the Jaina notions of time and the prevalence of different eras in different regions of India.[34] This leads him to the statement that 191 rulers of Kashmir had reigned for 4,109 years, 11 months and 9 days;[35] or, 'It is said that 2,355 years, 5 months and 27 days prior to this, the 40th year of the Divine Era, an ascetic named Mahaba lit the flame in a fire temple to worship God...'[36] Yet, slips are not infrequent. He dates the occurrence of the Hindu mythological Mahabharata war once at 5,691 years before his day, and at another place in the same volume at 4,831 years before.[37]

Unsurprisingly then, time, periodisation and chronology received varied treatment and stand in an asymmetrical relationship in the region and centuries that concern us, with the birth of Islam as the hegemonic temporal divide in history. Some attempts at deviation from it as did occur in India (and Iran) were in the form of defiance of this hegemony: important, intellectually creative but unenduring and uninfluential. Even as history remained and developed as an extremely important discipline in much of the world ruled by Muslim dynasties—Arabia, Iran and India—the notion of dividing it into ancient, medieval and modern periods was no part of this development. This notion was to come much later and at alien hands.

Even in Europe the tripartite periodisation has had a rather brief history. The term *modernus,* signifying 'modern', first appears in the sixth century A.D. in the meaning of 'recent' as distinct from the past,[38] a mere first step towards periodising history. It took another six centuries to invest the 'midterm' with a certain value: 'Two notable authors of the second half of the twelfth century stressing the modernism of their time—one to deplore it, the other to praise it—show the bitterness of the first phase of the quarrel between Ancients and Moderns', remarks Jacques Le Goff, who posits a 'series of successive modernities' instead of one clear break.[39]

The clear break and tripartite division was enunciated by the German, Cellarius, towards the end of the seventeenth century: *Historic antiqua* up to Constantine the Great; *historia mediiaevi* to the fall of Constantinople in 1453; and *historia nora* from 1453 onwards.[40] This was to become the convention in Europe, and with European expansion, in much of the rest of the world.

It was James Mill who brought the convention to India, in an anterior form of Hindu, Muhammadan and British periods, with his *The History of British India*, first published in 1817, though the notion of a Hindu and a Muslim India had already evolved, especially in the work of Sir William Jones.[41] The asymmetrical nomenclature—the first two periods defined by religious identities and the last by a secular, national identity—itself is a clue to Mill's utilitarian assumptions to which he was very strongly committed. The Hindu and the Muslim periods were thus not merely descriptive of the religion of the dominant ruling dynasties; they carried in them strongly pejorative undertones as the antitheses of the enlightenment informed by modern scientific rationality. Indeed, James Mill did not allow his derision of the premodern, and therefore (in his day) oriental irrationality, to remain a mere undertone; the point had to be driven home, often with a hammer.

Mill's work had a lasting influence on the writing of Indian history. As Ronald Inden observes, 'Throughout the nineteenth century, Mill's *History* remained the hegemonic textbook of Indian history. Later Indologists have either ... reiterated his construct of India or they have ... written their accounts as responses to it.'[42] Indeed, Mill has for long been looked upon as the culprit who foisted the notion of the Hindu and Muslim periods on Indian history which in turn generated the consciousness of religious solidarity of Hindu and Muslim communities only to culminate in 1947 in the partition of India along those dividing lines.[43] His action thus comes to be invested with both a long-term teleology and a suspicion of conspiracy, both of which tend to dilute the strength of the argument. As we have seen above, the notion of the Muslim period of Indian history was strongly, if implicitly, embedded in most histories written in that period. Once this category of historical periodisation became operative, the notion of a pre-Muslim or a Hindu period also got implicated even if neither term was ever used. Mill explicated what was implicit and for long familiar and counterposed it to his assumption of the utilitarian role of British rule in India; the long familiarity also found easy acceptance for his formal periodisation of India's history, virtually without resistance.

But then Mill and his many successors, British historians of India and more particularly British administrator–historians, were doing something more than merely explicating the implicit. If the court histories of the genre we have encountered above consensually accepted Islam as the dividing line in historical periodisation, historical causation in turn was posited in terms of human volition. The events of a reign unfold in the narratives as manifestation of the ruler's will, disposition or nature.[44] If the rulers' Muslim identity was one important dimension of the unfolding of these events, the wide range of their dispositions and natures was another. A flexible space thus inhered in the structure of causal explanation, large enough to accommodate alike an astonishingly 'secular' historian like Abul Fazl and a dogmatic Mulla Abdul Qadir Badauni, with a spectrum of others in-between.

However, once James Mill had shifted the emphasis from the rule of Muslim kings to 'Muslim rule' per se, all historical explanation came to be mono-locally centred on a highly essentialised Islam, eliminating in the process that vital space for the interplay of various elements and aspects in explaining the evolution of governance of an immensely diverse and complex society.[45]

The tripartite historical periodisation that Mill had introduced was to become hegemonic until well into the 1950s and beyond. Terms like 'Hindu Rule', 'Hindu Period', 'Hindu India', 'Muslim Rule', 'Muslim Period', etc., along with 'the British Period' came into common currency in learned works even when these works challenged the supremacy of Islam in the constitution of governance and placed much greater emphasis on the pursuit of personal or factional power by rulers and not always professedly on behalf of Islam. *The Foundation of Muslim Rule in India* by A.B.M. Habibullah and *Some Aspects of Muslim Rule in India* by R.P. Tripathi, classics of the ouevre of the past generation are two of several examples.[46] From the turn of the twentieth century, 'Ancient, Medieval and Modern India' came into use, Stanley Lane-Poole being the first to put the terms into circulation.[47] Its acceptance does not seem to have been immediate and complete, for less than two decades later Vicent A. Smith's influential *The Oxford History of India* while adopting 'Ancient India' for the early period, chose 'The Medieval Hindu Kingdoms' to designate the period between the death of King Harsha in A.D. 647 and the 'Muslim Conquest' and what we know as medieval India was described by him as 'India in the Muslim Period', followed by 'India in the British Period'.[48] But then even as the terms 'ancient', 'medieval' and 'modern' slowly gained currency, the basis for periodisation had not altered.[49] Within the university system, as in the professional world of historians, 'Ancient India' began with Harappa culture or the Indus Valley Civilisation as it was called since its archaeological excavation in the 1920s and terminated around the mid-eighth century A.D. with the end of the reign of King Harsha of north India. The 'Medieval Period' began either with Mahmud of Ghazni's invasion of north-western India in the first three decades of the eleventh century, or with the foundation of Muslim rule in [north] India in A.D. 1206, and usually terminated in A.D. 1707, the year of the death of the last of Great Mughals, Aurangzeb, or around the 1740s with the definitive collapse of the Mughal empire. 'Modern India' started its journey around the late eighteenth century, but effectively from the nineteenth century. The eighteenth century in particular inspired a rare unanimity among mutually exclusive schools of historians usually referred to as British Imperialist, Nationalist and Marxist, all of whom denounced it as the century of dreadful decline of empire, economy and social morality, the last almost always perceived as the unleashing of sexual libertarianism.[50]

The equation of ancient Indian history with the Hindu period and of medieval with the Muslim played a significant, though often conflicting role during the country's struggle for freedom from colonialism. Glorification and denunciation of India's remote as well as immediate past preceding the British conquest had both been part of the orientalist construction. If Sir William Jones upheld the achievements of the Hindus in early India and bemoaned their decline with the onset of the Muslim rule, James Mill inverted the picture if only to argue that even the more celebrated Muhammadan period was dismal compared to the benefits that the British had brought to the Indians. Admiration and contempt for India's past nearly always merged in the works of British historians and British administrator-historians in the ultimate legitimation of British rule.

These strands, however, had a different meaning of Indian historians. Glorification of ancient Indians'—inevitably Hindus'—achievements was constructed as the nationalist critique of the economic and cultural impoverishment of India following its subjugation to foreign conquest. The early author of this critique, R.C. Dutt, counterposed Hindu and British India and virtually skipped the Muslim period. But 'foreign conquest' came to encompass the medieval period as well, and hence the story of India's secular decline since then.[51]

The historians of medieval India had, however, to face a different set of problems. The history of medieval India became the battleground for the constitution and contestation of the 'two-nation theory' which culminated in the country's partition. The theory was based on the assumption of an exclusive and oppositional nature of the religion, culture, history and social structure of the two major communities, constituted in the perspectives of the twentieth century as nations. Contest to it came from the notion of a 'composite culture', a shared history and culture between the communities in which both had contributed and imbibed from each other. If the dividing lines of history were drawn across the Hindu and Muslim communities, the practicing historians were not so neatly divided, for Hindu and Muslim historians were fairly distributed on each side of the fence.

In some ways the fence on the battleground of medieval history mirrored the poltical battles being waged in the struggle against colonialism. The hegemonic dichotomy that came to characterise the internal cleavages of the struggle was imaged in the Congress versus the Muslim League opposition, posited by the Congress leadership as well as nationalist historians as nationalism versus communalism. The difference between the two was, however, one of strategy rather than of analytical category. The nationalism of the Congress comprised the notion of a composite culture and history shared by Hindus and Muslims alike. The slogn '*Hindu–Muslim bhai bhai* (Hindus and Muslims are like brothers) expressed this strategy in popular parlance; the Sanskrit phrase '*sarva dharma sama bhav*' (like treatment of all religions) was its rarefied conceptual version. The analytical category, however, remained the religious community identity. Hindus and Muslims were mobilised by the Congress as Hindus and Muslims, although as brothers.

The Muslim League, on the other hand, used the same category of mobilisation by discounting the shared history and culture and underlining innate hostility between two adversarial religions, a view also vehemently endorsed by Hindu 'communalists'. The step from a shared 'brotherhood' to enmity was a short and easy one, for, if the Congress and the Muslim League, or nationalism and communalism were empirically each others negations, conceptually they traversed much of the ground hand in hand. The shared conceptual, analytical category of the religious community established the two in a relationship of continuum rather than a dichotomy.[52]

This division was reflected in the writing of medieval Indian history, between the 'nationalist' and the 'communalist' historians. They pictured medieval Indian history either as a story of eternal bonhomie between the communities or of unrelenting conflict, often using the same data bases.

The growing influence of Marxist perspectives on Indian history writing, especially from the mid-1950s onward, reconstituted the problematics and therefore redefined the boundaries of the tripartite division. While several Marxist studies had appeared earlier, the publication of *An Introduction to the Study of Indian History* by the mathematician D.D. Kosambi in 1956 effected the paradigm shift. Although it was in exploration almost entirely given to 'ancient' India, a term that forms part of his next book's title, its influence was pervasive. Class displaced the religious community as the analytical category. If Kosambi's work provided an alternative broad framework for the study of Indian history, Irfan Habib's magisterial, *The Agrarian System of Mughal India,* 1963, gave it flesh and blood by its empirical richness and methodological sharpness.

New problematics around class structure and class struggles, technology and its relationship with social change, etc., created tensions vis-à-vis the old frame of historical periodisation which had essentially followed the contours of dynastic history, for the rhythms of social and economic change did not always coincide with those of dynastic displacements. However, the basic frame of the tripartite division was never seriously questioned, even as its boundaries were. The emergence of the concept of 'Indian feudalism' in D.D. Kosambi's and R.S. Sharma's works between 1956 and 1965 led to the conceptualisation of an 'early medieval India', a period whose origin is variously dated anywhere from the fourth century A.D. to the seventh, and terminating around the establishment of the Delhi Sultanate in A.D. 1206,[53] the beginning of 'medieval India'. 'Early medieval India' in some ways expands the temporal domain of medieval India, but, more important, emphasises the search for transitions in the socio-economic sphere. Its chief proponent, R.S. Sharma, had indeed sought to counterpose this period both to the ones that preceded and followed it by postulating it as the period of the efflorescence of Indian feudalism; but, looked at from another perspective, important and comprehensive developments during this period laid the foundation of much that was to characterise 'medieval' Indian social and economic structures, and, to a large extent, even state formation.[54]

These, however, were the debates of the 1950s to the 80s. The 1990s have again brought Indian historiography on the verge of another threshold, with emphasis on social and cultural profiles, power relations manifest in everyday life, within the family, inter-personal relationships and the study of space and time in historical contexts; equally, ecology is drawing historians' attention. These problematics by their nature defy tight temporal straitjackets. Explorations along these lines might lead to a far more effective questioning of the tripartite division than has hitherto been possible.

NOTES

1. Franz Rosenthal, *A History of Muslim Historiography,* Leiden, 1952: 13-14.
2. The histories have been a subject of several analyses in recent decades. See Peter Hardy, *Historians of Medieval India,* London, 1960; M. Hasan (ed.), *Historians of Medieval India,* Meerut, 1968; Harbans Mukhia, *Historians and Historiography During the Reign of Akbar,* New Delhi, 1976; Jagadish Narayan Sarkar, *History of History Writing in Medieval India,* Calcutta, 1977; Khaliq Ahmad Nizami, *On History and Historiography of Medieval India,* New Delhi, 1983. These follow earlier article-length studies: Hidayat Husain, 'Contemporary Historians of the Reign of Shah Jahan', *Islamic Culture,* 1941; A.B.M. Habibullah, 'A Re-evaluation of the Literary Sources of Pre-Mughal History', *Islamic Culture,* 1941; Shaikh Abdur Rashid, 'Zia-ud-din Barani: A Study', *Aligarh Muslim University Journal,* 1942; Mohammad Habib, 'Life and Thought of Ziauddin Barani' in M. Afsar Khan and M. Habib, *Political Theory of the Delhi Sultanate,* Allahabad, n.d.
3. Tarif Khalidi, *Arabic Historical Thought in the Classical Period,* Cambridge, 1994:115.
4. D.O. Morgan, 'Persian Historians and the Mongols' in D.O. Morgan (ed.), *Medieval Historical Writing in the Christian and Islamic Worlds,* London, 1982: 118–20.
5. There are two emphatic attempts at writing a 'world history': Minhaj al-Siraj's *Tabaqat-i Nasiri,* written in late thirteenth century A.D. and Abul Fazl's *Akbar Nama,* towards the end of the sixteenth. 'World history' for Minhaj comprised an account of the descent of humanity from Adam through Muhammad and the capliphs and the spread of Islam in the regions of West and Central Asia from where it had moved into northern India; for Abul Fazl, 'world history' was more a temporal than a spatial

category inasmuch as Akbar, the author's patron–ruler, was the 53rd descendant of Adam, unmediated by Muhammad and the caliphs, and was therefore the ruler of all humanity. The history of Akbar thus signals the culmination of all human history. For a discussion of both historians see Harbans Mukhia, *Historians and Historiography.*

6. Franz Rosenthal employs the term 'dynastic history' in the Arab context in his *Muslim Historiography*: 77.
7. Ibid.: 88, where he locates 'a sign of the influence of Persian national historiography', even though prior to the thirteenth century A.D. most works on Iran's history are written primarily in Arabic. See Bertold Spuler, 'The Evolution of Persian Historiography' in Bernard Lewis and P.M. Holt (eds), *Historians of the Middle East,* London, 1962: 126. R. Stephen Humphreys, however, draws attention to 'the new historiography' of the Middle Periods (from the ninth and early tenth centuries A.D.) written in both Arabic and Persian, *Islamic History: A Framework for Inquiry,* New York, 1995: 128–47. On Tabari's defence, Khalidi, *Arabic Historical Thought:* 78.
8. F. Rosenthal, *Muslim Historiography:* 71–72: Khalidi, *Arabic Historical Thought:* 73: Aziz al-Azmeh, 'Histoire et narration dans I'historiographie arabe', *Annales: Economies, Sociétiés Civilisations,* Mars-Avril 1986, 2: 418.
9. Aziz al-Azmeh, 'Histoire et narration': 420–21.
10. R. Stephen Humphreys, *Islamic History:* 130.
11. Khalidi, *Arabic Historical Thought:* 7. See also Aziz al-Azmeh, 'Chronophagous Discourse: A Study of Clerico-Legal Appropriation of the World in an Islamic Tradition' in Frank E. Reynolds and David Tracy (eds), *Religion and Practical Reason,* Albany, New York, 1994: 166, 167; and F. Rosenthal, *Muslim Historiography:* 18.
12. The argument is developed at some length in Harbans Mukhia, *The Mughals,* (forthcoming).
13. Mohammad Tavakoli–Targhi, 'Contested Memories: Narrative Structures and Allegorical Meanings of Iran's Pre-Islamic History' in his *Vernacular Modernity,* (forthcoming). An earlier version of it appeared in *Iranian Studies,* vol. 29 (1–2), 1996, 149–75; Khalidi, *Arabic Historical Thought:* 78–79.
14. Tavakoli–Targhi, 'Contested Memories'.
15. Abul Fazl, *Akbar Nama* (ed.), Maulavi Abd al-Rahim, II, Calcutta, 1881: 9–13; idem, *Ain-i Akbari* (ed.), H. Blochmann, I, Calcutta, 1872: 265–78.

16. Abul Fazl, *Akbar Nama,* II: 10, 18; *Ain,* I: 277–78.
17. Barbara W. Tuckman, *A Distant Mirror: The Calamitous 14th Century,* New York, 1978: 54.
18. Abul Fazl, *Ain,* I: 277.
19. Inayat Khan, *Shah Jahan Nama,* trans., A.R. Fuller, revised and edited by W.E. Begley and Z.A. Desai, Delhi, 1990: xix and 219.
20. Abul Fazl, *Ain-i Akbari,* II (ed.), H. Blochmann, Calcutta, 1877: 61–193.
21. Mulla Abdul Qadir Badauni, *Muntakhab,* III (ed.), Maulavi Ahamd Ali, Calcutta, 1869: 393–94.
22. Bakhtawar Khan, *Mirat al-Alam,* MS. No. Farsi Tarikh 51, Maulana Azad Library, Aligarh Muslim University, Aligarh, f. 185b.
23. Badauni, *Muntakhab,* I (ed.), Maulavi Ahamad Ali, Calcutta, 1868: 5, 7–8.
24. Paul E. Walker, 'Eternal Cosmos and the Womb of History: Time in Early Ismaili Thought', *International Journal of Middle East Studies,* vol. 9, 1978: 357; E. Goodman, 'Time in Islam' in Anindita Niyogi Balslev and J.N. Mohanty (eds), *Religion and Time,* Leiden, 1993: 138–62.
25. Louis Massignon, 'Time in Islamic Thought', *Man and Time,* Bollingen series, 30(3), 1957: 108–9. Goodman, however, suggests that discontinuous time is one among several strands of religious thought in Islam. Goodman, 'Time in Islam'.
26. Khalidi, *Arabic Historical Thought:* 8, 120.
27. Abul Fazl, *Akbar Nama,* I: 52.
28. Ibid.: 49–50.
29. Ibid.: 52.
30. Abul Fazl, *Ain,* I: 273.
31. *Babur Nama* (ed.) and trans., from the original Turkish by A.S. Beveridge, New Delhi 1970, reprint: 516–17.
32. Ibid.: 577.
33. Ibid.: 59, 100, 132.
34. Abul Fazl, *Akbar Nama,* I: 50–52; II: 11–12; *Ain,* I: 269–72.
35. Abul Fazl, *Ain,* I: 578.
36. Ibid.: 469.
37. Ibid.: 414, 516.
38. Jacques Le Goff, *History and Memory,* trans., Steven Rendall and Elizabeth Claman, New York, 1992: 27.
39. Ibid.: 28 and XII.
40. Henry E. Barnes, *A History of Historical Writing,* New York, 1962: 16.

41. J. Mill, *The History of British India,* ed. H.H. Wilson, 10 vols, London, 1858; J.S. Grewal, *Medieval India: History and Historians,* Amritsar, 1975: 10–11. For the prehistory and the formative influence of British rule in India on Mill's work, see J. Majeed, *Ungoverned Imaginings: James Mill's The History of British India and Orientalism,* Oxford, 1992.
42. Ronald Inden, *Imagining India,* Oxford, 1990: 45–46.
43. Thus, for example, in Romila Thapar, Harbans Mukhia and Bipan Chandra, *Communalism and the Writing of Indian History,* New Delhi, 1969.
44. For a detailed discussion of this argument see Mukhia, *Historians and Historiography.*
45. Harbans Mukhia, 'Communalism and the Writing of Medieval Indian History—a Reappraisal' in H. Mukhia, *Perspectives on Medieval History,* New Delhi, 1993. Also in this volume.
46. A.B.M. Habibullah, *The Foundation of Muslim Rule in India,* Allahabad, 1945(?) (date of the Preface to first edn); R.P. Tripathi, *Some Aspects of Muslim Rule in India,* Allahabad, 1936 (first edn).
47. Stanley Lane–Poole, *Mediaeval India Under Mohammadan Rule (A.D. 712–1764),* London, 1903. I am very grateful to Professor J.S. Grewal for drawing my attention to this important fact.
48. Headings of Parts/Chapters of V.A. Smith, *The Oxford History of India,* Oxford, first published 1917. Reference here is to the 1964 edn.
49. Lane–Poole himself was clear about the equation between Ancient/Hindu, Medieval/Muslim and Modern/British periods; see his Preface, iii. The equation has for long remained in circulation. Thus, to mention just one example, R.C. Majumdar, in a series of three lectures delivered in 1967, uses the terms interchangeably and quite unselfconsciously; see his *Historiography in Modern India,* London, 1970: 5–6 and *passim.*
50. For a brief summary of these perceptions, Urvashi Dalal, 'Delhi Society in the Eighteenth Century', Ph.D. dissertation, Jawaharlal Nehru University, New Delhi, 1998: Introduction.
51. Partha Chatterjee discusses this in the context of Bengal in his 'Claims on the Past: The Genealogy of Modern Historiography in Bengal' in David Arnold and David Hardiman (eds), *Subaltern Studies VIII,* New Delhi, 1994: 1–49. For an overview, Bipan Chandra, *Communalism in Modern India,* New Delhi, 1987: 209–36.
52. Harbans Mukhia, 'Communalism and Indian Polity', *South Asia*

Bulletin, 11 (1–2) 1991: 62–69. (The journal has since been re-christened *Comparative Studies of South Asia, Africa and the Middle East* and is published from Duke University, USA).

53. 'Early medieval India' has been used by several historians in different contexts and different meanings. For R.S. Sharma it coincides with the rise and growth of Indian feudalism between A.D. 300 and 1200 though his emphasis is on the centuries between the seventh and the eleventh; see his *Indian Feudalism c. 300–1200,* Calcutta, 1965. The term forms part of the title of B.D. Chattopadhyaya's recent anthology and covers roughly the same period, though he is no votary of feudalism in India; Chattopadhyaya, *The Making of Early Medieval India,* Delhi, 1994; in the Introduction, which seeks to historiographically contextualise the term, he expresses his discomfort with it but decides to use it for lack of a more appropriate alternative. A.B. Pandey's *Early Medieval India,* Allahabad, 1960, maps out the period from the advent of Islam in India in the early eighth century to the end of the Turkish regime of the Delhi Sultanate in 1526, with primary focus on dynastic history and a concluding chapter on early medieval society and government.
54. See the debate from 1981 to 1993 in *The Journal of Peasant Studies* originating with Harbans Mukhia's 'Was There Feudalism in Indian History?' in 1981, 3: 273–310, and B.D. Chattopadhyaya, 'Political Processes and the Structure of Polity in Early Medieval India' in his *The Making of Early Medieval India.*

4

The Celebration of Failure as Dissent in Urdu *Ghazal**

Recent years have brought a spate of serials centred on the theme of Urdu *ghazal* to the Indian television screens. The image of the *ghazal* in these serials is one of a kind of rhymed verse sung by courtesans in their *koṭhās* (residence-cum-performance locales), under the appreciative eye of the poet, and often lustful eye of a decrepit *zamīndār* whose purse is heavy but judgment is light. The singing is accompanied by some dancing, a few

---

* This paper has been long in coming. Earlier versions were experimented with in Seminars at the Indian Institute of Advanced Study, Shimla, Nehru Memorial Museum and Library, New Delhi, Allahabad Museum, Indira Gandhi National Centre for the Arts, Hindu College at the University of Delhi, my own Centre at JNU, and the Universities of Michigan and Pennsylvania at Ann Arbor and Philadelphia respectively. The discussion at each of these seminars greatly helped to sharpen arguments. Personal discussions with Professors Namwar Singh, Sadiqur Rahman Qidwai and Aslam Parvez were of immense help and I am extremely grateful to them for many suggestions. Muzaffar Alam and S. Ainul Hasan generously shared their knowledge of Persian literature with me and I remain deeply beholden to them. However, it was the stridency of Aijaz Ahmad's criticism at the Nehru Museum seminar, followed inevitably by an evening of shared drinks and recorded ghazals that added dimensions I had not thought of to begin with. So, special thanks to him. The translations of verses are, however, my own.

musical instruments being played by the courtesan's hangers-on, and unceasing rounds of liquor. The ambience in which the performance is enveloped is meant to convey what modern sensibilities would construe as decadence.[1]

This sensibility of decadence is reinforced by the coincidence of the efflorescence of Urdu *ghazal* in the eighteenth and the nineteenth centuries and what has for long been viewed by poets as well as historians as the crisis of Indian society, although the meaning of the term 'crisis' has undergone considerable mutation over time. If in the past, the collapse of the overarching Mughal state system was perceived as the trigger for the release of centrifugal energies that drove society into an impasse[2], for the present-day historians of the Aligarh Muslim University, the very imperial presence of the State in the seventeenth century was the springboard of an all-encompassing crisis in the following century.[3] But a sense of decline and decadence—with shaded zones in which the moral, the political and the social often dissolve into one another—seems to permeate the historians' vision of the era that saw the emergence of this new genre of poetry in India.

Yet, the *ghazal* is the very opposite of that image of decadence. Indeed its history, if not strictly speaking its origin, has given it one predominant idiom, that of dissent from what its creators had themselves perceived as a kind of decadence. 'Dissent', of course, could convey a range of meanings: the overt protest which leaves one in no doubt about the intent of the poet. Such, for example, is the tenor of an early verse of Jigar Moradabadi, not quite renowned for the poetry of protest:

Jo mahw-i jashn-i niẓām-i nau hain/pukār kar unsē kah rahā hūn//
Nichoḍte hain lahū g͟harībon kā / dast-i sarmāyadār ab bhī//

(My defiant call is addressed
to those immersed in the celebration of the new regime
That the capitalist's hand is
still merciless in squeezing blood out of the bodies of the exploited.)[4]

This paper will however focus on the subtle, implicit meaning of dissent, a meaning that is constructed as much as it is conveyed. A meaning that is nuanced.

The *ghazal*-form is one of rhymed verse, consisting of couplets whose number could vary with each composition.[5] Each couplet or *shi'r* is complete in form and meaning; often the mood of one *shi'r* in a *ghazal* differs from, or is even opposed to that of another. The *ghazal* therefore does not always have a single mood. It is essentially oriented towards a musical rendering, and therefore singing of all the couplets (*ash'ar*) of a *ghazal* in the same format does considerable violence to its very nature.

There is, however, a problem here: If the *ghazal* does not always have a single mood, doesn't the ascription of one single meaning—dissent, protest etc.—to its entire history become problematic? I would try to suggest that the wide range of moods and nuances in the *ash'ar* notwithstanding, the *ghazal*'s central categories—its imagery, symbols, emotions, above all its sensuality—have emerged and evolved through a history which has invested them with the meaning of dissent even when the context of its origin had yielded space to another.

The etymology of the word *ghazal* is 'talking to a woman about love'. *Ghazal* therefore is quintessentially love poetry; this makes it sensual poetry, though it usually stops short of crossing the threshold into the zone of Eros.[6] The aim of this paper will be to establish the social context of this love poetry and its sensuality.

The earlier explorations of the context of the overtly sensual tenor of *ghazal* have sought to root it in an empiricist mode of life's experience. Thus Khurshidul Islam and Ralph Russell first draw a rather gory profile of the inevitable tragic consequences of falling in love in medieval Indian society from which love had effectively been banished, and go on to explain the rise of the *ghazal* as an effusive manifestation of love's urges.

"Brought up in isolation from women, taught by society and his own emotions to believe in the overmastering power of love, fearful of the drastic reprisals he must face if he fell in love, himself believing that love is a danger to society, the lover is submitted to a strain which often proves literally unbearable and drives him mad. All such desperately intense emotions are expressed without restraint in the *ghazal*..." (Islam and Russell 1991: 98-9, 107-08).

At another place Ralph Russell confidently declares: "The central theme of the *ghazal* is love; and the love which it celebrates is, and in the society which produces the *ghazal* can only be, illicit love." (Russell 1992: 32).

Elaboration of this assertion comes a while later: marriage in medieval Indian society was purely utilitarian, devoid of tenderness; love could thus constitute an experience outside of the boundaries of marriage alone; hence it was illicit! Russell dares the Urdu-speaking scholars to admit this truth and reiterates the point: "I repeat, therefore, that the key to the understanding of the *ghazal* is the realization that it is the poetry of illicit love, of the love of a man for another man's betrothed or another man's wife" (Ibid., 1992: 33-5). Marion Molteno nearly reproduces the same argument: "Of all the emotions which are likely to have been suppressed in daily life and seek expression in poetry, the commonest is love.... Urdu love poetry appeals powerfully to anyone who has experienced the kind of love which brings disapproval from the society around them" (cited in Russell, 1992: 15).

Victor Kiernan, who has translated Muhammad Iqbal's and Faiz Ahmad Faiz's poetry into English, similarly traces, on a somewhat expansive contextual horizon, the overwhelming presence of love in *ghazal* to the absence of an actual experience of it in class-divided societies: "Romantic love between man and woman has been an instinct of every human community from the most primitive to the most refined.... But everywhere it has been hemmed-in by encroaching regulations and bans, very often following class division. In many regions, and in Asia at large by contrast with Europe, it came to be practically outlawed, and could hardly survive except in disguise. One cloak was supplied by the Sufi concept of the divine lover [around which the *ghazal* form had originated]" (Kiernan 1991: 14).

Kiernan goes on in the same vein: "There could be no full release for the less hardened among dominant classes from the morass of oppression and corruption in which they lived and moved and had their earthly being. Mystic poetry offered a substitute, escape from consciousness of the unpleasant realities, social as well as personal, that must have haunted them.... Sufi poetry was in essence the wail of an ossified society, a self-imprisoned civilization. The old order could only go on mouldering, all the worse attributes of the Asiatic state worsening as it grew more decrepit, until Western intrusion brought about a painful and costly new start" (Kiernan 1991: 15). See also Kiernan (1971: 36) where Urdu poetry has been envisioned as a safety valve.

Quite besides the somewhat questionable factual basis of the statement that the traditional Asian societies denied access to the experience of love to their men and women either on their own or in contrast with Europe,[7] the assumption here is that poetry, or for that matter any art form, is a mere reflex, a mirror image of one's actual sensual experience in real life. Thus both the expression as well as appreciation of a longing for love must be predicated upon an actual experience of love, manifest as sexual experience, or an actual denial of it, in real life. Presumably, then, societies that do not frown upon a free intermingling of men and women would be devoid of any artistic manifestation of the intense longing for love!

The empiricist underpinnings of this perspective are rather overpowering; there is no space here for any degree of autonomy of imagination, feeling, expression, even appreciation of the aesthetics of an art form without and outside of a 'material', i.e., physical experience of the kind which that art form seeks to communicate. Muhammad Sadiq, author of the standard *A History of Urdu Literature*, laments that "The poets take leave of facts and disport in the world of fancy and their greatness is measured by just how much they can indulge in ingenious invention" (Sadiq 1964: 34).[8] More important, there is no meaning imbedded in love poetry other than of corporeal love. It is hard not to be reminded of another positivist perspective which viewed religion as "but the reflex of the real world", an escape from the "real" life (Marx 1954: 79). Quite apart from the fact that romance, love, sexual pleasure were circumscribed with far greater fury by the Christian church in Europe from the inception to early modern centuries than by Islam or Hinduism in this part of the world, the very assumption that life, or the world, is divided into two halves—the "real"; i.e. material or sensual, and the cultural, or religious or aesthetic, that is at best "unreal" in the sense of being a mere reflex, or at worst a cloak or escape from that real world—is highly problematic, to put it mildly. It is not easy to understand how an aesthetic experience, or the feeling for beauty, is less real or a mere escape than the experience of making a living, for example or "sublimating" love in sexual intercourse; or a Sufi's ecstasy in what he experiences as his union with god any the less real, or a cloak, a surrogate sexual pleasure because he has been denied such pleasure in "real life".

This conception establishes a unitary meaning of love as purely corporeal and thus divests it of all its multiple nuances, its multifold ambiguities. For, love in Sufi discourse is an attribute of god, and the feeling of love in a human being is a manifestation of god's own existence. Indeed, Sufism consciously seeks to distance the experience of love from physical passion; it is cultivated and felt in the spirit (*rūh*) rather than in the body.[9] In Aijaz Ahmad's perception, "Urdu poetry ... never contemplates the experience of love in terms of a specific love relation." It is, for him, one of three questions that constitute the metaphysics of Urdu poetry, the other two being the nature of the universe and of god" (Ahmad 1971: xvi).

In medieval Hindi *sringār* poetry (poetry of romance), there is little space for the suppression of one's love for the sweetheart; indeed, it must constantly find utterance. The *ghazal*, on the other hand, sanctifies the concealment of one's love, keeping it a *rāz* (secret). The more the lover suppresses the manifestation of his love, the more he internalises it, the more he suffers the intense loneliness and sadness of love—that for him is the ultimate ecstasy, the supreme *gham* (the joy of eternal longing).

Neither of these conventional forms is a reflex of life's empirical experience; both are literary constructs whose significations go as much beyond life's quotidian existence as the limits of their own text. This paper therefore seeks to explore yet another facet of the expression of love and sensuality in the Urdu *ghazal* by locating it in an alternative social context. The context is one with two folds which mould *ghazal*'s history: Persio-Islamic lineage and Indian folklore.

Originating as part of *Qasīdah* (panegyric), with traces in Arabic literature, the *ghazal* developed as dissent from Islamic orthodoxy, but a dissent that remained internal to Islam, as another face of Islam, especially in Persian literary ambience.[10] By the time Urdu *ghazal* made its appearance, the Islamic context had considerably, though not entirely receded, for, this was also the time when renewed attempts were being made in India to assert an Islamic social and cultural identity to make up for the loss of 'Muslim' political power.[11] But the history of the *ghazal* had given protest against religious bigotry a hegemony that became supreme as well as autonomous. This hegemony was then easily transferred on to "secular" motifs either by altering the categories—imagery, metaphors, symbolisms etc.—or, more frequently, through a subtle change of nuances of old images, symbols, metaphors.

We might turn to a brief history of mutations within Islam for locating the origin of the *ghazal* in it. This context has not remained unexplored by scholars earlier, and some repetition of their researches could therefore perhaps be excused as necessary to make the point.

Islam, like every monotheistic religion, comprises two interrelated elements: universalism and protest, both manifest in its ideological underpinnings. The ideology of the meek inheriting the earth, as in Christianity, or of the existence of one god who looks after all his children with equal favour, as in Islam, constitutes a discourse in the true Foucauldian sense —the assertion of a new relation of social power.[12] This assertion invokes the universe of the "meek" and the deprived and counterposes an egalitarian ideology to one of dominance and subordination, drawing upon the dormant memory of tribal egalitarianism, much as secular ideologies, such as Marxism, were to do later on.

But the history of religions is also the history of strife, conflict, conquest and subjugation. It is more than ironic that a religion based upon universalism, protest and egalitarianism should culminate in conquest and subjugation; but then no egalitarian ideology creates, at least has ever empirically created, social equality. What it does create, however, is space for upward social mobility for those at the lower rungs of society. Islam created that space and unleashed enormous social energy.

Upward social movement itself inevitably generates consequential movement of social differentiation. Beginning with the assertion of tribal egalitarianism, the process of social differentiation and the history of the regions conquered by Arabic Islam eroded the fundamental tenets of Muhammad's discourse. Islam, thus face-to-face with tension between the inertia of existing structures and the momentum of the break, was going back upon itself, blurring the demarcating lines between continuity and change. But then this differentiation, the going back upon itself, was to create its own tensions and protests.

Early Islam thus witnessed a whole spectrum of dissensions—Shi'ite, Kharijite, Mu'tazalite.... Of these the last was an overt challenge that sought to subvert the newly emerged social differentiation and consequential hegemony; it combined arguments derived from Greek rationality and communitarian zeal and challenged the newly established social structure from below. It was more than a doctrinaire movement, being cast in an activist mould. It was therefore crushed with a heavy hand.[13]

There was, however, another mode of dissent, short on the activist front, but strong on the "moral" plane. It was far less virulent than the Mu'tazalite challenge; it did not seek to overthrow the new social regime, and bounded its protest within the given structure where it focused upon its 'impurities', and 'deviations' vis-à-vis the Islamic ideal. This was the Sufi protest.[14] Unlike the Mu'tazalite movement, which was strong, challenging, but short-lived, the less volatile Sufi protest proved far more durable, precisely for reasons of remaining internal to the system.

The Sufis, in focusing upon the impurities that had crept into Islam, were seeking to appropriate the legacy of Muhammad and his immediate successors, the pious caliphs, and thus highlighting the impieties of the present by contradistinction. The regime of Muhammad and the pious caliphs for long remained the reference point in both religious and secular literature in Islam.

The State, in Sufi discourse, constituted the chief deviation from Islamic puritanism and it thus became the focal point of disapproval expressed in various modes: one was to establish distance between oneself and the institutions and officials of the state. The Sufis were, by excluding themselves from the discourse of the state, expressing their disapproval of it; in a subtle way they were also excluding the state from their own discourse. But then the exclusion was always shaded with a certain ambivalence, for the Sufis did not question the existence of the state. In courting and practising poverty, they expressed disapproval of riches, but their doors were not closed to "unsought donations" (*futūḥ*) including at times from the rulers.[15] The monarchical form of governance, with all power vesting in the ruler, provided the prototype for the authority system that guided the functioning of their single monastic establishments or the whole 'order' of these establishments (*k͟hānqāhs* and *silsilahs*): the high estimate of the spiritual calibre of a Sufi was best expressed in analogy with the ruler—*Sultān al-Mashāikh* (Sultan amongst the shaikhs);[16] the practice of demarcated territorial jurisdiction of each *k͟hānqāh* copied the pattern of state administration.[17] At a certain stage, state officials began to maintain professional representatives (*vakīls*) to intercede on their behalf with the living or dead Sufis for their benediction, just as their *vakīls* protected their material interests at the imperial Court (Moini 1993: 155-63). The rulers on the other hand constantly treated the Sufi renouncers as their superior by visiting them in their hermitage, by giving them gifts and by expressing the wish to give up their kingdom and become *darvīshes*.[18] A certain element of symbiosis therefore moderated the tension of the Sufis' relationship with the state. The relationship was, in Akbar S. Ahmad's words, akin to "the opposition party to the establishment" (Ahmad 1988: 10, 90).

If this was one mode of expressing Sufis' disapproval of the state, the other—often an extension of the first—was to adopt stances very different from, at times even opposed to, the stances of the ruling class and, in particular, its ideological props, the *'ulamā*. The coalition between the ruler and the *ālim* is a later, logical corollary of the integration of political and religious authority in one person—first in Muhammad, then in the long line of his successors, the caliphs. It is with the establishment of *sult* (power) as the basis of governance that the Sultan and the Sultanate saw to the separation between the persons holding political and religious authority, partly as a reassertion of pre-Islamic Persian tradition and, to an even greater degree, the Turko-Mongol tradition in which Islam sat rather lightly at the surface under which a whole range of pagan religious forms and practices persisted.[19]

The Sufi thought and practice, originating in Arabia, found its efflorescence in Iran and India, its best literary manifestation being the Persian *ghazal*, the parent form of the Urdu *ghazal*. At the level of ideology, the Sufis counterposed the individual mystic experience to the argumentative theology of the *'ulamā*. Two world views were being constructed here: the world of the heart and that of the head, a durable dichotomy central to the *ghazal* poets. Thus Jalāl al-Dīn Rūmī, the greatest of mystic poets of the Persian language:

> *Bashūī ai aql dast-i khwīsh az man /*
> *ki dar majnūn paivastam man imrūz //*

(Draw away your controlling hand from me, Wisdom,
For, I am immersed in Majnūn this day)

The counterposition of the head and the heart is not one of rationality and irrationality, but of argumentation and feeling, of hegemonic ambition and universalism. The constructed realm of the head was contentious, fractious, domineering, which brooked no dissent; that of the heart experienced love, affection, humanism and was therefore universalist. One was a world of friction, conquest, hegemony; the other a world of harmony and peace amidst divergence. Hāfiz Shīrazī, who, besides Rūmī, was the other great poet of the Sufi genre in the Persian language, put this construction with the most charming simplicity:

Khalal pazīr buwad har binā ki mī bīnī
bajuz binā –i moḥabbat ki khālī az khalal ast

(Every foundation you see is vulnerable
The foundation of love alone is free of any disturbance)

The head vs. the heart or *khirad* vs. *junūn* dichotomy, characteristic of the *ghazal*, also implicated a dichotomy of elite vs popular cultures, the poet always upholding the latter with its universalist categories—love, affection, humanism, sorrow, pain etc. counterposed to the perceived elite categories of conquest and dominance, equated with the head. In the Persian poet Jāmī's *sh'ir*:

Darmāndah-i ṣalāḥ o fasad ham alḥaẓar
z īn rasamhā ki mardom-i āqil nihādah und

(Deprived of rectitude and corrupted with fear
This is where the people of wisdom have landed us)

The experience of the heart, counterposed to the argumentation of the head, found expression in the language of love, of romance. In the Persian *ghazal* compositions of the Sufis, god is mostly portrayed as the woman, the beloved, and man as the lover. The everlasting longing of the Sufi soul for union with god finds utterance in the longing of the lover for the beloved. The expression of intensely emotional devotion to god in terms of the human feelings of love between man and woman points to its popular origins, similar to expressions in other cultural zones, such as the Radha-Krishna legends in literature, painting and sculpture. The Radha-Krishna relationship, however, goes further than longing and the ecstasy of their union often finds expression in the orgasmic ecstasy of lovers after a long waiting and pining.[20]

In the *ghazal*, however, there is to be no union; for the poet, longing itself is the ecstasy, a value, an end. Thus *gham* (literally sorrow or pain, but better understood as "eternal longing"), central to the *ghazal*, is celebrated and courted rather than lamented and averted. Majnūn (the one possessed, the one obsessed with love for his beloved Laila in the Arab legendary romance) becomes the role model for the *ghazal* poet: a man in tattered clothes, the very image of total failure in life and even in love, yet a failure because of his obsession with love to the point of insanity, stones being cast at him, subject to social defamation, yet evoking a silent admiration for his magnificent obsession, his contempt of temporal success—this is the image the *ghazal*-poet most empathizes with. Majnūn of the *ghazal* is the very embodiment of *gham*, for which the poet longs forever. We have already heard Jalāl al-Dīn Rūmī exclaim his 'immersion' in Majnūn to the derision of Wisdom. Mirza Ghalib evokes the same empathy:

Main ne Majnūn pe laḍkpan mein asad /
sang uṭhāyā thā ki sar yād āyā //

[Even as I, a young lad, picked up a stone to cast at Majnun
The vision of my own bleeding head as I would grow up passed before my eyes (and the stone dropped from my hand)]

In the image of Majnūn, the poet was celebrating the humane 'insanity' of the lover and his world of complete failure in counterposition to the inhuman 'sanity' of the pursuit of success by the mighty and the dominant. *Gham*, eternal longing, itself implied the failure to unite with the sweetheart and as such stood for total failure in life, for the sweetheart could be anyone or anything—woman, god, revolution, humanity, a cause, whatever. *Gham* courts, dignifies and celebrates failure.

The courting and celebration of failure is a form of resistance, of disapproval, even of lampooning of the 'success' of Authority, secular or religious. The puritanical, forever-sermonizing *muḥtasib, wāiẓ, nāsīḥ, shaikh*—representing both religious and state authority—became special targets of ridicule and defiance:

Ze khānqāh be maikhānah mīrawad ḥāfiẓ /
magar ze mastī zuhd-i riyā ba hūsh āmad//

(Hafiz heads from the *khānqāh* to the tavern
If only to recover his senses after the moralist's hypocritical sermon)

Sauda, the eighteenth-century Urdu poet reverts to a theme common among poets of the *ghazal*: the moralist—*shaikh, muḥtasib*, etc.— sermonizing others on temperance, but himself stealing into the tavern:

Koī maikhāné se nāgah shām ko guzré jo shaikh
kyā kahūn Saudā jo rindon ne sulūk un sé kiyā

(Even as the Shaikh passed by the tavern in the eve
It's beyond Sauda to describe the treatment meted him by the tavern mates)

For Mir, Sauda's contemporary and trend-setter of Urdu poetry, 'ass' (*khar*) was the favourite, if a little impolite epithet for the *shaikh*. And Ghalib berates the *wā'iẓ* thus:

Kahān maikhāné kā darwāzā ghālib aur kahān wā'iẓ /
par itnā jānté hain kal woh jātā thā ki ham niklé //

(What! the *Wāiẓ* standing aface the tavern door!
But, believe me, Ghalib, I did see him stealing in as I departed)

Indeed, this lampooning of the religious moralist, standing-in for the *'ulamā*, is one of the invariable motifs of the *ghazal* poets, irrespective of their own predilections. For, life-principle, even a life steeped in immense agony is of cardinal faith for the poet. This upholding of life as the supreme principle is tantamount to denial of supremacy of even god and religion over it. For Ghalib:

Naghmahā –i gham ko bhī ai dil ghanīmat jāniyé
be ṣadā ho jāyegā yeh sāz –i hastī ek din

(Mercy be for the melody of life
Even for the melody steeped in agony
For, some day music will ebb away from this song)

Or, in a gem of a *sh'ir* Ghalib laments life's sorrows, life here impersonating more than himself:

Na gul-i naghmah hūn nah pardah-i sāz
main hūn apnī shikast kī āvāz/

(I am not the rose of melody, nor the sound of music
I am the echo of life itself that lies shattered)

Even as Ghalib hears the echo of life shattered around him, the imagery he draws upon is that of the colour of the rose of melody and the resonance of a musical instrument somewhere in the distance. The imagery of melody for life immersed in sorrow is common to both the couplets cited above.

Life in turn is perceived entirely in its sensual moment, counterposed to the chilling puritanism preached by the *muḥtasib,* hence by religious orthodoxy, carrying with it the authority of the State. This sensuality is expressed in a continuum from the seventeenth century poet Ja'far Zatallī's extremely "obscene" (i.e. sexually explicit) poetry, much like hardcore porn, to the subtle, elite poetry of Ghalib. Zatallī's 'obscenity' too is best appreciated as one that stands the puritanism of Aurangzeb's reign on its head, though he composes a poem in honour of the emperor as well (Ahmad, 1979). In a sophisticated mode, it is hard to locate a more aesthetic expression of sensuality than in Ghalib's *sh'ir*:

Gar hāth ko jumbish nahīn ānkhōn mein to dam hai
rahné dé abhī sā<u>gh</u>ar o mīnā méré āgé

(If life has ebbed away from my limbs the glow of desire still lingers in the eyes. Let the pitcher and the cup be before me)

If lampooning the *shai<u>kh</u>* etc. challenged institutional authority, the *ghazal* poets went beyond the institution and contested the ideological grounding of the *'ulamā's* version of Islam which brooked no dissent, for it is dissent, above all, that the *ghazal*-poets upheld and celebrated. For the *'ulamā* the truth of Islam was to be manifest in an act of conquest, subjugation and humiliation of people of other faiths, *kāfirs.* Ziā al-Dīn Baranī, the fourteenth-century historian was aghast that the Sultans of Delhi were content with the imposition of *jiziyā* on their non-Muslim subjects as an index of the Islamic nature of their state; they missed the real import of it, namely that the *kāfirs* must be humiliated for their refusal to convert to Islam (Baranī n.d. 44-7). In the celebrated conversation between Sultan 'Alā al-Dīn-Khaljī and a *qāẓī* of his empire, Mu<u>gh</u>īs al-Dīn, the *qāẓī* allegedly reprimanded the Sultan for collecting the revenue from the Hindus merely for filling up the state's coffers rather than as a means of humiliation for them. He even prescribed, in gory detail, the form of such humiliation: "While collecting the revenue, if the collector wished to spit into the *kāfir's* mouth, the *kāfir* should open his mouth to receive the spit. It is in such action that the glory of Islam lies" (Baranī 1862: 290).[21] In the reign of Sikandar Lodi, the *'ulamā* insisted on the execution of a Brahmin, Lodhan by name, who had the audacity to observe that both Islam and Hinduism were on a par as far as the Truth was concerned (Abdullāh 1954: 59-60). Akbar too, early in his reign, had to succumb, much against his will, to the pressure of Shaikh Abd al-Nabī, his *Sadr*, and order the execution of another Brahmin, who, the *Sadr* felt, had been less than respectful to Muhammad (Badāunī 1868: 80-2). The dichotomy between the Faith and *Kufr* was, for the *'ulamā*, permanent and indissoluble.

Not for the *ghazal*-poets, though. For them it was *'ishq* (Love), manifest as *g͟ham*, that stood above all other antagonisms and diluted, even dissolved them. For Mak͟hdūm al-Mulk

Har turā dar 'ishq-i mahkam shud qadam
dar guzasht aẓ kufr was aẓ islām ham

(Whoever sets his foot firmly in *'ishq*
Passes beyond the boundaries of *Kufr* and Islam)

Ghalib is equally attracted by the force of Islam and of *Kufr*:

Īmān mujhé roké hai to khīnché hai mujhé kufr
Ka'bah méré pīché hai kalīsā méré āgé

(Faith pulls me back
Even as Infidelity draws me with force
I stand transfixed
Between the Ka'aba and the church)

And more challengingly:

Khudā ké vāsṭé pardah nah Ka'abé se uṭhā zālim
kahin aisā na ho yān bhī vahī kāfir ṣanam niklé

(In God' s name draw not the veil away from the *Ka'aba*
Lest the selfsame *Kāfir* idol make its appearance underneath)

For Ghalib the very holiness of the *Ka'aba* itself is a mere cloak which is just as well left intact lest the truth, i.e. the *Kāfir* idol, be discovered as the foundation of the Faith!

Indeed, for the poets, *kāfir* becomes the greatest term of endearment, a synonym for the sweetheart. Thus for Mīr a fleeting glimpse of the *kāfir* idol's face is enough to forget all about Islam:

Dekhī hai jab se us buté kāfir kī shaql mīr
Jātā nahīn hai jī tunuk islām kī ṭaraf

(Ever since the *kāfir* idol's face passed before my eyes
My heart is no longer inclined towards Islam even a wee bit)

And Ghalib uses a delightful pun to express his love for the *kāfir* beloved:

Moḥabbat mein nahīn hai farq jīné aur marné kā
usī ko dekh kar jīté hain jis kāfir pe dam niklé

(Love erases the difference between life and death
I live by the sight of the *Kāfir* who takes my breath away)

However unlike in the history of the Persian *ghazal* in the Sufi milieu in which it engages in a fierce contestation of the *'ulamā*'s ground, Urdu *ghazal* developed in India when the Mughal empire was waning and any perception of the ascendancy of Islam could hardly be empirically sustained. Urdu *ghazal* is therefore far less attuned to the problems of spiritualism or Sufism or any form of religious philosophy than the Persian *ghazal* was (Russel 1992: 43), though of course Sufic undertones are easy to detect in the very notion of unbounded love for the sweetheart or of *gham* itself, reminiscent of the fundamental Sufi notion of *fanā'* (self-annihilation and immersion in the beloved, i.e. god). But then the operative categories of this poetry, once formed, transcended their immediate context and remained hegemonic even in other contexts.

The Urdu *ghazal* also evolved within the Indian folkloric milieu, far more permeable to pluralist cultural streams than several other civilizations.[22] Urdu *ghazal*, and Urdu literature in general, derives a great deal of its idiom from this milieu, even when its poetics are Persian in their origin. A remarkable testimony to the influences of this milieu is the 'Indianization' of even classic Persian texts, such as *Dāstān-i Amīr Hamza,* in its Urdu version.[23]

It is important to remember that Urdu was initially, and for very long time, the bazaar language, spoken by the common people and derided by the elite. It is equally important to remember that the early Urdu *ghazal*s were composed in the bazaar language whether in the Deccan or in Lucknow or in Delhi; consequently, not only the vocabulary and the idiom but the whole culture of the bazaar gets imbibed and reflected in this poetry, inviting derision of the elite Persian poets of the Court. J'afar Zatallī reflects the unpolished exuberance of that culture in Delhi. Through the eighteenth century, whether in the compositions of Delhi's Urdu poets like Najī, Fāyiz, Dard, Soz or of the great masters like Saudā and Mīr, the language continued to be heavily moulded by the one spoken in the streets. In the Deccan, at the hands of Qulī Qutb Shāh and Wajahī, it is the script, rather than the language, that showed any marked influence of the Persian *ghazal*. Thus in Qulī Qutb Shāh's couplet

'Ishq mein mast matvālī hūn Lālā
tūn ap adharān the munj kun denā pyālā

(Steeped I am in love, O Lālā
Place the cup of your lips on mine)

except for the Persian word *'ishq*, all other words are local and the whole structure of the sentiment (very inadequately carried in the translation) as well as the idiom are taken as if from the lore of Krishna. So too in Wajahī:

Piyā bin pyālā uchā jāye nā
Piyā bāj ek til jiyā jāye nā

(I can hardly lift the cup without my Love
I can hardly live a moment without my Love)

Interestingly, in both these couplets the subject is female expressing love for the male, akin to the Hindi tradition, instead of the other way around which came to characterize later Urdu *ghazal* (Sadiq, 1964, p. 45). It is with Mirza Ghalib that the language and the imagery came to acquire a heavy Persian garb.

Sensuality and the principle of the supremacy of life, or, if the term be permitted, life-principle, are essential characteristics of folklore. At the level of folklore, life-principle governs human relationship with divinity; there is no conception here of an Almighty God, with absolute authority over human life and human beings' unqualified subjection to it. On the contrary, human relationship with divinity is based on contractual terms with clear-cut material or sensual objects in view: birth of a son, cure from chronic ailments, plentiful harvest and, not infrequently, fall of calamity on one's adversary— all this in return for a price: donation to a tomb or a temple, feast for the gods, etc. (Mukhia, 1990). If the contract falls through, wholesome abuse of god follows in its train. At the elite level, the relationship is far more one-sided, though of course the dividing lines can never be very neatly drawn.

The 'secular' colour of Urdu *ghazal* may perhaps reflect the impact of this second source of its formation, the culture of the bazaar, particularly in view of the receding importance of Islam and the strong flavour of lampooning the ruler and the priest that marks folklore.

From both the Persian as well as the folklore lineages, Urdu *ghazal* drew upon the tradition of dissent to evolve its categories. So hegemonic did these become that even when rulers or priests themselves wrote the *ghazal*, the only categories available, and which they happily employed, were the ones that had the smell of ridiculing them.

NOTES

1. Much of this construction of decadence is indeed equated with 'excessive' sexual indulgence, perceived as 'moral' decline. Sir Jadu Nath Sarkar speaks of the setting-in of a 'moral canker in the Mughal Empire', manifest, among other things, as the 'sexual excess' and 'drug habit' of Muhammad Shah, last of the line of notable imperial rulers; see his *Fall of the Mughal Empire*, (Sarkar 1932, I: 5, 7). In Tara Chand's vision, in the 18th century '...an indescribable malaise had settled upon the spirit of India [and] a moral and intellectual canker was sapping its vitality', though his reference point is art and literature (Chand

1961, I, pp. 217-18). The *ghazal* itself has frequently been perceived as an index of medieval 'moral' decadence (See Sadiq 1964: 33-4).

However, doubts about the notion of decline in the 18th century began to be raised early. Hermann Goetz in his *The Crisis of Indian Civilization in the Eighteenth and Early Nineteenth Centuries* (Calcutta, 1938), conceded the decay of the imperial polity, but saw cultural efflorescence in the period. George D. Bearce too questioned the construction of decline in the sphere of culture and traced the notion to 'the historiography of nineteenth century utilitarians and reformers of Britain' reinforced by historians inspired by the freedom struggle; see his 'The Culture of Eighteenth Century India: A Reappraisal', *Proceedings of the Indian History Congress* (24th Session, 1961, pp. 287-96). More recently several valuable works of C.A. Bayly have opened the problematic of decline to an encompassing re-evaluation.

2. The classic argument in this genre was put forward by Sir Jadu Nath Sarkar (Sarkar 1932-50).
3. The leader of this group of distinguished historians is indisputably Irfan Habib, whose influential work, (Habib 1963) laid down the framework of the alternative argument, which, at least for Habib and his AMU colleagues, still remains like Caesar's wife—above the slightest suspicion. Any doubts raised by other historians are dismissed by a frantic wave of the hand. Thus, several recent papers published in the name of M. Athar Ali on India's 18th century exhibit a deep sense of insecurity at growing knowledge, insecurity that is manifest as aggressive, at times bemusing, reassertion of arguments that are at best passé; such, for example, is the debate on the somewhat sterile old dichotomies about India's 18th century being dark or bright or whether the Mughal empire was centralized or decentralized. See Athar Ali 1986-87:102-10; 1993: 699-710.

The formula applied in these articles is simplicity itself: 'While in India these conclusions [of Irfan Habib] received considerable acceptance and have received continuing confirmation from studies of documentary material from all parts of India, these views have been subjected to increasing suspicion by an ever larger set of Western scholars.' The world is thus neatly divided into the supporters and opponents of AMU historians [=Irfan Habib], a division that also coincides with the scholars' national identities! The demarcating line is, sadly, vitiated by some deserters like Muzaffar Alam and Chetan Singh; but then happily there is compensation, for Eric Stokes from the rival ranks can mercifully still be mobilized to AMU's rescue. At any rate, M. Athar Ali assures us that Alam's and Singh's scholarship is quite shoddy anyway, and all one needs to do is to 'blow away the smoke' of their 'verbiage' to reach the immovable rock of historiographical truth established 'since the early 1960s' [by Habib]. If one were to extend Professor M. Athar Ali's Indian vs. the Western scholars dichotomy just a wee bit, the validity of one's argument would then also be liable to the test of whether one was a North or a South Indian or a Hindu or a Muslim historian! See also Malik 1990: 3-35, for the dark vs. bright 18th-century debate.

4. Later on, realizing that such stridency was somewhat out of tune with the *ghazal*'s genre, Jigar republished it as a poem (*nazm*) rather than as a *ghazal*. See Qidwai 1991: 132. However, it is this poetry of overt protest that is the theme of Muhammad Hasan's study (Hasan 1977: 28-49).
5. Sadiq, however, observes that early on in the course of its evolution, the *ghazal* would usually comprise 'ten lines (five couplets) or so' (Sadiq 1964: 19).
6. Sadiq, however, has no doubt about the erotic nature of the *ghazal*: '. . . the ghazal ... is almost wholly erotic . . .' (Ibid: 16). The certitude indeed arises from Sadiq's reluctance to distinguish between sensuality and eroticism.
7. All the authors cited above have perceived the experience of love in purely corporeal, sexual terms. If one were to accept the articulation of the notion of love between man and woman exclusively in terms of sexual experience, the contrast then between Europe and India is indeed the other way round. For, it was the Christian Church in Europe which established a double association of sex with guilt and guilt with Eve, responsible for the fall of Adam from the Garden of Eden. Through the Middle Ages down to modern times the Church frowned upon sexual pleasure as sin, even when mediated through marriage. Simone de Beauvoir in her *Memoirs of a Dutiful Daughter* gives voice to this feeling inculcated in her through her family's surveillance of her sexuality in her childhood. For the Church's grave disapproval of any kind of joy in sex, see among many works Duby 1985; Klapisch-Zuber 1992; Goody 1983; Flandrin 1990: 44-71.

   In India, on the other hand, if Manu had a purely functional vision of sex which implicated the subjugation of woman to man, there was also the long libertarian tradition of which Vatsayayana's *Kāma Sūtra* is the best known, though not the only work. This tradition is placed in the Hindu religious mode in which *Kāma*, sexual pleasure, becomes an object of life's pursuit, Vatsayayana becomes a sage and temples are built with explicit sexual motifs. The tradition lays great stress upon sex as an object of pleasure for both the man and the woman; indeed, the man is enjoined upon to please the woman in every which way she can be pleased before, during and after love-making.

It was the perfect compatibility of the pursuit of sexual pleasure and devotion to god that was idolized by an eighteenth-century Hindi poet, Anand Kavi, in his composition *Koka Manjarī.* An illustration:

Manuj rūp hwai avtariyo teen vastu ké jog
Dravya upārjan, harībhajan aru kāmini ké sang bhog

(Man has taken his avatar for the sake of three objects
Earning wealth, worshipping god and making love to beautiful women)

The medieval Muslim Arabic text, *The Perfumed Garden* of Sheikh Nefzawi, also written in a religious mode, similarly emphasizes sex as an object of pleasure. See Fowkes 1987. The book also contains the translations of two other texts, The *Ananda-Ranga* of Kalyana Mall and *The Perfumed Garden,* all of them profusely illustrated with photo reproductions of erotic medieval Indian paintings and sculptures, themselves evidence of the relative absence of inhibitions about sex compared to Europe.

8. Sadiq's lament, however, lacks even in originality, for Ram Babu Saksena, in his *A History of Urdu Literature*, had already foreshadowed it: 'Facts were divorced from poetry...' (Saksena 1990: 21).
9. Of the immense amount of literature on this theme, see Corbin 1969: 221; Nurbakhsh 1992: xii; Burgel 1992: 64). William C. Chittick in his *The Sufi Path of Love: The Spiritual Teachings of Rumi,* deals with the theme of love in a chapter (Chittick 1983: 194-231). Mir Valihuddin traces the stages of the Sufi spiritual experience of love in *Love in its Essence: The Sufi Approach* (Valihuddin 1967).
10. See, for the most recent discussions of this aspect, essays by S. Hossein Nasr, Leonard Lewisohn, Annemarie Schimmel,

Johann Christoph Burgel and J. T. P. Bruijn in Lewisohn 1992.

11. Shah Waliullah's is clearly the most vigorous attempt to establish a homogenous cultural personality of the Indian Muslims under the hegemony of the *'ulamā's* vision. See Rizvi 1980; Umar 1993.
12. At the heart of Foucault's notion of discourse lies the question of relation of power whether between individuals, groups or institutions. Foucault has developed this notion in several of his writings, but see especially his 'Two Lectures' and 'Truth and Power' in Foucault 1980: 78-133.
13. For a discussion of various movements of sectarian opposition within early Islam, see Hodgson 1974: 241-79.
14. Although the study of Sufism has been carried out extensively, the best recent introduction to the theme is Chittick 1983.
15. The Naqshbandi order of the Sufis in particular had no problem with courting proximity to the rulers and partaking of their largesse. One of the leading figures of this order, Khwaja Ubaidullah Ahrar, justified such closeness with the ruler thus: 'Times have become very evil. If possible, there is no act better than serving at the court of the kings and rulers [through which] to assist the poor and the oppressed'. See Gross 1992: 163.
16. It is thus that among the most eminent saints of the Chishti order in India, Shaikh Nizamuddin Auliya is invariably addressed in Amir Khurd 1985.
17. Hasan Sijzi, *Fuwaid al-Fu'ad*, pp. 137-8 cited in Nizami 1974: 176.
18. A large number of Mughal miniatures depict the visits of imperial princes, and in some cases, of rulers themselves, to the hermitages with gifts. The depiction is nearly always suggestive of the superiority of the holy man and the acceptance of the subordinate position by the prince; for the prince is shown observing great decorum in the holy presence whereas the saint is shown care freely postured. Court historians like Shams Siraj Afif and Abul Fazl are forever keen to establish the affinity of the ruler of the day with the dervish. Emperor Babur reveled in the epithet *qalandar* (renouncer) and expressed his wish to hand over his throne to his son and become a dervish.
19. For the invocation of pre-Islamic cultural and political ethos of Iran, the best and most renowned work is of course Firdausi's *Shāh Nāmā*, (Firdausi 1967). For the Mongols, Morgan 1986.
20. Jaidev's twelfth-century work *Gītagovinda* is a classic in its genre, though a shade paler than the *Brahma-Vaivarta Purāna*. There is, besides, the *Sringār-ras* poetry of Bihari in the 17th century,

edited and translated into English by K. P. Bahadur (Bahadur 1990). A good number of the legendary Kangra paintings revolve around the Radha-Krishna romance and some of them leave nothing to the imagination.

21. Whether or not the conversation between the Sultan and the Qazi did indeed take place, the attitude attributed to the theologian echoes one that actually existed as such in Baranī's mind, for it closely parallels his observations in the *Fatāwa*.
22. Muhammad Sadiq is firm that Urdu *ghazal* owed nothing to India either in its motifs, or imagery or even in the flora and fauna of the land: everything about it was of Persian origin. Hence Sadiq finds Urdu *ghazal* rather boring, a kind of 'museum piece', (Sadiq 1964: 14-16). However several other critics and historians of literature emphasize the Indian social and linguistic landscape which nurtured the Urdu *ghazal*. See, for such views, Hussain 1983: 31-2; Suroor 1987: 27-8.
23. For a fascinating account of this transformation see Pritchett 1989: 67-75.

REFERENCES

Abdullah, 1954. *Tārīkh-i Dāudi*. Ed. S. Abd al-Rashid, Aligarh: Dept of History, Aligarh Muslim University.

Ahmad Akbar S., 1988. *Discovering Islam: Making Sense of Muslim History and Society*. London and N. Y.: Penguin Books.

Ahmad, Aijaz (ed.), 1971. *Ghazals of Ghalib*. New York: Columbia University Press.

Ahmad, Naim (ed.), 1979. *Kulliyāt-i Mīr Ja'far Zatalli*. Aligarh: Adabi Academy.

Ali, Athar M., 1986-87. 'Recent Theories of Eighteenth Century India', *The Indian Historical Review*, XII/1-2.

——— 1993. 'The Mughal Polity—A Critique of Revisionist Approaches', *Modern Asian Studies*, 27/4.

Amir Khurd, Khwaja Kirmani Nizami, 1985. *Siyār al-Auliyā*. Urdu tr. Khwaja Islam al-Din Nizami. New Delhi: Kitab Publishing House.

Badauni, Mulla Abd al-Qadir, 1868. *Muntakhab al-Tawārīkh*. Ed. Ahmad Ali and Lees. III. Calcutta: Asiatic Society of Bengal.

Bahadur, K. P. (tr.), 1990. *Bihārī: The Satsaī*. New Delhi: Penguin Books.

Barani, Zia al- Din, 1862. *Tārīkh-i Firūz Shāhī*. Ed. Sir Sayid Ahmad Khan. Calcutta: Asiatic Society of Bengal.

——— n.d. *Fatāwā-i Jahāndārī*. Tr. M. Habib and Afsar Khan as *Political History of the Delhi Sultanate*. Allahabad: Kitab Mahal.

Bearce, George D., 1961. 'The Culture of Eighteenth Century India', *Proceedings of Indian History Congress*, 24th session.

de Beauvoir, Simone, 1959. *Memoirs of a Dutiful Daughter*. Cleveland: Word Publishing Co.

Burgel, J. C., 1992. 'Ecstasy and Order: Two Structural Principles in the Ghazal Poetry of Jalal al-Din Rumi', in Leonard Lewisohn (ed.), *The Legacy of Mediaeval Persian Sufism*. London and New York: Khaniqahi-Nimatullahi Publications.

Chand, Tara, 1961. *History of Freedom Movement in India*. vol. I. Delhi: The Publications Division, Govt of India.

Chittick, William C., 1983. *The Sufi Path of Love: The Spiritual Teachings of Rumi*. Albany: State University of New York.

Corbin, Henry, 1969. *Creative Imagination in the Sufism of Ibn Arabi*. Tr. Ralph Manheim. Princeton: Princeton University Press.

Duby, Georges, 1985. *The Knight, The Lady and The Priest: The Making of Modern Marriage in Medieval France*. Tr. Barbara Bray. Harmondsworth: Penguin Books.

Firdausi Abul Qasim, 1967. *Shah Nama*. Tr. Reuben Levy, revised by Amin Banani under the title *The Epic of the Kings*. London: Routledge and Kegan Paul.

Flandrin, Jean-Louis, 1990. 'Contraception, Marriage and Love in the Christian West'. Tr. Monica Juneja, in Maurice Aymard and Harbans Mukhia (eds.), *French Studies in History*. vol. II. New Delhi: Orient Longman.

Foucault, Michel, 1980. *Power/Knowledge: Selected Interviews and Other Writings*, 1972-77. Ed. Colin Gordon. New York. Pantheon Books.

Fowkes, Charles (ed.), 1987. *The Illustrated Kama Sutra*. Tr. Sir Richard Burton. Middlesex: Penguin Books.

Goetz, Hermann, 1938, *The Crisis of Indian Civilization in the Eighteenth and Early Nineteenth Century*, Calcutta.

Goody, Jack, 1983. *The Development of the Family and Marriage in Europe*. Cambridge: Cambridge University Press.

Gross, Jo-Ann, 1992. 'Authority and Miraculous Behavior: Reflections on *Karamat* Stories of Khwaja Ubaidullah Ahrar', in Lewisohn (ed.), *The Legacy of Mediaeval Persian Sufism*. London and New York: Khaniqahi-Nimatullahi Publications.

Habib, Irfan, 1963. *The Agrarian System of Mughal India*. Bombay: Asia Publishing House.

Hasan, Muhammad, 1977. 'Urdu Mein Ehtejaji Adab'. *Asari Adab*, 29-30, May-Aug.

Hodgson, Marshall G. S., 1974. *The Venture of Islam.* vol. I. *The Classical Age of Islam.* Chicago: Chicago University Press.

Hussain, Syed Ehtesham, 1983. *Urdu Adab ki Tanqīdī Tārikh.* New Delhi: Taraqqi-i Urdu Board.

Islam, Khurshidul and Ralph Russell, 1991. *Three Mughal Poets: Mir, Sauda, Mir Hasan.* Delhi, reprint: Oxford University Press.

Jaidev, 1954. *Gitagovinda,* Chaturvedi, S. ed, Mathura: Pustak Mandir.

Kavi, Anand, n.d. *Koka Manjarī,* Delhi

Kiernan, Victor, 1971. *Poems by Faiz.* London: Allen and Unwin.

——— 1989. 'Persian Poetry and its Cosmopolitan Audience' in Christopher Shackle (ed.), *Urdu and Muslim South Asia. Essays in Honour of Ralph Russell.* (reprint, 1991). Delhi: Oxford University Press.

Klapisch-Zuber, Christiane (ed.), 1992. *A History of Women.* vol. II. *Silences of the Middle Ages.* Cambridge, Mass: Harvard University Press.

Lewisohn Leonard (ed.), 1992. *The Legacy of Mediaeval Persian Sufism.* London and New York: Khaniqahi-Nimatullahi Publications.

Malik Z. U., 1990. 'Core and Periphery: A Contribution to the Debate on the Eighteenth Century'. *Social Scientist,* 210/11, Nov.-Dec.

Mall, Kalyan, 1987. *Ananda Ranga,* in Fowkes, ed., *The Illustrated Kama Sutra.* Middlesex: Penguin Books.

Marx, Karl, 1954. *Capital,* I. Moscow: Progress Publishers.

Moini, S. Liyaqat H., 1993. 'The Hindus and the *Dargah* of Ajmer, A.D. 1658-1737: An Overview' in A. J. Qaisar and S. P. Verma (eds.). *Art and Culture.* Jaipur: Publication Scheme.

Morgan, David, 1986. *The Mongols.* Oxford: Basil Blackwell.

Mukhia, H., 1990. 'Indian Folklore and Peasant Mentality', submitted to Seminar on Peasant Culture and Consciousness, Bellagio.

Nefzawi, Sheikh, 1987. *The Perfumed Garden,* in Fowkes, ed., *The Illustrated Kama Sutra,* Middlesex: Penguin Books.

Nizami, K. A., 1974. *Some Aspects of Religion and Politics in India during the Thirteenth Century.* Delhi: Idarah-i Adabiyat.

Nurbakhsh, Javad, 1992. 'Two Approaches to the Principle of the Unity of Being', in Leonard Lewisohn (ed.), *The Legacy of Mediaeval Persian Sufism.* London and New York: Khaniqahi-Nimatullahi Publications.

Pritchett, Frances W., 1989. 'Emperor of India: Landhaur bin Sa'dan in the Hamza Cycle', in Christopher Shackle (ed.) *Urdu and Muslim South Asia. Studies in Honour of Ralph Russell.* New Delhi. Oxford University Press.

Qidwai, Sadiqur Rahman, 1991. *Tāsīr na ke Tanqīd.* New Delhi: Maktaba Jamia.

Rizvi, S. A. A., 1980. *Shah Wali-Allah and His Times*. Canberra. Ma'arifat Publications.

Russell, Ralph, 1992. *The Pursuit of Urdu Literature: A Select History*. Delhi: Oxford University Press.

Sadiq M., 1964. *A History of Urdu Literature*. London: Oxford University Press.

Saksena, Ram Babu, 1927. *A History of Urdu Literature*. Allahabad: Ram Narain Lal.

Sarkar, Jadu Nath, 1932-1950. *Fall of the Mughal Empire*. 4 vols. Calcutta:

Suroor, Al-i Ahmad, 1987. 'Ghazal ka Fun', in Kamil Quraishi (ed.), *Urdu Ghazal*. Delhi: Urdu Academy.

Umar, Muhammad, 1993. *Islam in Northern India during the Eighteenth Century*. New Delhi: Munshiram Manoharlal.

Valihuddin, Mir, 1967. *Love in its Essence: The Sufi Approach*. New Delhi: Indian Institute of Islamic Studies.

5

Communalism and the Writing of Medieval Indian History: A Reappraisal

Until very recently the writing of medieval Indian history primarily turned on an eloquent enumeration of the glorious achievements of great emperors; equally eloquent was the description of their failures. One way or the other, the emperor stood at the centre of all that was considered worthy of the historian's concern.

To a considerable extent this concern was inherited from the large number of Indian historians who wrote their books during the medieval centuries themselves, contemporaneously or near-contemporaneously with the events they had narrated, the contemporary historians as we call them. These contemporary historians were invariably members of the imperial or the provincial court and were often partisans of one or the other faction of the intrigue-ridden polity. Not seldom did they actually participate in the events they had described; equally frequently they or their friends or relations were eye-witnesses to such events. Inevitably, arising from each historian's predilections, his version of events was at considerable variance with those of the others even as they described the same events.[1]

Yet, there was much that they shared with one another. As members of the court, their attention was confined to their surroundings. The events they narrated were events in which the court's involvement was immediate and direct: accession of a ruler, rebellions against him, his conquests, administrative measures, punishments meted out by him as also rewards given, conspiracies hatched for or against him, his deposition or death, etc.[2] Even as the historians' sympathies varied, they were all concerned about the stability of the polity as a whole, though individually each might have liked it to lean in his direction, if only just a little.

Clearly the emperor was the pivot around which this whole polity revolved; he ruled on behalf of the entire ruling class, keeping all the factions together, dealing firmly with over-ambitious individuals or groups who tried to disrupt the overall unity and being benign to those who kept within the legitimate bounds. Understandably the emperors' actions drew a major share of contemporary historians' attention, both critical and appreciative, in medieval India.

Historians in medieval India also understood historical causation in terms of human volition or, at best, human nature or disposition. The understanding too had, in a manner, been conditioned by the historians' own daily experience. By virtue of their position in the court they were often participants in, or witnesses to, some of the events that formed part of their narrative. Their experience was that rebellions occurred when so-and-so had, of his will, decided to rebel; that a king was deposed when a group of nobles decided among themselves to terminate his reign; that an emperor engaged himself in extensive conquests owing to his virile nature; that another emperor followed a policy of treating all his subjects alike, irrespective of the distinctions of creed, for so enlightened was his disposition. Wilful decision, conditioned by the nature of each human being involved in the events with which the historians were concerned, formed the basic cause of the occurrence of those events, as our historians saw it. Ziaud din Barani, author of two of the most outstanding works of history around the middle of the forteenth century,[3] raised this understanding to the level of fine theory. Every man's nature, according to Barani, comprised contradictory qualities and the events in which a man was involved were a manifestation of those qualities. A balanced mixture of the contradictory qualities resulted in success, whereas an unbalanced mixture led inevitably to failure in life.[4]

Understandably, if the historians' own experience taught

them lessons in historical causation in their context, it was easy for them to explain similar events in the distant or near past in the same terms.

The explanation of historical causation in terms of human volition also implied the treatment of each historical event as a single, individual, independent event unrelated to the other events described in their works.[5] For in the absence of a structural analysis, the only other framework of historical explanation, within which all events together constituted an integrated pattern and thereby lost their individual identities, was the one in which divine will intervened to cause the occurrence of events. Medieval European historians' framework was indeed the prototype of such an explanation. Clerics as those historians were, their whole outlook on life and letters was influenced by the theological doctrine in which all that happened in the past and the present and was to happen in the future was predetermined by god's will; which in turn implied that the events of the past, the present and the future formed a tightly knit whole as the manifestation of god's wisdom, for surely no event could occur at random unless it had been assigned its due place in god's all-embracing plan.[6] But such was not the understanding of medieval India's courtier-historians, even when some of them happened to be theologians along with being courtiers and historians.[7]

If medieval Indian historians focused their attention on events pertaining directly or indirectly to the court and if they explained the occurrence of these events in terms of human will or nature, the ruler's will or nature would clearly occupy a critical element in the explanation in view of his pivotal position. The personal qualities of the ruler inevitably became the all-too-important factor in the whole framework of explanation. Indeed, the events that occurred during a reign were seen as the manifestation of the personality of the ruler.[8]

COMMUNAL AND IMPERIALIST HISTORIOGRAPHY

There was, too, an implicit communal undertone in this framework. If the ruler's disposition, his personal qualities, mattered all that much in the making of history, surely the fact that he was a Muslim ruling over a vast mass of Hindus would be a material factor in the whole assessment of history. And, of course, medieval centuries were not the time when the influence of religion had been eliminated from the thinking of humankind in any part of the world. It was easy therefore for some historians of medieval India to visualise contemporary history as the history of Muslim rule in India.[9]

Yet the framework of historical explanation in terms of human will/nature in its essentials contained a strong element of ambivalence that accommodated, for medieval centuries, a quite astonishingly secular historical thinking such as Abul Fazl's along with a fairly dogmatic Muslim statement such as Mulla Abdul Qadir Badauni's. Indeed the whole range of historical works written in medieval India swings in degrees from one to the other thinking, yet never overflowing the human will/nature syndrome.

This then was the ambivalent framework that British colonial historians had inherited from medieval India. It was, however, the singular mark of colonial historiography that it sought to eliminate the element of ambivalence from this framework, boldly explicate its latent communal undertone, and make a linear communal study of India's past the dominant, almost the exclusive, trend. Such was the end result of James Mill's periodisation of Indian history into Hindu, Muslim and British periods[10] which was to become the universally accepted periodisation for the study of Indian history for the next century and a half and continues to be nearly universally accepted in Indian Universities today though with a new nomenclature: ancient, medieval and modern periods. An even bolder and more deliberate attempt was made by Elliot and Dowson's eight-volume A *History of India as told by its Own Historians*[11] which was a translation of excerpts from Persian-language historical works of medieval India. The selection of excerpts left little to the reader's imagination: invariably the translated passages aroused communal passions. Apparently, Elliot knew what he was doing, for the professed purpose of all his intellectual labour was to 'teach the bombastic babus of India the virtues of good government they were enjoying' under the British rule compared to the misery of their fate when the Muslims governed them.[12] If Elliot succeeded eminently in achieving his objective of inflaming passions, it was largely because he had adopted a long familiar, durable framework but had drastically changed its emphasis.

The framework, however, still endured. Early in the twentieth century, especially during its second quarter, some historians vehemently contested the version of medieval Indian history that spoke only of Muslim rulers' oppression of the Hindus and of heroic Hindu resistance to it—the version given by British as well the Indian communal historians reflecting the communal wing of the Indian national movement. Communal historiography had a degree of variation in its outlook: Hindu communalism visualised the medieval centuries as a long period of alien Muslim dominance over the Hindus (the vast masses of the country's native people), the repeated attempts by the Muslim rulers to convert the Hindus to Islam or else to eliminate them and the heroic stubbornness of the Hindus in defence of their religion and the country's honour. Other stereotypes were also created: if the Hindus lost their battles to the Muslims, this was because of mutual dissensions;[13] if medieval Indian history was a story of unrelenting conflict between the two major communities, this was owing to the Muslims' determination to retain and assert their separate identity unlike their predecessors, the Greeks, the Sakas, the Huns etc, who also had emigrated from distant alien lands, but having once settled in this country had lost their independent identity in the mainstream of Indian (i.e. Hindu) life; Indian (i.e. Hindu) civilisation has always been known for its liberalism in embracing any element that comes to it with outstretched, friendly arms; it is the Muslims who refused to merge their separate identity in the mainstream of Indian (i.e. Hindu) life; indeed they sought to forcibly change the course of this stream. This was the origin of communalism in India, etc.[14] Muslim communalism, on the other hand, considered those reigns which overly asserted their Islamic identity as the peaks of Islamic glory. However, the basic assumption of both Hindu and Muslim communal historiography (as also the British) constituted the unity of their thought: they all visualised the Hindus and the Muslims in medieval India perpetually in conflict, deriving their evidence from the arena of political, indeed dynastic, history.

It was this notion of perpetual communal conflict in medieval India that the nationalist historians were contesting. They questioned the genuineness of the religious motivation of Muslim rulers of medieval India; they brought forth evidence to suggest communal harmony in medieval India; they emphasised the considerable extent of mutual interaction between the two large communities in the realm of ideas, in the realm of culture, in the realm of life-styles in the centuries past. It was from this emphasis that the concept of 'composite culture' was evolved.[15]

The contribution made by nationalist historians in secularising the study of medieval Indian history was by any standard extremely significant. However, they were contesting communal historiography really on the latter's terms. If communal historiography brought forth evidence to suggest Muslim oppression of Hindu subjects, nationalist historians cited cases of tolerance shown by Muslim rulers; if communal historiography highlighted instances of conflict between communities, nationalist historiography brought into relief other instances of cooperation between them. Both groups of historians studied mainly politico-administrative history and drew their evidence by and large from court chronicles. If communal historians overemphasised one part of evidence and covered up another, nationalist historians did much the same, though with a contrary, and admittedly more laudable, objective.

Clearly, this was rather a weak offensive against communal (and imperialist) historiography, for once the study of medieval Indian history in terms of the ruler's religious policy was conceded, the evidence overwhelmingly inclined towards the communal viewpoint. On this premise, nationalist historians, while lauding Akbar's achievements, handed over the other five-and-a-half centuries of 'Muslim' rule to communal historiography. It is interesting that when it comes to Akbar, the language of the nationalist and the communal historians becomes entirely interchangeable. This is essentially a communal vision, for by lauding Akbar's religious achievements, the validity of that historical methodology is established which seeks to evaluate all of medieval Indian rulers in terms of their religious attitudes. Akbar clearly becomes an exception, which merely proved the rule.

Fundamentally, therefore, even in nationalist historiography, the categories of historical analysis remained communal. So long as the categories of one's analysis remained Hindu and Muslim, whether one argued on behalf of communal conflict or communal harmony, one's thinking still remained limited to the confines of those communal categories. The logic of both the communal as well as the nationalist historians emanated from a common assumption of the existence of separate communal identities; so long as thinking was based on communal categories, this assumption was inescapable.

If there was no escape from this assumption, it was because this was in fact the assumption of the national movement itself and was common to both its nationalist and communalist wings. Both the chief antagonists during the national movement, the Congress and the Muslim League, proceeded with their politics based on the recognition of the existence of separate communities, the Hindus and the Muslims. The politics of one stressed rapprochement between them and that of the other their irreconcilability. The common basic assumption often permitted an easy transition from one to the other; a slight shift into each other's direction would often bring them to a common meeting ground; it also permitted easy shifts in individual loyalties. Starting from the basic assumption, from the very categories of social analysis and political agitation which were communal, the 'nationalist' politics as represented by the Congress carried far more than a 'tinge' of communalism;[16] communalism was indeed integral to that politics, through its silent, non-violent manifestation. The Muslim League, starting from the same categories of analysis, charted off to its not-so-silent manifestation. Conceptually, nationalism and communalism in India had much in common with each other even if historically they were each other's negation.

It was this dichotomy, conceptually questionable but historically significant, that was reflected in the dichotomy of communal and nationalist historiography of medieval India.

THE NEW SHIFT IN FOCUS

The circle was broken from the late 1950s onwards. This was the period when research was initiated on new themes altogether in which communal categories did not enter at all. These were themes like rural class structure, forms and magnitude of exploitation of medieval Indian peasantry, the significance of *zamindars* as a class, production technology, trade and commercial organisation etc. An important role in this shift of focus was played by research on what came felicitously to be called 'early medieval India' in Professor R.S. Sharma's terminology. This research made two significant contributions: one, it implicitly questioned the earlier, clearly communal, periodisation which divided medieval from ancient India at 1206 A.D., with the establishment of Delhi Sultanate, for it, again implicitly, opened up the possibility of seeing an extensive continuum of social and economic history from around the seventh or eighth to the thirteenth or fourteenth century, even as important changes occurred within the range of this continuum; two, it decisively shifted the emphasis from politico-administrative to socio-economic history, where communal categories in any case lost much of their significance.

As more research is done in newer areas, the very communal problematic—the relations between the Muslim dynasties and Hindu subjects or the extent of theocratic nature of the state in medieval India etc—is being marginalised. There has been of late a movement of the study of history of medieval

India towards society's lower rungs: a study of the actual labour processes in the field and the workshop, at the hands of the peasant and the artisan. This involves a complex interaction of areas of study: to begin with, the ecology of a region, the nature and the fertility of its soil, the availability of water for irrigation, the duration of the sunshine etc.; it also involves the given technology, the shape and size of the plough, the use of other implements and of course knowledge and practice of agricultural techniques such as crop rotation or preparing of manures of the treatment of plant diseases; above all, it calls for a study of social organization of labour utilisation: whether labour is servile or free, whether the system allows the actual producer freedom from extraneous control over his process or production or not, whether the system permits mobility to the peasant or not. The attempt is to study the production system in all its multi-faceted totality. Similarly, the labour of the artisan being examined.

The very complexity of this study allows religion merely the share that is its due in social life, along with the share of other elements, instead of giving it the overarching importance it had attained in the history writing of medieval India for so long. It is in this sense that history writing is becoming profoundly secular.

(*The paper seeks to reappraise the earlier essay, 'Medieval Indian History and the Communal Approach' in Romila Thapar, Harbans Mukhia and Bipan Chandra,* Communalism and the Writing of Indian History, *People's Publishing House, New Delhi, 1969*)

REFERENCES

1. The outstanding examples of the writings of Abul Fazl and Abdul Qadir Badauni, both courtiers of Akbar, represent an extreme case of variation in their versions of the same events; others would constitute somewhat milder examples.
2. There is at best a vertical growth in the contents of these works: from a mere narration of the stories of accession of rulers and their battles etc: such as in Minhaj us-Siraj's *Tabaqat-i Nasiri,* increasing information on allied themes such as administrative system, imperial policies, composition of nobility etc. begins to

get incorporated in their works, the two most outstanding examples of which are Zia ud-din Barani's *Tarikh-i Firuzshahi* for the Delhi Sultanate and Abul Fazl's *Akbar Nama* for Akbar's reign. There is, however, little horizontal growth in the contents of these works which would extend to matters of no immediate concern to the ruling class.

3. *Fatawa-i Jahandari*, English translation by M. Habib and Mrs. Afsar Khan under the title *Political Theory of the Delhi Sultanate*, Allahabad, n.d. and *Tarikh-i Firuzshahi*, Saiyad Ahmad Khan (ed), Calcutta, 1862. The whole of the *Tarikh* is yet to be translated from Persian into any other language though portions of it have been rendered into English by Elliot and Dowson and into Hindi by S.A.A. Rizvi.
4. Barani, *Fatawa-i Jahandari* (tr.), pp. 85-89.
5. Corroboration for this statement is found in the very style of writing of all medieval Indian historians. They break their narrative of history into regnal units and the reign of the contemporary ruler is mostly further broken into an annual chronicle. Within the regnal or the annalistic form, the narration of each event begins with the statement, 'and another event that took place during this reign (or in this year) was...' or 'another occurrence of this year was ...' One event having been described, they move on to the narration of the next event prefacing it with the same preamble.
6. See Collingwood, *The Idea of History*, Oxford, 1946, p. 55.
7. Pater Hardy, (*Historians of Medieval India*, London, 1960), has suggested that medieval Indian historians treated history as a branch of theology and that historical causation in their conception lay in divine will. Hardy appears to have overlooked the very substantial difference in the social, intellectual and political contexts as well as the social position of medieval Indian and medieval European historians in seeking to establish uniformity of historical approach between them.
8. For details of the argument advanced so far, as also for its empirical basis, see Harbans Mukhia, *Historians and Historiography During the Reign of Akbar*, Vikas, New Delhi, 1976.
9. Thus for example Badauni reconstructs the history of India from the day Islam had made its political appearance here. Significantly, he does not begin his book with the Muslim conquest of Sind, for 'Islam could not be stabilised in this region' after Muhammad bin Qasim's death; on the other hand, since it was 'Nasir-ud-din Subuktgin whose son was Sultan Mahmud

of Ghazni, who led annual expeditions to India with the intention of waging holy wars, and Lahore became the capital during the reign of his descendants, and moreover (since) Islam was never (thereafter) eliminated from this land', Badauni considers it proper to begin his history with Subuktgin. See his *Muntakhab al-Tawarikh*, vol. I, p. 8.

10. James Mill, *History of British India*, London, 1817.
11. Trubner and Company, London, 1867-1877.
12. Ibid., here vol. I, New Delhi reprint 2001, p. xxii.
13. The only available evidence for this all-encompassing theory is the alleged refusal of Jai Chand of Kannauj to come to the aid of Prithvi Raj Chauhan at the second battle of Tarain against Muhammad Ghori. Quite apart from the fact that one piece of evidence, even if true, does not substantiate a theory of such dimensions, this theory ignores the fact that Prithvi Raj did get help from other rulers. Secondly, the assumption underlying this theory is that individually the Indian rulers were quite weak vis-a-vis their alien adversaries, but collectively they would have been invincible. This assumption is made contrary to all available evidence which invariably points to many times more numerous Indian soldiers in the field of battle than the Turks. Clearly, addition of more solidiers could hardly have improved the prospects of victory. The causes of defeat lay elsewhere than in inferior manpower; they lay in the obsolete methods of utilising this manpower.
14. This appears a reasonable enough statement on the face of it. However, under it lies a methodological flaw and communal logic. The flaw rests on making a comparison between two incomparable phenomena. While the Greeks, Huns etc. have been identified on the secular basis of the country of their origin or of their race, Muslims have been given their identity in terms of their religion. Clearly, the two bases of identification are far from identical, and the comparison therefore is questionable. If however, identical bases of identification for all of them were adopted, the problem would be posed as follows: the Greeks, the Huns, the Sakas, the Scythians etc. came to India and over time lost their identity in the mainstream of Indian life: what about the Mamluks, the Khaljis, the Tughlaqs and even the Mughals? Have they retained their separate identity to this day, or has it been merged in the mainstream of Indian life? Evidently, the answer is quite unambiguous, for there is hardly anyone around to claim descent from all those dynasties that

had migrated to India in the medieval age and had ruled here for so many centuries. Where have the descendants of all those dynasties and their nobles gone? Surely they have merged their identity, like their predecessor-immigrants, in the mainstream of Indian life and enriched it in the process.

But then the whole argument in this unequal comparison is communal; not only does it identify Muslims on the basis of their religion, it also quietly identifies Indian mainstream with Hindu maintream. The argument is thus posed in veiled communal categories.

15. The concept of composite culture was the especial contribution of the Allahabad school historians: Professors Tara Chand, R.P. Tripathi and B.P. Saxena, in particular. Though Professor Muhammad Habib was situated at the Aligarh Muslim University, historiographically he too belonged to the same school.
16. Bipan Chandra, "Hindu Tinge in the National Movement" (mimeograph).

6

The Ram Janmabhoomi-Babari Masjid Dispute: Evidence of Medieval Sources

This paper is exclusively focused on the question: Was there a Ram temple underneath the structure known as the Babari masjid today? The reference point of this discussion is the evidence of medieval Indian sources.

The earliest evidence of the construction of the present structure at the site currently in dispute is inscribed on the walls of the building there in the form of two verses of three couplets each in Persian language—on the outer wall, enclosing the prayer hall, and on the wall inside, near the niche.

The verses that one encounters first, above the arch as one moves towards the hall, are not easy on the eye owing to the height of their placement Their text has, however, been reproduced by Mrs. A.S. Beveridge in one of several appendices to her translation of Babur's memoirs, the *Babur Nama.* She has also given a gist of these couplets along with an appreciation of their literary quality, though she refrains from fully translating them, as she does the other set. This verse, rendered into English, reads thus

> In the name of One who is Omniscient
> Creator of the Worlds, (but) Himself abode-less
> In salutation to the Prophet, beyond all praise
> The Chief among prophets of the two worlds
> Narrating to the world the story of Babur the Recluse
> Who has attained to the height of worldly success...

The verse is not quite complete as Mrs. Beveridge had

noted; she, however, cautioned against 'read(ing) any further meaning' into the verses because 'the language would not warrant it.'

The text of the other three couplets has now been rendered beyond one's reach with the installation of the idols of Ram, Sita and Lakshmana covering a good part of the rear wall. Mrs. Beveridge, however, once again comes to the rescue with her reproduction of both the text and a complete translation of this verse, which, with some slight modification, is as follows:

> By the command of Emperor Babur whose justice is an edifice reaching up to the very height of the heavens.
> The goodhearted Mir Baqi
> built this alighting place of angels
> May this goodness last forever! The year of its construction becomes manifest in saying
> May this goodness last forever.[1]

Thus Mir Baqi expressly states that he was carrying out Babur's command in erecting the structure for which he coins the felicitous phrase, the alighting place of angels, instead of a mosque. The phrase, meant to refer to the abode of god, for god is described in a comely term as abode-less, does justice to the Mir's poetic sensibility, even if the structure of the mosque itself has little aesthetic appeal in it. Clearly, the Mir was a better poet than architect! However, the structure itself leaves little room for doubt that it indeed belonged to a mosque with its three domes, each covering a court, the niche placed in the direction of the setting sun, the floor divided into individual spaces for the *namazis*. But the inscriptions do not state, or in any way indicate, that the mosque had been constructed at a site where there was an already existing structure, much less a temple of any sort; nor do they suggest that the place was invested with any sanctity by any set of people.

Babur himself records his visit to Ayodhya in 1528 twice on the same page of his memoirs, and states that he 'stayed a few days... in order to settle the affairs of Aud' (medieval Persian texts' synonym for Ayodhya). He does not let go even of such details as a hunt for which he had set out after a reconnaisance done on his behalf by one of his minions. But he shows no recognition of the existence of a Ram temple there and therefore, not surprisingly, makes no mention of any order for its demolition and the construction of a mosque instead, or anything else with a bearing on this affair.[2]

The next bit of our evidence from medieval sources comes from the *Ain-i Akbari* of Abul Fazl, compiled towards the end of the sixteenth century. Abul Fazl recognises Ayodhya as the city of Ram's residence, but does not locate any site of his birth, much less identify a temple built at such a site and makes no metion of Babari masjid at all. 'Auodhya', he says, 'is one of the largest cities of India' and goes on to record that 'In ancient times its populous site covered an extent of 148 *kos* in length and 36 in breadth, and it is esteemed one of the holiest places of antiquity. Around the environs of the city, they sift the earth and gold is obtained. It is the residence of Ramchandra who in the *Treta* age combined in his own person both the spiritual supremacy and kingly office'.[3]

If Babur as emperor, and Abul Fazl as a historian do not record the erection of the mosque at the site of a temple, they are not alone in their silence. None of Babur's imperial descendants, not even the bigoted Aurangzeb, himself responsble for the destruction of several temples and the construction of mosques in place of some of them, including the ones at Mathura and Kashi, ever reminisces about the building of the Babari mosque at the site; the place would clearly have been extremely holy to the Hindus and, for that reason if for no other, the erection of a mosque there would have given Aurangzeb considerable satisfaction, besides legitimising his own action at Mathura and Kashi. But he never says a word about it. Nor does anyone of the string of historians, all members of the imperial court, make any mention whatsoever of the mosque itself, much less of the destruction of a sacred temple to make way for it. Clearly, the mosque carried none of the significance that would have attached to it in the eyes of bigoted Muslims, had it displaced an ancient and extremely sacrosanct Hindu shrine. Among the historians of the imperial court, there was a whole range of hues, with a fair share of fanatical Muslims such as Mulla

Abdul Qadir Badauni, Imam of Wednesday's prayers at Akbar's court. Indeed, the Mulla wrote his three-volume *Muntakhab al-Tawarikh* in great anguish at what he perceived was the decimation of Islam at Akbar's and Abul Fazl's hands and looked back nostalgically upon the preceding reigns when Islam's glory had been manifest. The construction of Babari mosque at the site of a holy and ancient shrine of the kafirs would have gladdened his heart. But strangely, even he shows no awareness of such a happening.

If this is surprising, even more surprising is the complete absence of the mention of it in the works of any of the Hindi poets, most of them Hindus. Among them was Goswami Tulsi Das, an inhabitant of Ayodhya, who wrote his epic, *Ramcharitamanas,* and all his other poetry in his native Awadhi. A lifelong devotion to Ram had given him a rare boldness and legend has it that he curtly turned down an invitation from Emperor Akbar himself. The composition of the epic is dated in the 1570s, which places it within five decades of the construction of the mosque, i.e., within the poet's living memory.[4] Given Tulsi Das's devotion to Ram, the incident would have driven him hopping mad. But all we have from him is dead silence! Indeed, silence is all that we encounter in the imperial edicts, official histories and documents, literary works of all genres, European travellers' accounts...

The first clear, incontestable evidence that the mosque was built at the site of Ram's birth is contained in a document submitted to the Faizabad law-court by its superintendent (*darogha-i adalat*), one Hafizullah, in 1238 H./1822 A.D. A copy of this document, couched in perfect legalese, has been reproduced by Kamal al-Din Haidar in his *Qaisar al-Tawarikh.*[5] I give the English translation: 'The Jama masjid, constructed by Emperor Babur, is located at the *Janma Asthan,* that is, at the site of the birth of Ram, son of Raja Dasrat (and is) adjacent to the building of the Rasoi (kitchen) or Sita, wife of the above-mentioned Ram....' The document leaves one in no doubt about the linkage between the mosque and Ram Janmabhoomi; yet it does not mention any temple having existed at the site and having been demolished to make way for the mosque!

In the rest of the nineteenth century things moved fast and a Ram temple had found location in some versions of the dispute, of which there were several, and not all the disputants were votaries of non-violence.[6] However, this version was still shaky enough in the 1860s to have P. Carnegy conjecturing about the existence of a temple at the Janmabhoomi, building his conjecture on the black stone pillars embedded in the mosque, but not quite sure whether the temple was dedicated to Ram or to the Buddha, though at another place he does put it on record that the mosque had indeed displaced an earlier Ram temple and professedly bases his statement on 'locally affirmed' information, i.e., popular tradition.[7] By the turn of the twentieth century, by 1905 to be exact, the story had made its way into the Gazetteer of District Faizabad, though it was still talking vaguely of 'an ancient temple' being destroyed there.[8] Mrs. Beveridge picked up the story from the Gazetteer and turned it into a definitive account of the destruction of Ram temple and construction of the Babari masjid in its place. All she needed to do this decisive turn was not any piece of evidence but an assumption that Babur, by virtue of being a Muslim, must have been intolerant of any other religion and would have considered it his pious duty to convert a Hindu shrine into a mosque! In a footnote to her Appendix she observes: 'Presumably the order for building the mosque was given during Babur's stay in Aud (Ayodhya) in 934 AH. at which time he would be impressed by the dignity and sanctity of the ancient Hindu shrine it (at least in part) displaced, and like the obedient follower of Muhammad he was in intolerance of another Faith, would regard the substitution of a temple by a mosque as dutiful and worthy'.[9]

The demolition of the Ram temple and the construction of the Babari masjid then is an *inference,* not a *fact* ! It is an inference drawn from the fact of Babur being a Muslim. It is a pity that Mrs. Beveridge, of all persons, should have been the one to draw this inference after doing such a magnificent translation of the emperor's memoirs and going into minute detail of his life and career. For, while the Muslim rulers of medieval India comprised a wide spectrum of persons with an enormous variation in their natures and dispositions, from the innovative and adventurous Akbar to the cold and bigoted Aurangzeb, Babur, among them wasn't particularly renowned for his religious zeal or iconoclasm. A happy-go-lucky person, Babur was too fond of the good things of life—music, poetry, flowers, women, and not least, his cup of wine—to go for the puritannical exercise of demolishing temples and constructing mosques. Indeed, on his visit to Gwalior in September 1529, while he ordered the destruction of some erotic sculptures, for he was aghast at the sight, he made it a point to visit other 'idol-houses' of the town and reports 'enjoying the sight of these buildings'.[10] It is interesting that while Babur seldom fails to lay gardens wherever he goes and never fails to record it, he hardly ever refers to constructing a mosque or any other religious monument, including the one at Ayodhya.

At any rate, if one were to follow in the train of Mrs. Beveridge's logic that being a Muslim meant being a destroyer of other religions' places of worship, one would expect Babur to have proclaimed the demolition of the Ram temple and the construction of the mosque with great hyperbole, considering the antiquity and the dignity of the site, as she puts it. Aurangzeb was surely of the mould that Mrs. Beveridge ascribes to all Muslims; he demolishes temples, builds mosques in their places and leaves no one in doubt that he considers it one of his memorable achievements. The silence of Babur and of his descendants and of everyone else, on whichever side of the fence, until as late as the first quarter of the nineteenth century therefore does much damage to Mrs. Beveridge's logic.

It should be reasonable to argue that the entry of the story into a legal document of 1822 would point to a prehistory, that the story would have taken time to grow. There is, indeed, a strong popular tradition in the region that the Babari masjid stands at the site of Ram's birth and that it has displaced a temple dedicated to him and the historian must give to popular tradition due respect as a piece of evidence of another genre than documents. But popular tradition could either be a historian's subject of study as an indicator of popular mentalities, as a cultural phenomenon evolving over long stretches of time, itself a fascinating area of historical inquiry; or else, it must be rigorously historicised if it is to serve as an evidence for a particular historical event. To insist on popular tradition as the proof of the existence and demolition of a Ram temple and the building of the Babari masjid in the year 1528 is to misconstrue the nature of tradition as history, for between them the notion of time differs ever so widely. This is all the more so, for, as we have seen above, there is no indication of any kind during the seventeenth and a good part of the eighteenth century that any such belief existed then. The evidence of the 1822 document would indicate that the tradition that the mosque stood at the site of Ram's birth started growing sometime earlier, perhaps in the eighteenth century, and somewhere during the nineteenth century the site also came to be associated with a Ram temple. It would be extremely interesting to trace the evolution of this tradition in social, political and psychological setting apart from the setting of religious beliefs. But it would hardly serve as unimpeachable evidence for a particular event which had taken place anywhere between two and three centuries earlier!

One still has to contend with the black stone pillars embedded in the existing structure. P.Carnegy had noticed these pillars in 1870 and sought to conjecture the existence of a temple, as we have seen above. If Carnegy was not certain whether the carved pillars suggested a Ram or a Buddhist temple, no such doubt assails Dr. S.P. Gupta.[11] He is dead sure that the pillars supported an existing structure of Ram temple; the pillars were therefore *in situ.* This conclusion is, however, opened up to a little doubt by the fact that right at the entrance to the building which encloses the courtyard, two such pillars form part of the wall and the carving on them is totally dissimilar from each other. Indeed, of the fourteen pillars that have been used in the walls, the carving on ten is dissimilar and there is no order in which they have been placed. It is clear then that the pillars could not possibly have been *in situ,* that these had been brought over from somewhere around, even if they belonged to a temple, though the evidence for this is far from conclusive. At any rate, Gupta's certitude would have carried at least some conviction if he were able to make up his mind about the stuff the stone pillars are made of. For, on 2 December 1990 he had confidently announced that 'The blackstone is schistose of the black slate variety which is found only in the Garhwal-Kumaon region as far as U.P. is concerned'; less than a fortnight later, on 13 December, he, without any diminution of confidence, declared that 'while basalt is an igneous rock produced out of the lava of volcanoes, schistose, of which these pillars are made, is a sedimentary rock found at the bottom of the seas'![12]

REFERENCES

1. Babur Padshah, *Babur-Nama,* Eng. tr. A.S. Beveridge, Delhi reprint 1970, (first published 1922), tr's Appendix U. 'Buwad khair baqi' ('May this goodness last forever') gives the date of the construction, i.e., 935 H. or 1528 A.D.
2. Ibid, p. 602. Sushil Srivastava, however, somewhat stretches the evidence to dispute Babur's visit, in *The Disputed Mosque: A Historical Inquiry,* New Delhi, 1991, pp. 71-75.
3. Abul Fazl, *Ain-i Akbari,* Eng. tr., H.S, Jarrett, vol. II, Calcutta, 1849, p. 182.
4. Ram Kumar Verma, *Hindi Sahitya ka Alochnatamak Itihas,* Allahabad, 1971, p. 348.
5. vol. II, Lucknow, 1898, p. 117.
6. Sushil Srivastava has a useful and fair account of this evidence in his *The Disputed Mosque,* pp. 43-47.
7. P. Carnegy, *Historical Sketch of Fyzabad Tahsil, including the Former Capitals of Ajodhya and Fyzabad,* Lucknow, 1870, pp. 21 and 17.
8. H.R. Nevill, ed., *District Gazetteer of the United Provinces of Agra and Oudh, Fyzabad,* Allahabad, 1905, p. 173.
9. *Babur-Nama,* Appendix U. See also ibid, p. 656, fn.3 where she inserts '(marking the birth-place of Rama)' after citing Nevil's statement that Babur had destroyed the ancient temple.
10. *Babur-Nama,* pp. 611-613.
11. 'Ram Janmabhoomi-Babri Masjid: Archaeological Evidence, *Indian Express,* 2 December 1990.
12. Letter, *The Times of India,* 13 December 1990.

7

The Ideology of the Bhakti Movement: The Case of Dadu Dayal

The Bhakti movement has been variously interpreted by a number of historians. Mostly the movement has been studied in terms of its doctrines; at best attempts have been made to examine its influence on Hindu-Muslim relations in medieval India, or on the caste-system. Such examination, again, has largely been based on the profession of certain ideas by the leaders of the movement rather than on the sociological study of the impact of these ideas on the castes and communities in medieval India. However, McLeod has attempted a sociological study of the Sikhs in the time of Guru Nanak and Irfan Habib has tried to trace the origin of monotheistic movement of the fifteenth to seventeenth centuries to certain technological and economic changes during the thirteenth and fourteenth centuries.[1]

In the following pages an attempt will be made to examine the attitude of an extremely important leader of the Bhakti movement in the second half of the sixteenth century, namely Dadu Dayal, toward the State and various social classes. The significance of such a study perhaps lies in the fact that Dadu Dayal's attitude as that of the other leaders of the movement, would appear to be both a reflection as well as a determinant of current popular consciousness regarding the state and society, when we keep in mind the mass following of those leaders. Incidentally, this paper also seeks to explore medieval Hindi literature, in this case Dadu Dayal's *Granthavali*, as a source of information for understanding medieval Indian society.[2] The importance of this source for such a study cannot be overestimated, for a large portion of it, particularly the portion belonging to he Bhakti period of Hindi literature, is not only a non-official source but also the only mouthpiece of popular attitudes toward medieval Indian state and society.

Dadu was a spiritual descendant of Kabir.[3] He was born in 1544 A.D. most probably at Ahmedabad and he died, according to tradition, at Naraina village in Rajasthan in 1603 A.D. He was thus a contemporary of Akbar.[4]

Although Dadu appears to have travelled practically all over norhern India from Ahmedabad to Rajasthan then to Banaras and Bihar up to Bengal, he probably spent the major part of his life in Rajasthan.[5] It is, however, difficult to determine a chronology of his life, for he is very reticent in talking about himself and his disciples' accounts of his life contain much that is apocryphal.[6]

It is certain, however, that Dadu had a low-class origin, being a cotton-carder.[7] A number of editions of Dadu Dayal's works have so far been published[8] but the one prepared by Parshu Ram Chaturvedi and published by the Nagari Pracharini Sabḥa, Varanasi in 2023 V.S. (1966 A.D.) is based on a manuscript dated 1710 V.S. (1653 A.D.) probably to commemorate the fiftieth death anniversary of Dadu. The chronology of the verses, or the places where these verses were composed and recited are almost imposible to determine. Since Dadu was a preacher who covered a large area in northern India, the language of his verses must have varied according to the audience he was addressing. This is obvious from Dadu's use of *Khariboli,* Rajasthani, Panjabi, Gujarati and Persian languages; often there is a mixture of all these in one verse. Secondly, since the verses came spontaneously to Dadu as the vehicle of his discourse, the content must have varied from verse to verse even before the same audience. But in the MSS, the verses have been classified according to their content.

Dadu's verses have been preserved in two traditions—the oral (*maghazia*) and the written (*kagazia*).[9] The verses communicated orally have not yet been compiled. Kshiti Mohan Sen has estimated the number of orally communicated *padas* (a *pada* varying from 6 to 160 verses) alone at 20,000[10] whereas the number of *sakhis* (individual verses) is much larger. This estimate has been seriously questioned by Chaturvedi.[11] In the written tradition, however, among the better MSS. neither the number of verses varies very greatly considering that many of these are merely repetitions, nor do the content and language except for the substitution of some words for others without altering the meaning significantly.

One of the most significant concepts which emerge from Dadu's *Granthavali* is the concept of Guru. Man's approach to God is mediated through the Guru. 'Without the Guru even a hundred thousand moons and millions of suns cannot enlighten man's dark corners.'[12] 'With all the pools of water, the bird would remain thirsty if the Guru's grace is not available.'[13]

The Guru's power over man is thus absolute. Man's loyalty to the Guru is both personal[14] and total. At the same time the Guru on his part is benevolent to man; indeed, he merely acts as his guide[15] in the attainment of the ultimate objective, the *nirvana*.[16]

This concept of the Guru on the one hand holding absolute power over his disciples and on the other being benevolent towards them corresponds remarkably closely to, say, Abul Fazl's concept of the sovereign.[17]

The concept is further buttressed by Dadu's picturesque description of God and his court attended by all the grandeur of a great monarch.

Dadu variously refers to God as 'Sahib',[18] 'Sultan',[19] 'Maharaj',[20] 'the Rao of Raos'[21] etc. God's court contains all the regal paraphernalia—the slave-girls, the poets, the dancers, the drum-bearers, the treasury,[22] the messengers[23] etc. There are also the familiar officials in God's court—the Diwan[24] the news-writers[25] the courtiers who keep standing with folded hands[26] and the soldiers.[27] It is difficult for a person of low (spiritual) attainments to enter God's court where millions of gods keep standing with folded hands.[28] As one enters, one has to perform the *sajda*.[29]

The relationship between God and man is akin to that of master and slave. God is the master (*malik*) of the territory (*mulk*)[30] and man is His slave who owes Him undisputed loyalty.[31] Indeed, a truly loyal servant of God is one who would gladly accept even execution at His hands, or being drowned in a river or thrown down a hill.[32] Even the highest officials, including the khans, are accountable to Him.[33] His *firman* cannot but be obeyed, for it is so powerful as to turn a mountain into a rye and a rye into a mountain in an instant.[34]

On the other hand God's generosity towards his servants is unbounded. He is the protector of His servants,[35] He forgives them for all their shortcomings.[36]

It would be interesting to compare these ideas with those of Abul Fazl regarding the sovereign.

Kingship, for Abul Fazl, is a gift of God,[37] an emblem of the power of God.[38] His ideal king, Akbar, is referred to as the 'Lord of the Age whom the Almighty has given the power to conquer and has made the king of the world and its people...'[39] King being the shadow of God, he is answerable to Him alone and his power to rule over mortals is therefore absolute. Abul Fazl reinforces the king's absolutism further by advancing the concept of 'one rule, one ruler, one guide, one aim and one thought'.[40] This is tied up with the chief justification that Abul Fazl gives for the king's absolutism—the need to dispel any source of conflict in society, or, in other words, to maintain law and order in the given social and political set-up. 'If the majesty of royalty did not exist, how would various disturbances subside?'[41]—an idea very close to that of Dadu as we shall see later.

Abul Fazl pleads for unreserved loyalty to the king, particularly to Akbar. In fact any act not in complete conformity with such loyalty, and of course any act contrary to it, is bound to be visited by retribution.[42] Even among loyal men there are two types: those who are loyal due to some consideration and those who are 'noble truth-seekers who illuminate their altruistic hearts with the light of love and stand at the head of the chosen ones of God.'[43]

Abul Fazl's king is characterised by great generosity, besides majesty and absolute power. Abul Fazl quotes Akbar while pardoning the rebel Daud, 'We by virtue of our being the shadow of God, receive little and give much. Our forgiveness has no relish for vengeance.'[44] Abul Fazl himself attributes to the king *inter alia* qualities of 'paternal love towards the subjects,' and 'a large heart.'[45]

Given this correspondence between Dadu's concept of a majestic and absolute but benevolent God/Guru at the social level and Abul Fazl's similar concept of king at the political level, it is only logical that Dadu should admit the need for an absolute political authority. 'There would be peace', says Dadu, 'only if there is unity of political authority; if there is duality (of such authority), no one can remain happy due to the ensuing conflicts. With one political authority there is tranquillity in the city (kingdom); the king and the subjects are happy and there is light everywhere.'[46]

The other social classes and groups that have been referred to in the *Granthavali* are the Rana, the Rawat, the Sahu, the Sarraf, the trader, the *banjara* or the travelling merchant, the peasant and the weaver.

Dadu fully accepts the social function of all these classes and groups in the society of his day. In fact he uses the simile of God for almost everyone of them in different verses thus elevating their position in society. Nowhere does he make any specific complaint against the functioning of any one of them. At times he makes brief protest against some of them but in a very general way and that by implication. Thus, for example, he would rather that the ranas and raos along with the khans, control their ambition (lit. involvement) from outgrowing itself and 'covering the whole earth and the sky.'[47] Or, while he accepts the honourable social position of the rawat by calling himself a rawat of Raja Ram, he gives him an advice on self-control in order that the village be administered effectively. 'Dadu, rawat of Raja Ram, never forsake (His) name; take care of your soul and you can control the village (the body) better.'[48] It is obviously implied in this advice that not only did the rawat tend to transgress the area of his jurisdiction in dealing with the peasants, but that such transgression led to the ruin both of the peasantry as well as of the administrative authority, including the rawat, in the long run.

From the references made by Dadu to sections connected with trade and finance—the trader the sahu etc., it appears that Dadu gives them a place of high honour. He accepts the legitimacy of their business practices but only demands honesty of them in the interest of their business itself. That one should endeavour to get the maximum price for one's goods[49] and one should actively engage in speculation (*satta*) in order to enhance the price is a notion stressed by Dadu at more than one place. 'One who has devoted himself to God is in reality the wise one; engage in *satta* with the Creator if you want to sell at high price.'[50] 'Stake your head in speculation if you want to attain immortality.'[51] In fact anyone who does not look after his principal as well as his profit is a simpleton. 'Dadu, if you recite Ram's name you keep everything—your principal as well as your profit; if you do not recite it, you lose everything; awake O simpleton.'[52] Similarly the sahu or the money-lender is looked upon not as an expoliter but as a protector to whom the borrower is morally obligated. 'God gives (the money) to His servant to keep, the servant develops evil intentions (about the money). Dadu the whole money belongs to the Sah, to think of it otherwise is to deceive oneself.'[53] 'The head surrendered to Ram is the head which has acquired a protector; Dadu has returned (to God) what he had got from Him and is now free of debt. It is best to be the first to repay the dues to the lender and be free of debt; later on everyone repays one's debt anyway.'[54]

It is an indication of Dadu's appreciation of the role of wealth and money in society that he often resorts to measuring even spiritual attainments purely in terms of wealth, particularly jewels, pearls etc. God and the sadhu are often looked upon as jewellers in contrast to the ordinary man who treats the jewel (life) as a cowri and who carries away pebbles (the humdrum life) in the belief that these are jewels (the ideal, spiritual life).[55] It is, indeed, Dadu's belief that it is characteristic of the *kaliyuga* that the rich should become poor, and the poor rich, that the pure should become impure and the impure pure.[56]

However, Dadu advises the trader—and presumably the

others—to exercise self-restraint and not indulge in falsehood in their dealings and to be honest with the quality (and quantity) of his goods. This, indeed, would only enhance his trade.[57] It is only mildly implied here that the trader was not always fair in his transactions.

The only *sakhi* in which the *sarraf* as such is mentioned is not very significant except that the use of the term is recognized.[58] Similarly Dadu's references to agriculture and the cultivator are somewhat perfunctory in that he refers only to the need for irrigation and seeds for the purposes of cultivation.[59] These references do not yield any specific information in terms of agricultural practices or even the social condition of various sections in rural society except on some marginal points. Dadu's repeated emphasis on the need to give personal attention to cultivation by the land-owner in order to enhance the productivity of his land would perhaps suggest that lands deprived of such attention due to large-scale cultivation through agricultural labour tended to be relatively less productive. Indeed, Dadu employs the similes of God and *satguru* to refer to the cultivator who devotes such personal attention to his field and suggests that the crop growing from such labour would be ever-productive.[60]

In another context Dadu appears to suggest that twenty *biswas* of land was a source of enough prosperity to make the owner forget God.[61] But this is perhaps just a metaphorical use of the unit of measurement of land.

Dadu's references to the *banjara*[62] and the weaver[63] yield some slight information on the former's daily life and some of the latter's techniques of manufacture. However, none of these referenes have any social significance. The *banjara* arrives home early in the night, spends the second part of the night with his wife, lifts a big load and gets going in the third part and in the last part becomes a *'pir'* The night here signifies a life-cycle and the *'pir'* has been used satirically to refer to the *banjara's* old age when he cannot carry on his trade.

Dr. Tara Chand has dealt at some length with another aspect of Dadu's life and work, viz., his championing the synthesis of Hindu and Muslim cultures[64] and it is not necessary here to go into this discussion again. It might, however, be briefly stated that whereas at the political level Dadu conceives of his God in the image of the ruling king, at the social level he sharply attacks the orthodoxy of the conservative elements within the Hindu as well as the Muslim communities.[65] Indeed Dadu looks upon being a Musalman or a kafir as possessing or lacking certain virtues. 'Miyan Musalman really carries *kufr* in his heart, he has got involved in (worldly) matters and forgotten all about God (Rehman).'[66] 'Dadu kafir is one who tells lies, who does not keep his heart clean; (the kafir) does not recognize the Lord; he has in him all the lies and deception.'[67] 'He has no compassion nor affection in his heart, his heart is hard as the lightning, he should really be called a black kafir; Momin is really a different one.'[68]

Thus it would appear that Dadu generally accepts at the social level the ideals and the institutions of the ruling classes. He also accepts the class structure of society as it existed then. He would only like different classes to function more honestly and efficiently.[69] His thought is not the thought of protest but at best of resignation,[70] of avoiding any conflicts in society.[71] Dadu's thought therefore is not able to break the barriers of the ideology of the ruling classes; on the contrary, it is this ideology which percolates down to the social level and gets assimilated there in muted forms. Thus as Marx said, 'The ideas of the ruling class are in every epoch the ruling ideas,'[72] except when a given class seeks to overthrow the whole existing social structure and the conditions are ready for such change. And it was too early to expect Dadu, or for that matter the leaders of the Bhakti movement as a whole, to be the harbingers of this change, their great following among the masses notwithstanding.[73]

The mass-participation in the Bhakti movement during the fifteenth and the sixteenth centuries can perhaps be explained by the need for such re-adjustments within the caste-system as had been necessitated by certain economic and administrative changes in India following the establishment of the Turkish state. Irfan Habib has discussed technological changes as well as the new crafts that were introduced in India during the thirteenth and fourteenth centuries which considerably raised the productivity of labour in various spheres of production.[74] The high degree of administrative centralization in the same period ensured both relative stability and promotion of trade. Consequently, even some of the lower castes found themselves relatively affluent and therefore sought corresponding social status.[75] To a large extent this search is reflected in the forceful attacks on the caste system as a whole; Nanak even tried to put the idea of a casteless community into practice. But the effortlessness which characterized the re-instatement of caste even among the Sikhs suggests that its basis had never been fully demolished; at the very best a certain flexibility was allowed to creep into the system. It is interesting to consider the class-and caste-origins of the leaders of the Bhakti movement during the phase of massive popular support to it in north India, that is, during the fifteenth and sixteenth centuries. Kabir was a weaver, Nanak a petty-trader and Dadu a cotton carder along with a host of others like Dhanna, Pipa etc. of similar origins. More important, however, is the fact that it is the problems of the people of the lowers castes and classes that get reflected in their writings.

It is, however, significant that apart from their attacks on the caste, the complaints of economic oppression by the leaders of the Bhakti movement are made only against the lower rungs of administration—against the village headman in particular, or the accounts-keeper, etc.[76] Also that they prefer these complaints before none other than the king or the Diwan or before the idealized image of the king, viz., God. At times they fear that the Diwan might be dishonest as well, but they hardly ever express a grouse against the king. The mass participation in what appeared to them a movement of protest against the caste and economic oppression even though at the local level, and the simultaneous acceptance of the basic economic, political and even social structure as it existed then combined with the idealization of absolutism perhaps contributed on the one hand to peasant uprisings against the Mughal state later in seventeenth century and on the other to shaping the successor states in their internal organization as miniature imitations of the Mughal model.

REFERENCES

1. Yusuf Husain, *Glimpses of Medieval Indian Culture,* Bombay, 2nd edn., 1959, pp. 1-31, views the Bhakti movement as the result of the influence of the Islamic concept of the unity of God on Hindu polytheism; A.B. Pandey, *The First Afghan Empire in India,* Calcutta, 1956, pp. 256-90, looks upon it as the attempt of the Hindu community to reform itself in order to absorb the challenge posed by the Muslim political power and the Muslim attempts at dominating the Hindus in social and religious spheres; to I.H. Qureshi, *The Muslim Community of the Indo-Pakistan Subcontinent* (710-1947), The Hague, 1962, pp. 104-24, the Bhakti movement was a characteristically subtle attempt of the Hindus at luring the Muslims into its fold; K.S. Lal, *Twilight* of the *Sultanate,* Bombay, 1963, pp.291-315, considers the movement during the 15th century 'the silent revolution in Indian society' resulting from an interaction between Islamic, particularly Sufic, and Hindu ideas. Tara Chand in his classic study, *The Influence of Islam on Indian Culture,*2nd edn., Allahabad, 1963, sees in the movement two opposing schools of religious thought—the radical school represented by Kabir and the conservative one reprsented by Tulsidas, p. 145. For two different approaches see H.McLeod, *Guru Nanak and the Sikh Religion,* Oxford, 1968 and Irfan Habib, "The Historical Background of the Popular Monotheistic Movement of the 15th-17th centuries," (mimeo), presented to the Seminar on Ideas, Medieval India, University of Delhi, November, 1965.
2. There are very few specific pieces of information relating, for instance, to agrarian relations in the *Granthavali,* the kind of information that has been analyzed by Professor Irfan Habib, basing himself on the *Guru Granth Sahib,* in his "Evidence for Sixteenth Century Agrarian Conditions in the Guru Granth Sahib", *I.E.S.H.R.,* vol. I, no. 3, Jan-March, 1964, pp. 64-72. This paper therefore largely attempts to make a study of Dadu's general attitudes towards the various aspects of society for which there is information in the *Granthavli.* Since Dadu was both a follower of the popular movement that the Bhakti movement had become in medieval India, as well as its leader

with a great following of his own, it is obvious that his reflections were not merely personal but had a popular base.

3. Parshu Ram Chaturvedi, ed., *Dadu Dayal Granthavali,* Nagari Pracharini Sabha, Varanasi, 2023 V.S. (1966 A.D.), p. 92./verse 9.
4. Ibid, Introduction, pp. 1-2. Ram Kumar Verma places the date of his birth in 1658 V.S. (1601 A.D.) but goes on to state that he was a contemporary of Akbar. On the authority of Dadu's disciple, Jangopal, Ram Kumar Verma even claims that 'religious discussion used to take place between Akbar and Dadu.' See his *Hindi Sahitya ka Alochnatmak Itihas,* 6th edn., Allahabad, 1971, p. 273. However unless Dadu had these discussions with Akbar at the age of four, Akbar having died in 1605, the date of Dadu's birth given by Verma seems for off the mark although he has given the same date twice in the same paragraph.
5. Parshu Ram Chaturvedi, op. cit., Introduction, pp. 5-6.
6. *Shri Dadu Janmalila Parchi* of Dadu's disciple Jangopal and the *Bhaktamal* of another of his followers, Raghodass, both give very dubious information about Dadu's life. One has therefore to rely on scattered pieces of information to reconstruct whatever little can be reconstructed of his biography.
7. *Granthavali,* where Dadu refers to himself as a Pinjara, p. 455/verse 1 and Dhunia, p. 477/verse 1. Pinjara, according to the *Vrihat Hindi Shabdakosh,* Gyan Mandal, Banaras, 2009 V.S. (1952), means a cotton-carder. *Dabistan-i Mazahib* also refers to him as a *naddaf,* ed. Nazar Ashraf, Calcutta, 1809, p. 267.
8. Among others the following editions have so far been published: Sudhakar Dwivedi, ed., *Shri Dadu Dayal ki Vani,* Kashi Nagari Pracharini Sabha, 1906; Sudhakar Dwivedi, ed., *Dadu Dayal ka Sabad,* Kashi Nagari Pracharini Sabha, 1907; Chandrika Prasad Tripathi, ed., *Shri Swami Dadu Dayal ki Vani Ajmer,* 1964 V.S. (1907 A.D.); *Dadu Padsangrah,* Lahore, 1917, etc. Parshu Ram Chaturvedi's edition, which I have used for this paper, compares six MSS, and while preparing the oldest one for publication, the editor has given all the variaions in the other MSS in the footnotes.
9. Chaturvedi, op.cit, Introduction, p. 17.
10. Quoted in Ibid, Introduction, p. 17.
11. Ibid.
12. *Granthavali,* p. 7/58.
13. Ibid, p. 5/44.
14. Ibid, p. 2/4 'Dadu met the Guru with great ease and (the Guru)

embraced him; great kindness was thus shown to me by the kind one (the Guru) and all my lamps were lit.'

15. Ibid, p. 2/10 'When you meet the true Guru, he solves all your problems; he puts you on the boat and carries you across the river.' Or, ibid., p. 3/17. 'When one is drowning in the *bhau sagar* it is Satguru who rescues one; Dādu, meeting the Guru is meeting the boatman who will put you on to his boat.'
16. Dadu's description of the ultimate state of bliss is suggestive of *nirvana,* see Ibid, p. 392/35; at another place he even uses the term *nirvana* itself, p. 360/*pada* 15, verse 3.
17. This point will be discussed below.
18. *Granthavali,* pp. 148/11, 148/15, 18, 152/37, 38 etc.
19. Ibid, pp. 406/*pada* 20 verse 3, 434/1.
20. Ibid, p. 465/*pada* 3 verse 2.
21. Ibid, p. 348/*pada* 4 verse 1.
22. Ibid, p. 474-5/*pada* 19.
23. Ibid, p. 341/*pada* 8 verse 1.
24. Ibid, p. 488/*pada* 10 verse 3.
25. Ibid, p. 474/*pada* 19 verse 3.
26. Ibid, p. 470/*pada* 9 verse 2.
27. Ibid, p. 238/14, 239/19 where Dadu portrays God's servants as brave and loyal soldiers who are prepared to surrender their heads in God's cause.
28. Ibid, pp. 470-71/*pada* 9.
29. Ibid, pp. 35/67, 67/209,180/41 etc.
30. Ibid, pp. 428/*pada* 6 verse 2.
31. Ibid, p. 340/*pada* 6. 'God you are my master and I am your slave.' Indeed, the *Granthavali* is full of references where man is portrayed as God's slave.
32. Ibid, p. 478/*pada* 28.
33. Ibid, p. 360/*pada* 15 verse 3.
34. Ibid, p. 221/2.
35. Ibid, p. 294/33.
36. Ibid, pp.293/26, 312/*pada* 11 verse 1, 454/*pada* 2.
37. Abul Fazl, *Akbar Nama* (*AN*), Bib. Ind., vol. II, p. 285.
38. Abul Fazl, *Ain-i Akbari* (*Ain*), Blochmann (tr.), vol. I, Bib. Ind. 1927, p. 167.
39. *AN*, vol. II, pp. 128-29.
40. Ibid, vol. III, p. 4.
41. *Ain*, vol. I, Blochmann, ed., p. 2; Blochmann's translation has a slightly different version, p. 2.
42. *AN*, vol. III, p. 20.

43. Ibid, pp. 449-50.
44. Ibid, p. 97.
45. *Ain*, Blochmann (tr.) p. 3.
46. *Granthavali*, pp. 130-31/31-32.
47. Ibid, p. 253/68.
48. Ibid, p. 19/36.
49. Ibid, p. 170/6, 266/34 where man is advised to make effort to sell his (spiritual) wares at high prices.
50. Ibid, p. 19/34.
51. Ibid, p. 386/*pada* 22 verse 4: Immortality is the highest price for obtaining which speculation is the best method and therefore the stakes should be high.
52. Ibid, p. 20/40.
53. Ibid, p. 101/41.
54. Ibid, p. 241/38-39. Ram is looked upon both as the moneylender and the protector (*nath*).
55. Ibid, p. 162/122. see also pp. 265/25, 26, 27, 266/31 etc.
56. Ibid, p. 386/*pada* 23, verse 1.
57. Ibid, p. 266/34.
58. Ibid, p. 174/38.
59. Ibid, p. 303-05.
60. Ibid, p. 303/3. 'If the master (sahib) does not irrigate (his land), the plant would wither away. Dadu if the Lord irrigates (the land), the plant would keep on growing.' See also pp. 393/5, 6, 395/19 etc.
61. Ibid, p. 210/15. 'One who keeps his body tidy and absorbs himself in his twenty *biswas* (of land) and does not remember God, breaks the *Hadis*.'
62. Ibid, pp. 504-05.
63. Ibid, p. 438/*pada* 1.
64. Tara Chand, op. cit., pp. 185-86.
65. *Granthavali*, pp. 23-24, 153/43-44, 160/102-03, 459/*pada* 13, verse 2, 460/pada 14, verse 3 etc.
66. Ibid, p. 149/19.
67. Ibid.
68. Ibid, p. 275/34.
69. Ibid, p. 151/28.

    'Dadu, he is the Monin whose heart is soft like wax, who does not forget the Lord; who does not oppress (any one) and does not enjoy life sitting idly by (i.e. who does the work that is due from him); such a Momin will go to the heaven.' See also p. 182/50: 'Give to everyone what is his due and do some good to others; Dadu, that servant is best who does not carry any load (i.e., undue exaction from anyone) on his head.'

70. Ibid, p. 422/pada 4 and many other places. Dadu's ideal is the man living in the world but completely detached to it as lotus is in a pond.
71. Ibid, pp. 171-77, where Dadu forcefully disapproves of any kind of conflicts in society between sections or individuals.
72. Karl Marx, *German Ideology,* in Marx & Engels, *Selected Works,* vol. I, Moscow, 1969, p. 47.
73. Discussing the impact of the Bhakti Movement in Maharashtra, D.D. Kosambi remarks, 'The reform and its struggle was never consciously directed against feudalism so that its very success meant feudal patronage and ultimately feudal decay by diversion of a democratic movement into the dismal channels of conquest and rapine', *Myth and Reality,* Bombay, 1962, p. 35. With some qualifications this precisely is the point.
74. "Presidential Address", Medieval India Section, *Proceedings of Indian History Congress,* Varanasi Session (1969), Patna, 1970, pp. 139-61.
75. Irfan Habib, "The Historical Background of the Popular Monotheistic Movement." (mimeo), 1965.
76. Madhu Tandon, "Historical Analysis of Kabir's Poetry", unpublished M. Phil. dissertation submitted to the Jawaharlal Nehru University, 1974, pp. 79-80; Dadu Dayal *Granthavali,* pp. 19/36, 253/68.

8

Marx on Pre-Colonial India: An Evaluation

The basic elements that comprised Marx and Engels' understanding of Asiatic particularism *vis-a-vis* Europe were the following: the critical role of artificial irrigation in Indian agriculture for which, given the scale of its requirement, the State alone could have assumed the responsibility; independently of this, although operating in close collaboration with it, was the feature of the absence of private property in land; there were, besides, the numerous village societies, each being an isolated and economically self-sufficient unit where 'natural economy' persisted in the form of a unity between agriculture and handicrafts manufacture; outside of the village, commodities circulated in cities which by and large continued to remain parasitical; and this whole scenario was dominated by the despotic State hanging above, which collected the agrarian surplus in the form of tribute or tax that, at one stage in Marx's thinking, had assumed the characteristics of rent. All these elements together eliminated the possibility of any basic changes in the production system or the social organisation for centuries, until India's colonisation by Britain.

These characteristics together comprised what Marx had called the Asiatic mode of production.[1] Even though Marx had used the term 'Asiatic mode of production' only on two occasions, and Engels never, they do not appear to have changed their position on the characteristics and features that comprised this mode of production; indeed, they remained convinced of Asiatic particularism to the end.

Most of the elements that went into the making of Marx and Engels' understanding of Asia's history had been in circulation in Europe for varying lengths of time. The role of the State in maintaining hydraulic works for irrigation and navigation in Egypt, India and China had been emphasised by Adam Smith.[2] The notion of the absence of private property in land in Asia as the cause of Asiatic despotism had come to be established in Europe during the fourteenth century,[3] though several Eruopean travellers to India during the seventeenth century, and in particular Bernier, had done much to popularise the notion of the oriental sovereign being the master of all the land in his dominion.[4] Marx, like many others among his contemporaries, had picked up this notion from Bernier,[5] though he was aware of the raging controversy among British administrators and historians regarding the nature of land rights in India.[6]

The concept of isolated village societies, each economically and administratively a self-governing unit characterised by the unity of agriculture and handicrafts production,[7] again had a longish pre-Marxian history.[8] The notion of the State collecting taxes from the peasantry, taxes that also appeared as rent in view of the State's lordship over all land, had first been suggested by Adam Smith and later developed by Jones[9] and Marx,[10] although Marx was the one to emphasise the co-existence of commodity circulation in cities along with a natural economy in the villages.[11] The stasis of the East over a thousand years was the dominant notion of European thinking during the nineteenth century; so also was its corollary—the unleashing of the forces of progress in the Orient at Western hands.[12]

Marx absorbed all these elements which had originated in diverse sources and synthesised them into a distinct mode of production. It is not the objective of this paper to examine the validity of Marx's notion of the Asiatic mode of production or to discuss whether or not Marx, and Engels, had given up this notion at some stage of their lives. The attempt, on the other hand, will be to examine the significance of some of the individual observations of Marx on pre-colonial India and elaborate them with reference to empirical data, irrespective of the validity of Marx's own ideas. This is done on the assumption that the significance of Marx's observations is not dependent on his being right in each case; even when his own conclusions are patently questionable, the initial lead provided by his perceptions loses none of its value for understanding history.

I

The idea that India's agricultural production was possible only with large scale artificial irrigation, and this in turn necessitated State intervention, was first suggested by Engels to Marx.[13] Marx took to the suggestion enthusiastically in his article 'The British Rule in India'.[14] The theme continued to recur in both Marx's and Engels' writings—*Grundrisse, Capital* and *Anti-Duhring*.[15] Considering that Marx and Engels emphasised the gigantic scale on which artificial irrigation was required in India they might have had in mind canal and big tank irrigation for which state intervention would become necessary. Marx does in fact mention canals specifically in his article 'The British Rule in India' and in *Capital*, volume 1; Engels, however, makes a reference merely to the State's responsibility for 'the collective maintenancee of irrigation throughout the river valleys' which could either be canals or reservoirs where river water was stored. They should, at any rate, have been aware of water tanks for irrigation, for Marx cites an official House of Commons report published in 1812 and included in Campbell's *Modern India* (1852) in which reference is made to the Superintendent of tanks and water courses.[16]

The causal link that Marx and Engels had posited between irrigation and oriental despotism was abused by Karl Wittfogel, and this abuse has generally been recognised.[17] However, this recognition has also often led historians to deny the dire need for artificial irrigation in Indian agriculture or the State's contribution to it.[18] We shall discuss the signifinance of artificial irrigation for India's economic and social history later. For the moment let us merely note that the State in India did intervene in providing irrigation on a considerable scale. The famous Sudarshan Lake in South Gujarat was constructed by the Maurya rulers in the fourth century B.C., repaired by a Saka ruler in the second century A.D. and again by a Gupta ruler in the fifth century A.D. This lake thus has a long history of 800 years of service to agriculture. The Nandas had the construction of a canal in Orissa to their credit. This canal, too, survived for five centuries and was maintained by the local rulers. There is considerable evidence that either imperial or provincial dynasties undertook the construction and maintenance of reservoirs or canals for irrigation in various regions of early India: in South India in the Kaveri region, in Punjab, Rajasthan, Uttar Pradesh, Bihar and Bengal, in the Eastern Deccan and in Kashmir.[19] Megasthenes also reports the appointment of State officials for control over the distribution of canal water.[20] We are, of course, familiar with construction of canals for irrigation by Firuz Tughlaq in the second half of the fourteenth century and by Shah Jahan in the seventeenth century.[21]

Clearly then, Marx's and Engels' concern with the State's role in providing artificial irrigation was not without substance. However, their error lay in attributing exclusive responsibility to the State for providing such irrigation; in the process they overlooked the individual peasant initiative in tending his crop. It is in this basic error that the unfortunate causal link between irrigation and the notion of Oriental Despotism originated.

For artificial irrigation was not provided merely by grandiose projects like canals and artificial lakes but also by small tanks in the village (either maintained by village assemblies or by individuals) or wells. The humble *dhenkli* or *piccote,* a string at one end and a counterweight at the other, operating on the principle of the lever fixed between two vertical poles or a fork and drawing water from a shallow depth, surely required no heavy investment either of capital or labour.[22] Besides, there is the impressive progress of a three-stage development of water-wheels in North-West and North India between about the fifth or sixth century A.D. and the thirteenth;[23] and this progress is a remarkable testimony to individual enterprise. It is worthwhile keeping in mind that a water-wheel operating in one well could irrigate a number of fields in the neighbourhood; after the owner's field had been irrigated, water flowing from his water-wheel could be sold by the hour for use in the adjacent fields, much like what happens with tubewells in Punjab today.[24]

Unfortunately, while our historical records, whether inscriptions or texts, are eager to immortalise the construction of canals or lakes or big reservoirs by rulers, they are rather reluctant to take much notice of a well or a small tank or a small channel bringing water from the river to the field—works undertaken by anonymous peasants or even village potentates—unless these happen to enter into evidence in land sale-deeds where boundaries are strictly delimited or in cases of grave tension arising over the use of water. However, the rarity of references to such small-scale means of irrigation need not suggest the actual scarcity of these means. It is impossible to make even a rough quantification for the period before the eighteenth or nineteenth century; but it is perhaps not a gross overstatement to say that individual initiative was responsible for the substantial part of artificially irrigated agriculture in pre-colonial India. Individual initiative is also evident in the impressive increase in the number of crops grown before colonialism had eastablished itself here.[25]

As it happens, the failure of Marx and Engels to recognise individual initiative in providing irrigation led them to establish an avoidable causal relationship between irrigation and despotism; it also led them, and their contemporaries, to overlook the fact that rural India had been proceeding progressively with differentiation for over two millennia[26] and that artificial irrigation itself was one of the means of such differentiation. For, the construction of a well and the installation of a water-wheel, or the construction of a tank with sluice-gates, presupposed the availability of a certain amount of resources with the family undertaking such a project; on the other hand, the ready availability of water for its field would ensure returns to it which others, devoid of such resources, could hardly aspire to. Inevitably, the gap between the master of a well or a tank and his less fortunate brethren would tend to widen.

If Marx and Engels had erred in attributing to the State the exclusive responsibility for providing artificial irrigation, the fact that they assigned a critical role to such irrigation is nonetheless of singular importance for understanding India's social and economic history. For shaping any system of agricultural production, the regional ecology (nature of the soil, availability of water, duration of sunshine etc.), the given technology and the social organisation of labour utilisation must interact with one another. In early medieval Europe, where manure was the chief bottleneck in agricultural production and technology deficient, the lateral use of soil fertility became essential.[27] This necessitated the sowing of each seed at quite a distance from another; consequently vast fields were required to yield meagre amounts of produce. It is known, for instance, that up to the ninth century, a hundred acres of land were necessary to maintain one European peasant family.[28] The process of production was, therefore, extremely labour intensive. The demand for labour was concentrated in a few weeks, given the limited duration of sunshine. Medieval Europe sought to solve these problems by tying down peasant labour to *structured dependence* on the lords, of which serfdom was one, though the most important form.[29]

The high natural fertility of the Indian soil, given the availability of water, on the other hand, created a different kind of agrarian regime here. A much smaller field than in Europe, extending between 9 and 13.5 acres, sufficed to sustain an Indian peasant family.[30] Labour could also be spread out over time. It is, therefore, not the intensity of labour but of capital investment—in the form of irrigation devices or high value cash crops—which would enhance the value of one's yield. The nature of social conflicts generated in the process is, therefore, of a substantially different order than the one that medieval Europe had witnessed. In Europe social conflicts had led to the redistribution of the means of production themselves; this in turn, had led to the emergence of a new mode of production, the bourgeois mode, at the expense of the feudal mode of production; in India, the conflicts had remained confined to the redistribution of agrarian surplus, without subverting the production system as such, although within the system important changes did take place all the time.

II

Marx, like several others before him, had somewhat too readily accepted the notion of the unchanging East.[31] Basically, the absence of private property in land and the self-sustaining 'natural economy' of the Indian village, buttressed by the unity of agriculture and manufacture, had produced this condition of the 'unresisting and unchanging society.' Marx had noted the views in favour of the existence of private property but there is little reason to believe that he had himself been persuaded by them.[32] While continuing to stick to the notion of the absence of private property, Marx prevaricated between the State as the owner of land and ownership vesting with the clan or community.[33] Engels too at one place in the *Anti-Duhring* favours 'common ownership of the land' and at another refers indifferently to the village community or the State owning the land 'in the whole of the Orient'.[34] In 1888 he spoke of the 'village communities in which the land was communally owned' and characterised them as 'the primitive form of society all the way from India to Ireland.'[35] If he excludes any reference to the Asiatic mode of production from his *The Origin of the Family* and mentions instead 'the three epochs of civilization'—namely, slavery, feudalism and modern bourgeoisie—the context strongly suggests that he treated Asian history still as pre-history in terms of the origin and conflict of classes within it. His passage reads as follows:

> With slavery which reached its fullest development in civilisation, came the first great split of society into an exploiting and an exploited class. This split has continued during the whole period of civilisation. Slavery was the first form of exploitation, peculiar to the world of antiquity; it was followed by serfdom in the Middle Ages and by wage labour in modern time. These are the three great forms of servitude, characteristic of the three great epochs of civilization....[36]

Clearly, if Engels still considered India a society where 'the great split into an exploiting and an exploited class' had not yet occurred he could hardly have included its history among the epochs of civilisation.[37]

However, irrespective of whether Marx and Engels favoured State or communal property, their basic position till the very end denied the existence of private property in land. This was combined with the notion of unity between agriculture and manufactures and self-sufficiency of the village as a unit.[38] Hence the characteristic of changelessness in India's pre-colonial history in contrast to the rapidly changing stages of historical development in Europe—slavery, feudalism and modern capitalism.

The notion of significant changes in pre-colonial India's economy and society is a recent entrant in Indian historiography and no hard effort is called for to explain Marx's ignorance of it. Clearly, Marx's and Engels' notion of changelessness in Indian society has little chance of survival in the face of recent research. Yet, the significant difference implied by Marx in the pace and nature of changes in pre-colonial Indian society *vis-a-vis* pre-modern Europe remains an important pointer to the different paths of development that these societies have followed for entering into the modern world.

Europe's stages of historical development—slavery, feudalism and capitalism—are clearly enough marked and almost universally accepted. It is also nearly universally accepted that in India the changes that occurred in the production system and social organisation, important as these are, do not mark comparably distinct discontinuities. Changes in India are long drawn and gradual; they have the effect of modifying the existing production techniques and social organisation of production; but they rarely overthrow an existing social and economic structure and replace it by a new one, by a new mode of production. This is especially true since the seventh century A.D.

It is now commonly accepted that the post-Vedic society in North India witnessed, on the one hand, considerable expansion of agriculture and, on the other, the emergence of sharp social differentiation. Although individual landholdings, tilled by family labour, appear to have formed the dominant pattern,[39] in the Buddhist literature we meet with large farms, sometimes tilled by as many as 500 ploughs, employing a gang of wage labourers.[40] The *Arthasastra* also speaks of state farms worked by 'slave labourers and prisoners.'[41] In the post-Mauryan period share-cropping and debt-bondage appear to have grown in importance as the basic forms of labour.[42] In the Gupta and post-Gupta times we hardly come across any reference to large farms, whether owned by individuals or the State; on the other hand the *sudras* were gradually being transformed into petty producers. By the first half of the seventh century, most, if not all, *sudras* had become peasants.[43] This consolidation of petty peasant production, in the midst of a highly stratified rural society, provides the social context of individual peasant initiative in extending cultivation through the development of irrigation devices and the adoption of new crops, to which we have referred earlier.

This consolidation was accompanied by a significant change in the form of exploitation. From now on, while the peasants' process of production, including their labour, was under their own control, they were subjected to parting with their surplus produce in the form of revenue paid to the State. With the relationship of exploitation pivoted on the appropriation of the surplus produce, conflicts between peasants and the State inevitably arose on the quantum of the surplus so appropriated; these conflicts had little bearing upon the production system. As a consequence of these conflicts the means of production were not redistributed until after the onset of colonialism; what was distributed and redistributed was the peasants' surplus produce. It was thus that even when the crisis created by such momentous events as the collapse of the Mughal empire, occurred during the early eighteenth century, the empire was succeeded by the resurgence of the class of zamindars everywhere; the crisis, in other words, led to the resurgence of an old property form rather than the emergence of a new one.

It is therefore arguable that without the intervention of European colonialism, there was little chance of the development of capitalism in the late medieval Indian economy.[44] The medieval Indian economy was characterised by the following features—high fertility of land, low subsistence needs of the producers, consequently a high level of exploitation of the peasantry yielding an enormous amount of surplus to the ruling class, and finally, peasants' freedom of control over their process of production. These features, especially the last, ensured a degree of steady development of the productive forces; simultaneously, they ensured a relative stability of the production system which would not be subjected to violent upheavals. The social conflicts, being confined to the appropriation of surplus, were such in nature that their resolution did not require the overthrow of the given structure.[45]

It is this essential divergence in the paths of development followed by medieval Europe and pre-colonial India that Marx had emphasised, perhaps even over-emphasised. It is hardly necessary to accept Marx's own assumptions and follow his own argument in order to appreciate the significance of his critical perception. Surely, this is a theme that calls for a much more detailed examination than has yet been done.

III

We have noted in the foregoing Marx's adherence to the notion of the absence of property in land in India. However, Marx made a real break in dealing with the problem when he transferred this attention to the use of, rather than merely the title to, land. The use of land in Marx's understanding ranged from communal cultivation to individual possession and cultivation. In 1853 Marx stated: 'In some of these communities the lands of the village are cultivated in common, in most cases each occupant tills his own field.'[46]

In the *Grundrisse*, Marx refers to communal property actually realising itself in labour either in the form where 'the individual with his family work independently on the lot assigned to them' or through 'the communality of labour itself as in a few clans in India'.[47] In *Capital* he speaks of:

> Those small and extremely ancient Indian communities, some of which have continued down to this day, are based on possession in common of the land.... The constitution of these communities varies in different parts of India. In those of the simplest form the land is tilled in common, and the produce divided among the members.[48]

The question of the use of land is indeed one of critical significance; it is far more important than the question of ownership. Ownership is essentially a legal category, particularly as it is articulated in terms of land's alienability: If one has the right to alienate one's land, that is proof of one's ownership of it. But then alienation of land itself is expressive of a situation where demand for land outstrips its supply; where, in other words, a market for land has to some extent developed. In the context of land being available aplenty (such as the one in pre-colonial India) and the consequent absence of developed land market, the very search for the articulation of one's proprietary right in land in terms of the right to alienation would appear anachronistic. It is perhaps far more useful, in such a context, to examine the nature of land use and the form of organisation of labour for production.[49] This is indeed what Marx sought to do when he concerned himself with the problem of communal or individual cultivation of the land.

The manner in which land is tilled depends upon a number of factors: the ecology, the technology, the availability of man-power in a region, and, above all, the social or human intervention in organising forms of labour utilisation. Even with comparable ecologies and technologies, one society might organise its labour for production quite radically differently from another.

In pre-colonial India, the organisation of labour for agricultural production was predominantly in terms of family labour from seventh century A.D. onwards, as we have noted earlier. On the farms of big land owners, labour was hired[50] and at times even forced.[51] This labour, both on the peasants' fields and on larger farms, was supplemented by the labour of the menial castes who were paid an extremely meagre share of the produce in return.[52] This collective control of the lower castes' labour exercised by the entire cultivating community irrespective of its own differentiation, is the specific Indian solution to the problem of meeting the labour demand of the production system.

The control over labour was exercised through the operation of the caste system which excluded the menial castes from the right to own and cultivate land for themselves, and this in the context of enormous land abundance. It was thus that the availability of agricultural labour was determined by social laws and customs in a specific Indian form of non-economic coercion.

Marx, perhaps, did not have the communal control over the lower castes' labour in mind when he spoke of either communal or individual cultivation. Yet, we owe this problematic to his insight, to this attempt to understand the working of the system of agricultural production rather than merely the question of ownership of landed property. This problematic, indeed, is one that has still to be fully examined. It calls for an estimation of the labour input in agricultural production on a regional basis; it also calls for attempts to understand the form of lower castes' resistance to the grossly unjust social restrictions on their access to land when so much of land was there for the asking. Besides, the reasons for the durability of the caste system and its relationship with changes in the production system and forms of labour utilisation are aspects that have been so little examined, even though, clearly, they are crucial to any understanding of pre-colonial economy and society in India. Both Marxism and the historiography of India will be the richer if some of these problems that had occupied Marx are subjected to a far more detailed examination than has yet been done, even if Marx's own observations have to be modified in the end, or abandoned altogether. For Marx, after all, was too great a thinker to be right all the time.

REFERENCES

1. Karl Marx, A *Contribution to the Critique of Political Economy* (hereafter *MCCPE;* Moscow, 1970), 'Preface,' p. 21; and Karl Marx, *Capital,* vol. I (Moscow, 1954), p. 79.
2. Perry Anderson, *Lineages of the Absolutist State* (London, 1975), pp. 466 ff. and Marian Sawer, *Marxism and the Question of the Asiatic Mode of Production* (The Hague, 1977), p. 29.
3. Ibid, pp. 6 f.
4. Thomas Roe, *Journal,* in *Chrchill's Collective Voyages,* vol. I (London, 1732), p. 729; Tavernier, *Travels in India,* vol. I (New Delhi, 1977), p. 260; Manucci, *Storia do Mogor,* vol. 2 (London, 1907), p. 44; and Bernier, *Travels in the Mogul Empire* (New Delhi, 1972), p. 204.
5. K. Marx to F. Engels, 2 June 1853, in K. Marx and F. Engels, *Seleccted Correspondence* (hereafter MESC; Moscow, 1975), p. 75.
6. See K. Marx to F. Engels, 14 June 1853, ibid, p. 80: 'As to the *question of property,* this is a very controversial one among the English writers on India. In the broken hill-country south of Krishna, property in land does seem to have existed' [emphasis original].
   In 1858 too, he showed recognition of disputes that had been continuing on this question in India; see his 'Lord Canning's Proclamation and Land Tenure in India,' in Karl Marx, *The First Indian War of Independence* (hereafter *FIWI:* Moscow, n.d.), pp. 161-63. For details of this controversy, see Lawrence Krader, *The Asiatic Mode of Production: Sources, Development & Critique in the Writings of Karl Marx* (Assen, 1975), pp. 37-85.
7. K. Marx to F. Engels, 14 June 1853, *MESC,* pp. 79 f; K. Marx, 'The Future Results of British Rule in India,' *FIWI,* pp. 36 f; K. Marx, *Grundrisse* (Harmondsworth, 1975), pp. 473, 485 f and 493; *Capital,* vol. I, pp. 375 f; *Capital,* vol. III (Moscow, 1971), pp. 333 and 786 f; and F. Engels, *The Origin of the Family, Private Property and the State* (Moscow, 1968), p. 156.
8. While the notion of the self-sustaining village society had been advanced by Mark Wilks in his *Historical Sketches of the South of India* (London, 1810), vol. I, pp. 177 f, and was taken up by *The Fifth Report from the Select Committee on the Affairs of the East India Company* in 1812, it was Richard Jones who first developed the notion of the unity between agriculture and handicrafts; see Lawrence Krader, op.cit., pp. 53-55. This theme was then elaborated by Marx in *Capital.*

9. L. Krader, op. cit., pp. 39f and 41.
10. *Capital*, vol. III, pp. 790f.
11. *Capital*, vol. I, pp. 375f.
12. G.W.F. Hegel, *The Philosophy of History* (New York, 1944), pp. 142, 161 and 163; M. Sawer, op. cit., pp. 26 and 30f. For the inevitability of India's subjection to Europe as a condition for the former's progress, see G.W.F. Hegel, op.cit., p. 142; K. Marx, 'The Future Results of British Rule in India', *FIWI*, pp. 33-40; and M. Sawer, op.cit., p. 26.
13. F. Engels to K. Marx, 6 June 1853, *MESC*, p. 76.
14. K. Marx, 'The British Rule in India'. *New York Daily Tribune*, 25 June, 1853, written by Marx on 10 June 1853 reproduced in *FIWI*, p. 16.
15. *Grundrisse*, pp. 473 f; *Captital*, vol. I, p. 514; and F. Engels, *Anti-Duhring* (Moscow, 1954), p. 249.
16. *FIWI*, p. 19.
17. Perry Anderson, op.cit., pp. 487-91; Marian Sawer, op.cit., p. 49; and Irfran Habib, 'An Examination of Wittfogel's Theory of Oriental Despotism,' *Enquiry* (New Delhi), 6, pp. 54-73.
18. R.S. Sharma, 'Stages in the Evolution of Early Indian Society' in G.P. Sinha (ed.), *The Man and the Scientist* (Delhi, 1979), p. 205.
19. Nand Kishore Kumar, 'Hydraulic Agriculture in Peninsular India, (c.300 B.C. to 1300 A.D.), *Proceedings of the Indian History. Congress*, 1979 (Delhi, 1980), pp. 211-214.
20. R.C. Jain (ed.), *McCrindle's Ancient India as Described by Megasthenes and Arrian* (New Delhi, 1972), p. 86. I owe this reference to my colleague Dr. B.D. Chattopadhyaya.
21. T. Raychaudhuri and I. Habib (eds.), *Cambridge Economic History of India* (hereafter as *CEHI;* Cambridge, 1982), vol. I, pp. 49 and 216.
22. Henry Yule and A.C. Burnell, *Hobson-Jobson* (New Delhi, 1979), S.V. *Picottah.*
23. B.D. Chattopadhyaya, 'Irrigation in Early Medieval Rajasthan', *Journal of the Economic and Social History of the Orient*, vol. 16 (2 & 3), pp. 298-316; and Irfan Habib, 'Presidential Address' to the Section on Medieval India, *Proceedings of the Indian History Congress*, 1969 (Delhi, 1970).
24. That water from a well was shared and the wheel 'leased out' is evident from early medieval evidence, one of which allows a land-grantee a one-third share of the water of the attached well and another of actual leasing out of a water-wheel (see B.D. Chattopadhyaya, op.cit., pp. 311 and 314 f).

25. Harbans Mukhia, 'Was There Feudalism in Indian History?' *The Journal of Peasant Studies,* vol. 8(3), 1981, n. 213.
26. Uma Chakravarti, 'Slavery and Bondage in Ancient India' (forthcoming); Irfan Habib, 'The Peasant in Indian History', in *Social Change in India* ("Social Scientist Marx Centenary Volume", vol. I, Trivandrum, 1983), pp. 40f: and *CEHI,* vol. I, pp. 54f, 174-77, 221f, 240 and 247.
27. Charles Parain, 'The Evolution of Agricultural Technique', *Cambridge Economic History of Europe,* vol. I (Cambridge, 1966), pp. 133 f and 145 f; Marc Bloch, *French Rural History* (London 1976), p. 25; G. Duby, *Rural Economy and Country Life in the Medieval West* (London, 1968), pp. 24 f; and Lynn White Jr., *Medieval Technology and Social Change* (London, 1973), pp. 41-43 and 53.
28. R.H. Hilton, *Bond Men Made Free* (London 1973), p. 28.
29. Harbans Mukhia, op.cit., pp. 274-77.
30. R.S. Sharma, *Light on Early Indian Society and Economy* (Bombay, 1966) pp. 62 and 73; and Puspa Niyogi, *Contributions to the Economic History of Northern India* (Calcutta, 1962), p. 97 and n.
31. K. Marx, 'The Future Results of British rule in India' *FIWI,* pp. 33f. Cf. Montesquieu's statement: 'The laws, customs and manners of the Orient—even the most trivial, such as mode of dress—remain the same as they were a thousand years ago,' as cited in Perry Anderson, op.cit., p.464. Also cf. James Mill's view that the Asiatic social system 'was one in which all progress hand ceased thousands of years ago', see Marian Sawer, op. cit., pp. 30f. Again witness Hegel: '...the Hindoos have no History in the from of annals [Historia]... they have no History in the form of transactions [*Regestrae*]; that is, no growth expanding into a veritable political condition'; see G.W.F. Hegel, op. cit., p. 163.
32. We have noted earlier that in 1853 and 1858 Marx had recorded the view that private property in land did exist. In 1879, again, in his resumé of M. Kovalevsky's book, *Communal Landholding,* Marx noted the emergence of individual private family property 'in the modern sense.' But then, as Daniel Thorner cautiously remarks 'From the materials currently available to us we cannot tell whether Marx was simply summarising Kovalevsky or simultaneously expressing agreement with him that the Indian village community had undergone a series of transformation,' see Daniel Thorner, 'Marx on India and the Asiatic Mode of Production', *Contributions to Indian Sociology,* vol. 9, December 1966, pp. 61f.

33. In his letter dated 2 June 1853 addressed to Engels, Marx had entirely appoved of Bernier's view that the king in India was 'the sole and only proprietor of all the land'; see *MESC*, pp. 76f. In 1857-58 Marx, it seems had shifted decisively to the 'clan or communal property'; see *Grundrisse*, pp. 472 f and 484. He repreated this view in 1859 and 1867; see *MCCPE*, p. 33, and *Capital*, vol. I, pp. 77 f. In the third volume of *Capital*, drafted between 1863 and 1867, Marx again implicitly reverted to the position that the sovereign had been the proprietor of the soil in India; see *Capital*, vol. III, p. 791.
34. F. Engels, *Anti-Duhring*, pp. 224 and 244f. respectively.
35. Footnote added by F. Engels to the English edition (1888) of *The Communist Manifesto*, as cited in Daniel Thorner, op.cit., pp. 59 f.
36. F. Engels, *The Orgin of the Family, Private Property and the State* was first published in 1884. Another edition, revised by Engels hismelf, was brought out in 1891. Reference is made here to the Moscow reprint (1968) of this edition; see p. 172.
37. Eric Hobsbawm also feels that the fact that in *The Origin of the Family* Engels made no allusion whatsoever to the Asiatic mode of production can probably be explained by the reason that it was omitted by Engels 'as belonging to the pre-history of "civilisation",' for Engels came to hold that slavery, serfdom and modern wage-labour had been 'the three great forms of servitude, characteristic of the three great epochs of civilization'; see E.J. Hobsbawm (ed.), 'Introduction,' *Karl Marx: Pre-Capitalist Economic Formations* (first published in 1964; reprint New York, 1971) p. 51n. Irfan Habib somewhat severely calls this explanation of Hobsbawm 'rather strained'; see Irfan Habib, 'Marx's Perception of India,' *The Marxist*, vol. I (1), July, September 1983, p. 115n.
38. K. Marx to F. Engels, 14 June 1853, *MESC*, p. 80; 'The Future Results of British Rule in India,' *FIWI*, pp. 36 f: *Grundrisse*, pp. 473, 486 and 493; *Capital*, vol. I, pp. 357 f; *Capital*, vol. III, pp. 333 and 786f; and F. Engels, *The Origin of the Family*, p. 156.
39. Uma Chakravarti, op.cit., pp. 21-23.
40. P.C. Jain, *Labour in Ancient India* (New Delhi, 1971), pp. 44 f.
41. R. Shamasastry (tr.), *Kautilya's Arthasastra* (Mysore 1967), p. 129.
42. Uma Chakravarti, op.cit., pp. 38 f and 45 f.
43. R.S. Sharma, *Indian Feudalism* (Calcutta, 1965), pp. 61-63.
44. Irfan Habib, 'Potentialities of Capitalistic Development in the Economy of Mughal India,' *Enquiry*, Winter 1971, pp. 1-56.
45. Harbans Mukhia, op. cit., p. 293.

46. K. Marx to F. Engels, 14 June 1853, *MESC*, p. 80.
47. *Grundrisse*, pp. 473 and 477.
48. *Capital*, vol. I, p. 357.
49. Harbans Mukhia, op.cit., p. 290.
50. Dilbagh Singh, 'Tenants, Sharecroppers and Agricultrual Labourers in Eighteenth Century Eastern Rajasthan *Studies in History*, vol. 1(1), 1979, p.39.
51. Harbans Mukhia, 'Illegal Extortions from Peasants, Artisans and Menials in Eighteenth Century Eastern Rajasthan', *Indian Economic and Social History Review*, vol. 14(2), April-June 1977, pp. 231-45.
52. In two rare documents of 1752 and 1766 pertaining to Eastern Rajasthan, their share has been estimated at 0.6 per cent and 0.9 per cent respectively; see Dilbagh Singh, 'Local and Land Revenue Administration of the State of Jaipur (c 1750-1800)', [New Delhi: Jawaharlal Nehru University, unpublished Ph.D dissertation], p. 53.

Economy and Society

9

Was There Feudalism in Indian History?*

To discuss a problem such as 'Was There Feudalism in Indian History?' one should, in fairness, begin by defining one's terms. What, in other words, is feudalism? Unfortunately the answer to this simple question varies with the historian who makes the attempt.[1] If there is no universally applicable definition of feudalism, there is an objective reason for it, which has critical significance for our argument: feudalism was not a world-system; capitalism was the first world-system.[2] It follows therefore that there is no universally applicable abstraction of feudalism as there is of capitalism. When we speak of capitalism in its abstract form, as generalised commodity production where labour itself is a commodity[3] we do so because of our awareness that all of humanity was, during the nineteenth and twentieth centuries, subjected to the force of this production system through different stages of antecedent developments. Feudalism, on the other hand, was, throughout

* An earlier version of this paper was first read as the Presidential Address, Medieval India Section, Indian History Congress, 40th Session, 1979. It was later discussed in three seminars respectively organised by the School of Social Sciences, Jawaharlal Nehru University, New Delhi; Department of History, Erasmus University, Rotterdam; and Society for the Study of Feudalism, Sorbonne, Paris. I was fortunate to receive written or oral comments from Maurice Aymard, Guy Bois, Barun De, Irfan Habib, R.H. Hilton, Iqtidar Alam Khan, Frank Perlin, Burton Stein and Immannuel Wallerstein; it is a privilege to acknowledge my debt of gratitude to them all.

its history, a non-universal, specific form of socio-economic organisation—specific to time and region, where specific methods and organisation of production obtained.[4]

It is necessary to lay stress on this point here, for it is lost sight of when feudalism is defined as a system based on 'non-economic compulsion' or as a 'redistributive world system' or in even more general terms as an agrarian economy with a fairly cohesive ruling class siphoning off the agrarian surplus through the use of overt or covert force.[5] These definitions seek to identify an entire social and economic structure in terms of the political or juridical basis of the exploitation of the primary producer, the peasant; they do not take into account the totality of the production system. They seek to identify a mode of production by merely referring to the relations of exploitation. Secondly, these definitions are so broad as to cover all pre-capitalist systems in one sweep, for all precapitalist societies were characterised by primarily agricultural production, unequal division of property and non-economic coercion by the ruling class which appropriated the peasants' surplus in a variety of forms—rent (in labour, cash or kind) or revenue or in the form of servile or bonded labour. The use of the term 'feudal' in such a broad sense fails to demarcate the specifics of the feudal social and economic organisation from the prefeudal ones in Europe and from other, non-European medieval social and economic systems.[6] It therefore does not explain much.

I shall in the following pages try to establish these demarcating lines by suggesting the specificity of feudalism to western Europe between the fifth or the sixth century and the fifteenth. Feudalism also developed in its classic form in eastern Europe between the sixteenth and the eighteenth century and possibly in Japan during the Tokugawa regime in particular. I am, however, constrained to leave these regions out of the discussion in this paper, hopefully without causing much harm to my argument. Since western Europe always provides the reference-point for any discussion of feudalism in India, or, for that matter, elsewhere, I shall also attempt a comparison between medieval western Europe and medieval

India. The focus of this comparison will be on the respective conditions of labour which are determined by interaction between nature and social organisation and which, in turn, determine the dominant characteristics of a social formation.

I

Feudalism, like other social formations before or after it, was a transitional system. As such it stood mid-way in the transition of the west European economy from a primarily slave-based system of agricultural production[7] to one dominated by the complementary classes of the capitalist farmer and the landless agricultural wage-earner, but in which the free peasantry also formed a significant element. It is necessary to suggest here that the term 'free peasant' as used in this paper is not concerned with the legal freedom of the peasant to alienate his proprietary rights in land or implements or the usufruct of his land; it is even less concerned with the absence of legal restriction on the peasant's mobility. Legal restrictions on the alienation of land acquire social significance only in the context of a fairly developed land market, just as legal restrictions on peasants' mobility become important only if there is a developed labour-market so that the peasant, by being made immobile, is deprived of a competitive price for his labour. In the absence of these features of developed land and labour markets—which, indeed, characterised the era of the rise of capitalism and were thus bound to be absent earlier—not all the legal freedoms would make much difference to the fate of the peasant. The economic, rather than the legal, significance of the term 'free peasant' therefore denotes a peasant who, quite independently of his social or juridical status, earns his and his family's subsistence off his own (including his family's) material resources and labour. In other words, he (or his family) does not render labour to any one else either in performance of labour service (for purposes of production) or for wages. This does not, of course, exempt him from the obligation to part with his surplus produce in the form of taxes to the State, or, on its behalf, to its officials. Nonetheless, he retains complete control over the process of production on his land through his (and his family's) labour[8] and is assured of a relatively more certain, though perhaps no higher level of subsistence[9] than peasants who are 'unfree'.

As slavery became an increasingly uneconomic element in the production process of late Graeco-Roman antiquity[10] the European slaves, freedmen and, for reasons of growing insecurity, allodialists with varying resources were transformed into different strata of dependent peasantry.[11] This transformation never succeeded in eradicating social and economic differences within the class of peasants;[12] nor were the allodialists completely eliminated from any region in any period.[13]

With slavery becoming increasingly unproductive and the capitalist farmer, along with the landless agricultural worker co-existing with free peasant economy still to develop a long way in the future, the feudal economy came to be characterised by an intermediate and transitional feature which formed the core of the feudal mode of production in its early phase: in the early feudal economy the peasant, irrespective of his social or juridical condition, came to acquire certain hereditary rights for the use of land and other resources even when they belonged to the lord; on the other hand, his and his family's labour potential was always in excess of the resources on which it could be fully expended. In general, as Georges Duby has put it, with the exception of a stratum of the class of allodialists, the area of arable land cultivated by the tenanted manses, varying greatly in size, 'was always less than the amount of land which in theory corresponded to the physical capacity of a peasant family'.[14] One could perhaps add that this would be equally true of small peasant families, legally free but economically dependent on the sale of their labour to supplement their income from the land and that the limitation of resources would include agricultural implements and draught animals, in addition to land.

This hiatus between the labour potential of a peasant family and its resources (used for production) appears to have constituted the distinctive characteristic of the feudal mode of production in its formative stages; it enables us to distinguish the feudal mode of production from the slave and the capitalist modes in Europe[15] and from other medieval economies in different regions of the world.[16] The agrarian economy of the ancient Graeco-Roman region depended largely on the separation of the producer from the means of production under conditions of slavery facilitating the appropriation of his entire labour by the owners of the latifundia. Capitalist agriculture, on the other hand, is characterised by the separation of the producer from the means of production under the conditions of a wage labour-market, so that surplus value is appropriated by kulaks through the sale of the produce. Co-existing with it, though far from being its equal, is free peasant production with regional and temporal variations. In the feudal system in its classic form, the producer is neither completely separated from the means of production, nor is he an independent economic being. Indeed, it is via this intermediate feature that the west European economy effected its transition from slavery to capitalism, This feature formed the objective basis of the appropriation of the peasants' surplus labour by the feudal lords primarily for purposes of agricultural production.

Non-economic coercion by the feudal lords, then, consisted of a system of exploitation of the structured labour surplus, or excess of the labour potential of the peasant family over its resources. This hiatus formed the basis of the availability of labour for the cultivation of the lord's demesne through forced labour or, marginally, hired labour. This form of coercion became part of the conditions of labour and subsistence, and hence far more effective than any amount of overt force. The dependence of the entire peasantry (including the serfs, but barring a stratum of allodialists) on the lords was thus structured in the production-process, for the lord controlled, even if only partly, the use of labour-time for production on the peasant's manse.

This view of feudalism based on *the structured dependence of the entire peasantry on the lords* (with the only exception of the crust of independent allodialists) enables us to take into account the dynamism of feudal society and to understand its development during the eleventh, twelfth and thirteenth centuries and its decline in the fourteenth as the culmination of peasant resistance generated in the course of the daily toil in the field during the preceding centuries. For, this dynamism was also structured in the hiatus between the peasant family's labour power and its productive resources.

For, the surfeit of labour power of the peasant family and the lord's demand for it were not quite symmetrical. In a system of agricultural production based on an intensive use of labour (including the wastage of labour in traversing vast fields), where the returns on labour were abysmal and where the period available for agricultural operations was brief, the input or withdrawal of even small amounts of labour made considerable difference to output, whether on the lord's demesne or the peasant's own manse. Hence a silent struggle between the lord and the peasant to push the limits of the surfeit labour in the one's or the other's direction. This silent class struggle occurred in the actual process of tilling the soil.[17] If the lord imposed rigorous supervision over the peasant's toil, the peasant had on his side inertia and deception and, of course, the merciful incompetence and corruptibility of the supervisory staff. If the lord endeavoured to exact labour beyond the time that the peasant could spare from the cultivation of his own land, the peasant was also constantly on the watch for opportunities to steal from the lord's time and devote it to his own manse. Such opportunities were not rare, particularly at the peripheries of manor where supervision was less rigorous, or wherever the peasant manse might lie adjacent to the demesne.[18]

The labour-intensive nature of agricultural production was conditioned by a number of factors. The chief constraint upon medieval European agriculture was the lack of manure.[19] The implements used were relatively primitive,[20] and even the draught power of the animals was underused owing to defective methods of harnessing them;[21] this limited the period for which land was under the plough. All these factors necessitated extensive cultivation, and the seeds had to be spread out on the field, the deeper fertility of which remained unutilised. Extensive cultivation in turn meant wastage of labour in traversing long distances on the field itself and from the nucleated village settlements to the outlying fields.[22] Thus in the few weeks available for actual cultivation there was great demand for manual labour on which agricultural practices were so heavily dependent.[23] This might perhaps explain the relative stability of village settlements in western Europe during the eighth, ninth and tenth centuries,[24] for agricultural operations at every level, from the lord to the humble peasant, required a stable supply of labour.

This great demand for manual labour in turn conditioned some other aspects of early feudal society; labour services were so organised as to place the heaviest burden on those with least resources—those who had nothing else to give except labour with bare hands.[25] It is in this context that the question of population also asumes a peculiar complexity. For medieval Europe, in what Marc Bloch has called the 'first feudal age', was both over- and under-populated at the same time. It was over-populated during the larger part of the year when peasants had little to do and had to subsist off the forest products such as wild fruits, honey and wild animals and were periodically wiped out by famines,[26] but during the brief period when agricultural operations were to be carried out there was an acute scarcity of labour.[27]

If this scarcity was to be overcome, it would be necessary to make a more intensive use of soil-fertility and to forge some labour-saving devices. West European society as a whole was thus poised for technological development with a direct bearing on agriculture.[28]

The centuries after 1000 A.D. witnessed technical development which related primarily to implements and agricultural practices; manuring remained almost as meagre as earlier. Most of the tools and techniques that spread widely in western Europe during the first three centuries of the second millennium A.D. had been known to Europe in theory or practice for varying lengths of time, though their application had been very limited. Only in this period did conditions evolve for their wide social acceptance.[29] On the whole this era was marked by a 'technical dynamism'.[30]

The agricultural progress of these centuries, particularly of twelfth and thirteenth, following the use of better implements and practices and a more effective use of human and animal labour, led to a phenomenal rise in the productivity of land and labour. The seed:yield ratio which stood at 1:1.6 or at best at 1:2.5 during the ninth and tenth centuries came to stand at 1:4 during the thirteenth.[31] The magnitude of this advance can be assessed from the fact that a rise in the ratio from 1:2 to 1:3 would double the amount of food available for consumption. This continued to be the average ratio until the sixteenth century in many regions of western Europe and in some of them even up to the nineteenth.[32]

Indirectly, following a rise in the productivity of land, the size of holding necessary to maintain a peasant family declined sharply from about a hundred acres a manse on an average in the ninth century to anywhere between twenty and thirty in the thirteenth.[33] While the ninth century was characterised by the existence of full manses, in the twelfth century the quarter manse had become the standard unit of a tenure.[34]

Reduction in the size of the holding minimised the wastage of labour in agricultural production; the rise in productivity on the other hand stimulated the growth of population. The availability of greater amount of food (and particularly vegetable proteins) made possible by agricultural progress should have allowed population to grow at the lower end of society where scarcity of food grains and proteins was a constraint on reproduction. The relative decline in the frequency and intensity of famines during the first three centuries after 1000 assisted in population growth at the peasants' level; later on, during the fourteenth century, when food again became scarce and famines resumed their dismal visitations with customary ferocity, it was at the peasants' level that death took its largest toll.[35] Life expectancy also appears to have risen from about 25 years in the Roman Empire to 35 in England of the thirteenth century.[36] However, the problem of the growth or decline of population is not related merely to the productivity of land; the uncertainty of production, and even more important, the unequal distribution of produce (and resources in general) played a more decisive role.[37]

At any rate even though the benefits of the rise in productivity were differentially distributed, the rural poor also shared in it and were assured of a certain amount of secure nutrition; this was not a negligible impetus to human multiplication. Duby has noted that the influx of men to the towns during the centuries of agricultural progress originated in villages with more generous harvests.[38] There is a consensus among historians that between 1000 and 1300 there was considerable growth of population.[39]

Many of these developments—diminution in the amount of land necessary to provide subsistence to a peasant family, the more effective use of soil-fertility through better tools and techniques, the rise in population—caused extensive land-reclamation in Europe, starting hesitantly in the late tenth or early eleventh century and reaching its peak in the second half of the twelfth. In the thirteenth century it began to taper off and was gradually replaced by increased pastoral activity.[40] Initially it was the peasants who reclaimed land in search of lessening their encumbrances.[41] Group-migration from old villages notwithstanding, the consequence of the land-reclamation movement was individualisation—both of the holdings and cultivation.[42] Individualisation was also reflected in the break-up of the large kinship groups into nuclear family units.[43]

The movement for land-reclamation was soon taken over by the lords and it became far more organised.[44] There was, however, a distinction in the condition of peasants on the two types of land reclaimed. On the piece cleared by himself, the peasant had a greater autonomy and therefore lighter burdens; on the lord's reclaimed land, on the other hand, the peasant's dependence and burdens were greater, though in comparison to peasants in the old villages they were substantially lighter.[45]

The conditions of labour in west European countryside had changed. As the productivity of land rose with the introduction of relatively capital-intensive technology, the price of land and implements also rose; on the other hand, the demand for manual labour declined. Concurrently, the burden of forced labour now shifted from bare manual work to work with a plough-team;[46] it shifted, in other words, from the lowest rung of society to a rung or two above it. The peasant also, seized by the legitimate desire to raise more produce from his own land, became increasingly reluctant to render labour service.[47] Thus upaid labour was once again becoming an uneconomic proposition in west European history, as it had earlier become under slavery. On the other hand, the growing peasant population made labour available in the expanding labour-market. It was thus that the process of 'commutation' of forced labour into payments in cash and kind started. There was, besides, the process of 'enfranchisement' whereby the dependent peasant purchased his freedom ('the franchise') off the lord. Indeed, the lords encouraged commutation and enfranchisement, for these brought them ready incomes, whereas they could hire in the expanding labour-market such labour as they required for the cultivation of their estates. The peasant, for his part, also welcomed commutation or enfranchisement.[48] Payment of a fixed amount of cash or kind in rent, wherever it was so fixed, would enable him to devote more attention to his own manse and he would be the exclusive beneficiary of increased production or higher prices. Franchise would permit him to become independent once and for all, so that he could look after his land or migrate to places where he would obtain the highest price for his labour. However, some caution is called for in assessing the progress of commutation and enfranchisement. These did not proceed in a linear progression; there was many a reversal on the way.[49] Nonetheless there was definitive lightening of the peasant's many burdens.

Commutation and enfranchisement made a differential impact on the different strata of feudal lords. Whereas the seigneurs[50] still had various sources of their income intact—the right to mint coins, the administration of justice[51] which was being increasingly used to collect fines, the establishment of 'monopolies'[52]—the smaller lords with no seigneurial authority had increasingly to shift to new forms of subsistence. They took to cultivating the demesne with their own, and hired, labour and selling the produce in the market[53] which was increasingly influencing the patterns of agricultural production. The agricultural progress of the eleventh, twelfth and thirteenth centuries had considerably increased the marketable surplus in the countryside and this in turn led to a noticeable growth of trade and urbanisation in this period. On the other hand, trade and urban centres began, to an extent, to determine the patterns of production in the countryside. Of course, the demand for agricultural produce was growing in rural areas as well wherever the landless agricultural worker, being paid his wages in cash, had to buy his subsistence. Rural artisans were similarly placed.

The problem of the role of trade and towns in the decline of feudalism in Europe has been examined by many historians and it is not necessary to go into the highly controversial theme here.[54] It does, however, appear on balance that the main direction of peasant migration in western Europe in the first five centuries after 1000 A.D. had been within the countryside itself. By and large, it was the land with lesser encumbrances that beckoned the peasants to uproot themselves from their old villages and resettle at long distances; the town played at best a marginal role in this movement. Indeed, when the west European peasantry broke into rebellion of literally continental dimensions during the fourteenth century, one of their chief demands was the right to free mobility, whereas most cities on the continent looked on passively whenever they did not help the lords suppress these uprisings.[55]

The changes in the west European countryside then, which had resulted from the interaction of the developing social structure and the given means of production in the first feudal age, undermined the very basis of feudal society. These changes had, above all, led to a process of differentiation in the countryside and the emergence of the complementary classes of the kulak and the landless agricultural worker together with as a subordinate element and with great regional variations—the free peasant.[56]

With the increased marketable surplus in the countryside, trade began to assume increasing importance in the west European economy from the eleventh century,[57] though it had never been absent earlier.[58] The use of the horse shoe-nail in this period greatly improved transport which in turn assisted in the promotion of trade.[59] There were, of course, considerable regional and local price variations and local price fluctuations. The short-term price fluctuations, however, occurred in the background of a long-term average price-rise. The twelfth and thirteenth centuries were marked by a rise in production followed by a rise in prices.[60] Clearly, demand was growing faster than the supply.

Conditions were thus very favourable for production for the market. Both productivity and prices were rising. Labour could be hired, wages would decline as the demand for foodgrains rose—both resulting from a growing population. It was also possible, of course, on some manors to combine production for the market with the use of the serf's unpaid labour.[61] These conditions began increasingly to drive agricultural production into the patterns of commerce and this in turn lent strength to the process of differentiation.

There were many sources of the rise of the class of kulaks, the most important amongst them being the bigger lords' agents or bailiffs etc.[62] These agents, often originating at the lower rungs of society,[63] were familiar with agricultural practices first hand; they did not, however, consider touching the plough beneath their dignity; nor did they scruple to grab money at every opportunity whether from the peasants, the lords, the merchants or from God's own house, the Church.[64] Their power over the peasants corresponded to the lord's power.[65] But there was an incipient conflict between them and their masters. For, as commercialisation of agriculture proceeded, the agents took the lord's demesne on 'farm' or gradually purchased land. On this they employed their own and family labour supplemented by hired labour, with a view to selling its produce. They were thus emerging as alternative bases of economic power within feudal society. This class of much-maligned *nouveaux riches*, of low social origins and moderate cultural tastes, the butt of the aristocracy's ridicule,[66] driven by the desire for profit—this class formed one of the chief dynamic elements in the later medieval economy of western Europe.

Besides the agents, the small lords, pushed by the need to sell in the market but constrained by the limits of their resources, found themselves alongside the bailiffs.[67] There were also the merchants, urban and rural, who entered the area in search of profit.[68] They 'farmed' fragments of large estates which the lords were willing to hand over to them when feudal rents were declining.[69] They gradually purchased land on which they employed hired labour, the produce being sent to the market. They tried to expand the scale of production by re-investing the returns.[70]

Some peasants were also able to rise. The number of such peasants was rather small and at any rate they were, in most cases, better off at the starting point than those from whose ranks they had arisen. Some cases of peasants taking the lord's demesne on 'farm' have also been noted.[71]

The small and marginal peasants, on the other hand, by and large, became landless agricultural workers; to use the new, capital-intensive, technology, the small (and marginal) peasant had to depend upon loans. He had also to borrow money if he desired his franchise, or if he migrated elsewhere where he would need sustenance for the initial breathing period. He was thus subject to stiff borrowing conditions, imposed either by the merchant-moneylender or the lord. The former would buy off a part or whole of the peasant's surplus produce in advance repayment of the loan or the interest and thus deprive him of the advantage of price-rise; the lord, on the other hand, would impose stiff conditions, including, at times, labour services.[72] Real freedom came only to those peasants who had their own resources to buy it.[73] The lord also adjusted to the economic benefits of the age by replacing hereditary tenancies with fixed-time tenures and gradually even the latter with tenancies-at-will so that at each renewal of a tenure the advantage of any rise in productivity or prices could accruc to him.[74]

The small and the marginal peasants were thus subject to the pressure of many forces. Deprived of the protection of the lord, the village community or even his own group of kinsmen, the slightest vagary of production or prices would compel this peasant to sell or forfeit his mortgaged land and implements and he would immediately go reeling into the ranks of the landless looking for work in the labour market. It is perhaps true that socially the small peasant suffered a depression in his status on losing his bit of land but economically, even as a landless agricultural wage-earner, he was better off than he was as a small peasant.[75] But this situation could last only so long as the society as a whole registered economic progress. With the slightest setback in the economy, those who were at its lower end had to pay the heaviest price. Famine would make its terrible appearance and wipe out large numbers of resourceless peasants. [76]

It was thus that the feudal society was growing and, in the process, giving birth to two inter-related classes, and reviving an older one in greater strength, which were to destroy the parent structure through various stages and forms of struggle. The initial thrust for capitalist development originated in the countryside.

The agricultural progress of the twelfth and thirteenth centuries consisted primarily of extension of the arable into the forest and the pasture; and it had also reduced the period of the fallow thereby utilising the existing soil fertility more intensively. This could, however, go on only up to a point, for a shrinking pasture would reduce the animal population which in turn would diminish the quantity of manure, scarce as it already was. The forest on the other hand, also maintained a delicate ecological balance which would be disturbed by cutting down trees in large numbers. Besides, apart from wood, the demand for which was on the increase,[77] they provided supplementary food to both men and animals.

Historians are generally agreed that agricultural progress had begun to recede from the beginning of the fourteenth century all over western Europe, though the intensity of the recession varied regionally, for the land reclamation movement during the preceding two centuries had overreached itself.[78] Given the unequal distribution of resources, the declining yields from the more marginal of the reclaimed lands were beginning to weaken and sweep off numbers from the poorer strata.[79] The availability of labour was itself, perhaps, inhibiting any further technical development.

The fourteenth century witnessed great social upheavals. There was also considerable ecological disturbance which was reflected in an appreciable fall in the temperature and continuous rainfall for long periods such as in 1315-17. Famines resumed their dismal visitations and there was a series of epidemics. The famine of 1315-17 deprived western Europe of a tenth of its population.[80] The Black Death of 1348-50 was only one in a series of disasters, though the most catastrophic of them;[81] it wiped out anywhere between a quarter and a half of the population. Nor did the epidemics cease after this terrible toll. Thus, even assuming a lower death rate of 25 per cent in 1350, the west European population had lost 40 per cent of its strength during the course of fourteenth century,[82] even if we assume that those who suffered acute malnutrition but still survived could be counted as full members of the work-force.[83]

The immediate consequence of these disasters was a price-scissors effect: the prices of foodgrains fell owing to a fall in demand, but wages and the prices of industrial goods were on the rise.[84] This was a direct challenge to the lords' standards of living, for their incomes from the land were declining but the cost of agricultural production and prices of luxury goods were rising. This should have reinforced the process of differentiation within the class of landlords, for the smaller ones, with no other source of income than land, were ruined more easily than the bigger ones who could still rely upon court-fines, monopolies etc.[85] Land was also available more freely now and in this way the free peasantry reemerged in strength.[86]

The aristocracy, on the other hand, took resort to war and plunder. Everywhere in western Europe this was a period of extensive wars—the Hundred Years' War in France, the Wars of the Roses in England, in Germany and Italy, in Spain and Flanders. Even the resurgence of the State during this period added its weight to the crisis by raising the level of its demand for taxes.[87]

But then it was not these developments which created the

'general crisis' of feudalism. Feudal society had, in the past, been familiar with over-population, wars, famines and deaths. The general crisis was, on the other hand, the result of the determination of men to get over the impasse according to their situation in society.[88] The class of feudal lords, faced with declining incomes and rising expenditures, still commanded the power of the State and took resort to an overt use of it. The State, which was reviving all over western Europe at this time, intervened on behalf of the lords by fixing wages at the pre-Black Death level, and by legally restricting peasant mobility—unlike in the first feudal age when peasant immobility was part of the production system. This was a challenge to the landless wage-earner, the small and marginal peasant who earned their living in part by selling their labour, and the emerging class of kulaks who hired labour and therefore required a mobile peasantry. The 'feudal reaction' assumed similar forms everywhere.

The peasantry, on the other hand, was so situated as to be able to defend its gains much more forcefully than ever before, for demand for labour was much greater than the available supply. The desolate lands also provided the opportunity to those peasants who had the other necessary means to emerge as free peasants. The peasantry thus responded to the 'feudal reaction' by bursting out in a string of rebellions everywhere in western Europe.[89]

The fourteenth century saw a series of minor peasant uprisings and some really massive rebellions, spread all over the hundred years. A remarkable feature of these great rebellions was that most of them occurred in the most prosperous rural regions of western Europe and were led by the most prosperous sections of the peasantry: the Flanders rebellion of 1323-27, the Grand Jacquerie of 1358, north of Paris; the Tuchin movement in central France from the 1360s to the end of the century, and, of course, the great peasant uprising of 1381 in the East Anglia region of England. The fifteenth century witnessed the massive outburst of the *remensas* of Catalonia.[90] Germany also had a series of peasant uprisings in the fourteenth and fifteenth centuries.[91]

It is also remarkable that in regions where poverty

prevailed, the peasantry remained passive. In central Italy, rent-racking of the peasantry led to decline in the rate of growth of population, but, sadly, engendered no rebellion.[92] When the Grand Jacquerie was up in arms in the region north of Paris, one of the most prosperous regions in European countryside, the area to the south-west of Paris, where poverty reigned, remained inert.[93]

The peasantry was thus rising to defend the gains it had made thanks to the emergence of a new mode of production in the countryside;[94] for rebellions occurred by and large in those areas where the emergence of the new mode of production was more pronounced, and peasants were acquiring self-confidence, so essential to the act of rebellion, which, after all, is an act of great humanism.

By the end of the fourteenth century the failure of the feudal reaction had become apparent.[95] From the beginning of the fifteenth century western Europe started to recover its bases of strength. The ground for this recovery had been prepared by the preceding 'crisis' that had undermined much of the economic and social system which had become outmoded by its own tremendous onward movement. The attainment of the abstraction of capitalism was yet a long way off;[96] but movement had been set firmly in its direction.

II

Expression of grave regret over the lack of adequate information on almost all crucial points of the social history of ancient and medieval India is perhaps the inevitable starting point of all historical research on these periods. The poverty of information gets even more hurtful when it stands face-to-face with the almost embarrassing riches of evidence on medieval Europe. If, therefore, what follows in the pages below appears to be a string of conjectures and speculations, at least part of it could perhaps be blamed on the collective misfortune of historians that so little of the evidence from India's ancient and medieval centuries has survived.

If the meaning of the term 'feudalism' differs from one

historian to another, as we noted earlier, it follows that the period of the history of a country—in this case India—characterised as feudal would also vary widely according to each historian's understanding of feudalism. Thus while some Soviet historians of India have found traces of feudalism in the *Arthasastra* of Kautilya,[97] for R.S. Sharma Indian feudalism originated in the fourth century A.D., reaching its peak during the eleventh and twelfth centuries.[98] With the establishment of the Delhi Sultanate, for political and economic reasons, feudalism, in B.N.S. Yadava's view, began to decline.[99] The distinguished Russian historian of the nineteenth century, M.M. Kovalevski, on the other hand, believed that the process of 'feudalisation' in India started precisely with the 'Muslim conquests'.[100] For D.D. Kosambi, whose writings on Indian history justly enjoy a privileged status, the feudal system broke down around the middle of the seventeenth century, under Aurangzeb;[101] Col. James Tod, on the other hand, was witness to the functioning of what he believed was the classic form of feudalism in Rajasthan in the early nineteenth century.[102]

The point of comparison in the works of the historians mentioned above, and of many others who have considered the problem of Indian feudalism, invariably rests in medieval western Europe. This is understandable, for, so long as we remain concerned with the question, 'Was there feudalism in India?', we must seek to answer it in the light of the most developed form of feudal social organisation, which was west European. This comparison is quite independent of the answer to the question raised here. It is thus that Tod compared early nineteenth century Rajasthan with the west European feudal system as described in Hallam's *Middle Ages* (published 1824),[103] and found that four of the six elements which comprised feudalism were prevalent in Rajasthan.[104] D.D. Kosambi also drew upon Marion Gibb's *Feudal Order* and Maurice Dobb's *Studies*.[105] R.S. Sharma and B.N.S. Yadava have repeatedly referred to western Europe by way of comparison.[106] It is in relation to medieval Europe that Satish Chandra finds, 'in many respects' a similarity in the Indian concept of landownership.[107]

D.D. Kosambi provided a fresh outline for the study of

Indian feudalism—his famous concept of feudalism from above and feudalism from below[108]—an outline that was unfortunately found inadequate by some other historians.[109] It was Professor R.S. Sharma who first made a systematic study of Indian feudalism in his book and in various articles.[110] Professor B.N.S. Yadava has added a great many detail to Professor Sharma's work by studying northern India in the early medieval period, particularly during the twelfth century.[111]

The main theme in the works of Professor Sharma and Professor Yadava is woven around the assumed antagonism between trade and urban life on one hand and feudalism on the other,[112] and, particularly, the rise in importance of landed intermediaries owing to an increasing number of grants of land by the state to its officials and to the Brahmans in charity; this resulted in the subjection of the peasantry to the intermediaries and in the peasants' dependence on them. R.S. Sharma visualises the development in India of almost all components of west European feudalism—serfdom,[113] manor,[114] self-sufficient economic units,[115] the process of feudalisation of crafts and commerce,[116] apart, of course, from declining trade and urbanisation. The elements which had allegedly undermined the European feudal structure, namely, the revival of trade and towns, flight of the peasants to the towns to escape excessive impoverishment at the hands of the lord and the process of commutation of forced labour into monetary payments—all these, in Professor Sharma's view, developed in India also and similarly undermined Indian feudalism.[117] Indeed, the only important determinant of European feudalism which Professor Sharma could not trace in India was foreign invasions[118]—and B.N.S. Yadava has made up even this deficiency by drawing attention to the barbarian, particularly the Hun, invasion of India which shattered the lame Gupta empire and contributed to the rise of feudalism. 'The Gurjara-Pratihara empire', says Yadava, 'arose in Northern India like the feudal Frankish Carolingian Empire'.[119] Of all these, the most critical element of Indian feudalism, in Professor Sharma's and Professor Yadava's view, consisted of the growing dependence of the peasantry on the landed intermediaries following the grant of more and more rights to them by the state. The dependence was manifested in terms of increasing restrictions on the peasant's mobility and his subjection to forced labour, in turn, was becoming increasingly intensive.[120]

It is not possible here to go into all the points made by Professor Sharma and Professor Yadava in establishing the similarity between Indian and European feudalism; at any rate, it is hard to have to disagree with the work of such eminent historians. I would confine my comments to some of the important arguments advanced in support of an Indian feudalism.

The alleged antagonism between feudalism and the trade-urbanisation complex has been a matter of great dispute between historians ever since Henri Pirenne's days; increasingly, however, the two are being seen as less incompatible than was the case in the 1930s and the 1940s—a point that we have noted earlier. At any rate, even in terms of historical evidence, D.C. Sircar and, more effectively, B.D. Chattopadhyaya have questioned the extent of the decline of trade and urbanisation in the period concerned.[121]

More important, however, is the fact that while R.S. Sharma and B.N.S. Yadava have established considerable similarity in the features of Indian and European feudalism, the one basic difference appears to have been overlooked by them: in Europe feudalism arose as a result of a crisis of the production relations based on slavery on one hand and changes resulting from growing stratification among the Germanic tribes on the other, the two coming into what Perry Anderson calls a 'catastrophic collision of two dissolving anterior modes of production—primitive and ancient'.[122] In other words, European feudalism developed essentially as changes at the base of society took place; in India, on the other hand, the establishment of feudalism is attributed by its protagonists primarily to state action in granting land in lieu of salary or in charity, and the action of the grantees in subjecting the peasantry by means of legal rights assigned to them by the state. It is, indeed, a moot point whether such complex social structures can be established through administrative and legal procedures.

Above all, however, it is the concept of the peasantry's 'dependence' that appears to be of uncertain value in the context in which it has been used. The evidence marshalled by Sharma and Yadava at best establishes the increasing *exploitation* of the peasantry; dependence, on the other hand, should consist of an extraneous control over the peasant's process of production, and this has yet to be proved in the Indian context. If one speaks of European peasants' 'dependence' on the lord, it is primarily because such dependence had become rooted in his very conditions of labour, as we have seen in section I above. The critical element in such dependence was the diversion of at least a part of peasant's labour from his own process of production to that of the lord. It is doubtful whether this could be said of India. The nature of forced labour in India—of which there is considerable evidence throughout her history—is in its very essence different from that in Europe, for in India it is very rarely used for purposes of production.[123] There is, indeed, an objective reason for the absence of serfdom in Indian history, for conditions of production in India did not require serf-labour, as I shall try to argue below. Thus forced labour in India remained, by and large, an incidental manifestation of the ruling class' political and administrative power rather than a part of the process of production.

Certain specific features of Indian agrarian history could, perhaps, be clearly enough established, even though only a small segment of it has been studied. The fetility of Indian soil in general appears to have been far higher than that of Europe until as late as the nineteenth century.[124] Nature, on the other hand, permitted the Indian peasant to subsist at a much lower level of resources than his European counterpart. Secondly, and in part conditioned by the factors just mentioned, Indian agrarian history has been characterised predominantly by a free peasantry (in the economic rather than in the legal sense).

A number of indicators point to the high fertility of land in India, though, of course, there was considerable regional variation.[125] The cultivation of two crops, of one crop in each field, every year, which even the spread of the three-field rotation in Europe from the tenth or the eleventh century onwards could not ensure, was a feature of Indian agriculture from at least the Vedic period onwards.[126] Indeed, three crops are also mentioned in our sources which do not appear to treat the phenomenon as exceptional. It is quite difficult to establish whether every field yielded two or three crops a year; some of the references do clearly suggest that such indeed was the case, though it may be rash to accept their suggestion for all soils. Obviously, some lands did bear crops twice or thrice a year.[127]

But even if we were to ignore this evidence, the outstanding fact still remains that no field remained uncultivated for more than a part of the year, something even the three-field rotation was unable to achieve in late medieval Europe. Indeed, the negligible incidence, if not the complete absence, of the system of fallowing in ancient and medieval India is a remarkable testimony to the high fertility of the Indian soil. Historians, while using the term 'fallow', have almost invariably referred in fact to either virgin or abandoned lands, or, at best, lands withdrawn from cultivation for brief periods, which corresponds to permitting the land a lea.[128] Fallow land, unlike the virgin or the abandoned land, is an integral part of the cycle of cultivation. Indeed, it has to be ploughed more often than the land sown, for its soil must be repeatedly pulverised and weeds ploughed back or burnt down to be turned into green manure or potash. The practice of the fallow obviously suggests a soil that is quickly exhausted; the lea, or a brief withdrawal of the plough from the field, on the other hand, would be adequate for a soil relatively less prone to exhaustion. William Tennant, writing at the end of the eighteenth century, noted that '...the Indian allows it (his field) a lea, but never a fallow', though he ascribes this to the general backwardness of Indian agricultural techniques.[129] Some other evidence also suggests the practice of the lea, but rarely of the fallow. The *Ain-i Akbari* describes the second of its four categories of land as one that '(the peasants) do not cultivate for a time and thereby increase its strength'.[130] The *Risaala-i Ziraat* also mentions the prevailing practice, in the second half of the eithteenth century in Bengal, of the cultivation of fields in alternate years.[131] It is quite possible, of course, that instead of following the practice of the fallow, it would be simpler to abandon the exhausted fields and reclaim new ones, for, after all, there was no scarcity of land.[132] But there is very little evidence to suggest that it was widespread. Indeed, the reclamation of land is, after all, a costly process and would hardly be resorted to unless the cost of the restoration of soil-fertility through the use of manure outweighed the cost of reclamation. And manure, as Irfan Habib reasonably argues, should have been available in far greater quantity in the centuries before the beginning of the twentieth than after it.[133]

The system of manuring appears to have developed into a fine art if we go by the minute details of the methods and ingredients of preparing manures for different plants. It is far from certain whether Vedic Indians practised manuring.[134] But the *Arthasastra,*[135] the *Brhatsamhita,* the *Agni Purana,*[136] the *Krsi-Parasara*[137] and the *Upavana-Vinoda,*[138] among others, describe in very great detail the elements of which manures were made. The elements varied from cow-dung and goat's and sheep's droppings to the fat of the pigs[139] and the flesh of the cows;[140] green manure and mixture of honey and clarified butter with some other elements have also been recommended. Some of these preparations were meant for treatment of seeds before they were sown to ensure better germination.

Nor were the agricultural implements and practices too primitive for their age. Almost definitive evidence of the use of the plough has been uncovered at a pre-Harappan site, Kalibangan in Rajasthan, belonging broadly to the first half of the third millennium B.C.[141] The Vedic age, of course, used the plough,[142] and it has naturally continued in use ever since. The size and weight of the plough varied from region to region and, perhaps, from one stratum of the class of agriculturists to another.[143] It is true, as Elliot so derisively states, that the Indian plough—'simple...and wretched in construction'—merely scratched the topsoil,[144] but this appears to have been primarily due to the fact that the fertility of most soils in India lies at the surface.[145] Elliot himself noted that 'when anything like a mould-board is required, the people have sufficient ingenuity to frame one'.[146] Construction of a deep-penetrating plough should not have been beyond their capability, if it were required.

The literature of successive periods refers to many other implements used for agricultural production, besides the plough. The Vedic literature mentions the sickle and the sieve;[147] the *Ramayana* of Valmiki refers to the spade.[148] The *Amarkosa* speaks of the hoe and the harrow besides mortar and pestle for separating the grain from the chaff, and the winnowing fan etc.[149] The *Krsi-Parasara* gives, with many details, the names and the dimensions of various parts of the plough.[150] From about 600 B.C. the use of iron in making agricultural implements appears to have been on the increase.[151] It is, on the other hand, difficult to establish the origin of the seed-drill but this important device which, in Elliot's words 'has only within the last century been introduced into English field husbandry...has been in use in India from time immemorial'.[152]

Experts in agriculture recommended the ploughing of the field more than once, sometimes as many as five times.[153] It is not easy to say how far the recommendations were actually heeded, but Grierson did notice the ploughing of the field five times in modern Bihar,[154] although, of course, it might be a phenomenon of recent origin. Weeding was to take place twice.[155] Given the two or three crops in the year, crop rotation was 'practically a gift of nature and to know the combination which best suited particular soils would have been a matter of experience'.[156] The system of transplantation was also known;[157] and so was the treatment of diseased plants.[158]

It is in irrigation that the most important technological advance has been registered in ancient and medieval Indian agriculture. The *Rgveda* mentions some devices for water-lift (probably from a tank), but the technical details of these are as yet unknown.[159] The *Arthasastra* also refers to several methods of obtaining irrigation water from rivers, lakes, tanks and wells;[160] the Mauryan state apparently imposed a heavy irrigation cess—ranging from one-fifth to one-third of he produce[161]—even when the sources of water were privately owned.[162]

It was the spread of the noria from about the seventh century and of the Persian wheel from around the time the Delhi Sultanate was established in north India, that appears to have made a critical difference to the extension of agriculture at least in the Punjab,[163] the fertility of whose soil Abul Fazl considered unrivalled.[164] The canals, on the whole, appear to have been marginal to agricultural production. Firuz Shah Tughlaq[165] and Shah Jahan[166] did order the construction of canals, but for all practical purposes canal irrigation appears to be a more recent phenomenon.

If, owing to the natural richness of the soil and the relatively efficient tools and techniques, agricultural productivity in India was high, the subsistence level of the peasant was very low—thanks to climatic conditions, and, as we shall argue later, social organisation. Consequently, the amount of land considered necessary for the subsistence of a peasant family in India was estimated at anywhere between nine and fourteen acres in the fifth century B.C.[167] Unfortunately, there is little evidence to go by for the later periods of our history on this point, but unless we assume a significant decline in soil-fertility or rise in the subsistence level, this size of landholding was hardly likely to have changed drastically. Indeed, such a landholding, with traditional implements and practices, but with a reasonably assured supply of irrigation water, should even today earn the peasant family the pittance that it needs to survive and reproduce itself.

The relatively small size of holdings in India had the principal effect of averting the wastage of labour in the process of production which occurred in Europe; consequently far less labour was required for agricultural operations here. Moreover, these operations could be spread over a much longer period in the course of the year than in western Europe. Thus there does not appear to have been a highly concentrated demand for large amounts of labour during brief periods. It is thus that the absence of serfdom in Indian history, except for some marginal incidence[168] becomes intelligible. Indeed, even Sharma and Yadava are led by their evidence to conclude that serfdom was far from being the dominant feature in India.[169] For the process of production in India did not create an acute scarcity of labour; enserfment of the peasant therefore was hardly necessary. It is not as if the ruling class or the state in India was more compassionate to the primary producer than the feudal lords or the medieval state in Europe; it resorted even to enslavement of the peasants and the artisans[170] whenever it felt the need. But such need arose rarely and for brief periods of time.

When historians, therefore, describe the Indian peasant as a serf[171] or a 'near-serf', they do so primarily on the basis of legal restrictions imposed on his mobility, the absence of the right to free alienation of land, and, of course, his subjection to the rendering of forced labour.[172]

It is true that the state in India, concerned as it primarily was with the collection of revenue from land, made it obligatory on the part of the cultivator to keep his field constantly under the plough. The *Arthasastra* recommends that the 'lands may be confiscated from those who do not cultivate them and given to others; or they may be cultivated by village labourers and traders, lest those who do not properly cultivate them might pay less (to the government)'.[173] The *Arthasastra* also places restrictions on the free alienation of land or the free mobility of peasants, once again with a view to preventing the loss of revenue: 'Tax-payers shall sell or mortgage their *Brahmadeya* or gifted lands only to those who are endowed with such lands; otherwise they shall be punished with the first amercement. The same punishment shall be meted out to a tax-payer who settles in a village not inhabited by tax-payers'.[174] The state was advised even to compel the peasants to grow an additional crop on their fields if the king found himself financially straitened.[175] Manu prescribes the imposition of a fine on a cultivator who does not cultivate his field in proper time nor guard the crop against animals.[176] All this, however, did not violate the owner's title to the land even if it had been cultivated by another.[177] Indeed, the period for which the title remained legally valid went on increasing from 10 years at the time of Manu (c.second century A.D.) to 105 years in the thirteenth century, with limits fixed at 20 years,

60 years and 100 years between these dates.[178]

Thus, when Aurangzeb's *firman* to Muhammed Hashim[179] on one hand recognised the peasant ownership of land[180] (including the right to sell or mortgage it[181]) and on the other advised the use of persuasion and, if necessary, compulsion, to have the peasant till his land, it was really reiterating a very ancient Indian position.[182] If the state asserted its right to ensure uninterrupted cultivation of land, or to collect the revenue due to it even when the peasant neglected to cultivate his field,[183] or else to have the land tilled by another in case the owner had fled, the extent of its actual enforcement would vary from one situation to another. In the seventeenth century when the incidence of desertion of land had assumed serious dimensions, the state's insistence on its right became more emphatic.[184]

However, one aspect needs to be kept in view while discussing the problem of peasant immobility: we can hardly speak of a developed labour-or land-market in ancient and medieval India, though hired agricultural labour and instances of sale or mortgage of land have been mentioned in our sources.[185] Thus, it is primarily the economic, more than the legal, limitations on mobility which confined the peasant to his village,[186] though, of course, we must not visualise the ancient and medieval Indian peasant as completely immobile. Even if we were to accept state intervention in uniformly enforcing restriction on the peasant's movement or on his right to freely alienate his land, his mastery over the means and the process of production still remained intact, provided, of course, that he cultivated his field (in such manner as he chose) and paid the revenue to the state or its assignees.[187] It is true, as many historians have pointed out, that the pre-modern Indian peasant did not enjoy modern or bourgeois proprietary rights in land, for he could not freely alienate, abandon or abuse his land;[188] obviously no historian expects the peasant to have enjoyed such a right. But then is it merely a legal problem? If, by some stretch of the imagination, these legal rights could be granted to the peasant of the ancient and medieval past, would they have made a material difference to his situation, other things remaining the same—when he could rarely find a buyer for his land or labour or when he could not easily give up cultivation for some other occupation? At any rate, the absence of these rights did not deprive him of control over his field or the plough or—above all—his labour.

And it is in this sense that we have earlier defined a free peasant, following Marx's insight. The question of the legal ownership of land, which has been discussed by a very large number of historians of ancient and medieval India,[189] and the other legal rights carries, at best, a moderate significance in the actual socio-economic context.

In this sense, free peasant production appears to have been consolidated in post-Maurya times. In the Buddhist literature large farms are met with, sometimes with as many as five hundred ploughs, tilled by a gang of hired labourers.[190] The *Arthasastra* also speaks of state farms worked by 'slaves, labourers and prisoners'.[191] But in Gupta and post-Gupta times these large farms, whether owned by individuals or by the state, are no longer referred to; instead, there is the transformation of the *sudras* into petty producers. By the first half of the seventh century most, if not all, *sudras* had become peasants.[192] In part, at least, the spread of peasant production appears to have been due to the state policy of extending cultivation. The Maurya state undertook to settle new villages, or resettle deserted ones, 'either by inducing foreigners to immigrate' or by transferring excess population from the densely populated regions of the kingdom.[193] But individual reclamation of land may have become more common in post-Maurya times—a phenomenon reflected in the formulation of the *bhumicchidranyaya*: the field belongs to him who first removes the weed, as the deer to him who first shoots it.[194] It is reasonable to assume that with the spread of the noria and Persian wheel, to which reference has been made earlier, considerable reclamation should have taken place at the hands of those who could afford the price of the apparatus.[195] The medieval Indian state gives the impression of extreme keenness to extend cultivation if only because more evidence has survived from this period. Thus the grants made by the state in charity comprised two equal halves of cultivated and waste lands.[196] Among the duties of the revenue-collector of the Mughal state enumerated in the *Ain* is reclamation of wasteland for cultivation and prevention of arable land from falling waste.[197] Various other officials and semi-officials were similarly charged: the Karoris,[198] the Zamindars,[199] even the Jagirdars.[200] Thus when Aurangzeb's *firman* to Muhammad Hashim unambiguously recognises the peasant's title to land reclaimed by him,[201] it merely establishes the continuity of a very old Indian practice of encouraging the extension of cultivation by individual peasants.

The primarily free peasant form of agricultural production gradually evolving from post-Maurya times, thus characterised the agrarian economy of pre-modern times.

It is no longer necessary to try to prove the existence of stratification in the ancient and medieval Indian countryside, for there is now hardly any dispute about it. The caste-system in particular appears to have maintained economic and social disparities, especially in making landless agricultural labour available for the cultivation of the lands of big land-owners.[202] When, therefore, we speak of free peasant production, it is by and large in terms of its primacy in the production system.[203]

If the Indian peasant's control over the process of production demarcated him from his medieval European counterpart, there is little reason to believe that he also enjoyed a higher standard of living. We have noted earlier that nature in India allowed the peasant to subsist off very meagre resources; what nature permitted as the minimum level was made the maximum by social organisation. There are continual references in our sources to the heavy demand of revenue and other taxes from the peasants and the consequent miserable level of their existence. The Pali texts draw a pitiful picture of peasants' poverty.[204] Kautilya prescribes between one-fifth and one-third of the produce as irrigation cess, even when the source of irrigation is privately owned, as we have noted earlier.[205] As R.P. Kangle argues, with the *bhaga* or land revenue being fixed at one-sixth, the total would amount to one-half of the produce for peasants paying one-third as irrigation cess.[206] The law-books had 'unalterably' laid down the rate of land revenue demand in the range of one-twelfth to one-sixth depending on the nature of the soil and its yields. Yet the actual collection varied between one-tenth and one-third according to the status of the ruler. Indeed, a specimen document in the *Lekhapaddhati* reveals that at times up to two-thirds of the produce was being collected in the eleventh and twelfth centuries.[207] In the *Sukranitisara,* different portions of which belong to centuries after the eleventh, the recommended land revenue rates vary between one-sixth and one-half of the produce.[208] King Lalitaditya of Kashmir (eighth century) gave advice to his heirs which Sultan Balban was to repeat in turn to his own heirs, five centuries later: Do not allow the villagers to accumulate more than they need for bare subsistence lest they revolt.[209] D.C. Sircar and B.N.S. Yadava have enumerated the formidable number of taxes and cesses collected from peasants and artisans[210] and if Professor Yadava reaches the conclusion that 'mostly the peasants appear to have been left with a bare margin for subsistence'[211] in the twelfth century, he is by no means overstating the case. It is in continuation of this tradition that the Sultans of Delhi and the Mughal emperors collected anywhere between a quarter and a half of the produce as revenue from land.[212] It is possible, of course, that with technical progress such as the introduction of the noria and the Persian wheel and with great diversification of crops,[213] the value of produce from the land increased and the state raised its demand for revenue, but this is an aspect that needs to be carefully examined before a statement can be made with confidence.[214]

The characteristics of agrarian history discussed above—high fertility of land, low subsistence level and free peasant production—also explain the relative stability in India's social and economic history. It is, after all, true that there has hardly been any concentrated social effort caused by acute tensions to change completely the means, the methods and the relations of production. Indeed, barring the *arghatta* (noria) and the Persian wheel, one can hardly speak of a major break in the means of agricultural production. It appears that the features we have discussed above have some relationship with the absence of these major breaks. In India, unlike Europe, there appears to have been no prolonged and acute scarcity either of labour or production; the routine increase in demand could perhaps have been met by the routine extension of agriculture.

Thus with a high quantum of agrarian surplus available in the form of land-revenue and cesses etc. to the state—which formed the chief instrument of exploitation[215]—because of high fertility of land and the low subsistence level of the peasant,[216] a kind of equilibrium existed which facilitated the state's appropriation of the peasants' surplus in conditions of relative stability. Whenever the state tried from time to time to trespass upon the limits of the equilibrium, the peasantry reacted by either abandoning cultivation or even resorting to violence.[217] But it needs perhaps to be admitted that such cases of active resistance were rather rare, and, except for the peasant rebellions of Aurangzeb's reign, remained largely localised. For, once the state's instrusion had been resisted, balance was again restored.

In combination with this factor, the peasant's independent control over his process of production eliminated the possibility of acute tensions which might have necessitated significant changes in the entire system of production. The conflicts that characterised the economic history of pre-British India were conflicts over the distribution and redistribution of the surplus rather than over a redistribution of the means of production, which had changed the face of the medieval European economy.[218] The conflicts over the redistribution of the surplus were resolved by and large within the existing social framework. It is thus that even when the Mughal empire was collapsing, one gets the impression that the class of zamindars at various levels was turning out to be the main beneficiary emerging in strength.[219] Medieval Indian society did not have enough tension in it to lead it to the bourgeois system of production.[220]

To argue against the notion of an Indian feudalism need not lead one to the acceptance of the Asiatic mode of production.[221] Indeed, the concept of the Asiatic mode of production is predicated upon the absence of private property in land,[222] which is far from the generally accepted view among Indian historians today. It is evident that a wide range of social formations have existed in the world prior to their subjection to the universality of capitalism, and this range cannot be exhausted with the concepts of feudalism and the Asiatic mode of production. Irfan Habib has questioned the validity of the concepts of feudalism and the Asiatic mode of production for Indian history[223] and has suggested a neutral term, namely, the Indian medieval economy.[224] I have perhaps been quite rash in emphasising free peasant production as the characteristic feature of the Indian medieval economy. But a critique of the existing straitjackets of feudalism and the Asiatic mode of production may have this much to recommend it: it might clear the path in search of a typology more specific to pre-British India. Additionally, it might draw us away from Euro-centrism in the study of history.[225]

REFERENCES

1. Marc Bloch's classic description of the fundamental features of European feudalism is well-known everywhere: 'a subject peasantry; widespread use of service tenement (i.e. the fief) instead of a salary, which was out of the question; the supremacy of a class of specialised warriors; ties of obedience and protection which bind man to man and, within the warrior class, assume the distinctive form called vassalage; fragmentation of authority—leading inevitably to disorder; and, in the midst of all this, the survival of other forms of association, family and state, of which the latter, during the second feudal age, was to acquire renewed strength', *Feudal Society,* tr. L.A. Manyon, Chicago, 1964, p.446. To Joseph R. Strayer and Rusthton Coulborn 'Feudalism is primarily a method of government, not an economic or a social system, though it obviously modifies and is modified by the social and economic environment', 'The Idea of Feudalism' in R. Coulborn, ed., *Feudalism in History,* Princeton, 1956, p.4. For Henri Pirenne feudalism was 'closed estate economy where production was largely for consumption and trade was practically absent', *Economic and Social History of Medieval Europe,* tr. I.E. Clegg, London, 1958, (first published 1936), pp.7-12. Even historians sharing a common analytical

methodology, namely Marxism, have understood feudalism in a very wide range of meanings. Thus, whereas Paul Sweezy's conception of feudalism is virtually akin to that of Henri Pirenne, in R.H. Hilton, ed., *The Transition from Feudalism to Capitalism,* London, 1976, pp. 33-56 and 102-08, Maurice Dobb equates it with serfdom, *Studies in the Development of Capitalism,* revised edition, London, 1963, reprint 1972 (first published 1946), pp. 35-37; for Perry Anderson it was 'the specific organisation in a vertically articulated system of parcellized sovereignty and scalar property that distinguished the feudal mode of production in Europe', *Lineages of the Absolutist State,* London, 1977 (first published 1974), p. 408.

In the Indian context R.S. Sharma characterises the period between 300 and 1200 A.D. as feudal when he finds most features of west European feudalism having developed here, *Indian Feudalism c.* 300-1200, Calcutta, 1965, pp. 1-2, 7, 16, 52-3, 63-4, 154, 158, 271 etc. S. Nurul Hasan, on the other hand, calls medieval India feudal even though she 'did not have *any* of the characteristics of western European feudalism', *Thoughts on Agrarian Relations in Mughal India,* New Delhi, 1973, p. 2, (emphasis added).

2. Clearly other pre-capitalist universal categories such as 'stone age', 'bronze age', etc. do not stand in the same class as a highly organised mode of production with an advanced social organisation.
3. Karl Marx & F. Engels, *Selected Works,* vol. I, Moscow, 1969, pp. 160-62.
4. Cf. the perceptive remark of Jean Suret-Canale: '*By its very nature,* capitalism, as well as being one of the great stages of human progress, also assumes a universal value, destroying or reducing to the status of residual survivals the previous modes of production. *A fortiori,* such universality appertains to socialism. But one cannot project this universality of the last two stages of social development on to the history which precedes them', cited in Marian Sawer, *Marxism and the Question of the Asiatic Mode of Production,* The Hague, 1977, p. 208 (emphasis original).
5. Thus Maurice Dobb, equating feudalism with serfdom, explains the latter term as a type of exploitation that is enforced and perpetuated through 'so-called "extra economic compulsion" in some form', *Capitalism, Development and Planning,* New York, reprint 1970, pp. 2-3. R.H. Hilton also accepts the equation of

serfdom with 'non-economic compulsion', though he does not define feudalism as the equivalent of serfdom, Hilton, ed., *Peasants, Knights and Heretics*, Cambridge, 1976, p. 4 'Redistributive world system' is Immannuel Wallerstein's term. This world system is based on a mode of production wherein 'a surplus is extracted from agricultural producers normally in the form of tribute to sustain an imperial (or state) bureaucracy at a given level of consumption', 'From Feudalism to Capitalism — transition or transitions?, *Social Forces*, vol. 55, no. 2, December 1976, p. 281 n2. This term is as general as 'non-economic compulsion' or 'pre-capitalist society', and is therefore hardly superior to it. S. Nurul Hasan understands feudalism to mean a primarily agrarian economy where the surplus is appropriated by a 'fairly closed' ruling class through both non-economic coercion and the role played by it in agricultural as well as the subsidiary handicrafts production, *Thoughts*, pp. 1-2.
Perry Anderson has sharply criticised universalist definitions of feudalism, which, with suitable modifications, would equally appertain to different regions of the medieval world, *Lineages*, pp. 401-12. His criticism arises from the assumed similarity of the 'infrastructure' of economies in different parts of the pre-capitalist world, economies that are imprecisely defined by and large in terms of 'large landownership with small peasant production, where the exploiting class extracts the surplus from the immediate producer by customary forms of extra-economic coercion—labour services, deliveries in kind, or rents in cash—and where commodity exchange and labour mobility are correspondingly restricted', ibid, p.401. He suggests that since '*all* modes of production in class societies prior to capitalism extract surplus labour from the immediate producers by means of extra-economic coercion... pre-capitalist modes cannot be defined except via their political, legal and ideological superstructures, since these are what determine the type of extra-economic coercion that specifies them. The precise forms of juridical dependence, property and sovereignty that characterise a pre-capitalist social formation, far from being merely accessory or contingent epiphenomena, compose on the contrary the central indices of the determinate mode of production dominant within it', ibid, p. 404 (emphasis original). Anderson himself defines feudalism, as we have noted earlier, as the specific organisation of the seigneurial and serf classes 'in a vertically articulated system of parcellized sovereignty and

scalar property that distinguished the feudal mode of production in Europe', ibid., p. 408. Quite apart from the problem with defining a mode of production (even a pre-capitalist one) in terms of the politico-legal specifics, into which we need not go here, Anderson has unnecessarily accepted the notion of similarity between the 'economic infrastructures' of different medieval regions. The similarity exists only when the definitions are wide, and therefore, futile, enough to cover all of these economies (definitions such as 'non-economic coercion'); in fact the histories of these medieval regional economies have followed quite divergent paths even when they were all primarily agrarian economies and even when surplus was extracted through non-economic compulsion in all of them. Japan's feudalism is the only one outside Europe the genuineness of which is accepted by most analysts from Karl Marx to Marc Bloch to Anderson himself, although even there divergent opinions have not gone unrecorded. See Karl Marx, *Capital*, vol. I, Moscow, 1954, p. 718n; Marc Bloch, *Feudal Society*, pp. 446-47, 452; Perry Anderson, *Lineages*, pp. 413-17, 435-61. Frances V. Moulder on the other hand suggests that certain similarities in the political structure between Tokugawa Japan and European feudalism notwithstanding, Japan's history was closer to China's than Europe's, *Japan, China and the Modern World Economy: Towards a Reinterpretation of East Asian Development c. 1600 to 1918*, Cambridge, 1977, pp. 25, 71-90. In India the chief protagonists of an 'Indian feudalism' seek to establish the system's kinship with its European counterpart not so much in terms of the 'economic infrastructure' as in politico-juridical and ideological terms in consonance with unequal social distribution of property, though they make do with a simple, rather than a fanciful, language. See R.S. Sharma, *Indian Feudalism*, and 'Problem of Transition from Ancient to Medieval in Indian History', *The Indian Historical Review*, vol. I, no. I, March 1974, pp. 1-9; B.N.S. Yadava, *Society and Culture in Northern India in the Twelfth Century*, Allahabad, 1973. Prof. R.S. Sharma's persuasive scholarship has indeed inspired a large body of literature on Indian 'feudalism' written along the lines suggested by him.

6. Thus is S. Nurul Hasan able to use the terms 'feudal' and 'pre-capitalist' as synonyms: 'the Mughal system was feudal and pre-capitalist in character', *Thoughts*, p. 3.
7. There are, of course, divergent opinions regarding the primacy

of slavery in the economy of Graeco-Roman antiquity. A.H.M. Jones and R.H. Hilton believe that the ancient economy was dependent on the majority of small independent peasants rather than larger latifundia cultivated by salves. See Jones, 'The Economic Basis of Athenian Democracy', *Past and Present*, No. 1, Feb. 1952, pp. 13-31, and Hilton, *Bond Men Made Free: Medieval Peasant Movements and the English Rebellion of* 1381, London 1973, p. 10. M.I. Finley, on the other hand, suggests the ratio of slaves to free citizenry at around 3 or 4 :1 in the fifth or fourth centuries B.C., precisely the period Jones is concerned with, 'Was Greek Civilisation Based on Slave Labour?', *Historia*, VIII, 1959, pp. 58-59 cited in Perry Anderson, *Passages from Antiquity to Feudalism*, London, 1974, pp. 22-23, n. Anderson himself suggests a ratio of 3:2 after considering various other estimates, ibid.

8. This is essentially how Marx had understood the term, *Capital*, vol. III, Moscow, 1971, pp. 804, 807.
9. 'Subsistence' as a Marxian concept includes 'the maintenance and reproduction of the producer', Marx, *Capital*, vol. I, p. 512. Clearly subsistence needs would vary from region to region according to the climate and from class to class according to custom. They would also vary with time as nature's productive capacity is utilised more fully. But in any pre-socialist society, given the class division, they are likely to approximate more closely to 'the natural wants imperatively calling for satisfaction' (ibid) at the lower end of society than at the middle and higher ends.
10. M.I. Finley, *The Ancient Economy*, London, 1973, pp. 85-87: Marc Bloch, *French Rural History*, tr. Janet Sondheimer, London, 1976, p. 68; Bloch, 'The Rise of Dependent Cultivation', in M.M. Postan, ed., *Cambridge Economic History of Europe*, vol. I, 2nd edn., Cambridge, 1966, p. 248; Georges Duby, *Early Growth of European Economy: Warriors and Peasants from the Seventh to Twelfth Century*, tr. Howard B. Clark, New York, 1974, p. 40 (hereafter *Warriors and Peasants*); Perry Anderson, *Passages*, pp. 18, 25-28, 79, 82.
11. Marc Bloch, *Feudal Society*, pp. 171-73; Bloch, 'The Rise of Dependent Cultivation', pp. 255-56; Bloch, *French Rural History*, pp. 72-74, 76-77, 85-90; Georges Duby, *Rural Economy and Country Life in the Medieval West*, tr. Cynthia Postan, London, 1968. pp. 33-35; Duby, *Warriors and Peasants*, pp. 88-89; R.H. Hilton, *Bond Men Made Free*, pp. 33-35; Perry Anderson,

Passages, p. 149.

12. Marc Bloch, *Feudal Society*, p.180; G. Duby, *Warriors and Peasants*, pp.40, 87-88, 90-91; Perry Anderson, *Passages*, p.148; R.H. Hilton, *Bond Men Made Free*, pp. 42-44.
13. Marc Bloch had once argued that in England, where feudalism was much more thoroughgoing because of being imposed from above after the Norman conquest, the spread of the manor completely wiped out all traces of allodial property, *Feudal Society*. pp. 187-89, 244, 248. More recently it has been suggested that feudal land tenures, along with other feudal institutions, had developed in England before the Conquest which only accentuated their further development, while features of the pre-feudal past continued to exist as subsidiary elements; see J.O.Preswich, 'Anglo-Norman Feudalism and the Problem of Continuity', *Past and Present*, no. 26, 1963, pp. 39-57.
14. G. Duby, *Rural Economy*, pp. 33-35, 40
15. Maurice Dobb did make this distinction in terms of unfreedom of the serf as the reflection of a property relation which asserted itself as a direct relationship between rulers and servants, *Studies*, p.35. This distinction hinges on the juridical basis of unfreedom rather than on the economic basis, though it does have economic 'content' as Dobb asserted. More important, while the equation of feudalism with serfdom may faithfully describe the numerical preponderance of serfs in the production system, the bi-polar division between lords and serfs excludes from its purview the vital multi-polar tensions which were leading the feudal society on to hectic growth, and, ultimately, to its decline. Dobb's bi-polar division of feudal society explains feudalism's decline in terms of impoverishment of the peasantry owing to the lord's demand for more revenue; this explanation assumes a static level of production. In fact, feudalism declined owing to its tremendous onward march. For a detailed review of Maurice Dobb's argument, see Harbans Mukhia, 'Maurice Dobb's Explanation of the Decline of Feudalism in Western Europe—a Critique', *The Indian Historical Review*, vol. 6, nos. 1-2, 1979-80.

    We have already commented on Perry Anderson's delimitation of west European feudalism's specificities, which, indeed, are such that pre-thirteenth century early medieval India, at least, can find herself comfortably placed there much against Anderson's will.
16. China is another major region of the world which is said to

have had its feudalism, beginning with the Chou dynasty in about 1050 B.C. The distinguished Chinese historian, Wu Tak'un has, however, questioned the validity of the concept of Chinese 'feudalism', 'An Interpretation of Chinese Economic History', *Past and Present*, no. 1, Feb. 1952, pp. 1-13.

17. F.L. Ganshof and A. Verhurlst, 'France, the Low Countries and Western Germany', *Cambridge Economic History*, pp. 314-15.
18. G. Duby, *Warriors and Peasants*, pp. 89-90, 94-95.
19. Charles Parain, 'The Evolution of Agricultural Technique' *Cambridge Economic History*, pp. 133-34, 145-46; Marc Bloch, *French Rural History*, p. 25; G.Duby, *Rural Economy*, pp. 24-25; Duby, *Warriors and Peasants*, p. 169.
20. Charles Parain, op.cit., pp. 128-29, 148-57; G. Duby, *Rural Economy*, pp.17-21; Lynn White Jr., *Medieval Technology and Social Change*, London, 1973 (first published 1962), pp. 41-43, 53.
21. Charles Parain, op.cit., pp. 144-45; Lynn White, op.cit., pp. 59-60.
22. Marc Bloch, *Feudal Society*, pp. 60-61; G. Duby, *Rural Economy*, pp. 6, 14.
23. G. Duby, *Rural Economy*, p. 18; Charles Parain, op.cit., pp. 129-31, 152-53,157-59.
24. G. Duby, *Rural Economy*, pp. 6-7, 14-15.
25. Marc Bloch, *French Rural History*, pp. 72-74; G. Duby, *Rural Economy*, pp. 40-42; R.H. Hilton, *Bond Men Made Free*, pp. 61, 85-86.
26. G. Duby, *Rural Economy*, pp. 12-15; G. Duby, *Warriors and Peasants*, pp. 78-83.
27. G. Duby, *Rural Economy*, pp. 38-39, 48-49.
28. Marc Bloch and G. Duby have argued that the incentive for technological development came from the lord's estates. See Bloch, 'Medieval Inventions' in his *Land and Work in Medieval Europe*, tr.J.E. Anderson, London, 1967, p. 182, and Duby, *Warriors and Peasants*, pp. 95-96, 177, 229-30. For the suggestion that the society as a whole created this development, see Harbans Mukhia, 'Maurice Dobb's Explanation', pp. 166-67.
29. Perry Anderson, *Passages*, p. 183.
30. Lynn White, op.cit., p. 88.
31. G. Duby, *Rural Economy*, pp. 25-27; 103; C. Parain, op.cit., p. 125; Lord Beveridge, 'The Yield and Price of Corn in the Middle Ages', in E.M Carus-Wilson, ed., *Essays in Economic History*, vol. I, London, 1966. (first published 1954) pp. 15-16.
32. G. Duby, *Rural Economy*, p. 102.

33. R.H. Hilton, *Bond Men Made Free,* p. 28. The manse comprised the amount of land necessary to maintain one household at subsistence level; it therefore differed from region to region according to soil-fertility and customary subsistence needs of the peasant family unit. See Robert Latouche, *The Birth of Western Economy,* tr. E.M. Wilkinson, London, 1961, p. 82 and A. Gurevich, 'Representations of Property during the High Middle Ages', *Economy and Society,* vol. 1, Feb. 1977, p. 8.
34. G. Fourquin, *Lordship and Feudalism in the Middle Ages,* tr. Iris and Lytton Sells, London, 1976, p. 168.
35. G. Duby, *Rural Economy,* pp. 294-95.
36. R.S. Lopez, *The Birth of Europe,* London, 1967, p. 398, cited in Perry Anderson, *Passages,* p. 190.
37. E.A. Kosminsky suggests, in passing, the significance of unequal distribution of property in feudal society in this context, 'The Evolution of Feudal Rent in England', *Past and Present,* no. 7, April 1955, p. 22.
38. G. Duby, *Warriors and Peasants,* p. 198-99.
39. J.C. Russel, *Late Ancient and Medieval Populations,* Philadelphia, 1958, pp. 102-13; Russell, 'Population in Europe', in Carlo M. Cipolla, ed., *The Fontana Economic History of Europe,* vol. I, London, 1972, pp. 39-40; M.M. Postan, *The Medieval Economy and Society,* London, 1975 (first published 1972), pp. 35-36, J.Z. Titow, 'Some Differences Between Manors and their Effects on the Condition of the Peasant in the Thirteenth Century', *Agricultural History Review,* vol. X, no. 1, 1962, pp. 1-2; Maurice Dobb, *Studies,* p. 47; Marc Bloch, *French Rural History,* p.16; Duby, *Rural Economy,* pp. 119-22.
40. G. Duby, *Rural Economy,* pp. 81-87; Duby *Warriors and Peasants,* pp. 119-210.
41. Hermann Aubin, 'The Land East of the Elbe and German Colonization Eastwards', *Cambridge Economic History,* pp. 455-56; E. Miller, 'The English Economy in the Thirteenth Century: Implications of Recent Research', *Past and Present,* no. 28, July 1964, p.33; Patricia Croot and David Parker, 'Agrarian Class Structure and Economic Development', *Past and Present,* no. 78, February 1978, p. 39; G. Duby, *Warriors and Peasants,* pp. 201, 208.
42. B.K. Roberts, 'A Study of Medieval Colonisation in the Forest of Arden, Warwickshire', *Agricultural History Review,* vol. XVI, 1968, p. 102; Leopold Genicot, 'Crisis: from the Middle Ages to Modern Times', *Cambridge Economic History,* pp. 733-34; Ganshof and Vershurlst, op.cit., pp. 297-98; G. Duby, *Warriors*

and Peasants, p. 205.

43. Marc Bloch, *Feudal Society*, pp. 137-41; Joan Thirsk, 'The Family' *Past and Present*, no. 27, April 1964, pp. 117-22. Laslett, however, is reluctant to accept the notion that changes in family structures correspond to social transformations, *The World We Have Lost*, cited in Hans Medick, 'The proto-industrial family economy: the structural function of household and family during the transition from peasant society to industrial capitalism', *Social History*, vol. 1, no. 3, October 1976, pp. 292-93.
44. G. Duby, *Warriors and Peasants*, pp. 205-08.
45. G. Duby, *Rural Economy*, p. 77.
46. Ibid, pp. 115-16, 207-8.
47. Ibid, pp. 207-08, 263-64; Lynn White, op.cit., p. 65. Andrew Jones argues that labourers' perquisites had to be created in England during the thirteenth and fourteenth centuries to obtain speedy and efficient use of customary labour, 'Harvest Customs and Labourers' Perquisites in Southern England, 1150-1350; the Corn Harvest', *Agricultural History Review*, vol. XXV, 1977, p. 14.
48. Marc Bloch, *French Rural History*, pp. 106-12; G. Duby, *Rural Economy*, p. 208; Duby, *Warriors and Peasants*, pp. 91-92.
49. M.M. Postan, 'The Rise of a Money Economy' in Carus-Wilson, ed., op.cit., vol. I, p.7; R.H. Hilton, 'Freedom and Villeinage in England' in Hilton, ed., *Peasants, Knights and Heretics*, p. 181; P.D.A. Harvey, 'The English Inflation of 1180-1220', in ibid, pp. 74-75; G. Duby, *Warriors and Peasants*, p. 222; E.A. Kosminsky, 'Services and Money Rents in the Thirteenth Century', in Carus-Wilson, ed., *Essays in Economic History*, vol. II, 1966 (first published 1962), pp. 39-42 where he suggests that villeinage remained a more important part of labour supply on the larger estates while the smaller ones depended more on hired labour.
50. Among the lords were the seigneurs; or the banal lords, whose authority was derived from their exercise of the *ban*, theoretically the king's power to give orders, but actually usurped by lords from the eighth century onwards. Since it was by nature an arbitrary power, its flexibility as a source of income and authority was much prized by the seigneurs who had both land and men within their jurisdiction. Then there were the landlords whose control extended to the land. Besides, there were the non-territorial lords who derived their income from the right to collect taxes, tithes etc. a right they had either earned or had simply usurped. See Marc Bloch, *Feudal Society*, p. 251; J.S. Critchley, *Feudalism*, London, 1978, p. 67; G. Duby, *Warriors*

and Peasants, pp. 174-77; Guy Forquin, op.cit., pp. 133-36.

51. The power to administer justice was as stratified as the class of lords; see Critchley, op.cit., p. 57; also Marc Bloch, *French Rural History*, pp.78-80; Guy Fourquin, op.cit., 185-86; G. Duby, *Warriors and Peasants*, pp. 211-13, 227, 249-51.
52. The 'monopolies' comprised the mills for grinding corn, the oven for baking bread, the winepress for the grapes, and the bull and boar for replenishing the livestock of the village, etc. The monopolies were fiercely contested by the peasants; see Marc Bloch, *Land and Work in Medieval Europe*, pp. 135-68; Bloch, *Feudal Society*, p. 251; G. Duby, *Warriors and Peasants*, pp. 222-23, 227-29.
53. E.A. Kosminsky, 'Services and Money Rent', op.cit., pp. 46-48.
54. However, the paper on 'Maurice Dobb's Explanation' referred to earlier discusses this question in some detail on pp. 174-75.
55. R.H. Hilton, *Bond Men Made Free*, pp. 128-29, 130, 132 and 206-7 where Hilton discusses the attitude of the urban bourgeoisie towards the Grand Jacquerie, the Catalan *remensas*, the Tuchin rebellion and other peasant movements respectively.
56. L. Genicot and G. Duby have discussed this process of differentiation in considerable detail and with impressive clarity. See L. Genicot, op.cit., and Duby, *Rural Economy*, passim.
57. G. Duby, *Rural Economy*, pp. 126-65.
58. See for the existence of money and exchange in classical feudalism of earlier centuries Marc Bloch, 'Natural economy or money economy: a pseudo-dilemma', in his *Land and Work in Medieval Europe*, pp. 230-44. Witold Kula, constructing a 'model' of feudal economy, suggests the existence of 'monetary' and 'natural' sectors within every feudal 'enterprise' big or small, *An Economic Theory of the Feudal System*, tr. Lawrence Garner, London, 1976, p. 133.
59. R.S. Lopez, 'The Evolution of Land Transport in the Middle Ages', *Past and Present*, no. 9, April 1956, p. 24. Marc Bloch notes the construction of a large number of bridges all over Europe during the twelfth century, *Feudal Society*, pp. 69-70.
60. G. Duby, *Rural Economy*, p. 302-05; Perry Anderson, *Passages*, p. 191. The rise in agricultural prices was especially sharp in England between 1180 and 1220; see P.D.A. Harvey, 'The English Inflation 1180-1220' in *Peasants, Knights and Heretics*, pp. 57-58.
61. G. Duby, *Rural Economy*, pp. 263-64; M.M. Postan, 'The Rise of a Money Economy', op.cit., p. 7.
62. The large size of the noble or clerical domains within the range

of 2,000 to 4,000 acres necessitated the recruitment of bailiffs to supervise production, storage, consumption, sale etc. For the size of the estate, Perry Anderson, *Passages,* p. 140. See also Guy Fourquin, op.cit,. p. 172; G. Duby, *Warriors and Peasants,* pp. 467-47, 229; G. Duby, *Rural Economy,* pp. 228-31 and passim. In Duby's *Rural Economy,* scattered at many places, is perhaps the best account of the transformation of the class of agents into rich farmers or kulaks.

63. Marc Bloch, *French Rural History,* pp. 191-92; G. Duby, *Warriors and Peasants,* p. 47; Henri Pirenne, op.cit., pp. 60-61.
64. G. Duby, *Warriors and Peasants,* p. 229; Duby, *Rural Economy,* pp. 219, 245.
65. G. Duby, *Rural Economy,* pp. 244-45.
66. G. Duby, *Warriors and Peasants,* pp. 257-58.
67. E.A. Kosminsky, 'Services and Money Rents', op.cit., pp. 46-48; Kosminsky, 'The Evolution of Feudal Rent', op.cit., p. 35n; G. Duby, *Rural Economy,* p. 247; Duby, *Warriors and Peasants,* pp. 176-77.
68. Guy Fourquin op.cit., pp. 80-82; G. Duby, *Rural Economy,* p. 129.
69. L. Genicot, op.cit., pp. 715-16.
70. Marc Bloch, *French Rural History,* p. 124.
71. G. Duby, *Rural Economy,* p. 236.
72. Ibid, pp. 252-59, 285. The intensification of labour services on the English estates towards the end of the thirteenth century has been sufficiently highlighted by Kosminsky, 'Services and Money Rents', op. cit., pp. 46-47, and Hilton, 'Freedom and Villeinage in England', op.cit., pp. 181, 184.
73. G. Duby, *Rural Economy,* pp. 256-57.
74. Ibid, pp. 257-58.
75. L. Genicot suggests that during the fourteenth and the fifteenth centuries the small landowners suffered a depression and the landless agricultural workers and marginal farmers registered an improvement in their economic conditions, so that 'at the end of the Middle Ages not the whole but the greater part of the rural population shared approximately the same economic standard of life', op.cit., pp. 728-31. See also G. Duby, *Rural Economy,* pp. 152, 280, 305.
76. G. Duby, *Rural Economy,* p. 286.
77. Ibid, pp. 141-45.
78. Ibid, pp. 317 ff.; Perry Anderson, *Passages,* pp. 197-99; Marc Bloch, *French Rural History,* pp. 17,112; M.M. Postan, *The Medieval Economy and Society,* pp. 63-79; R.H. Hilton, *Bond Men*

Made Free, p. 16; E. Miller, 'The English Economy of the Thirteenth Century', op.cit., p. 38. Guy Bois makes the point in the classic Marxist idiom: 'Above all, the system had exhausted its possibilities for expansion in a virtually complete conquest of the cultivable area', 'The Transition from Feudalism to Capitalism', (mimeo), presented to the Indo-French Seminar on the same theme at the University of Delhi, Jan. 1979, p. 21.

79. G. Duby, *Rural Economy*, pp. 294-95.
80. For disturbed ecological balance etc., Perry Anderson, *Passages*, pp. 198-99; for famines and epidemics, G. Duby, *Rural Economy*, p. 295. Also Ian Kershaw, 'The Great Famine and Agrarian Crisis in England 1315-22' in Hilton ed. *Peasants, Knights and Heretics*, pp. 85-132.
81. Philip Ziegler, *The Black Death*, London, 1970 (first published 1969); Perry Anderson, *Passages*, p. 201.
82. J.C. Russell, *Late Ancient and Medieval Populations*, p. 131.
83. Duby suggests that the middle-aged resisted epidemics with greater strength, *Rural Economy*, p.308. This should reflect the decreasing resistance of the younger generation perhaps because of diminishing nourishment owing to the declining returns from the land. Slicher van Bath very sensitively discusses the physical and mental consequences of prolonged malnutrition, *Agrarian History of Western Europe*, 500-1850, tr. O. Ordish, London, 1963, pp. 11-84.
84. Thus, for example, while between the thirteenth and the mid-fifteenth century agricultural prices fell by 10 per cent, wages rose by 250 per cent, R.H. Hilton, *Bond Men Made Free*, p. 154; Genicot, op.cit., pp. 684,692,694; G.Duby, *Rural Economy*, pp. 307-08, 320; Guy Bois, 'Note on the movement of prices in feudal economic systems', (mimeo), p. 2.
85. G. Duby, *Rural Economy*, p. 316.
86. Cristobal Kay, 'Comparative Development of the European Manorial System and the Latin American Hacienda System', *Journal of Peasant Studies*, vol. II, no. 1, October, 1974, p. 72,
87. L. Genicot, op.cit., pp. 699-700; Guy Fourquin, op.cit., p. 210.
88. Guy Bois, 'Transition' op.cit., pp. 21-26; R.H. Hilton, 'A Crisis of Feudalism', *Past and Present*, no. 80, August, 1978, pp. 11-18.
89. R.H. Hilton, *Bond Men Made Free*, pp. 85ff.
90. Ibid; G. Duby, *Rural Economy*, pp. 332-35.
91. Peter Blickle, 'Peasant revolts in the German empire in the late Middle Ages', *Social History*, vol. IV, no. 2, May 1979, pp. 223-39.
92. Perry Anderson, *Passages*, p. 199 and n.

93. R.H. Hilton appears to be astonished that 'the impoverished and badly harassed area to the south west of the city—precisely where one would expect an explosion of pure misery—was virtually untouched by the rebellion', *Bond Men Made Free*, p. 117.
94. Ibid, pp. 82, 89-90, 94.
95. Perry Anderson, *Passages*, p. 293.
96. Maurice Dobb justly considers the fifteenth and the sixteenth centuries 'transitional' between feudalism and capitalism, *Studies*, p. 20.
97. V.I. Kalyanov and I.P. Baikov cited in B.N.S. Yadava, 'Some Aspects of Changing Order in India, during the Saka-Kusana Age' in G.R. Sharma, ed., *Kusana Studies*, Allahabad, 1968, p. 80. For Baikov the exploitation of the two lower *varnas* or castes by the higher ones constituted feudalism.
98. R.S. Sharma, *Indian Feudalism*, pp. 1-76, 210-62.
99. B.N.S. Yadava, *Society and Culture*, pp. 172-73.
100. Daniel Thorner, 'Feudalism in India', in R. Coulborn, ed., op.cit., pp. 143-45.
101. D.D. Kosambi, *An Introduction to the Study of Indian History*, 2nd revised edn., Bombay 1975 (first published 1956), pp. 391-92.
102. Col. James Tod, *Annals and Antiquities of Rajasthan*, ed. W. Crooke, vol. I, London, 1920, pp. 155-56, 182-83, 190.
103. Tod, op.cit., p. 154. Interestingly, Hallam's work still provides the reference point at least to D.C.. Sircar, *Landlordism and Tenancy in Ancient and Medieval India as Revealed by Epigraphic Records*, Lucknow, 1969, p. 36.
104. Tod, op.cit., p. 190.
105. D.D. Kosambi, *An Introduction etc.* pp. 353-55 and 403n. See also his *The Culture and Civilization of Ancient India in Historical Outline*, reprint, New Delhi 1972, (first published in 1970), pp. 23-24.
106. R.S. Sharma, *Indian Feudalism*, pp. 1-2, 16, 34, 63-64, 84, 154. 208 etc; B.N.S. Yadava, *Society and Culture*, pp. 171-72, 175-80 etc.
107. Satish Chandra, 'Some Aspects of Indian Village Society in Northern India During the Eighteenth Century', *Indian Historical Review*, vol. 1, no. 1, March, 1974. p. 51.
108. D.D. Kosambi, *An Introduction &c* chs. 9 and 10.
109. For a critique of this concept see Irfan Habib, 'Marxist Interpretation' *Seminar*, 39, Nov. 1962, pp. 36-37.
110. R.S. Sharma, *Indian Feudalism;* 'Problem of Transition', op.cit.;

'Origins of Feudalism in India', *Journal of the Economic and Social History of the Orient*, vol. 1, 1957-58, pp. 297-328; 'Indian Feudalism Retouched' (review article), *Indian Historical Review*, vol. 1, no. 2, Sept. 1974, pp. 320-30 etc.

111. B.N.S. Yadava, *Society and Culture*. Yadava's numerous articles rarely go beyond the arguments and evidence of his book.
112. Thus the decline of trade—both internal and international—and, following it, the decline of urban centres is seen by R.S. Sharma as evidence of the rise of feudalism in post-Gupta times, and the revival of trade and city life, of feudalism's decline, *Indian Feudalism*, pp. 65-73 and 242-62. For a similar assumption of a trade-feudalism dichotomy in B.N.S. Yadava's work see his *Society and Culture*, pp. 172-73 and 'Immobility and Subjection of Indian Peasantry in Early Medieval Complex', *Indian Historical Review*, vol. 1, no. 1, p. 27. Unfortunately, Yadava has misunderstood Moreland's phrase 'peasants' payments' in cash as 'the regular practice of payment to the peasants in cash', which contributed to the growth of economic mobility; Moreland was referring to the revenue paid *by* the peasants to the state or its agents. See W.H. Moreland, *Agrarian System of Moslem India*, Allahabad, 1929, p. 204 and Yadava, 'Immobility and Subjection', p. 27.
113. *Indian Feudalism*, pp. 53-59, 118 and passim.
114. Ibid, pp. 74, 271.
115. Ibid, p. 71, 241, 271.
116. Ibid, pp. 238-41.
117 For revival of trade and towns, ibid, pp. 242-62; flight of peasants to towns p. 244; commutation, pp. 242-44, 262.
118. Ibid, p. 74.
119. B.N.S. Yadava, *Society and Culture*, pp. 137-39.
120. R.S. Sharma *Indian Feudalism*, pp. 50-53, 121-22, 243, 283; R.S. Sharma, *Light on Early Indian Society and Economy*, Bombay, 1966, p. 73; B.N.S. Yadava, *Society and Culture*, pp. 163-73; Yadava, 'Immobility and Subjection', pp. 21-23.
121. D.C. Sircar, 'Landlordism Confused with Feudalism', in Sircar, ed., *Land System and Feudalism in Ancient India*, Calcutta, 1966, pp. 58-61; Chattopadhyaya, 'Trade and Urban Centres in Early Medieval North India', *Indian Historical Review*, vol. 1, no. 2. Sep., 1974, pp. 203-19. See also M.R. Tarafdar, 'Trade and Society in Early Medieval Bengal', *Indian Historical Review*, vol. IV, no. 2, Jan.1978, pp. 274-86.
122. Perry Anderson, *Passages*, p. 128.

123. Forced labour rendered gratis appears to have been absent in the pre-Mauryan period, P.C. Jain, *Labour in Ancient India,* New Delhi, 1971, pp. 242-43; in the Mauryan period compulsory labour was used for purposes like the construction of state buildings, though it is not clear whether it was paid for or unpaid, ibid., and G.K. Rai, 'Forced Labour in Ancient and Early Medieval India', *Indian Historical Review,* vol. III, no. 1, July 1976, pp. 26, 37. By the first century A.D. *visti* had acquired the characteristics of unpaid compulsory labour. Its scope began to expand even as a wider section of the people was subjected to the exactions under this heading; forced labour came to acquire a permanence in Indian Society that is exceeded only by the caste system, for we find continuing references to it throughout the ancient and medieval periods; see R.S. Sharma, *Indian Feudalism* pp. 48-53, 121-22, 242-43; Irfan Habib, *Agrarian System of Mughal India,* Bombay, 1963, pp. 150, 239, 248; H. Fukazawa, 'A Note on the Corvee System (Vethbegar) in Eighteenth Century Maratha Kingdom', in *Science and Human Progress* (Essays in Honour of the late Professor D.D. Kosambi), Bombay, 1974; Harbans Mukhia, 'Illegal Extortions from Peasants, Artisans and Menials in Eighteenth Century Eastern Rajasthan', *Indian Economic and Social History Review,* vol. XIV, no. 2, April-June 1977, pp. 231-45; Henry Elliot, *Memoirs of the History, Folklore and Distribution of the Races of the North-Western Provinces of India,* ed., John Beames, vol. II, London, 1859, p. 232. While forced labour was used for a variety of purposes like the construction of forts, repairs of roads, carting of goods of the King's officials etc., there is very meagre evidence of its use for agricultural production. R.S. Sharma cites only one source—the *Kamasutra*—where peasant women are required to work on the village headman's fields, apart from cleaning his house, carrying things from and into his house etc., *Indian Feudalism,* pp. 51-52. But quite apart from the vagueness of the reference to peasant women working in the village headman's fields, one of a whole range of their tasks, even the interpretation that those women were rendering forced and unaid labour has been questioned by G.K. Rai, 'Forced Labour', op.cit., p. 30. There is some primary evidence for the existence of forced labour for agricultural production such as in the *Bhagvata Purana* (not later than 800 A.D.) cited in G.K. Rai, op.cit., p. 33, and some village level documents in Rajasthan cited in Harbans Mukhia, 'Illegal Extortions', p. 233. But on the whole its incidence is quite

marginal and even Professor Sharma agrees that serfdom had not become 'a common trait of the Indian agrarian system in medieval times', 'Indian Feudalism Retouched' op.cit., p. 328. Curiously, it is the artisans who were continually subjected to forced labour from the post-Gupta period. In the *Arthasastra* they are treated as independent, *Kautilya's Arthasastra* tr. R.Shamasastry, Mysore, 8th edn. 1967 (first published 1915), book IV, ch. I, pp. 229-32; but from the post-Gupta period, particularly from the sixth century, the artisans were attached to merchants and were liable to render forced labour, R.S. Sharma, *Indian Feudalism*, pp. 69-73. In the seventeenth century we still find them being subjected to forced labour, this time by the nobles; F. Bernier, *Travels in the Mogul Empire 1656-68*, tr. A. Constable, London, 1916, pp. 228-29 and Ali Muhammad Khan, *Mirat-i Ahmadi*, vol. 1, ed. Nawab Ali, Baroda, 1928, p. 260. The phenomenon is somewhat curious because there is little evidence of the scarcity of artisan labour. Of course, forced labour was not necessarily unpaid labour and there is considerable amount of evidence of wages being paid to artisans. See, for example, F. Pelsaert, *Jahangir's India*, tr. W.H. Moreland and Peter Geyl, Cambridge, 1925, p.60, and *Waqai-Ajmer-wa-Ranthambor*, transcript, Andhra State Archives, Hyderabad, p. 227.

124. Elliot, for once championing the cause of India against a compatriot, argued in 1859 that the average produce of the Province of Allahabad was *double the average* of the scientific cultivators of England; he also noted the decline in soil fertility in his own day, *Memoirs*, vol. II, p. 341 and n. (emphasis original).
125. Thus, while Abul Fazl speaks in glowing terms of the fertility of the *suba* of Lahore, he is far less enthusiastic about the provinces of Gujarat and Ajmer, see *Ain-i Akbari*, ed. Blochmann, Calcutta, 1867-77, vol. I, pp. 538, 485 and 505 respectively.
126. The *Taittiriya Samhita* makes a clear reference to the harvesting of two crops of corn in a year from the same piece of land apart from beans and sesamum; this would naturally imply crop rotation, see S.P. Raychaudhuri, L. Gopal and B.V. Subbarayappa, 'Agriculture' in D.M. Bose, S.N. Sen and B.V. Subbarayappa, eds., *A Concise History of Science in India*, New Delhi, 1971, p. 353 (hereafter *History of Science*); P.C. Jain, *Labour in Ancient India*, pp. 35-36. A.K. Ghosh and S.N. Sen accept the two crops but are less certain about rotation, 'Botany: Vedic

and Post-Vedic period', *History of Science*, pp. 377-78. References to two crops can be found continually since the *Taittiriya Samhita:* in Megasthenes' account, Puspa Niyogi, *Contributions to the Economic History of Northern India,* Calcutta, 1962, p. 20; in Kautalya's *Arthasastra,* pp. 131-32; in the *Brhatsamhita* of the Gupta period, S.P. Raychaudhuri, et.al., 'Agriculture', op.cit., p. 361; in the *Ain,* vol. 1, pp. 304-36 where all the revenue rates of Akbar's reign are mentioned for two crops—the winter and the spring.

127. Panini (c. 400 B.C.) refers to three annual crops, see P.C. Jain, op.cit., p. 50; *Ain,* vol. 1, p. 389 (*suba* Bengal where rice was harvested thrice), p. 473; (*suba* Khandesh where jowar—a millet—was similar reaped thrice) and p. 513 (*suba* Delhi). The sources that leave one in no doubt regarding the cultivation of two or three crops in a year in the same field are: *Taittiriya Samhita* and *Ain,* vol. 1, p. 389 (Bengal *suba*). The *Arthasastra* on the other hand, suggests the use of compulsion by the state to grow a second crop on the field if the state's interest so required, p. 273.

128. Thus in the law-book of Narada (Gupta period) a tract of land that had not been cultivated for a year is defined as *ardhakhila,* Puspa Niyogi, *Contributions,* p. 21, and as *khila* if it had been uncultivated for three years, R.S. Sharma, *Indian Feudalism,* p. 35. *Khila* is then rendered as 'fallow' by Professor Sharma, though Niyogi prefers 'half-waste' for her *ardhakhila.* Prof. Sharma also renders *bhumicchidra* as fallow, *Indian Feudalism,* p. 36, though the context clearly points to virgin land. R.P. Kangle in fact translates *bhumicchidra* as 'land which cannot be used for agriculture because it is unsuited for it', *The Kautilya Arthasastra,* part III, Bombay, 1965, p. 174. See also Niyogi, *Contributions,* p. 69. D.C. Sircar has a section entitled 'Reclamation of Fallow Land' which would appear curious but for the fact that 'fallow' denotes virgin or deserted land to most historians of ancient India. See Sircar, *Landlordism and Tenancy,* p. 4; P. Niyogi, *Contributions,* p. 1; B.P. Mazumdar, *The Socio-Economic History of Northern India (1030-1194 A.D.),* Calcutta, 1960, p. 175. See also D.C. Sircar, *Indian Epigraphical Glossary,* Delhi, 1966, for *khila* (rendered: uncultivated land, fallow land), p. 157 and *khila-ksetra* (rendered: fallow land), p. 157. To S.P. Raychaudhuri it appears that the system of fallowing was known in the age of the *Yajurveda,* though, unluckily, he says nothing more about it, in Raychaudhuri, ed., *Agriculture in Ancient India,* New Delhi,

1964, p. 81. However, even some of the later works dealing exclusively or partly with agricultural practices make no mention of the genuine fallow. See, for example, the *Arthasastra,* the *Krsi-Parasara,* ed. and tr. G.P. Majumdar and S.C. Banerji, Calcutta, 1960, and Sarngadhara, *Upavana-Vinoda,* ed. & tr. G.P. Majumdar, Calcutta, 1936. The estimates of the date of *Krsi-Prasara* vary widely between 1300 B.C., the post-Vedic but pre-Christian era, and between 100 and 600 A.D; see S.P. Raychaudhuri, 'Land Classification in Ancient India', *Indian Journal of the History of Science,* vol. I, no. 2, Nov. 1966, p. 107; A.K. Ghosh and S.N. Sen, 'Botany: Vedic and Post-Vedic Period', *History of Science,* p. 379, and G.P. Majumdar, 'Introduction', *Krsi-Prasara,* p. VI, respectively. Some of the recent secondary works also discuss the whole range of agricultural operations in ancient India but do not refer to fallow; see, for example, B.N.S. Yadava, *Society and Culture,* pp. 256-62. If modern historians have used the term 'fallow' for virgin or deserted lands, or for the lea, it is obviously because the genuine fallow hardly existed.

129. William Tennant, *Indian Recreations; consisting chiefly of strictures on the Domestic and Rural Economy of the Mahomedans and Hindoos,* vol. II, Edinburgh, 1804, p. 16.

130. *Ain,* vol. I, p. 297. This category is named *parauti.* However, the third category, *chachar,* is so classified when it falls out of cultivation 'owing to excessive rain or inundation', ibid., p. 301; and the last, *banjar,* land when it loses its productive capacity through inundation, ibid. Thus, barring *parauti,* the forced exclusion from cultivation of the other categories of land is due to circumstances extraneous to the cycle of production. Indeed, the first class of land, *polaj,* is that which is never allowed to lie uncultivated, ibid., p. 297, and the other lands are to be slowly encouraged to develop into *polaj* class, by means of progressive taxation keeping pace with the diminishing period of their non-cultivation, ibid, pp. 301-02.

131. *Risaala-i Ziraat,* Edinburgh University Library Persian MS. No. 144, ff. 6b-7a.

132. Irfan Habib, *Agrarian System,* p. 23 and n. Irfan Habib's informant speaks of the customary practice in Gorakhpur, eastern U.P., of reclamation of new land once the old soil had spent its fertility. The period is early nineteenth century. Mufti Ghulam Hazarat, the informant, however, makes it a point to highlight the low fertility of the region where the practice

prevailed.

133. Irfan Habib suggests the following logic: Since in Mughal times between one-half and three-quarters of the land was cultivated compared to the area of such land at the beginning of the twentieth century, keeping in view regional variations, the medieval Indian peasant should have had at his disposal extensive wastelands and forests and therefore more cattle and drought animals. He could also have burnt firewood and used animal dung for manure. See Irfan Hibib, *Agrarian System*, pp. 53-54, 55-56, 116, and 'Potentialities of Capitalistic Development in the Economy of Mughal India', *Enquiry*, new series vol. III, no. 3, Winter 1971, p. 4. If this were so of medieval India, it should have been truer of the earlier period.
134. A.K. Ghosh and S.N. Sen appear to be doubtful, 'Botany: Vedic and Post-Vedic Period', *History of Science*, p. 377.
135. P. 132.
136. B.N.S. Yadava, *Society and Culture*, p. 257.
137. Pp. 74, 78.
138. Pp. 81-83.
139. *Arthasastra*, p. 132.
140. P.C. Jain, op.cit., pp. 60-61.
141. B.B. Lal, 'Perhaps the Earliest Ploughed Field So Far Excavated Anywhere in the World', *Purattatva*, no. 4, 1970-71, pp. 1-3. Professor Romila Thapar drew my attention to this evidence, for which I am extremely grateful.
142. P.C. Jain, op.cit., pp. 32, 34; S.P. Rychaudhuri, et.al, 'Agriculture', *History of Science*, p. 352, R.S. Sharma, *Light etc.*, pp. 55-56.
143. The *Atharvaveda* refers to ploughs driven by six and twelve oxen, P.C. Jain, op.cit., p. 35. There are references to the yoking of 6, 8, 12 and even 24 oxen to the plough, R.S. Sharma, *Light etc.*, p. 57. The *Krsi-Parasara* in a colourful verse suggests that 'a plough is said to have eight bulls, six for the cruel and two for the cow-killers', p. 73. Abul Fazl implies that a peasant having four oxen for his plough was too poor to be taxed, *Ain*, vol. 1, 287.

    The regional variation in the shape of the plough as used today has been recorded by Jaya Datta Gupta and B.N. Saraswati, 'Ploughs and Husking Implements', in *Peasant Life in India*, Memoir No. 8, Anthropological Survey of India, Calcutta, 1961, pp. 25-29. The regional variation in the weight of the plough was noted by N.G. Mukherji, *Handbook of Indian Agriculture*, Calcutta, 1915, pp. 93 and 99 where the ploughs of Bengal and Bundelkhand are respectively estimated at 1.25 and

3.5 maunds. It is perhaps not unreasonable to assume that these variations are a legacy of the distant past.

Panini divides agriculturists into three classes according to the type of plough they used and whether the plough belonged to them or not, P.C. Jain, op.cit., pp. 48-49.

144. Elliot, *Memoirs,* vol. II, pp. 340-41.
145. This was the conclusion reached by the Royal Commission on Agriculture in India, *Report,* London, 1928, pp. 110-12 cited in Irfan Habib, *Agrarian System,* p. 24 n.
146. Elliot, *Memoirs,* p. 340 n.
147. S.P. Raychaudhuri, et.al., 'Agriculture', *History of Science,* p. 352.
148. D.R. Chanana, 'The Spread of Agriculture in the Ganges Valley,' *Contributions to Indian Economic History,* no. 2, 1963, p. 115n. The Pali texts also refer to the spade, P.C. Jain, op.cit., p. 43.
149. S.P. Raychaudhuri et.al., 'Agriculture', *History of Science,* p. 360.
150. Op.cit., pp. 74-75.
151. R.S. Sharma, *Light etc.* pp. 57, 60-61.
152. Elliot, *Memoirs,* vol. II, pp. 341-42.
153. According to Panini, the field was at times ploughed twice and at others thrice, P.C. Jain, op.cit., p. 49; Kautilya suggested ploughing the field 'often', *Arthasastra,* p. 129; The *Krsi Parasara* recommends five ploughings for abundant crops, p. 77.
154. Grierson, *Bihar Peasant Life,* 2nd edn., Patna, 1926, p. 172, cited in A.K. Chaudhuri, *Early Medieval Village in North-Eastern India (A.D. 600-1200)*, Calcutta, 1971, pp. 153-54.
155. *Krsi-Prasara,* p. 82.
156. Irfan Habib, *Agrarian System,* p. 26; also B.N.S. Yadava, *Society and Culture,* p. 257.
157. *Krsi-Prasara,* pp. 80-81.
158. The *Vrksayurveda,* also attributed to Parasara, author of *Krsi-Prasara,* deals with the treatment of plants, as the title suggests, A.K. Ghosh and S.N. Sen, op.cit., p. 379.
159. S.P. Raychaudhuri et.al. 'Agriculture', op.cit., pp. 353-54.
160. P. 131.
161. Ibid.
162. R.P. Kangle, op.cit., p. 174.
163. Irfan Habib, 'Presidential Address', *Proceedings of Indian History Congress,* 31st Session, Varanasi, 1969, pp. 149-55.
164. *Ain,* vol. I, p. 538.
165. Zia-ud-din Barani, *Tarikh-i Firuz Shahi,* ed. Saiyad Ahmad Khan, Calcutta, 1862, p. 367-71; Shams-i Siraj Afif, *Tarikh-i Firuz Shahi,* ed. M. Wilayat Hussain, Calcutta, 1888-91, p. 127.
166. Sujan Rai Bhandari, *Khulasat-ut Tawarikh* ed. Zafar Hasan, Delhi,

1918, pp. 29-30, 36-37.

167. Baudhayana suggests a holding of six *nivartanas* for the purpose, R.S. Sharma, *Light etc.* p. 62. A *nivartana*, according to Professor Sharma, comprised roughly an acre and a half, ibid., p. 73. Puspa Niyogi on the other hand suggests, on the basis of a longish discussion with many impressive details, that a *nivartana* was equal to 40,000 cubits, *Contributions*, p. 97, and n. That would bring it close to 2.3 acres.
168. The Malabar Kannamkar, for example, tied to the land and working for the *janmi* landowners, could come near the category of serfs.
169. R.S. Sharma: 'On the whole while a great part of the time and energy of European peasants was consumed by their work on their master's fields the peasantry in India gave most of their time to their own fields, of the produce of which a considerable share went to the holders of the grants and other intermediaries; on the contrary, the number of free peasantry seems to have been far greater', *Indian Feudalism*, p. 75; also *Light etc.* p. 83. B.N.S. Yadava: 'Thus the Sudra peasants cannot be equated with the unfree serf of Medieval Europe', in D.C. Sircar, ed., *Land System and Feudalism*, p. 94; also *Society and Culture*, p. 171 and 'Immobility and Subjection', op.cit., p. 25.
170. The state farms of the Mauryas were cultivated by slaves, amongst others, *Arthasastra*, p. 129; artisans were enslaved by the Sultanate of Delhi during the thirteenth and fourteenth centuries, Zia-ud-din Barani, *Tarikh-i Firuz Shahi*, pp. 313-14. See also Irfan Habib, 'Economic History of the Delhi Sultanate—An Essay in Interpretation', *Indian Historical Review*, vol. IV, no. 2, Jan. 1978, pp. 292-94, 297.
171. R.S. Sharma, *Indian Feudalism*, pp. 56, 118-24. In a recent article Prof. Sharma describes the Indian peasants as having been reduced to the position of 'semi-serfs as a result of numerous impositions made on them', 'Indian Feudalism Retouched', op.cit., p. 327.
172. Irfan Hibib, *Agrarian System*, pp. 115-16, 118; 'Economic History of the Delhi Sultanate', p. 298. Irfan Habib does not consider forced labour an important element in this situation.
173. P. 46.
174. P. 197.
175. P. 273.
176. Cited in B.P. Mazumdar op.cit., p. 171.
177. *Arthasastra*, p. 197.

178. R.S. Sharma, *Indian Feudalism,* pp. 149-50.
179. Ali Muhammad Khan, *Mirat-i Ahmadi,* pp. 268-72.
180. Ibid, article III.
181. Ibid, articles XIII and XVI.
182. Zafarul Islam reasonably questions Irfan Habib's suspicion of the testimony of the *firman*. While Irfan Hibib thought the order had little relevance to the agrarian conditions in India for it was expressly drafted to set out the laws of the Shariat, *Agrarian System,* p. 113, Zafarul Islam, comparing its provisions with those of Islamic law, suggests its specific late seventeenth century relevance to India, 'Aurangzeb's Farman of Land Tax—An analysis in the Light of the *Fatawa-i-Alamgiri', Islamic Culture,* vol. 52, no. 2, April 1978, pp. 117-26. It is possible to trace these provisions back to the *Arthasastra* and to later Hindu law-books.
183. Aurangzeb's *firman* to Muhammad Hashim, article II.
184. Besides the *firman* to Muhammad Hashim, Article II, B.R. Grover has brought to light pieces of evidence from Shah Jahan's reign wherein the Desais were charged with resettling in their original homes tenants who had migrated to some other villages, 'The Position of the Desai in the Pargana Administration of Subah Gujarat under the Mughals', *Proceedings of Indian History Congress,* twenty-fourth session, Delhi, 1961, p. 152. Grover's evidence comes from some Persian documents located in Paris. The Desais, however, used persuasion and reassurance rather than coercion in carrying out their duties; but then the line between the two is very thin.
185. *Arthasastra,* p. 213; P.C. Jain, op.cit., pp. 236-39 for regulation of wage-payments by law-gives of the Gupta age; Irfan Habib, *Agrarian System,* p. 120. For sale of land, see *Arthasastra,* p. 197; D.C. Sircar, *Land System and Feudalism,* p. 12; R.S. Sharma, *Indian Feudalism,* pp. 36,149; B.R. Grover, 'Nature of Dehat-i-Taalluqa (Zamindari villages) and the Evolution of the Taaluqdari System During the Mughal Age', *I.E.S.H.R.,* vol. II, nos. 2 and 3, April and July 1965, p. 261.
186. R.S. Sharma, 'Indian Feudalism Retouched', p. 329; 'In fact even without compulsion peasants and artisans had no option but to stick to the village for the set up being the same everywhere, migration to another village could not materially change the situation.' B.N.S. Yadava stresses the role of ideology more than of law in enforcing immobility, *Society and Culture,* p. 166.
187. R.S. Sharma and B.N.S. Yadava have merely *inferred* that the state's grant of villages, enumerating a number of rights

transferred to the intermediaries, should have led to the creation of dependence of the peasants on them. This is by no means certain. Villages, according to Professor Sharma's own evidence, were donated even by private individuals, *Indian Feudalism*, p. 61; these individuals were clearly in no position to change class relations in the countryside. As D.D. Kosambi remarks with characteristic perception, 'The recipients of a whole village gained at most the rights the state would normally claim. That is, they collected the taxes already fixed by usage.
No portion of the tax was to be passed on to the state or any state official, but the donee had not the right to increase such taxes, nor any property rights over land and cattle', *An Introduction etc.* p. 321. At any rate the creation of peasant's dependence implies changes in the processes and relations of production and these can hardly be brought about by administrative fiat.

188. D.D. Kosambi, *An Introduction etc.*, p. 323; Irfan Habib, *Agrarian System*, p. 115; S. Nurul Hasan, *Thoughts*, p. 3.
189. Historians, too numerous to be referred to here, have discussed the question of land-ownership confining the options by and large to the state and the peasant. Communal ownership is definitively ruled out by all. Various combinations of the state's and the peasant's rights have also been suggested. Thus D.C. Sircar urges that it was the king who in theory owned the land and the cultivators were his tenants. However, they held permanent occupancy rights and the king was not expected to evict them, *Landlordism and Tenancy*, pp.1-3. B.N.S. Yadava believes that royal ownership and private individual ownership of land were not mutually exclusive in the context of the land system of the twelfth century, *Society and Culture*, p. 254. For medieval India, B.R. Grover has strongly argued in favour of peasant-proprietorship of land, 'Nature of Land-Rights in Mughal India', *I.E.S.H.R.*, vol. I, no. 1, 1963, pp. 2-5; 'Dehat-i-Taaluqa', pp. 261-62. Irfan Habib, on the other hand, while accepting the notion of private property in land, qualifies it with the absence of the right to free alienation etc. as we have noted above. Noman A. Siddiqi goes to the extent of denying to the peasants the right to sell or mortgage land, *Land Revenue Administration under the Mughals*, Bombay, 1970, pp. 11,16.
190. P.C. Jain, op.cit., pp. 44-45.
191. P. 129.
192. R.S. Sharma, *Indian Feudalism*, pp. 61-63. Elsewhere, Professor

Sharma remarks of the post-Gupta period: 'Perhaps the major portion of land continued to be in the possession of free peasants, who paid revenue directly to the State', *Light etc.*, p. 83. Professor Sharma, of course, appears to derive his definition of free peasantry from Fa-hsein who states that 'only those who till the king's land pay a land tax' and that they are free to go and stay as they please, ibid.

193. *Arthasastra*, p. 45
194. Manu, cited in P.C. Jain, op.cit., p. 51.
195. Irfan Habib, 'Jatts of Punjab and Sind', in Harbans Singh and N.G. Barrier, ed., *Essays in Honour of Dr. Ganda Singh*, Patiala, 1976, pp. 92-103.
196. *Ain*, vol. I, p. 199.
197. Ibid, pp. 285-86.
198. Abdul Qadir Badauni, *Muntakhab ut-Tawarikh*, vol. II, Bib. Ind,. p. 189.
199. B.R. Grover, 'Dehat-i-Taalluqa', p. 262.
200. See the 'Yad-dasht-i-izafa-i-dehat' (memorandum regarding newly settled villages) of Shah Jahan's time in Ziauddin Ahmed Shakeb, ed., *Mughal Archives*, vol. I, Hyderabad, 1977, p. 295; also pp. 36-45. The fact that such memoranda were to be submitted enumerating the number and location of newly settled villages suggests that the official injunction to extend cultivation had to be taken seriously.
201. Article V: 'Whoever turns (wasteland) into cultivable land should be recognised as its owner (*malik*) and should not be deprived (of land)'.
202. Irfan Habib, *Agrarian System*, pp. 121-22.
203. R.S. Sharma, *Indian Feudalism*, p. 75; R.S. Sharma, *Light etc.* p. 83; B.N.S. Yadava, *Society and Culture*, p. 171; S. Nurul Hassan, *Thoughts*, p. 18.
204. P.C. Jain, op.cit., 131.
205. *Arthasastra*, p. 131.
206. Op.cit., p. 174.
207. B.N.S. Yadava, *Society and Culture*, pp. 297-98.
208. Puspa Niyogi, *Contributions*, p. 180.
209. D.D. Kosambi, *An Introduction etc.* p. 365; D.C. Sircar, *Land System and Feudalism*, p. 21. For Balban's similar advice see Zia-ud-din Barani, op.cit., pp. 100-101.
210. Sircar, *Landlordism and Tenancy*, pp. 66-79; Yadava, *Society and Culture*, pp. 288-301.
211. *Society and Culture*, p. 301.

212. Irfan Habib, 'Potentialities etc' pp. 1-12,27; *Agrarian System,* pp. 192-96. Irfan Habib suggests a major new argument that the Delhi Sultanate created 'an entirely new kind of agrarian taxation in India. Once implanted, the single massive land-tax was to last in India till practically the first half of this century. The State would henceforth regularly claim the bulk of the peasants' surplus....', 'Economic History of the Delhi Sultanate', p. 297. The bulk of the surplus was, indeed, claimed by the Sultans, but in view of the evidence available for the pre-Sultanate period, particularly for the eleventh and twelfth centuries, we need really to be more certain whether they were doing anything unprecedented.
213. Even if we took only foodgrains into account, the increase in their number over the centuries has been very impressive. Thus, while barley, wheat and rice are referred to in the Vedic literature, R.S. Sharma, *Light etc.* pp. 56, 58, the *Arthasastra* enumerates many crops, some of which remain unidentified, and the number of grains comes to about ten, p. 131. A twelfth century work refers to twenty-four kinds of foodgrains, P. Niyogi, *Contributions,* pp. 23-24. The *Ain* has revenue-rates against twenty-nine varieties of grains and fourteen vegetables, vol. I, pp. 298-301. Even of the same grain, a large number of varieties gradually began to be cultivated. We are informed that around the twelfth century fifty varieties of rice were grown in Bengal, B.N.S. Yadava, *Society and Culture,* p. 258. Abul Fazl makes nearly the same point when he remarks that if a single grain of each kind of Bengal rice were collected, a large vase would be filled up, *Ain,* vol. I, p. 389.
214. The water-wheel might have had a three rather than a two stage history which Irfan Habib has so painstakingly reconstructed. *The arghatta* (or the noria) had buckets attached to its rim and was thus functional only on surface water in a pool or on the bank of a river. It also had to be manually operated. The fully developed Persian wheel, on the other hand, was an animal-powered, geared machine which collected water from a well in its bucket chain attached to the rim. A technologically intermediate stage appears to have consisted of the water-wheel, with a bucket chain but without the gear. It was manually operated and drew water from wells. A three stage history of water-wheel, if valid, should suggest not only a longer period of development of this irrigation device but also a wider social participation in the process of its development, for a larger

number of peasants could perhaps afford the wheel available in a wider range. The consequent rise in the productivity of land should also have had its impact on the process of state-formation between the seventh-eighth and the fourteenth century. The establishment of a highly centralised state-structure, collecting at times as much as a half of the peasant's produce as revenue in the thirteenth and early fourteenth century, was perhaps not an act of conquest but the culmination of a process that started during the seventh century or thereabout. The first to notice the rise in productivity, owing to the spread of irrigation, were the village potentates and they might also have been the first to demand a greater amount of the peasant's produce in revenue. The state would take its own time to wake up to this new reality; but once it did, it introduced an element of systematisation in the appropriation of the peasant's increased surplus, through a relatively efficient, and highly centralised, administrative apparatus. The establishment of this state can thus be seen as the culmination of a process that developed from the bottom upwards rather than from top downwards.

Clearly, this is still the very initial outline of a hypothesis and much research is called for to arrive at a conclusion.

215. Irfan Habib, *Agrarian System,* p. 257. Irfan Hibib makes this remark in the context of medieval India, but this would as well be true of the earlier period irrespective of direct collection of revenue by the state-officials or on its behalf by assignees.

216. Bhimsen, a late seventeenth-century chronicler, grasped this point in his description of Tanjore: in the whole world nowhere else are there so many temples, he says. The reason for the building of these temples he assigns to the very high fertility of land—producing four crops a year—and the abysmal standard of peasants' subsistence which he describes in detail and 'without exaggeration'. Consequently, 'a large revenue is raised, the amount of which is known only to the Recording Angel', *Nuskha-i Dilkusha,* tr. Jadu Nath Sarkar, Bombay, 1972, pp. 193-94.

217. In the *Mahabharata,* Bhisma says, 'If the king disregards agriculturists, they become lost to him, and abondoning his dominions betake themselves to the woods', cited in P.C. Jain, op.cit., p. 54; in the eleventh century Ksemendra bemoans the fact that the poor, with malice towards the property of the rich, were turning violent, B.N.S. Yadava, 'Problem of Interaction between Socio-economic Classes in the Early Medieval

Complex', *Indian Historical Review,* vol. III, no. 1, July 1976, p. 55; the Kaivarttas in east Bengal took to arms to resist the increasing state oppression in the last years of the eleventh century, R.S. Sharma, *Indian Feudalism,* p. 268; the peasantry of Doab revolted in the second quarter of the fourteenth century against the state's excessive exactions, Zia-ud-din Barani, op.cit., pp. 472-73; for the documentation of the widespread peasant rebellions of the second half of the seventeenth century, see Irfan Habib, *Agrarian System,* pp. 330-51.

218. It has been argued that Indian feudalism comes closest to European feudalism of the twelfth century, B.N.S. Yadava, *Society and Culture,* p. 171. Quite apart from the validity of this comparison in terms of historical evidence which is by no means conclusive, even if such evidence were conceded, a momentary convergence between two social systems following independent paths of historical development can hardly justify the conclusion that they were both marked by the same characteristics.
219. It is too early to be definitive about it, but some work on different regions of eighteenth century India is in progress at the Jawaharlal Nehru University to test this hypothesis.
220. For a persuasive argument regarding the absence of any potential for capitalist development in the Mughal economy, see Irfan Habib, 'Potentialities etc'.
221. Irfan Habib vehemently questions the validity of the notion of the Asiatic mode of production; see his 'Problems of Marxist Historical Analysis', *Enquiry,* n.s. vol. VII, no. 2, Monsoon 1969, pp. 52-67. For a recent re-statement of the rejection of this notion see Bipan Chandra, 'Karl Marx, His Theories of Asian Societies and Colonial Rule' (mimeo). Unfortunately, in Bipan Chandra's discussion of ancient and medieval Indian history there is hardly a statement that can go uncontested. Marian Sawer has in her *Marxism and the Question of the Asiatic Mode of Production,* referred to earlier, made a very interesting study of the history of this concept and the recent political context in which it has been discussed.
222. R.A.L.H. Gunawardana suggests that Marx had at some point abandoned the notion of the absence of private property in land in India, 'The Analysis of Pre-Colonial Social Formations in Asia in the Writings of Karl Marx', *Indian Historical Review,* vol. II, no. 2, Jan. 1976, pp. 365-88. Gunawardana has in this connection drawn attention to evidence hitherto overlooked by historians. It remains true, however, that this evidence belongs to the period

between 1853 and 1858; on the other hand in his writings of the latter phase of this period and afterwards Marx continued to insist on the absence of private property in land in that he spoke of its communal ownership; *Grundrisse,* tr. Martin Nicolaus, London, 1973, pp. 472-73; *A Contribution to the Critique of Political Economy,* Moscow, 1970, p. 33 n. (where Marx says that 'primitive communal property... is still in existence in India'); *Capital,* vol. I, pp. 357-58.

223. 'Problems of Marxist Historical Analysis'.
224. 'Economic History of the Delhi Sultanate', p. 298.
225. Whenever we discuss the question of feudalism in any country and in any period, medieval western Europe inevitably provides the point of reference for such a discussion, whatever be our answer to this question. One can, of course, see the justice of comparing the history of other countries with that of western Europe in modern times for it was, after all, in western Europe that capitalism arose which was later to encompass the whole world; but it is difficult to see the logic of such a comparison in the ancient and medieval periods when it might only persuade us to ask questions which have so little relevance to our history. It is possible, of course, to speak of regional variations of feudalism. One could thus argue in favour of an Indian feudalism, a Chinese feudalism, a West Asian feudalism, etc. apart from the west European and the Japanese ones. However, I visualise two reservations with respect to this argument. First, the use of a common denominator for the whole range of regionally and temporally variant socio-economic systems could hardly be justified unless one could establish a fundamental similarity underlying these variations—a similarity that is precisely defined. Secondly, quite apart from the fact that feudalism as a category achieves universality only through the looseness of its definition, the very search for a universal category, equally applicable to different medieval regions, is based on the assumption that the medieval world was one world sharing a common socio-economic system. We thus attribute to the medieval world characteristics which more appropriately belong to the nineteenth and twentieth centuries.

10

Peasant Production and Medieval Indian Society*

I feel truly overwhelmed by the generosity of response to my paper, 'Was There Feudalism in Indian History?' published in this journal four years ago, and I greatly value the privilege of entering the beautiful world of academic dispute, a world aesthetically far more satisfying than one of unanimity or forced consensus.

Since both agreement and disagreement of contributions to this volume extend to specific points as well as the general approach of that earlier paper, I visualise two options before me: to take up each point, especially if it is in dispute, and abandon, modify or reiterate it; or else, to keep the discussion to the main theme or themes of all our debates and going into detail only when indispensable for the argument. Without

---

* Apart from the stimulus of the contributions to the special issue of the *Journal of Peasant Studies* on 'Feudalism and Non-European Societies', this article owes much to discussion and argument with successive generations of my students at JNU and to long conversations with Krishna Bhardwaj, S. Bhattacharya, B.D. Chattopadhyay, Suvira Jaiswal, Majid Siddiqi, C.N. Subramaniam and Romila Thapar. The substance of its argument was also presented at a delightfully informal gathering of historians, economists and sociologists at the Nehru Memorial Museum and Library, New Delhi. To all these friends I repeat those simple and therefore beautiful words in gratitude: 'thank you'.

overlooking the fact that the detail and the main theme cannot always be counterposed, I yet choose the latter option, largely because I have not the competence to cover the breathtaking range of issues and evidence that the six contributions have marshalled, and in part because interest in these issues is unlikely to be confined to a small group of specialists familiar with, or eager to pick up every little detail.

I

It had been stated earlier almost as an axiom scarcely capable of generating much controversy that since capitalism was the first world system, feudalism could only be treated as a system that was specific to a region and a period. Anticipating a comparison between the 'universal' aspect of feudalism and the universality of stone age, bronze age etc., the comparability of these utterly dissimilar phenomena itself had been called into question [*Mukhia,* 1981: 273 and n. 2].

I was clearly a little too optimistic about the innocuous nature of the statement, much as Frank Perlin is today, for 'no one seems [to him] to claim for feudalism the status of a world-system' [*Perlin,* 1985: 94]. R.S. Sharma does indeed make such a claim with the argument that certain variations notwithstanding, feudalism in different medieval regions did possess some essentially similar characteristics and that, much like tribalism, stone age and so on with all the internal variations within each, it cannot be denied the status of a world system [*Sharma,* 1985: 19-20].

Arif Dirlik has in turn perceptively argued that universalisation of the concept of feudalism has actually followed in the footsteps of the historical universalisation of capitalism [*Dirlik,* 1985: 198] and that it is the 'essentialist' rather than the structuralist view of feudalism that earns for it the status of a world system; in the process the 'essence' of feudalism becomes so loose as 'to accommodate disparate economic and social structures' [1985: 212-15]. He also makes a distinction between the 'universal' and the 'global' aspects of a phenomenon, though unfortunately he does not elaborate it fully [1985: 198].

Clearly then the argument about the universality of feudalism has followed two different notions of what constitutes a world system and I should like to elaborate my own notion. The classic Marxian formulation that capitalism is the first world system follows the logic that, with the spread of capitalist production and distribution on a world scale, the economies of all the different regions of the world, irrespective of their own stages of development, were integrated under the hegemony of the capitalist mode of production, and this integration was not a contingent but a structural phenomenon that inhered in the specificity of the capitalist mode of production. It is the ever expanding scale of production and distribution resulting from *generalised* commodity production and based on wage labour that give capitalism the necessary dynamism to bring the world under its hegemony. While commodity production and wage labour were either separately or together not unknown to several civilisations since antiquity, *generalised* commodity production through wage labour was characteristic of capitalism alone.[1] Clearly then, pre-capitalist systems, though by no means static, did not possess the internal dynamism that would give them the hegemony we have been speaking of; in this sense they were incapable of becoming world systems.

It then remains to speak of a pre-capitalist system as a world system only by way of noting similarity of some or the other features amongst regional economies; the 'essentialist' approach. Usually similarity is observed in the fact that these were agrarian economics and that surplus, irrespective of its form, was appropriated from the primary producer through non-economic coercion. All this is true enough of all post-slave and pre-capitalist societies. But then for the very same reason focusing on these general features and treating them as the hallmark of feudalism reduces feudalism to a catch-all category; such a category can hardly serve as a rigorous definition capable of distinguishing one medieval society from another. We can speak of any pre-capitalist system as a world system only by reducing both the categories (of the world system and the pre-capitalist system) to considerable flabbiness. Is it not curious that even those of us who insist on rigour and precision in defining capitalism are willing to lower our guards when dealing with post-slave and pre-capitalist systems and deposit all of them under the residual category of feudalism?

R.S. Sharma has buttressed his notion of 'Indian feudalism' by restating the argument of regional variants within the broad framework of feudalism [*Sharma,* 1985: 20-21].[2] If at the starting point this broad framework covers under its umbrella nothing more than general features such as agrarian economy and surplus appropriation through non-economic coercion, it can hardly take into account distinctive, and perhaps critical considerations such as production processes, social organisation of labour and concrete forms of non-economic coercion, for it treats all forms of non-economic coercion as equivalent and interchangeable. And loose as the category of the broad framework of feudalism is, its heuristic utility is further compromised as we qualify it in regional contexts. We thus face the problem of either to dilute the already vague category of feudalism, or to dump under its banner such diverse social and economic structures that even this vague category can encompass only with discomfort. Besides, can we really terminate the category with the notion of regional variants? Logically, sub-regional variants are bound to follow in the footsteps of regional variants of this world system *ad infinitum,* further compromising it at every stretch. What then remains of the concept of feudalism as a social structure capable of illuminating all, or most, of the medieval world's variant regional and sub-regional economies? Indeed, the very search for such a universal pre-capitalist category appears to be anachronistic, for it follows in the aftermath of universalisation of capitalism in both history and historiography [*Mukhia,* 1981: n. 225; *Dirlik,* 1985: 198].

It is not our intention to question the very notion of regional variations in a pre-capitalist society, for surely scarcely any region would be a replica of another ecologically, economically or in terms of social organisation. Variation could be a feature of the chronology of development of regions, or of its pace or even of its direction. But then it is useful to distinguish between the notions of regional variation embedded in the structuralist and the 'essentialist' conceptions of feudalism (an insight we own to Dirlik).

Marxists have usually understood feudalism in terms of politico-juridical specifics of non-economic coercion of surplus-appropriation, the divergence of their views on the universality of feudalism notwithstanding. Thus Anderson [1977: 404], Gottlieb [1984], Sharma [1985: 20] and Perlin [1985: 105, 110] have so defined their approach to feudalism. Valuable as this insight is, it nevertheless creates some further problems, for it implies that:

(a) underneath variations in the politico-juridical specifics lay a uniform production system over time and space;
(b) variations in the forms of non-economic coercion (rent in labour, kind or cash or collection of revenue) notwithstanding, these were equivalent and interchangeable; it thus treats feudalism as a static system;
(c) the historians' attention be focused on the relation of exploitation as the explanatory category for social change even at the expense of the totality of the production system; and
(d) the state (or ruling class) was the prime mover of pre-modern historical change; to the extent that the peasantry showed signs of dynamism this was in response to state action.

I should like to suggest that these problems could perhaps be resolved if we altered our perspective somewhat.

In the paper 'Was There Feudalism in Indian History?' and in a companion paper, 'Maurice Dobb's Explanation of the Decline of Feudalism in Western Europe — A Critique' [*Mukhia*, 1979-80: 154-84] I tried to view things in an alternative perspective without making any explicit statement to the effect. I should now like to elaborate its implications, since each one's perspective after all determines the structure of one's argument.

This alternative perspective focuses on interaction amongst the following three factors:

(a) the ecology of a region;
(b) the given level of technology at a point of time in the region; and
(c) the social organisation of labour utilisation.

The ecology of course is given to us by nature and it differs to a greater or lesser extent from one region to another. The nature of the soil and its suitability for the cultivation of some rather than other crops, the availability and types of sources of water supply, the topography and the duration of the sunshine are the starting points of peasants' labour, although they might to an extent alter the nature of some of these (e.g. soil and water sources) over a pretty long stretch of time. Technology on the other hand is a largely socially conditioned factor and the level of technological development in a society would depend, on the one hand, on the social perception of ecology and on technological expertise (in other words, on knowledge) and, on the other on the forms of labour utilisation in that society. Thus even between regions of similar ecology, the level of technology might vary, given different social conditions; or, for that matter, even within the same region, knowledge and utilisation of techniques would differ from one stratum of society to another.

A more decisive intervention, however, occurs in the organisation of labour utilisation, even though in pre-capitalist societies non-economic coercion would characterise all forms of labour use. To an extent, the form would depend on ecology, technical level of a society and the demand and supply of labour in a region; but above all it would depend on the balance of power in that society, a balance that is not determined by the state or the ruling class alone. Slavery, serfdom or wage labour surely did not come into existence at the will of the ruling class; the silent and at times overt resistance of those who too possessed an enormous reserve of power, through being producers of society's wealth, also determined the form of social organisation of labour; their role would be particularly important in the process of transition from one such form to another. On the other hand, the social organisation of labour utilisation would give us significant clues to the nature of the state presiding over the society.

This perspective I believe, comprises a totality although it would be hard to locate the three factors in a permanent hierarchy for none of them is privileged to determine the others in every circumstance.

In this perspective the economic infrastructures underlying medieval polities, far from exhibiting any degree of uniformity, would bring into high relief their deep-seated variations. Even within the same region changes in production processes over time could be detected with greater certainty and their implications for the other factors could perhaps be established. The succession of different forms of non-economic coercion (rent in labour, cash or kind or straight-forward collection of revenue) would rather suggest considerable changes in production processes, techniques, the demand and supply of labour and not least the influence of the market. To treat all these forms as equivalent and interchangeable, in isolation from the production system, would be tantamount to ignoring all these changes and treating the whole span of feudal economy as much the same from the beginning to the end. It is thus that historical change is better understood in the context of the entire system of production rather than merely as a process of stimulus-response relationship between the state and, in the case of medieval societies, the peasantry. Treating the state as the prime mover of social change attributes far too much of motive force to it. No society functions at the diktat of the ruling class, but rather through a balance between the power exercised at many levels—political, military, juridical and administrative power, the power of leadership of communities and not least the power that peasants (in medieval societies) commanded by virtue of carrying out the production processes. The dynamism for social change thus originates in friction at all the multifarious joints in society, and each social stratum participates in it, however differential its contribution.

Above all, this perspective by insisting on placing the precise form of non-economic coercion in the context of the production system and by distinguishing each form from the others—irrespective of the order of their succession, or even in the case of their coexistence in different regions—is able to focus on the form of peasants' resistance to their exploitation. The peasant who has to render labour rent would resist the lord in the very process of cultivating the demesne through lethargy, stealing of the lord's time, and by being careless. But a peasant who has to pay rent in cash can hardly adopt the same technique of resistance; he will have to haggle with the lord over the payment of money after the crop has been harvested and sold in the market. Or when he pays rent in kind, he takes resort to attempt at concealing part of the produce from the lord's or his agent's eye or bribing the agent.

The case of the revenue-paying peasant of medieval India is even further apart. The revenue was collected from the village as a unit after the crop had been harvested and each peasant had to contribute his share to it according to the size of his holding, though the rate per unit of land was the same for all. This implied that the Indian peasants' resistance took place outside the production process over the quantum of revenue demand and that, of necessity, this resistance had to be collective in nature, involving a major or at least a considerable part of the village society. This would be unlike the early medieval European peasants' resistance in the very process of production which therefore made his resistance more individual in nature, though of course on certain issues, such as the community's rights to pastures, there would be collective pressure.

Thus, whether peasants' resistance takes place in the very process of production or outside it, or whether there is a succession from one form of resistance to another, makes a vital difference to the history of that production system. Therefore when R.S. Sharma asks, 'if parts of the products are placed at the disposal of the grantee, what is the difference between enjoying the means of production, that is land, and the fruits of production?' and adds, 'Land does not mean anything without its products' [*Sharma*, 1985: 30], he is overlooking the critical difference, namely, the form of peasants' resistance which must correspond to the concrete form of non-economic coercion.

It was this totality that the definition of feudalism as 'the structured dependence of the entire peasantry on the lords' had sought to capture; the hiatus between the labour potential of each peasant family and its resources was a condition of feudalism and the 'structured dependence' its distinctive characteristic. The notion of 'the structured dependence' was posited in the context of the production system which in turn was visualised as transitional, though the transition was ascribed to class struggle, at times silent, imperceptible, inherent in the daily toil on the field, and at others in the form of violent outbursts. It is difficult to agree more with Wickham's perception that 'it is over the control of production that the dynamic of class struggle in feudalism is most actute' [*Wickham*, 1985: 186]. It was in contrast with this feature that the medieval Indian peasantry was characterised as a 'free peasantry' whose process of production was free of extraneous control and whose class struggle therefore was of a different order from that of feudal lords and peasants in Europe. We shall return to this below.

The role of ideology in class struggle, irrespective of its form, remains to be examined, though Marxist historians in general have largely ignored this vital question. However, my own neglect of it was not in any way an indication of its secondary importance; nor was it due to any implicit conception that 'the material base' must first be sorted out before attention is turned to the ideological superstructure. It was in fact born of my greatly limited familiarity with the theme.[3] Nor is there much secondary literature on this theme, Marxist or non-Marxist, on which one could draw in the Indian context. References to the role of ideology in early and medieval Indian society or brief discussion of it [*Chattopadhyaya*, 1977: 276-86; 1980-1981: 15-23; and mimeo: 29; *Sharma*, 1985: 36], however tend to treat it as a kind of conspiratorial creation of the ruling class implanting its own ideology on to peasants' (or artisans') mind and thereby impeding the growth of peasants' class consciousness and consequent class struggle. Thus R.S. Sharma observes: 'Classes with conflicting interests were kept together through the performance of *puja, japa, vratas, tirthas, samskaras, prayaschitas*[4] and through prospects of heaven and hell. The all-pervasive influence of astrology (*jyotisa*) and that of the doctrine of Vedanta kept the people reconciled to their lot. All factors brought people of opposite interests together' [*Sharma*, 1985:36].

This is rather a partial vision, for it does not explain why the peasants came to accept an ideology so alien to their interests. It tacitly assumes that since the ruling class has at its disposal considerable intellectual, among other resources, it develops a sophisticated ideology to defend its own interest which it then imparts to the peasantry. Since the peasantry can hardly be expected to command similar intellectual resources, it is in no position to resist the alien ideology. Support for this view could perhaps be drawn from Marx and Engles' observation: the ideas of the ruling class are in every epoch the ruling ideas: i.e. the class which is the ruling material force of society is at the same time its ruling *intellectual* force [*Marx and Engels*, 1972:44, emphasis in original].

I believe it amounts to considerable disrespect to the intelligence of peasants to treat them merely as victims of ruling class conspiracy. This is not to deny the influence of the ruling class ideology on peasants' minds, but to suggest that peasants accept that part of the ruling class ideology which corresponds to their daily experience; they do not accept all of alien ideology. Thus, for example, the medieval Indian peasant was renowned for his fatalistic attitude, an attitude which would reconcile him to considerable adversity. In that measure this mode of rationalisation strongly buttressed the dominance of the ruling class. But the peasant would accept the notion of fatalism only when his crop had failed, for he had no one else to blame for it. Unlike the medieval European peasant whose process of production was under control of the lord and who therefore had a visible target in case of crop failure, the Indian peasant's process of production being free from such extraneous control—a point I shall return to later in this article—he could hardly lay the responsibility for it at the door of any individual or institution; an invisible factor such as fate then came handy as an explanation. But the same peasant refused to blame his fate if the state or its agent demanded more revenue than was customary; he stood up for his rights, sometimes by submitting petitions, at other times by threatening to give up cultivation, at still others by actually migrating to other areas or into the forests and finally by taking up arms. This time his enemy stood before him, and one could hardly trace a sign of the fatalistic attitude in him.

But then the role of ideology can hardly be understood in terms of a one-to-one correspondence with the material interest of one or another class [*Poulantzas*, 1978: 28-46; *Geertz*, 1964;47-75], much as R.S. Sharma and I have sought to do. At any rate the formation of ideology as part of culture is seldom a one-way process, originating at the top and flowing downwards; it usually evolves out of a complex interaction between rituals, beliefs and ideas of all the different strata of society.[5] Frank Perlin's contribution to this volume did set out to examine concretely the role of ideology in late pre-colonial Maharashtra society outside of this one-to-one correspondence [1985: 132-140]. His insight does considerably deepen our understanding of that society, but it is doubtful whether historical explanation merely in terms of the notion of 'brotherhood' among the *vatandars* of Maharashtra is an adequate substitute for the Moreland/Habib/Mukhia orthodoxy.

II

Between 1965 when R.S. Sharma published his *Indian Feudalism* and now ('How Feudal was Indian Feudalism?' in this volume) there has happily been a remarkable change in his notion of what constituted Indian feudalism. In the book Sharma conceived of it almost as a carbon copy of the Pirennean version of the rise and decline of feudal economy in Western Europe, and he made a point-by-point comparison with Europe, employing all the terms, categories and institutions in reference to which the Pirennean School had analysed feudalism in Europe: decline of trade, manor, serfdom, commutation of labour services into cash payment, revival of trade and urban centres, and so on. And if he did not find the Germanic invasions of Europe replicated in India, B.N.S. Yadava, another erudite proponent of the notion of Indian feudalism, drew attention to the Hun invasions of north India at about the same period of time [*Mukhia,* 1981:301, n. 106, for references]. Sharma's article in this volume, on the other hand, marks a search for a genuinely 'Indian' variant of feudalism, though in regard to the application to India of some of the important categories of European feudalism—such as serfdom—he takes somewhat ambivalent positions.[6] Nor has he revised his chronology, so that Indian feudalism in his view originated about the fourth or fifth century AD, as trade and urban centres declined and tapered off by the eleventh or twelfth century when trade and the process of urbanisation once again revived. His argument is still focused on land assigned by the state to grantees. Along with land was assigned 'blanket authority' over peasants, which leads Sharma to conclude that this blanket authority 'may have' included the right to peasants' labour for purposes of agricultural production [1985: 27, 32]. He speaks of a 'social crisis' and 'a crisis in production relations' created by the resistance of 'the lower orders' to performing the functions assigned to them which led to 'changes in the mode of production' whereby peasants were subjected to more arbitrary and greater exploitation in the period of Indian feudalism [1985: 33-4]. Subject to numerous exactions, the Indian peasant was living at the bare level of subsistence by the twelfth century [*Yadava,* 1973: 301].

The early medieval period in India (c. fifth to twelfth century AD) was also the period of considerable technological and economic growth, especially in the sphere of agricultural production.[7] R.S. Sharma has graphically captured some of this progress in his contribution to this volume [1985:36-7], and he observes that: 'This period was undoubtedly an age of larger yield and a great agrarian expansion.' Burton Stein has similarly located impressive expansion of agriculture in early medieval south India [*Stein,* 1980: 68-9]. Technological and agricultural progress is also indicated by the three stage evolution of the water-wheels which drew water from wells [*Mukhia,* 1981:309, n. 214; Habib, in *Raychaudhuri and Habib* (eds.), 1982, I: 49]. Irrigation was (and still is) the chief bottleneck in agricultural expansion in India and the use of well-irrigation, through water-wheels and several other devices, brought this vital element within reach even of small peasants. The construction of wells should have induced both an extension and an intensification of cultivation; the amount of water required for irrigating each crop could also be regulated and overdosing of crops with water thus prevented; this would imply a more organised method of agricultural production. The bricklined wells were particularly capital intensive;[8] this fact itself should lead the cultivator towards the production of high value crops [*Williamson*, 1931: 621]. There was, besides, considerable effort undertaken by the imperial and provincial states to provide irrigation by digging canals and huge lakes [*Kumar*, 1979: 211-14].

Agricultural progress in this period is also indicated by the growing number of new crops and an increasing number of varieties of old crops. There is evidence of the cultivation of rice (in Kathiawad region), wheat, barley, sesamum, peas and cotton in the Harappa culture. The *Rg Veda* refers to five crops: barley, sesamum (of the black and the white-seeded varieties), cucumber, bottlegourd and sugar cane; it makes no reference to wheat, rice or cotton, though the term for barley (*yava*) was possibly used as a generic term for corn and might have included wheat. The later Vedic texts such as the *Atharva Veda* and the *Taittiriya Samhita* do however mention rice; barley and wheat are mentioned in the *Atharva Veda* and beans and sesamum in the *Taittiriya Samhita*. Pearl-millet was perhaps a gift of Africa to India in the PGW phase. The *Arthasastra* mentions 17 kinds of crops of which some 10 were foodgrains, and rice was of two varieties. By the twelfth century AD 24 to 25 kinds of food crops, including vegetables and fruits, were being cultivated. In addition, new varieties of some crops were being produced. A medieval text, the *Sunya Purana*, tells us that more than 50 varieties of rice were being grown in Bengal. If we extend our survey to the end of the sixteenth century, the number of crops had risen to more than 40, though of course there was regional variation in both the number and types of crops. This number was not exceeded even in the 1920s.[9]

All this constitutes an impressive record of progress. However, if the very scale of state effort in encouraging agricultural expansion has ensured its transmission to historical record, the contribution of individual peasants, small and big, has largely, and unreasonably, remained unsung. However humble the individual contribution, the totality of it all would be no less substantial than that of the state's contribution. Of the 528 wells in a group of 18 villages that we have noted above, only 41 or 7.76 per cent were after all brick-lined; the rest were just shafts dug into the soil until the water table was reached. They would serve for a couple of years and then collapse, to be replaced by other such shafts—clearly the work of very small peasants who could not afford the cost of brick-lined wells. Yet, must we scoff at their effort? Or, for that matter, at the effort of the better-off strata of peasants who provided leadership in this agricultural progress by experimenting with water-wheels, tanks and, not least, new and often capital-intensive crops? Down to the early twentieth century, by which time the scale of state intervention in agricultural production had grown much larger, the *Report of the Royal Commission on Agriculture* was appreciative of the great significance of the smaller irrigation works and urged the government to pay more attention to them [1928: 338-9]. The early medieval and medieval Indian peasantry clearly possessed a much grater degree of dynamism than has usually been granted by historians until very recently [*Mukhia*, forthcoming b].

But then how does one square the growing subjection of peasants to the blanket authority of the grantees and their ever increasing exploitation in all conceivable forms in the period of Indian feudalism (for such is the picture that R.S. Sharma has given us) with this record of considerable agricultural progress in which the same down-and-out peasants played such a significant role? One could perhaps ascribe the peasants' effort to the pressure of the grantees. But then in so doing one must also assume peasants' utter helplessness in the face of this pressure—rather a doubtful assumption in view of the power they commanded by virtue of their control over the production process. It is also doubtful if peasants would make all the extra investment of capital and labour merely to meet the increasing demand of revenue or rent with little or no benefit accruing to them, and that not for a year of two but over centuries.

The picture of extensive land grants and the ensuing subjection of peasants' almost unrestrained exploitation by grantees creates some other problems as well. This picture really hinges on the assumption of the king's unreserved right of ownership in land. This assumption, which R.S.Sharma makes [1985: 22], can be sustained only by ignoring an enormous amount of evidence to the contrary.[10] Besides, since the Delhi Sultanate, successor to the era of 'Indian feudalism', bears no evidence of such grants of land, along with the assignment of 'blanket authority' over peasants, are we to hail the Sultanate as the liberator of the oppressed peasants whose obligation was now more or less limited to the payment of specified taxes? This is a scenario that is unlikely to make a strong appeal to Irfan Hibib, among others, for he has argued over the years that the establishment of the Delhi Sultanate in the beginning of the thirteenth century marked a new stage in the history of India by stretching the level of peasants' exploitation to its highest pitch, a feature that was to characterise the history of all the subsequent centuries down to India's independence [*Habib,* 1978: 297-8].

Above all, since in R.S. Sharma's perception Indian feudalism had declined by the eleventh or twelfth century AD with the revival of trade and urban centres, how are we to characterise the six centuries falling between its decline and India's colonisation? Surely not as an era of capitalist development! Sharma of course has always restricted his researches to the terminal date of the twelfth century AD at one end, though at the other he has extended his study to prehistoric civilisation; he might thus claim immunity from having to characterise the post-twelfth century Indian social formation. But then all of us must reckon with the logic of our argument.

One might perhaps get around this problem by extending the period of Indian feudalism to the end of the seventeenth of early eighteenth century, the eve of the beginning of colonisation, and some historians have indeed done so, even though their problematic was different [thus *Kosambi,* 1975: 391-2; and one *D.N. Jha,* 1979: 16].

In a way, the breathtaking simplicity with which a period of five or six centuries is just added on to the life of Indian feudalism is by itself a sad comment on the lack of rigour in the concept of Indian feudalism. But even if one were to concede these centuries, it still remains for us to explain the transition of a society characterised by a highly disintegrated administrative organisation, decline of trade and virtual disappearance of currency, decline of urban centres and the almost unrestrained subjection of peasants to exploitation at will by the land grantees (all in the early medieval period), to a highly centralised administrative system covering a vast empire, with a strong base of commodity production in agriculture and handicrafts and a vibrant currency system, and an almost extravagant number of towns and a peasantry whose primary obligation was to pay a fixed number of taxes, even if these taxes deprived it of the bulk of its surplus produce (characteristics of the late sixteenth and the whole of the seventeenth century),[11] all of it within the framework of Indian feudalism.

It is of course true that European feudalism too was not the same from one end of its duration to the other and the memorable division Marc Bloch had made between the First and the Second Feudal Ages has lost none of its validity, even though a great many parts of the picture he drew of feudal society have been substantially modified. But then it is also true that the processes which have transformed the first into the second feudal age have more or less clearly been identified in the historiography of European feudalism so that it is easy to visualise the changes in the later medieval Europe as the cumulative effect of the tensions which had characterised early medieval society. It is also easy enough to see that all these changes from the fifth to the fifteenth century had occurred within the structure of feudalism, although those very changes subverted the structure in the later Middle Ages.

If the historiography of Indian feudalism could establish such or similar order of linkages which would explain the transition of early medieval Indian society to the society of the seventeenth century, it could command a strong case in its favour. However, as we have seen above, even the story of the transition of (north) India from the eleventh or twelfth to the thirteenth century runs into awkward moment; the long-term transition is an item that has not yet even been placed on the historians' agenda. In such a situation the addition of five or six centuries to Indian feudalism would hardly amount to more than an intellectual sleight of hand.

If the concept of Indian feudalism is riddled with potholes, 'the Indian medieval economy' or the 'medieval Indian system' suggested by Irfan Habib [1978: 298; 1985: 49] also is not without problems. In putting this notion forward Habib has not discussed its characteristics; as such it remains a descriptive, empiricist rather than an analytical category. But it is possible to put together in outline certain of the characteristics of the medieval Indian economy as visualised by Habib over the past two decades. These are as follows.

(a) The predominance of peasant production in the context of a stratified agrarian economy. The peasants, however, were 'no better than semi-serfs' for they 'were not masters of their domicile'. They were therefore to be brought back to their village by officials if they deserted it for whatever reason [*Habib,* 1982: 11, 20, 25; *Raychaudhuri and Habib* (eds.), 1982, I: 54].

(b) Increasing pressure being exerted by the state, ever since the establishment of the Delhi Sultanate, on peasants in that the bulk of peasants' surplus was now collected as revenue increasingly in cash. This was a point of departure in Indian history and continued to be its characteristic feature down to India's independence in 1947.

(c) The growing impoverishment of the peasantry owing to increasing demand of the ruling class for revenue. This in turn inhibited major technological and economic breaks, by denying to possible new technological devices a receptive market and ensuring abundance of artisan labour supply at low cost [*Hibib,* 1963: 317-51; 1971].

In 1963 when Irfan Habib published his *Agrarian System of Mughal India* a major change in historians' perception of medieval Indian rural society was introduced. Until then that society had usually been perceived in terms of an egalitarian structure by virtue of the absence of property in land; Habib on the other hand portrayed a highly stratified society, a picture that has come to stay. His emphasis on the primacy of peasant production was also a valuable contribution to our understanding. Problems, however, arise in considering his notion of semi-serfs. Legal restriction on the free mobility of peasants is a feature first encountered in the *Arthasastra.* But the restriction was motivated entirely by the anxiety of the state to ensure continuity of cultivation and avert the loss of revenue. It was for this reason that the *Arthasastra* did not permit tax-paying peasants to settle 'in a village not inhabited by tax-payers' [*Kautilya's Arthasastra.* 1967: 197]. Indeed, it even advised the state to compel cultivators to grow an additional crop on their fields if its financial needs so required [1967: 273].

Manu, the great law-giver of the second century AD, prescribed the imposition of a fine on a cultivator who did not cultivate his field in good time nor protect the crop against animals [*Mazumdar,* 1960: 171]. But the most graphic evidence of this comes from a document of the second half of the fourteenth century, when the peasants of one village, part of whose revenue had been assigned to a trooper, migrated to another and the trooper insisted on their return on the ground that the claim was not on the 'ownership of their persons' but the right to collect the assigned taxes from them [*Raychaudhuri and Hibib* (eds.), I: 54]. Clearly then as long as taxes were paid, which the peasants must pay whether or not they had cultivated their fields, they could not be subjected to any other restrictions. We shall have to loosen the meaning of serfdom or even semi-serfdom considerably to equate it merely with legal restriction on free mobility of peasants, irrespective of its context.

At any rate, a little caution is in order in treating legal restriction on peasant mobility as evidence for the actual absence of such mobility. Indeed, after characterising peasants as semi-serfs owing to the lack of mastery over their domicile, Irfan Habib observes, 'An interesting feature of agriculture during Mughal times was the mobility of the peasantry' [*Raychaudhuri and Habib* (eds.), 1982, I: 218], and in support cites the oft-quoted statement of Babur, 'In Hindustan hamlets and villages—even towns—are depopulated and set up in a moment!' Habib reasonably explains this as being possible because of the large areas of virgin land available in most regions during the sixteenth and seventeenth centuries. Surely, by that logic even larger areas of virgin land should have been available as we go back in time and therefore the possibility of peasant migration was likely to have been greater in the preceding centuries.

Irfan Habib has pioneered research in the production technology of medieval Indian agriculture, as in several other areas, which has immensely enriched our understanding of India's medieval past. Yet the great significance he attaches to the maximisation of land revenue collection with the establishment of the Delhi Sultanate bears little relationship to the system of agriculture production. If the state's revenue demand under the Sultanate had risen, it could have done so either in a greater or lesser measure of correspondence with a rise in production levels, or as a result of an exercise of sheer will on the part of the ruling class, whether or not peasants obtained their subsistence. If indeed production levels had not registered any marked growth and peasants were compelled to pay much higher amounts in revenue to the Sultans (as Habib strongly implies in treating the establishment of the Delhi Sultanate as a major break in the history of the appropriation of peasants' surplus), surely they must have remained considerably under-exploited in the preceding centuries. And yet the picture of peasantry drawn by R.S. Sharma, B.N.S. Yadava and others, as seen above, is hardly one of a cheerful, prosperous peasantry in those centuries. It was, we are told, making do with a bare margin of subsistence in the twelfth century, just prior to the establishment of the

Sultanate. It is of course, true that the pre-Sultanate states collected the bulk of peasants' surplus under numerous heads and the Sultanate did so under a single head; but is that an important enough difference to demarcate a new stage in the country's history commencing with this change?[12]

The growing state pressure for a rising revenue demand also resulted, in Irfan Habib's view, in a kind of leveling effect over the various strata of peasantry. Habib has rightly pointed out the regressive nature of Mughal land revenue demand which appropriated the surplus at uniform rates irrespective of peasants' individual resources. Indeed, at times this demand was made even more regressive by differential revenue rates in inverse relation to peasants' resources and caste status [*Singh,* 1976: 301-2]. Given a stratified peasantry and regressive taxation, the increasing pressure itself should have promoted relative differentiation. It is therefore not easy to reconcile the notions of stratification and levelling effect except by positing a highly progressive taxation—hardly a viable proposition.

If the peasantry remained highly stratified, that should by itself be a strong argument for the existence of a responsive market for new, even capital-intensive, technological devices if they were otherwise useful. Indeed, as we have noted above, in promoting agricultural progress in particular, individual peasants at all levels played a significant role. However, technological and economic progress can seldom be judged with reference to the last peasant or artisan. The leadership is usually provided by their upper strata and it tends to percolate downwards; and medieval India was not devoid of such strata. If therefore, medieval Indian economy did not undergo a basic transformation and did not move on to the stage of capitalism, it is hardly owing to uniform absence of purchasing power by the Indian peasants. Nor need we hold the abundance of cheap artisan labour responsible for the absence of major labour-saving technological breaks. We have it on the authority of Joseph Needham that several purely labour saving devices were developed in China in the context of labour aundance [*Needham,* 1979: 33-4]. Later in this article we shall try to explain the absence of the basic transformation of medieval Indian society in terms of the nature of social conflict embedded in that society.

Several problems we have discussed originate in the fact that these concepts have as their focus the relationship between the state and the peasantry, in which the state always commands the initiative.[13] This almost amounts to looking at peasants from the foot of the throne, as it were. The historian's sympathy rests quite obviously with the peasants, but their role in historical change is recognised only when eruption of their anger comes to notice in dramatic uprisings in reaction to excesses of the state. In the process, the peasantry's role in silently, almost imperceptibly changing production technology, its role in silently, equally imperceptibly resisting exploitation in the very process of production through daily toil or outside it, in various forms, which really create the setting for violent outbursts—these features of historical change are relegated to secondary significance.

It was this historical change that the notion of 'free peasant economy' in medieval India had sought to capture. Free peasantry is a category open to different interpretations. For Irfan Habib such free peasantry existed only in the era immediately preceding the development of capitalism in Europe [1985: 49]. Long and Richardson [1978], on the other hand, have postulated the existence of free peasantry engaged in subsistence agriculture in several pre-capitalist societies. Wickham in his article in this volume has drawn our attention to the useful category of tied but free peasantry in Ottoman Turkey [1985: 181]. Indian historians have usually understood the freedom of peasants in terms of their legal right to unrestricted mobility, a view which had come in for some questioning, following which the term had been defined with reference to the presence or absence of extraneous control over the peasants' process of production.[14] The free peasant neither rendered his nor his family's labour to anyone in any form for purposes of production, nor employed outside labour; he cultivated his family farm with his own family's labour and resources, within of course the universal constraints of the regional ecology.

There is however the utilisation of the labour of menial castes in the field by the entire community of cultivators irrespective of its own stratification. Their labour was made available by denying them access to land, even in the context of land abundance, through the working of the caste system (Habib, 1963: 121-2; 1982: 14, 18). It is tempting to attribute the growth of this class of 'an ostracised rural proletariat', as I. Habib calls it, to the proliferation of untouchable castes in ancient and early medieval India. It is curious however that growth in the number of untouchable castes in ancient and early medieval India not withstanding—a theme on which Vivekanand Jha has done such impressive research [1975: 14-31]—no contemporary evidence from this period has yet been cited to the effect that the caste system (or the state) denied them the right to hold land.[15] The history of this, one of the most significant developments in India's past, which is also a feature specific to Indian society, is therefore far from clear even in outline. One could perhaps draw some inferences to this end from the available evidence; but surely for studying such a major development, which is unlikely to leave any aspect of society untouched, one must have something more substantial than inferences to depend upon.

In view of the sharp criticism made by R.S. Sharma and Burton Stein of the degree of freedom the medieval Indian peasant enjoyed over his process of production, I realise that the case had probably been overstated, if unintentionally. No freedom in any society is absolute, surely not one that concerns the production system, so critical to the existence of the entire society. Several restraints would influence a peasant's decision to go on cultivating a particular crop or changing over to another: his familiarity with the technique of producing one or another crop, the capital and labour needs of a new crop, the pattern of demand in the neighbouring market, the availability of the requisite amount of water and so forth, and it is always worth while keeping these in mind while speaking of peasants' freedom. But then several, if not all, of these would restrain agricultural production in all societies at the hands of all strata of agriculturists, even if differentially. The fact that the Indian peasant today continually faces the uncertainty of power or diesel supply to run his tubewell should hardly lead us to describe him as an unfree peasant. The question of freedom or unfreedom of a particular class or stratum of society must surely be distinguished from universal restraints.

In this qualified sense production at the hands of the 'free peasant' that we have been speaking of or 'the independent producer' as Irfan Habib calls him, came to be consolidated by the seventh century AD, accordingly to R.S. Sharma's testimony.[16] Clearly this could only be the culmination of a long-drawn out process with considerably regional variation; indeed, through the whole of the early medieval and medieval periods the system of agricultural production based on free peasant labour was confined at best to north India. South India, especially its most fertile region, the Kaveri delta, retained a distinct form of agricultural production and labour organisation, a form that was subverted only in the twentieth century, as Burton Stein has shown in his article for this volume [1985: 73,75-6, 85]. It might of course be added that along with communal control over land expressed in the periodic redistribution of fields there had also emerged individual land ownership in the region [*Karashima*, 1984: 16-17].

Uma Chakravarti has, in an excellent article [forthcoming], graphically traced the changes in the forms of labour used for agricultural production in ancient India. The early Buddhist literature introduces us to differentiated agrarian society where individual land holdings had become quite familiar. In the Buddhist texts we also come across large farms at times requiring 500 ploughs for tilling, for which the labour of *dasas*, *kammakaras* and *porisas* (usually translated as slaves, labourers and servants) was employed. Understandably, these texts also record the first appearance of the word *dalidda* (extremely poor people). Large state farms are also mentioned in the *Arthasastra* and these were worked by 'slaves, labourers and prisoners' [*Kautilya's Arthasastra*, 1967: 129]. At the same time the *Arthasastra* sought to regulate the relationship between master and slave [*Chakravarti*, forthcoming: 31-2]; masters were clearly encountering considerable resistance from slaves, enough to require state intervention. From the Mauryan period onwards, debt bondage, wage-labour, and share-cropping appear to have grown in importance [*Chakravarti,* forthcoming: 38-9]. In the Gupta and post-Gupta periods our evidence does not speak of large farms, either state owned or private; on the other hand the *sudras* were being transformed into petty peasants, a process completed by the first half of the seventh century AD, as we have seen above.

The consolidation of petty peasant production, however, occurred in the context of *a growing complexity of social stratification,* and this becomes increasingly evident from the inscriptions of this period. To a degree, the grants in revenue and land made by the state created the strong class of intermediaries who gradually acquired hereditary titles to them—the class which was itself highly stratified and which was to be known by the generic term of 'zamindars' from the thirteenth century onwards. On the other hand stratification would proceed at the other end too, with the upper strata of the class of landowners interposing themselves between the state and the rest of the peasantry, a process described by D.D. Kosambi as 'feudalism from below' [1975: 295-6]. In incorporating them into the class of intermediaries the state would perhaps give merely formal sanction to a *fait accompli.* This was particularly true of tribal chiefs whose tribes would merge with organised agrarian society through either the use of force or by more peaceful 'persuasion' [*Sharma,* 1969: 16]. In a number of cases spread over different regions of early medieval India the growing pace of stratification led to the establishment of new ruling lineages arising from the agrarian base.[17]

In speaking of the consolidation of petty peasant production, therefore, we can hardly view it as a substitution for stratified agrarian society. The emphasis on petty peasantry is an emphasis on the significant element of change which, starting earlier, had become crystallised by the seventh century AD.

This scenario seems to provide the social context in which the agricultural progress of early medieval centuries becomes intelligible. The absence of extraneous control over the peasants' process of production at all levels of stratified rural society (with all the qualifications that have been suggested) led them to participate in the 'great agrarian expansion' that R.S. Sharma speaks of. However, starting with unequal resources, different strata of agriculturalists would benefit differentially from the expansion, so that the very process of agricultural progress would further promote stratification and generate new forms of rural tensions. In a regional study, though of much later period, the whole spectrum of such tensions has been brought alive and it has been shown that disputes were not only economic in nature [Bajekal, 1980]; quite possibly the nature of tensions would vary over time and space but, equally possibly, with growing stratification and widespread agricultural progress, tensions would arise at a number of joints in that society.

Yet if I highlight the freedom of peasants' control over their process of production as the chief element of change that had occurred by the seventh century which was to characterise the social history of most parts of India down to the colonial era, it is to bring into relief the specific form of exploitation. In my earlier article it had been suggested that medieval Indian economy was characterised by high fertility of land, low subsistence needs of the peasants (and consequent high level of exploitation of peasantry yielding a very large amount of surplus to the ruling class), and peasants' freedom of control over their process of production. It was on the basis of this last feature that the medieval Indian peasant had been defined as a free peasant. R.S. Sharma's argument that the early medieval peasants' process of production, among other things, was subjected to the control of the grantees is merely an inference derived from his picture of the general subjection of peasantry to the authority of the grantees (which 'might even enable the beneficiary to force the peasant to work in his field' or the grantees 'may develop a natural tendency to control the process itself on which the nature and amount of yield depend') [*Sharma*, 1985: 27]. Surely the very absence of definitive evidence to substantiate such a vital feature of our social history should justify some doubt about the viability of this argument.

The free peasant system of production decisively laid down the chief form of exploitation: from now on, peasants were to part with their surplus produce in payment of revenue to the state, in kind or cash. With the relation of exploitation firmly based on the appropriation of revenue, conflicts between peasants and the state arose on the question of revenue so appropriated. It is significant that most evidence of peasant protest in any form from the early medieval period onwards relates to the amount of revenue demand.

Burton Stein has made an extremely important and valid criticism of an element that the description 'free peasant economy' seems to ignore. Having posited a crucial binary relation of exploitation between the revenue-paying free peasant and the revenue-appropriating state ('the chief instrument of exploitation'), it remains for us to characterise the nature of the state as well. Besides, Stein rightly asks, can one really speak of the state of India over all its different regions and long stretches of time in the singular? This really is a profound problem; it is also perhaps least researched in Indian historiography. If therefore what follows is rather elementary, to an extent it is due to the hitherto general neglect of the problem by historians.

In a sense in defining free peasant economy as one in which the peasant paid revenue to the state but did not have to contend with extraneous control over his process of production, a definition of the state was also implied. The state exercised non-economic coercion to collect revenue from peasants and distributed it among different strata of the ruling class, according to *a hierarchy of their rights in the produce of land.* The state's occasional grant of loans to peasants and digging of some canals notwithstanding, it remained by and large uninvolved with the processes of production. Its coercive power was therefore never rooted in production system.

This, along with maintenance of law and order, seems to be the basic characteristic of the state's relationship with the peasant for nearly a thousand years preceding India's colonisation. Given this characteristic there was considerable variation in the extent of territorial or administrative control of the succession of imperial and regional states in India over this period, the complexion and composition of the higher echelons of the ruling class, the degree of cohesion or conflict amongst the ruling strata, and so forth. Besides, even a grand state of imperial dimensions was able to establish its overarching presence in the regions only with considerable degree of variation, often compromising with and incorporating in its interstices regional and local customs and institutions. Thus an imperial state system such as the Mughal system would not be exactly the same in one region as in another. With all these qualifications, however, the early medieval and medieval Indian state existed primarily to collect revenue for maintaining a ruling class which remained alien to the actual process of production.

Clearly this is a description of the functions rather than a characterisation of the nature of the medieval Indian state. The notion of the tribute-gathering state is also a mere description with the added disadvantage that the tributary mode of production,[18] in which it operates, covers not one but several systems of production over different regions and periods. On the other hand Burton Stein's characterisation of the medieval state in south India as the 'peasant state' is original enough to have led to considerable discussion in India. Yet, in depositing all the different strata of landowners in the homogeneous category of peasant as far as their control over state power is concerned, and in sidestepping the problem of the nature of state's coercive power with reference to surplus appropriation, Stein's conception of the state itself becomes severely handicapped.

We are thus back to the problem of characterising the Indian state (or states) in our period. I should confess that describing the state comes easier than giving a name to it, and we all might perhaps begin our search for a name by trying to explicate what we understand by the state in early medieval and medieval India. The search is going to be long indeed.

The notion of the free peasant system of production where the state appropriates revenue allows us to visualise a continuum from early medieval India into the early colonial era; it also allows us to study the nature of changes taking place within the continuum. The free peasant production ensured a degree of gradual, steady development of the production forces. Impressive as this development was, we could hardly speak of it at any stage in this period as a fundamental transformation of the production system. Its pace was evened out by the long time span so that we would be hard put to point to a cluster of changes in a relatively brief period that would lead the economy and society to a new stage, comparable to stages of development in European history.[19]

The explanation for this perhaps lies primarily in the nature of social conflict characteristic of that system of production. The medieval Indian peasant was, to be sure, heavily exploited. Indeed, it is possible to argue that, given the high fertility of the Indian soils and low subsistence level which nature in most parts of the Indian subcontinent permitted, the state collected from the peasants much greater amount of surplus than the feudal lords were able to do from their peasants in Europe. Yet once exploitation of the peasantry had come to be pivoted on revenue collection, conflict between peasants and the state came to the fore only after the production process had been completed, for the conflict related to the quantum of revenue demand. In other words the nature of social conflict remained extraneous to the production system. In early medieval western Europe social conflict inhered in the very process of production, in which all the different strata of rural society had a degree of involvement; consequently, a resolution of it was possible only in the transformation of the production system and redistribution of the means of production, giving rise to new classes. In medieval India on the other hand social conflict was limited to the distribution and redistribution of the surplus; the means of production did not get redistributed. Even a grave political crisis, such as the collapse of the mighty Mughal Empire in the early eighteenth century, was neither the effect nor the cause of social upheavals rooted in the redistribution of the means of production or the emergence of new property forms.[20] Social tensions arising from upheavals in the class of zamindars (subordinate revenue appropriators) as often corroded the strength of the Mughal empire as peasant uprisings did and these upheavals frequently occurred in the relatively prosperous regions of the Empire. The model of peasant rebellions led by the zamindars against the Mughal state's ever rising level of exploitation which Irfan Habib had posited in 1963, when tested against village level evidence in a small region of north India, did not yield positive results. Except for the alliance between the Jat zamindars and Jat peasants, where caste clearly cemented their bond, in other sub-regions either such a bond was absent or else zamindars and peasants were at loggerheads with each other even when both of them were rebelling against the state.[21] At any rate, what did emerge from the debris of the Empire was the resurgent class of zamindars everywhere, a class that was older than the Mughal empire and the Delhi Sultanate.

It is therefore arguable that, given these features of the system of agricultural production and of the nature of social conflict, medieval Indian society, far from being static or stagnant, was yet unlikely to have undergone a transformation whether or not colonialism had intervened.[22]

NOTES

1. 'Generalised commodity production where labour is a commodity' is merely the abstraction of the capitalist mode of production. Prior to arriving at the point of abstraction a society might pass through various combinations of production and market relations so that commodity production could be combined with slavery, bonded labour, sharecropping etc. It is of course useful to distinguish between 'purely' capitalist relations of wage labour and generalised commodity production and combination of pre-capitalist production relations with generalised commodity production. It is equally useful to keep in mind the direction of the drift of these combinations. If the drift is towards the abstraction of capitalism, one could perhaps speak of a decisive tendency towards the development of capitalism even prior to its reaching the point of abstraction.
2. Sharma gets the impression from n. 225 of 'Was There Feudalism in Indian History?' that I had supported the notion of regional

variants of feudalism. I regret having given him this impression, for I had in that longish note actually questioned even the methodology of positing regional variants of feudalism outside Europe.

3. I made an attempt to understand the nature of popular ideology in medieval Hindi literature in Mukhia [1978]. Its success was rather moderate and at any rate I was unable to pursue it further.
4. Respectively: worship, repeated uttering of a sacred name or verse, fasts or domestic rituals, pilgrimages, rituals connected with life-cycle and penances.
5. Duby [1968: 3-10], in the west European context, and Chattopadhaya [1983: 8] for India. Indeed, the Hindu religious systems incorporate a large number of tribal gods, goddesses and rituals.
6. Thus, on p. 24 in this volume Sharma treats the early medieval Indian peasant as almost a serf; on p. 30, the peasant is no longer treated as a serf; but on p. 32 serfdom is described as an important feature of early medieval society in India.
7. Curiously, the editors of *The Cambridge Economic History of India* [*Raychaudhuri and Habib*, 1982, I: xiii] insist on characterising the period as a 'long period of economic decline' even in the face of considerable research supporting agricultural progress.
8. As late as the second half of the seventeenth century only 41 and out of 528 wells in 18 villages of a *pargana* (revenue and administrative unit) in eastern Rajasthan were brick-lined. Information kindly given by my collegue Dr. Dilbagh Singh.
9. For evidence see Mukhia [forthcoming a].
10. Some of the evidence has been cited in Mukhia [1981: 209, 307, n. 189]; a far more impressive amount of evidence has been collected by Lallanji Gopal in his 'Ownership of Agricultural Land' [1980: 42-89]. An important source giving rise to the controversy is the refusal of most historians of ancient India to distinguish between a land and a revenue grant and treating all as land grants along with which all the king's sovereign rights over peasants were alienated. L. Gopal has made the distinction and has therefore reached an altogether different set of conclusions. It is of course essential to make the distinction in order to delneate the form of peasant resistance.
11. For the summary discussion of these characterics, see Raychaudhuri and Habib (eds.) [1982, I]. See also the review of this book in *The Indian Economic and Social History Review*, vol. XXI, no. 1 (1984. pp. 111-27).

12. Irfan Habib does indeed seem to think so in Habib [1982; 27, n. 187.]
13. R.S. Sharma indeed makes explicit in his article for this volume what had earlier been merely implicit in his argument, namely that the state could call into existence a social structure. In support he mentions the examples of the Norman Conquest of England which had led to the imposing of feudalism from above, and colonial conquest in India [1985: 20, 33]. Irfan Habib similarly refers to the 'influence' of the Barbarian invasions of Europe and the Norman Conquest of England on the development of feudalism for drawing a parallel with the Turkish conquest of India and the consequent inauguration of a 'separate formation' [1985: 51].

    The old view that English feudalism was the creation of the Norman state had been upheld by Marc Bloch in *Feudal Society* [1964: 187-9, 244, 248] and Guy Fourquin in *Lordship and Feudalism in the Middle Ages* [1976:76], though Fourquin's concern was with the lord-vassal relationship. This view has however been subjected to questioning lately and it has been argued that feudal land tenures as also feudal institutions and military obligations had preceded the Conquest of England and continued thereafter. See for a critical assessment of this literature, J.O. Prestwich [1963: 39-57]. Barbarian invasions and the evolution of feudal system in western Europe were similarly preceded by the growing disintegration of the society in antiquity and the beginning of its transition to feudal society, a theme discussed so well by Perry Anderson in *Passages from Antiquity to Feudalism* [1974: 15-172]. The view that colonial society in India was the creation of the colonial state is also being slowly questioned; see S.Bhattacharya [1979: 103 and 1984].

    The point, however, is not to deny the *influence* of the state on social developments but to express doubt whether such influence can be equated with the state's *creation* of a social formation. The evolution and maturation of a social formation is after all a very complex phenomenon in which almost every conceivable element would play its part, however differentially; to attribute it entirely to the will of the state might perhaps amount to an unjust degree of simplification.
14. Mukhia [1981: 274-5, 290-91]. Irfan Habib also suggests that the medieval Indian peasant 'was an independent producer' in 'Forms of Class Struggle in Mughal India' [1980: 3].
15. Since my familiarity with ancient Indian History is based on

secondary sources, I requested three of my colleagues, B.D. Chattopadhyaya, Suvira Jaiswal and Romila Thapar, each a distinguished historian of ancient India, to help me out with primary evidence on this point; each has reported failure.

16. Sharma, in *Indian Feudalism* [1965: 61-3]. The second edition of this book is a marginally revised version of the first.
17. Thus the Gurjara-Pratihara lineage arising in Rajasthan and extending at one stage to Bengal [*Chattopadhyaya*, 1983: 14]; in south India the Vellalas, primarily peasants, had given rise to warriors from amongst their ranks [Stein, 1980: 187-8]; the Chandellas too are said to have belonged to Gond or Bhar tribes and risen to become a substantial ruling lineage in Central India [*Thapar*, forthcoming: 12-13]; the Reddys of Andhra were a low caste landowning community who rose to form the ruling stratum [*Jaiswal*, 1979-80: 35].
18. Currie [1980]. Ms. Currie was kind enough to send me a copy of her paper.
19. It has been suggested by Suvira Jaiswal that such an argument might amount to treating European developments as 'exceptional and unique' which in turn would be a Eurocentric vision of history [*Jaiswal*, 1979-1980: 19 n.3]. I believe the 'rule' for Marxists is that all societies change and progress through social contradictions to which no society would be an exception, and neither Europe nor India was such an exception, certainly not the one in my vision. However, this 'rule' does not extend to a uniform pattern of development laid down by Europe even prior to the rise of capitalism: in the pre-capitalist world there was no 'rule' and no 'exception' as far as the patterns or stages of development were concerned in that different societies followed different paths into the world of capitalism/colonialism.
20. In a refreshing and original article, 'The Middle Classes and the Mughal Empire', Iqtidar Alam Khan has indeed argued for the existence of the 'middle classes' (or 'the middle stratum') in medieval India [1975: 113-41]. However the 'middle classes' he has described were, despite some tensions, perfectly compatible with the agrarian economy of which they were a part; there was little possibility of their being 'the harbingers of a truly industrial bourgeoisie.'
21. See for a more elaborate argument and evidence Rana [1981: 287-326].
22. This was basically also the argument of my earlier article [*Mukhia*, 1981: especially 292-3], where an attempt was made

to define the nature of social tensions in medieval India rather than to deny their existence or their intensity. Somehow Irfan Habib in his paper for this volume has seen in that argument an 'idyllic picture of pre-colonial India' for which he finds little justification in historical evidence and directs us to his own variant reading of the evidence set out in his *Agrarian System.* His own conclusion is that '... there were just as intense contradictions as anywhere else; but that these were different in nature and consequences from the contradictions leading to capitalism in Europe' [1985: 49]. One is left wondering, then, doesn't his own conclusion come perilously close to the one he has sought to dismiss by nothing more, as it were, than a wave of his hand?

REFERENCES

Anderson Perry, 1974, *Passages from Antiquity to Feudalism,* London.

Anderson, Perry, 1977, *Lineages of the Absolutist State,* London.

Bajekal, Madhavi, 1980, 'Rural Disputes in Eastern Rajasthan in the Eighteenth Century,' M.Phil. dissertation, Jawaharlal Nehru University.

Bhattacharya, S., 1979, 'Notes on the Role of the Intelligentsia in Colonial Society: India from Mid-Nineteenth Century,' *Studies in History,* vol. 1, no.1.

Bhattacharya, S., 1984, 'S.G. Deuskar Lecture', Centre for Studies in Social Sciences, Calcutta.

Bloch Marc, 1964, *Feudal Society,* Chicago.

Chakravarti, Uma, forthcoming, 'Slavery and Bondage in Ancient India.'

Chattopadhyaya, B.D., 1983, 'Political Processes and Structure of Polity in Early India: Problems of Perspective', Presidential Address, Ancient India Section, Indian History Congress, 44th Session.

Chattopadhyaya, Debiprasad, 1977, *Science and Society in Ancient India,* Calcutta.

Chattopadhyaya, Debiprasad, 1977, 'Science, Philosophy and Society in Ancient India', *The Indian Historical Review,* vol. VII, nos. 1-2 (July-Jan).

Chattopadhyaya, Debiprasad, mimeo, 'Technology and Society in Ancient India.'

Currie, Kate, 1980, 'Problematic Modes and the Mughal Social Formation', *The Insurgent Sociologist,* vol. IX, no.4.

Dirlik, Arif, 1985, 'The Universalisation of a Concept From 'feudalism' to 'Feudalism' in Chinese Marxist Historiography', *The Journal of Peasant Studies,* vol. 12, nos.2 and 3 (Jan./April).

Duby, Georges, 1968, 'The Diffusion of Cultural Patterns in Feudal Society', *Past and Present,* no. 39 (April).

Fourquin, Guy, 1976, *Lordship and Feudalism in the Middle Ages,* London.

Geertz, Clifford, 1964, 'Ideology as a Cultural System,' in *Ideology of Discontent* (ed. D. Apter), New York.

Gopal, Lallanji, 1980, 'Ownership of Agricultural Land', *Aspects of the History of Agriculture in Ancient India,* Varanasi.

Gottlieb, Roger, S., 1984, 'Feudalism and Historical Materialism: A Critique and a Synthesis' *Science and Society,* vol. XLVIII, no. 1, pp. 1-37.

Habib, Irfan, 1963, *The Agrarian Systems Mughal India,* Bombay.

Habib, Irfan, 1971, 'Potentialities of Capitalistic Development in the Economy of Mughal India,' *Enquiry,* New Series, vol. III, no. 3 (Winter).

Habib, Irfan, 1978, 'Economic History of the Delhi Sultanate—An Essay in Interpretation,' *The Indian Historical Review,* vol. IV, no. 2 (January).

Habib, Irfan, 1980, 'Forms of Class Struggle in Mughal India' (mimeo), paper presented to the Indian History Congress, 41st Session.

Habib, Irfan, 1985, 'Classifying Pre-Colonial India,' *The Journal of Peasant Studies,* vol.12, nos.2 and 3 (Jan./April).

Jaiswal, Suvira, 1979-1980, 'Studies in Early Indian Social History: Trends and Possibilities', *The Indian Historical Review,* vol. VI, nos. 1-2 (July/Jan.).

Jha, D.N., 1979, 'Early Indian Feudalism: A Historigraphical Critique', Presidential Address, Ancient India Section, Indian History Congress, 40th Session.

Jha, Vivekanand, 1975, 'Stages in the History of Untouchables', *The Indian History Review,* vol. II, no.1 (July).

Karashima, N., 1984, *South Indian History and Society: Studies from Inscriptions A.D. 850-1800,* New Delhi.

Kautilya's Arthasastra, 1967, (trans. R. Shamasastry).

Khan, Iqtidar Alam, 1975, 'Presidential Address', Medieval India Section, *Proceedings of Indian History Congress,* 36th Session.

Kosambi, D.D., 1975, *An Introduction to the Study of Indian History,* Bombay.

Kumar, Nand Kishore, 1979, 'Hydraulic Agriculture in Penisular India (c.300 B.C. to 1300 A.D.)', *Proceedings of the Indian History Congress,* 40th Session.

Long and Richardson, 1987, 'Informal Sector, Petty Commodity Production and the Social Relations of Small Scale Enterprise' in *The New Economic Anthropology* (ed. John Clammer), New York.

Marx, Karl, and Friedrich Engels, 1972, *On Historical Materialism*, Moscow.

Mazumdar, B.P., 1960, *Socio-Economic History of Northern India (1030-1194 A.D.)*, Calcutta.

Mukhia, Harbans, 1978, 'The Ideology of the Bhakti Movement—The Case of Dabu Dayal', in *History and Society: Essays in Honour of Professor Nihar Ranjan Ray* (ed. D.P. Chattopadhyaya), Calcutta, pp. 445-54.

Mukhia, Harbans, 1979-1980, 'Maurice Dobb's Explanation of the Decline of Feudalism in Western Europe — A Critique', *The Indian Historical Review*, vol. VI, nos. 1-2 (July-Jan).

Mukhia, Harbans, 1981, 'Was There Feudalism in Indian History?', *The Journal of Peasant Studies*, vol. 8, no.3 (April).

Mukhia, Harbans, forthcoming a 'Agricultural Technology in Medieval North India', paper submitted to the Seminar on Technology in Medieval India, Birla Industrial and Technological Museum, Calcutta (to be published in Proceedings of the Seminar).

Mukhia, Harbans, forthcoming b. 'Marx on Pre-Colonial India: An Evaluation', presented at the Karl Marx Centennial International Seminar, University of Burdwan (to be published in Proceedings of the Seminar).

Needham, Joseph, 1979, *The Great Titration: Science and Society in East and West*, London.

Perlin, Frank, 1985, 'Concepts of Order and Comparison with a Diversion on Counter Ideologies and Corporate Institutions in late Pre-Colonial India.' *The Journal of Peasant Studies*, vol. 12, nos. 2 and 3 (Jan/April).

Poulantzas, Nicos, 1978, *State, Power, Socialism* (trans, Patrick Camiller), London.

Prestwich, J.O., 1963, 'Anglo-Norman Feudalism and the Problem of Continuity', *Past and Present*, no. 26 (November).

Rana, R.P. 1981, 'Agrarian Revolts in Northern India during the late 17th and early 18th century', *The Indian Economic and Social History Review*, vol. XVIII, nos. 3-4.

Raychaudhuri, Tapan and Irfan Habib (eds.), 1982, *The Cambridge Economic History of India*, vol. I, Cambridge.

Report of the Royal Commission on Agriculture, 1928, London.

Sharma, R.S., 1965, *Indian Feudalism,* Calcutta.

Sharma, R.S., 1985, 'How Feudal was Indian Feudalism?' *The Journal of Peasant Studies,* vol. 12, nos. 2 and 3 (Jan/April).

Singh, Dilbagh, 1976, 'Caste and Structure of Village Society in Eastern Rajasthan during the Eighteenth Century,' *The Indian Historical Review,* vol. II, no.2 (January).

Stein, Burton, 1980, *Peasant State and Society in Early Medieval South India,* New Delhi.

Stein Burton, 1985, 'Politics, Peasants and the Deconstruction of Feudalism in India,' *The Journal of Peasant Studies,* vol. 12, nos. 2 and 3 (Jan/April).

Thapar, Romila, forthcoming, 'Legitimation by Descent: The Kshatriya Varna in Northern India,' typescript, to be published in *Annales.*

Wickham, C.J., 1985, 'The Uniqueness of the East,' *The Journal of Peasant Studies,* vol. 12, nos. 2 and 3 (Jan/April).

Willamson, A.V., 1931, 'Indigenous Irrigation Works in Peninsular India', *The Gegoraphical Review,* New York, vol. XXI, no.4 (October).

Yadava, B.N.S., 1973, *Society and Culture in Northern India in the Twelfth Century,* Allahabad.

11

Illegal Extortions from Peasants, Artisans and Menials in Eighteenth Century Eastern Rajasthan*

In the context of increasing attention being paid by historians to problems of medieval Indian rural society, an attempt has been made in this paper to examine the illegal extortions made from the peasants, village menials and artisans by the dominant groups with whom they come into immediate contact, viz., the jagirdars, the zamindars, the *ijaradars* (revenue farmers) and state officials like the *amils*, the *faujdars*, etc. The term 'illegal' denotes such extortions as were made in contravention of the custom accepted by the victim as well as by the state; and 'extortions' might be in the form of forced labour (*begar*), carrying away of peasants' bullocks in lieu of

---

* I am extremely grateful to my colleague Dr. Dilbagh Singh for introducing me to the documents on which this paper is based and for generously helping me with many suggestions as well as sharp criticisms. I have also drawn considerably on his unpublished doctoral dissertation, 'Local and Land Revenue Administration of the State of Jaipur (c. 1750-1800)', submitted to the Jawaharlal University in 1975. I have had the benefit of discussing an earlier version with my colleagues at a faculty seminar and with Amit Bhaduri separately; their criticisms have been of great help.

I am deeply obliged to the Director and the staff of the Rajasthan State Archives, Bikaner, for extending the maximum cooperation for my work.

labour or taking away the goods manufactured by the artisans without payment and in various other forms. Incidentally, light is also thrown on the 'legal' form of forced labour and other obligations owed by the lower sections of village society to the dominant groups.

The evidence on which this paper is based is in the form of copies of *chithis* (letters) preserved in the Jaipur Records section, *Daftar Diwan Huzuri,* Rajasthan State Archives, Bikaner. The *chithis* were written by the *Diwan* of the Jaipur state to its officials, particularly the *amils;* each *chithi* contains the substance of a complaint received by the *Diwan* and his instructions thereon.

We were able to trace 48 *chithis* pertaining to extortions after a fairly intensive search. Our evidence, therefore, does not constitute a selected sample; this is all the evidence we could lay our hands upon for our region and period.

This paper has been divided into two sections. In Section I the evidence has been arranged and presented without much comment. However, notice has been taken of the widening scope and increasing intensity of illegal extortions from peasants, artisans and menials from about the middle of the eighteenth century. In Section II an attempt has been made to explain the causes of this intensification in terms of changes in the agrarian economy as well as the devolution of administrative authority from the state's capital to the *parganas.*

I

While the phenomenon of extortions, legal as well as illegal, was widespread within the region, its exact forms had considerable sub-regional variations. Our documents clearly indicate that extortions considered customary in one *pargana* faced resistance for being illegal in another.[1] Incidentally, this fact limits the utility of single documents to a certain degree, for each document reflects at best the conditions in the *pargana* from which it had originated and therefore no wider generalization regarding the prevalence of specific forms of extortions can be based on individual *chithis.*

Some degree of forced labour, or *begar*, and some other extortions were sanctioned by custom and recognized by the state (of Jaipur) in the territories directly or indirectly under its control as well as by those subjected to such extortions. Custom subjected the village menials, socially and economically the most depressed section in the village,[2] to the largest burden of extortions particularly in the form of *begar*. Whereas the artisans were usually exempt from any form of extortion[3] and the cultivators were subject to rendering a few specified services like providing milk and curds to the jagirdar at the time of harvest or for entertaining his guests,[4] or inviting the zamindar and his family to a feast on the occasion of a wedding in a peasant household[5] or paying him a cess for permission for such a marriage[6] or providing cots and beds for his guests on the occasion of a wedding in his family[7] or in some areas rendering *begar* to the jagirdar at sowing and harvest time,[8] the menials were required to render it to all dominant sections of the village society gratis. Their readiness to flee their villages on a number of occasions owing to excessive *begar* also suggests its high incidence.[9]

The extortions could be divided into two categories: those used for the purposes of (agricultural) production; and other non-production forms.

Under the first category, the cultivators (indifferently called *raiyati* or *paltis* in our documents)[10] were required to render *begar* to the jagirdar in some areas,[11] though in other areas the imposition of any kind of *begar* on cultivators was disallowed by custom and therefore by the state.[12] The zamindar was entitled to *kotri ki begar* though not everywhere, as noted earlier. It is possible that in cases where the cultivators did render *begar*, both the jagirdar and the zamindar were entitled to it. There is a large number of complaints from the village menials being harassed with demands of *begar* by the jagirdar, the zamindar, the *amil* and the *faujdar*, etc., beyond the customary limit.[13] Possibly part of the customary *begar* rendered by them might have been in the form of agricultural labour on the zamindar's and perhaps the others' lands and another part in some other forms like carting.

We have earlier noted the non-productive forms of extortions like the provision of milk and curds, cots and beddings, etc. The village menials were *inter alia* required to carry the jagirdar's and possibly the others' belongings up to a distance 5 *kos* (about 10 miles) from the village.[14]

Besides, almost anybody could be compelled by the *amils* to purchase agricultural products collected by them as revenue in kind.[15] Refusal to buy these could result in the imposition of a tax or a cess. Another minor form of extortion was forcing the barbers of the village to supply *pattal* (a kind of plate made by joining together large leaves on which food is served), *datun* (twigs to serve as tooth-brush) and earthen lamps to the *amil* and other officials.[16]

The eighteenth century witnessed an attempt by the officials as well as other dominant sections in the village to extend the scope and intensity of extortions. Whether such an attempt is exclusive to that century or is a continuation of earlier efforts, it is difficult to state categorically. However, the number of complaints begins to grow considerably from the 1730s and particularly rapidly from around the middle of the century as the following table would show:

Period	*Number of Complaints*
1700-10	Nil
1711-20	1
1721-30	2
1731-40	6
1741-50	17
1751-60	6
1761-70	16

Note: Our documents do not go beyond 1770.

The peasants and village menials increasingly complain of transgression of the customary limits by almost all dominant sections in almost all forms of extortions. Apart from excessive *begar*, they complain of other undefined forms referred to as 'different kinds of harassment' (*tarah tarah ki khechal*). Thus, the zamindar in the village Niworo, *pargana* Chatsu was forcing the peasants to render *begar* in 1753, even though the village custom did not entitle him to it.[17] The peasants of village Khurnala, *pargana*, Mauzabad, complained in 1754 that whereas custom required them to provide cots and beddings for the zamindar's guests or on the occasion of wedding in his family, he was forcing them to render *begar* and was carrying away their bullocks in lieu of it presumably for cultivating his own land.[18] The same zamindar was also trying to extort *kotri ki begar* from the village to which he was not entitled.[19] A complaint against the extortion of begar from the cultivators by the zamindar in village Kheri Ram ki, *pargana* Mauzabad, is recorded in 1770.[20] Apparently, the zamindar was committing serious enough violation of the custom to be ordered to give an undertaking that he would not resort to it in the future. In another instance the local zamindar also began to harass the peasants in an indirect way: by extorting *begar* from the menials who where supposed to serve only the peasants.[21] His own customary entitlement to the menials' *begar* extended only to the area settled by him. His attempt to stretch this right had resulted in the flight of the menials from the village and the complaint by the *patel*, the *raiyat* and the *mahajan* was followed by orders to the *amil* to reassure the menials and bring them back.

The jagirdar on his part was also trying to extend his right to customary extortions in various petty ways. Apart from his attempt to extort *begar* from groups like the peasants and even *mahajans*, to which he was clearly not entitled,[22] he tried to force the village menials to render *begar* to him round the year, though he was entitled to it only for specific jobs on specific occasions.[23] He also tried to ensure regular supply of milk and curds throughout the year from the peasants though they were required to provide him with these only at the time of harvesting or to entertain his guests.[24] Even in areas where the jagirdar was entitled to *begar* from the peasants at harvest-time, he was making an effort to convert it into a constant feature the year round.[25] And whereas the zamindar, in one case mentioned earlier, had carried away the peasants' bullocks, the jagirdar in village Kherla, *pargana* Paonta, carried away some of the peasants themselves and held them in captivity to extort *begar* from them.[26] In another case the jagirdar forced the *chamars* to carry his belongings beyond the customary limit of 5 *kos*.[27]

The *amil* was entitled to customary *begar* from the village menials.[28] But when in one case he forced the *chamars* to go to the neighbouring village and render *begar* there, they took to flight. The *amil,* with supreme indifference to the finer points of caste-status, forced the Brahmins, the Mahajans and the Meenas to substitute for them.[29]

Besides the *amil,* the *faujdar* also had a right to the menials', 'customary' *begar*.[30] But these officials, taking advantage of what might have been their general entitlement to *begar* from the menials, were trying to extend it to areas which had been specifically exempted from it. Thus in 1762 when the menials had fled the village Kheri, *pargana* Bahatri, due to famine, and others from some neighbouring villages had migrated there, the *amil* and the *faujdar* tried to extort *begar* from them even though the menials of that village had been exempted from it as per the *sanad* given to them.[31]

Even the *ijaradar* (revenue-farmer), whose official position allowed him only the right to collect revenue on a short or long-term contract with the state,[32] felt confident enough in *qasba* Pahari in the pargana of the same name to carry away the peasants' carts and bullocks in *begar*.[33]

Among the village menials, the barbers as a caste appear to have been the greatest sufferers from illegal demands of *begar* made by almost everyone in a position to dominate over them. Thus in 1726 the barbers of *qasba* Phagi and (some) villages of *pargana* Phagi lodged a complaint against all officials who were forcing them to provide *pattal, datun,* and earthen lamps to a limit that they found unbearable.[34] Similarly in 1734 the barbers of village Dhigraya and Bahmanvas in *pargana* Ghazi ka Thana complained against the jagirdar and the *patel* for making them carry water for them and against government officials for extorting *begar*.[35] In the same year the *amil* of *qasba* Toda Rai Singh in the *pargana* of the same name was accused of extorting excessive *begar* from the barbers apart from coercing them to provide *pattals* to him so much so that they threatened to desert the *qasba*.[36] The *amil* was instructed by the Diwan of the state to desist from making such demands. In 1751, the same complaint was repeated against the *amil* on the plea that the barbers of the *qasba* had never rendered *begar* and the *sanad* to that effect notwithstanding, the *amil* was persisting with his demands.[37] Possibly sometime between 1742 and 1751 they had acquired a *sanad* of exemption from *begar* as a counterpoint against the *amil's* persistent extortion. Interestingly the agents of the Marathas, who were in possession of *qasba* Toda Rai Singh in the middle of the eighteenth century, had extended similar claim to *begar* from the barbers as the *amils* under the Rajput rulers had done.[38] In all probability the Marathas' demands were in addition to those of the *amil*, for the instruction given to him on the barbers' complaint required him not only to refrain from demanding *begar* for himself but also to prevent the Marathas from doing so. Even so, the barbers of that *qasba* appear to have got no respite, for there is still another repetition of the complaint four years later, with similar instructions again being sent to the *amil*.[39]

It is vis-a-vis the artisans that the extension of the scope of extortions is the most spectacular, perhaps because this category of village inhabitants had been by custom exempt from such extortions with a few minor exceptions like the potters who were required to carry water for the village watchman.[40] Significantly over one-third of the complaints in our documents originate from the class of artisans. Whereas in the case of the peasants and menials (except the barbers) an established custom was being stretched here and there, groups like the artisans faced an utterly new phenomenon, likely to turn into 'custom' unless resisted at the outset. For the absence of customary obligations of any kind, apart, of course, from the payment of taxes, on the part of the artisans might precisely have been the reason why almost every local official—the *amil*, the *faujdar*, the *kotwal* and 'all officials'[41]—made an attempt to lay claim to the artisans' goods and services gratis whenever an opportunity arose. They also tried to extend their hold over practically every group among the artisans in one way or another—goldsmiths, calico-printers, tailors, oil-pressers, cotton-carders, carpenters, tanners, blacksmiths, potters, etc.

The extortions from the artisans were either in the form of *begar*, or coercing them into parting with their products without payment; quite often it was both. *Begar*, again, could be either in the form of service rendered by them according to their profession, or a different kind of service altogether.

Thus in 1737 the oil-pressers, the carpenters, and the potters along with the barbers of *qasba* Gijgarh, *pargana* Gijgarh, lodged a complaint against the local *kotwal*.[42] While the oil-pressers where being forced to supply 10 *sers* of oil every month without being paid for it, the others found the burden of *begar* having now become unbearable. The *amil* was accordingly instructed to prevent the *kotwal* from extorting any *begar* and for paying the artisans both for their goods as well as services. In 1739, the goldsmiths of *qasba* Niwai, *pargana* Niwai, reported that the *faujdar* had issued a warning that anyone wishing to get ornaments made should do so with his prior permission.[43] No reason for this extraordinary order has been mentioned. However, since the state refused to uphold the order, it had presumably been issued on the *faujdar's* own initiative possibly to punish the goldsmiths for refusing to accept some of his unreasonable demands or to pressurize them into acceding to such demands.

The *faujdar* of pargana Pidani was, however, a little more circumspect in making demands on the *qasba's* calico-printers and tailors for rendering him *begar* and supplying him with chintz gratis; he first falsely charged them with having committed rape.[44]

In 1741 the tailors of *qasba* Chatsu were being forced by the *amil* of the pargana to clean the fortress and the local pond, besides rendering other kinds of *begar*.[45] At the same time the oil-pressers of the *qasba* were being subjected to rendering *begar* to an unbearable degree.[46] The oil-pressers, besides carrying on their caste-profession, were also engaged in the privileged *gharuhala* cultivation[47] and were on both counts exempt from *begar*. Complaints of excessive begar were also received from the oil-pressers of *qasba* Phagi, similarly engaged in *gharuhala* cultivation (1741),[48] cotton carders of *pargana* Phagi (1741)[49] both against the *amils*, two carpenters of village Choru of the same *pargana* against the *faujdar* and the *amil* (1743),[50] carpenters of *qasba* Toda Raj Singh against the *amil* (1742),[51] tailors and calico-printers of village Manoharpur, *pargana* Sawai Jaipur against the *amil* (1742),[52] carpenters, blacksmiths and potters of *qasba* Ghazi ka Thana and some neighbouring villages against the *faujdar* and the *amil* (1742);[53] and the *panchas* of the caste-panchayat of the calico-printers of *qasba* Pidayan against the *faujdar* and the *amil* (1743).[54] The last mentioned complaints also reported that their cots and beddings were being carried away by the *walahis*[55] presumably on orders from the *faujdar* and the *amil*. Similarly there are cases of harassment of artisans on other counts. A goldsmith of *qasba* Amer, *pargana* Amer, complained of a cess being imposed on him in 1740 which no one in his family had paid during the past four generations.[56] The tailors and calico-printers of village Manoharpur, *pargana* Sawai Jaipur, were being forced by the *amil* to pay tax on their huts along with having to render *begar* in 1742 though they had never been subject to either.[57] The tailors of *qasba* Toda Rai Singh were compelled in 1764 to purchase agricultural goods by the *amil* who had collected these as revenue in kind.[58] This in addition to their cots and beddings being carried away.

An interesting indication of carting as a form of illegal *begar* is given in an early document of 1726. The *chithi to* the *amil* of *pargana* Sanganer instructs him to arrange carts for transporting bricks and lime for constructing a fort there. 'The charge for transport,' it says 'must be settled with the cart drivers with their full consent; no compulsion should be used, though you should try to save the government's money.'[59] Obviously, the *amils* were a little less likely to be so considerate to the cartmen when their own goods were to be transported.

These extortions often led to a conflict of interest not only between the victims and the dominant groups but even amongst members of the dominant groups themselves, for extortion by one would lead to denial of it to another; in the case of a jagirdar or *ijaradar* it might even cause a decline in his revenue. In the process some of them would appear to champion the cause of the peasants, artisans and menials against exploitation by other groups. Thus in 1741 one Abhai Singh Naruka, who was jagirdar of a large part of a village and *ijaradar* of the remaining part, complained that the *amil* was causing him harassment by extorting illegal *begar* from the village.[60] Similarly the jagirdar of village Niworo in *pargana* Chatsu complained against the zamindar's extorting *begar* from the cultivators in 1753.[61] The jagirdar of village Kherli in *pargana* Bahatri reported that the menials of his village having fled due to famine, their brethren from some other villages had migrated there and the *faujdar* and the *amil* were trying to extort *begar* from them, from which the menials of that village had been exempt.[62] Obviously, the *amil* and the *faujdar* were interpreting the exemption to apply to particular persons belonging to menial professions, whereas the jagirdar felt that the exemption was granted to the village as such. The state upheld the latter's interpretation. Interestingly, the *patel* almost invariably sided with his village in the complaints against extortions.

The conflict of interests among the dominant groups could at times bring some relief to those subjected to extortions. In an interesting case the zamindar in village Subrai, *pargana* Ghazi ka Thana, complained in 1765 that the *ijaradar* of his village had threatened to impose fine on any menial who rendered *begar* to the former.[63] His complaint was, however, admitted by the state and *begar* was resumed. The respite to the menials was, therefore, short-lived.

II

Irfan Habib mentions that zamindars and the state officials in the Mughal empire were entitled to *begar* rendered by the menials in the form of carrying their goods and acting as guides, besides assisting the *madad-i maash* grantees during their *shikar* expeditions.[64] It was however, 'as a rule an exceptional form of labour imposed upon some inhabitants by the authorities, rather than a regular part of productive work'.[65] In our region and period, however, there is both a slightly greater variety as well as greater intensity even in the customary *begar*, for not only the peasants, besides the menials, are subject to it in some areas but the participation in agriculture production is also a form of forced labour. It is not possible to determine the share of forced labour relative to hired, family or tenant labour in agricultural production and it is likely that this share was not decisive. But as a phenomenon it did exist.

The complaints particularly of *begar* originate from territories under almost every form of administration in eastern Rajasthan—territories that form the *watan* of Jaipur's rulers, those given in jagir to them and those taken by them from the imperial jagirdars on *ijara*. This fact, along with some variation in the forms and incidence of extortions compared to the Mughal empire (as well as the Maratha kingdom) would perhaps suggest that such extoritions had preceded as well as survived the integration of the Jaipur state with the empire. The state in its turn appears to have accepted the local custom in this regard instead of formulating a uniform law for all its territories.

Once the extortions in the form of forced labour and other forms were built into the social and administrative structure to ensure the predominance of the dominant sections of society, an attempt by them to extend the 'customary' limits became almost inevitable. A study at the level of political and administrative institutions and policies is likely to ignore this aspect, for the extension of the limits takes place primarily at the local or village level where the peasants, artisans, and menials as the producers of society's wealth come into immediate contact with those who appropriate their surplus.

As we have seen above, some degree of *begar* and a few other minor extortions like the supply of milk and curds and cots and beddings on specific occasions were sanctioned by custom. The scope and intensity of these extortions registered an upward trend as the century advanced. It is likely that the actual incidence of this developing trend was far greater than has been recorded. For, it may perhaps be assumed that the number of complaints made, on which this paper is based, would be considerably smaller than the actual number of cases of illegal extortions. One may also assume that the complaints would be made by and large in cases of gross violation of the custom; the milder violations would have gone unreported.

It is important to note that the intensification of exploitation of the peasants, artisans, and menials in these forms of extortions took place at the hands of almost everyone in a position to make a demand, whether he was the *amil*, the *faujdar*, the jagirdar or the zamindar or even the *ijaradar* at the local level. However, the largest share in this process of intensification was taken by the state officials. Two-thirds of the complaints are against the *amil* and other officials whose responsibility it was to check any excesses on the inhabitants within their jurisdiction. The attitude of the state was at best lukewarm except where actual flight of peasants, artisans or menials, or even a threat of such flight, occurred. In a case of flight of peasants or artisans the revenues of the state declined directly, and when the menials fled, the decline was indirect on account of fall in production owing to the non-availability of their labour. However, in no case is there any punishment mentioned against illegal extortions. It may be suggested that the state policy was likely to have been to control the exploitation of the peasants etc. by any one socially and politically dominant section in the interests of the entire ruling class. Whether the state was actually able to exercise the control would depend on a number of factors at any given time, primarily on the state of the economy and the degree of political and administrative control.

The agrarian economy of eastern Rajasthan appears to have witnessed two phases from c. 1650 to the end of the eighteenth century. The first phase covers nearly a century and the second roughly half that period.

The first century of this period registers a degree of advance both in terms of agricultural production as well as of an upward price mobility.[66] There is a certain increase in the production of cash crops in the *kharif* (autumn) season; but the proportion of crops in the *rabi* (spring) harvest grows as compared to the *kharif* harvest as a whole. The *rabi* crops in this region require a considerable scale of investment. The availability of additional investible surplus would thus be indicated. The price-rise, similarly, tended to benefit the peasantry, though the benefits would naturally be shared unequally by its different sections. The preference of the cultivators to pay the revenue in cash during the first century of our period (by shifting to *zabti* crops, the revenue from which was collected in cash)[67] and the substitution of kind for cash (and a shift back to *jinsi* crops for which revenue was paid in kind during the latter half of the eighteenth century when prices were on the decline)[68] is an interesting testimony to the additional surplus left with them by the price rise.

The second phase of the agrarian economy saw a reversal of these happy trends. Both the scale of agricultural production and the prices suffered a decline. The prices register a downward trend from the 1740's.[69] The decline in production is slightly harder to pinpoint in the time-sequence, but the trend is unmistakable during the second half of the eighteenth century.[70] The decline in the production of commercial crops in the *qasbas* is particularly marked and this in turn would adversely affect the artisans.[71]

The change in the economy must have affected the entire countryside in this region, though, once again, the impact on various classes, and sections within each class, would be quite differential, the worst shock falling on those who were in least position to absorb it. For, this half century bears unmistakable testimony to growing poverty in the countryside and increasing indebtedness of the small peasants and possibly other poorer sections.[72] A preliminary analysis of the innumerable documents of this period also suggests that famines began to make their appearance with greater frequency during the latter half of the eighteenth century in our region.[73] It is significant to note, however, that the decline in prices accompanies an overall decline in agricultural production including foodgrains.[74] This would indicate a fall in demand owing to a fall in the purchasing power even as the goods were becoming scarcer. It should not be far fetched to assume that the first to suffer from the fall in purchasing power were those who needed it most for their sheer survival.[75]

Consequent to these developments, the relationship between the various classes and between their sections in the countryside would have been considerably altered leading to a greater dependence of the small peasants, artisans and the menials on those who could provide them with the means of subsistence.

This was perhaps the setting to the attempt by almost all socially and politically dominant groups to extend the 'customary' limits of extortions. To this the decline of the state's control over its administrative apparatus also contributed.

Even as the Mughal empire was declining, some of its constituent units showed remarkable tenacity in retaining intact, in varying degrees and for varying periods of time, the administrative system they had inherited from the empire. The Jaipur state was one of these units. During the reign of Sawai Jai Singh (1700-43), the state extended the territory under its jurisdiction by various means, attained great cultural heights and retained a degree of control over its administrative machinery.[76] After his reign, however, the state declined steeply. The successful Maratha raids into this territory were both a reflection and a partial cause of this decline.

The consequent laxity in central control within the state led to a localization of administrative authority. It is a reflection of such localization of authority that the Diwan's instructions to the *amils* on complaints of excessive extortions from peasants etc. were at times disregarded and complaints had to be repeated.[77] Even in the normal course the local officials would not scrupulously refrain from taking advantage of the growing vulnerability of peasants, artisans and menials accompanied by the officials' growing autonomy; a further temptation was added by the frequent transfers, particularly of the *amils.* On an average the *amil* stayed in one pargana for three years.[78] The *amils,* who mostly belonged to the caste to *sah* (*sahu,* money lender), possessed an additional influence on the higher echelons of administrative authority on account of money lent to many of the local nobles.[79] It would therefore have required a man of exceptional integrity not to take advantage of his brief stay in a *pargana* in every way including stretching the limits of extortions which custom had sanctioned him. It is to be expected that the gains from illegal extortions would be shared unequally among the various strata of the dominant sections, the most influential getting the largest share. Of the 48 complaints, 32 are against the *amils* and other officials like the *faujdar* and the *kotwal;* of these 32, twenty had originated from the artisans in qasbas where the *amils* usually resided. The *amils,* and to an extent their junior colleagues, the *faujdars* and the *kotwals,* were most admirably situated to derive full advantage from the growing dependence of peasants, artisans and menials and their own increasing authority.

The nature of the economy also perhaps favoured the *amils* and other officials as far as the distribution of additional extortions among the various dominant sections was concerned. The agrarian economy of medieval India was essentially a free peasant economy,[80] and the use of forced labour for agricultural production was perhaps marginal at best. It is possible that labour-scarcity was not a crucial problem in medieval Indian agriculture which might have necessitated the institutionalization of forced labour; such labour as was required could be obtained from the class of menials—among them the landless agricultural workers such as the *chamars*—in return for meagre payment in kind. The primary form of enhanced extortions could therefore be in using forced labour for unproductive purposes and taking away of goods without payment. And the *amils* and other officials being in possession of administrative authority, and with rare direct involvement in agricultural production, were most favoured by the situation to take the major share of illegal extortions, though the other groups also benefited from these.

The growing inability of the state to check its officials from making illegal demands left the peasants, artisans and menials with their own capacity of passive or active resistance to put a brake on these demands. The resistance could take the form of either actual flight from the village or a threat to that effect. It is interesting that in case of flight, the Diwan invariably issued stiff instructions to the officials to bring the fleeing group back, obviously by accepting its conditions. The humiliation of its officials implied in this was of little concern to the state where its basic economic interests were involved; in the bargain it could appear as the defender of its underprivileged subjects.

REFERENCES

1. Thus, for example, while the peasants were obliged to render *begar* to the jagirdar at harvest time in village Chatrpura, *pargana* Chatsu, *chithi* dt. Chaitra Sudi 6, Vikrami Samvat (V.S.) 1825/ A.D.1768, the jagirdar at village Khurnala, *pargana* Ghazi ka Thana was denied such *begar, chithi* dt. Magh Sudi 1, V.S.1811/ 1754. Similarly, while the zamindar was entitled to *Kotri ki begar,* (forced labour at the harvest-time and sundry other services) in the area settled by him in some regions, *chithi* dt. Chaitra Sudi 15, V.S.1825/1768 addressed to the *amil, pargana* Ghazi ka Thana, in others he had no such entitlement, *chithi* dt. Sawan Vadi 12, V.S.1811/1754 pertaining to village Khurnala *pargana* Mauzabad. Indeed, even within the same *pargana,* Mauzabad in this case, *kotri ki begar* was not allowed in some villages, ibid., and allowed in some others, *chithi,* addressed to *amil* dt. Paush Vadi 7, V.S. 1827/1770. The instances of village-level variations in custom are, however, rare.
2. Socially, the menials belonged to the lowest rungs of the caste hierarchy. Economically, for rendering assistance to the peasants at sowing at the harvest times, they received a paltry share of the produce. In two rare document of 1752 and 1766 of parganas Malarna and Tonk, their share has been estimated at 0.6 per cent and 0.9 per cent respectively. See Dilbagh Singh, op.cit., p. 53. Besides, they had to render *begar* to various sections of society as will be discussed below. Significantly, the menials were also known as *begaris,* ibid; also Irfan Habib, *Agrarian System of Mughal India,* Bombay, 1963, p. 150n., and H. Fukazawa, 'A Note on the Corvee System (Vethbegar) in Eighteenth Century Maratha Kingdom', *Science and Human Progress* (Essays in honour of the late Prof. D.D. Kosambi), Bombay 1974, p. 12.
3. In all our documents pertaining to the artisans, their claim to exemption from any extortion has been upheld by the state. Only in one document the potters are required to carry water for the village watchman, *chithi* dt. Asadh Vadi 13, V.S. 1799/ 1742 relating to villages Dhingraya and Bahmanvas in *pargana* Ghazi ka Thana.

4. *Chithi* dt. Vaisakh Sudi 15, V.S.1826/1769 pertaining to village Mundawari, *pargana* Malarna.
5. *Chithi* dt. Sawan Sudi 1, V.S. 1811/1754 pertaining to *pargana* Mauzabad, quoted in Dilbagh Singh op.cit., p. 85.
6. *Chithi* dt. Paush Sudi 14, V.S.1820/1763 pertaining to *pargana* Chatsu.
7. *Chithi* dt. Sawan Vadi 12, V.S.1811/1754 pertaining to village Khurnala, *pargana* Mauzabad.
8. *Chithi* dt. Chaitra Sudi 6, V.S.1825/1768 pertaining to village Chatrpur, *pargana* Chatsu. .
9. Five of our documents mention actual desertion by the menials and artisans and in nine others the threat of flight by various groups is implied in their declaration that 'they cannot carry on any longer' on account of the burden of extortions. The menials complained only of *begar;* at any rate they had nothing else to give.
10. For a discussion of these terms, see Dilbagh Singh, op.cit., pp.28-43.
11. *Chithi* dt. Chaitra Sudi 6, V.S.1825/1768 pertaining to village Chatrpur, *pargana* Chatsu.
12. *Chithi* dt. Magh Sudi 1, V.S.1811/1754 pertaining to village Khurnala, *pargana* Ghazi ka Thana.
13. The evidence for this will be cited below.
14. *Chithi* dt. Magh vadi V.S.1820/1763 pertaining to *qasba* Baswa, *pargana* Bahatri. Also Irfan Habib, op.cit., p. 248.
15. For a definition of such forced sale, known as *padna,* see *chithi* dt. Asoj Sudi 6, V.S.1794/1737 addressed to the *amil, pargana* Niwai. The agent of the jagirdar of village Sakarkhawda, *pargana* Chatsu, complained in 1749 that the *amil* was imposing *padna* (probably on the village), *chithi* dt. Maghshri Vadi 5, V.S.1806; the tailors of *qasba* Toda Raj Singh lodged a similar complaint against their *amil* in 1764, *chithi* dt. Jeth Sudi 6, V.S. 1821.
16. *Chithi* dt. Asoj Vadi 7, V.S.1783/1726 pertaining to *qasba* Phagi and villages in *pargana* Phagi; *chithi* dt. Paush Sudi 13, V.S.1799/1742 pertaining to *qasba* Toda Raj Singh, *pargana* of the same name.
17. *Chithi* dt. Maghshri Sudi 3, V.S.1810.
18. *Chithi* dt. Sawan Vadi 12, V.S.1811.
19. *Chithi* dt. Sawan Sudi 1, V.S.1811.
20. *Chithi* dt. Paush Vadi 7, V.S.1827.
21. *Chithi* dt. Jeth Sudi 7, V.S.1825/1768. The complaint pertains to village Todah, *pargana* Ghazi ka Thana.

22. *Chithi* dt. Magh Sudi 5, V.S.1819/1762 relating to village Khurnala, *pargana* Mauzabad.
23. *Chithi* dt. Vaisakh Sudi 15, V.S.1826/1769 pertaining to village Mundawari, *pargana* Malarna.
24. Ibid.
25. *Chithi* dt. Chaitra Sudi, V.S.1825/1768 pertaining to village Chatrpura, *pargana* Chatsu.
26. *Chithi* dt. Vaisakh Sudi 15, V.S.1821/1764.
27. *Chithi* dt. Magh Vadi 7, V.S.1820/1763.
28. *Chithi* dt. Jeth Sudi 13, V.S.1820/1763, pertaining to village Abhaneri, *pargana* Lalsot.
29. Ibid.
30. This is implied in the specific exemption granted to the menials of village Kherli, *pargana* Bahatri from rendering *begar* to the *amil* and the *faujdar, chithi* dt. Bhadon Vadi 6, V.S.1819/1762.
31. Ibid.
32. See Dilbagh Singh, 'Ijara System in Eastern Rajasthan (1750-1800)', *Proceedings of Rajasthan History Congress,* vol.VI, 1973, pp. 60-69.
33. *Chithi* dt. Sawan Sudi 3, V.S.1817/1760.
34. *Chithi* dt. Asoj Vadi 7, V.S.1783.
35. *Chithi* dt. Asadh Vadi 13, V.S.1799.
36. *Chithi* dt. Paush Sudi 13, V.S.1799.
37. *Chithi* dt. Sawan Sudi 2, V.S.1808.
38. Ibid.
39. *Chithi* dt. Phagun Sudi 8, V.S.1811/1754.
40. *Chithi* dt. Magh Sudi 5, V.S.1789/1732 relating to *qasba* Niwai, *pargana* Niwai.
41. The potters referred to in the preceding footnote complained against 'all officials' who were forcing them to carry water whereas custom required them to carry water only for the village watchman.
42. *Chithi* dt. Phagun Sudi 12, V.S.1794.
43. *Chithi* dt. Magh Sudi 12, V.S.1796.
44. *Chithi* dt. Chaitra Sudi 9, V.S.1798/1741.
45. *Chithi* dt. Paush Vadi 2, V.S.1798.
46. *Chithi* dt. Asadh Sudi 8, V.S.1798/1741.
47. The *gharuhala* cultivators, also known as *riyayatis* or those allowed concessions, paid substantially less revenue to the state than the ordinary cultivators, the *raiyati.* See Dilbagh Singh, 'Local and Land Revenue Administration,' pp. 16-17. His statement that the *gharuhala* concessions were confined to the

higher castes such as the Brahmins, the Rajputs and the Vaisyas (Mahajans, taken as a caste not as a profession) and holders of superior rights such as the *patels*, the zamindars, etc. when engaged in agriculture, pp. 11-12, needs to be slightly qualified in view of two of our documents' reference to oil-pressers being *gharuhala* cultivators. Of course, the available evidence still overwhelmingly supports Dilbagh Singh's conclusion.

48. *Chithi* dt. Sawan Sudi 3, V.S.1798.
49. *Chithi* dt. Sawan Sudi 6, V.S.1798.
50. *Chithi* dt. Chaitra Vadi 12, V.S.1800.
51. *Chithi* dt. Asadh Vadi 7, V.S.1799.
52. *Chithi* dt. Asoj Sudi 5, V.S.1799.
53. *Chithi* dt. Kartik Sudi 14, V.S.1799.
54. *Chithi* dt. Phagun Sudi 8, V.S.1800.
55. 'Walahis' skinned the dead animals.
56. *Chithi* dt. Sawan Sudi 9, V.S.1797.
57. *Chithi* dt. Asoj Sudi 5, V.S.1799.
58. *Chithi* dt. Jeth Sudi 6, V.S.1821.
59. *Chithi* dt. Phagun Sudi 9, V.S.1783.
60. *Chithi* dt. Phagun Vadi 1, V.S.1798, relating to village Rudaheli *pargana* Paunkhar.
61. *Chithi* dt. Magh Sudi 3, V.S.1810.
62. *Chithi* dt. Bhadon Vadi 6, V.S.1819/1762.
63. *Chithi* dt. Jeth Vadi 6, V.S.1822.
64. Irfan Habib, op.cit., pp. 150 and 248.
65. Ibid, p. 239; H. Fukazawa op.cit., p. 121, for similar nature of *begar* in the Maratha kingdom during the eighteenth century.
66. See S. Nurul Hasan, K.N. Hasan and S.P. Gupta, 'The Pattern of Agricultural Production in the Territories of Amber (c.1650-1750)', *Proceedings of the Indian History Congress*, 28th Session at Mysore, Aligarh, 1966, pp. 244-64; S. Nurul Hasan and S.P. Gupta 'Price of Food Grains in the Territories of Amber (c.1650-1750),' *Proceedings of the Indian History Congress*, 29th Session at Patiala, Patna 1968, pp. 345-68. A summary of S.P. Gupta's conclusion to the same effect in his unpublished doctoral dissertation 'Land Revenue System in Eastern Rajasthan' is also given in Dilbagh Singh, 'Local and Land Revenue Administration,' p. 161.
67. S. Nurul Hasan, K.N. Hasan and S.P. Gupta, op.cit., p.245.
68. Dilbagh Singh, 'Local and Land Revenue Administrations p. 151.
69. S. Nurul Hasan and S.P. Gupta, op.cit., p. 353 and passim; Dilbagh Singh, 'Local and land Revenue Administration,' p. 154.

70. Dilbagh Singh, 'Local and land Revenue Administration,' pp. 106, 110-11, 113, 161.
71. Ibid, p. 112.
72. Ibid, p. 113. Also Dilbagh Singh, 'Rural Indebtedness in Eastern Rajasthan during the Eighteenth Century', *Proceedings of Rajasthan History Congress,* vol. VII, 1974, pp. 83-89.
73. S.P. Gupta and Dilbagh Singh, 'Famines in the Territories of Amber (c.1660-1770),' *Proceedings of Rajasthan History Congress,* vol. VIII, 1975.
74. Dilbagh Singh, 'Local and Land Revenue Administration,' p. 161.
75. It is not necessary to go into the causes of this development in the economy, for we are here concerned merely with the fact of economic decline in the countryside. Dilbagh Singh has, however, attributed it to the Maratha invasions and consequent disinclination on the part of the peasants to invest in the *rabi* season; see his 'Local and Land Revenue Administration', p. 111.
76. For a detailed and competent, though a little adulatory study of his reign, see V.S. Bhatnagar, *Life and Times of Sawai Jai Singh, 1688-1743,* Delhi, 1974.
77. Among our documents there is only one case of actual repetition of a complaint, that by the barbers of *qasba* Toda Rai Singh against the *amil's* extortion of *begar,* referred to earlier. But eight other documents give a warning against such repetition suggesting that the incidence of repetition was considerable.
78. See Dilbagh Singh, 'Local and Land Revenue Administration', pp. 416, 464-69.
79. Dilbagh Singh, 'The Role of the Mahajan in the Rural Economy of Eastern Rajasthan during the 18th Century,' *Social Scientist,* May 1974.
80. Irfan Habib, op.cit., 114-15; S. Nurul Hasan, *Thoughts on Agrarian Relations in Mughal India,* Delhi 1973, p. 18.

12

The *Risāla-i Zirā't** [A Treatise on Agriculture]

INTRODUCTION

The *Risāla* is an interesting document in several ways but principally because it draws us away from the grand imperial heights and introduces us to the ground realities, particularly in the realm of revenue administration. It gives us a fascinating

---

* In 1980 I came across the *Risāla* at the Edinburgh University Library, though I had seen references to it earlier. Thanks to the generosity of the Homi Bhabha Fellowship Council, Bombay, which financed the visit as part of a Fellowship, I was able to obtain a microfilm copy. I had been interested in translating the brief MS. and had indeed prepared a draft soon after. The draft was seen by S. Bhattacharya, B.B. Chaudhuri, Barun De and Peter Marshal, all of whom made some very valuable comments and suggestions. I acknowledge with gratitude help rendered by them. My very special thanks go to Professor Nurul Hasan, then Vice-President of the Council of Scientific and Industrial Research, whom I approached with some trepidation, for I could not expect any substantial share of his time. But time is what he gave me most generously of and made some extremely useful suggestions. Several long discussions with him were an unforgettable experience, particularly as I realised that, above all his other commitments, the historian in him is ever ready to respond to the first call. After the draft had been commented upon, it lay in cold storage until my friend Rajat Datta, who had earlier used it for a couple of his writings, discovered the Murray papers. He passed on

picture of the wheels within wheels that operated in the working of that administration.

We know precious little about the author of this all-too-brief document, comprising 19 folios in all, the date of its composition or even about its regional context. Its language is simple and prosaic, picking up a little style towards the later folios; there is also a good mixture of Indian words. The manuscript, probably the original, is located at the Edinburgh University Library;[1] there is no known copy of it anywhere.

The author frequently mentions Bengal as the region of his reference, though Professor Peter Marshal, in a personal communication, suspects that he was actually talking of Bihar. This, on account of the names of crops, which Marshal believes are more characteristic of Bihar than of Bengal. There are too references to Azimabad, i.e. Patna, and Buxar. Marshal also suggests that *muqarrarī* (fixed revenue) tenures are characteristics of Bihar and that the term *mustajir* (revenue-farmer) is not widely used in Bengal. However, one could still reasonably stick to Bengal as the area with which the author was concerned, irrespective of his own regional or linguistic background. His persistent reference to Bengal makes it hard to assume that he actually had Bihar in mind. The crops that he mentions are also grown in Bengal. Indeed, his somewhat contemptuous references to wheat, always followed by a dismissive 'etc.' ('March-April is the season for the cultivation of wheat etc. In Bengal, the cultivation of paddy is predominant and that of wheat etc. is secondary...') suggests that he actually had Bengal in mind rather than Bihar where the cultivation of wheat is not so insignificant. As for the terms, these are all

---

all information on the *Risāla* to me with characteristic kindness and kept egging me on to give finishing touches to the translation. This endeavour therefore owes a great deal to him. I also double-checked the meaning of some terms with my colleague, Dilbagh Singh, and I thank him for the assistance. Whenever in doubt I could always draw upon Muzaffar Alam's mastery of Persian and he let me do so with cheer; I am ever so grateful to him.

standardised Persian administrative terms used nearly uniformly in almost all parts of the Mughal dominion; at any rate, the author, a high revenue official, as we shall see below, would have used them virtually by force of habit. And the mention of Azimabad and Buxar is in the nature of references to 'other' lands [...the province (*sūbāh*) of Azimabad, '...moneylenders from Buxar'].

Going by the details about revenue officials in the village and the frequent reference to *ijārādāri, mathaut* and *abwāb* in the *Risāla*, the impression about its terrain of reference being Bengal becomes stronger, for, this would point to a region where both the Mughal revenue system had taken root and experiments under the *Nizāmat* system had been made. The text is nearly silent on *jāgīrdārs* as an important element in rural society. This is not surprising in view of Murshid Quli Khan's attempt to convert the *sīr-i hāsil parganās* of Bengal into the *khālisā,* not so much for the rulers in Delhi, but more to establish financial basis for the *Nizāmat* which he was creating in the first quarter of the eighteenth century, as Professor Abdul Karim has shown in his *Murshid Quli Khan.* Murshid Quli's administration involved strict control over the smaller *zamīndārs* and the flight of the *jāgīrdārs* from Bengal into Orissa. By the end of the eighteenth century, Bengal was clearly a *jāgīr*-free area in contrast to Bihar where references to *al-tamghā jāgīrs* continue well into the 1780s and 1790s.

The chronological location of the *Risāla* has been open to even wider ranging speculation. Professor Irfan Habib unhesitatingly places it 'c.1750'. In his view 'The preface shows it was written in Bengal probably a little before the British conquest'.[2] Professor Zahiruddin Malik, who has translated some excerpts from the *Risāla,* is nearer the mark when he observes that '...the subject-matter treated clearly shows that it was composed between the years 1765-1772'.[3] For, any careful reading of the text would have left one with little doubt that this is a post-*Dīwānī* document. Professor Nurul Hasan, in a personal communication, brought it further forward to the 1780s, though he would place it *before* 1785. He took his cue from the opening statement of the text that it had been 'written for the English (*sāhibān-i ālīshān*)'.[4] He also kindly deciphered for me the seal in Persian on the flyleaf. This is the seal of James Graham dated 1200 A.H./1785-86 A.D.

Professor Hasan was nearly right. But thanks to the discovery made by Dr. Rajat Datta, the MS. can now be definitively dated. It was in 1998 that Dr. Datta, then working for his doctorate at King's College in London, brought to my notice a hitherto unknown MS. in the collection known as 'Murray Papers on the Revenues of Bengal' in the Home Misc. Series of the India Office Library and Records (MS. no. 68). Murray, a somewhat conscientious official of the East India Company, felt concerned at the gap between the expectation of revenue from Bengal and its actual collection. He studied the problem in some detail and 'by a very long perseverance, obtained lights, which appear to me to be extremely interesting. I found the most important of them comprised in a Persian Treatise, written at my request, in the year 1785, by a native of Rank, a man of great experience and ability, who had been long in high office in the Administration of the Revenues....' So there it is, the *Sāhib*[5] whose suggestion the author of the *Risāla* acknowledges as the stimulant to his endeavour and the man, though still unidentified, who complied with the suggestion. To a longish note expatiating on his concern over the loss of revenue and, of course, the welfare of the 'natives', Murray also appends his own English translation of the 'Substance' of the Treatise. The remarkably accurate version does him credit; there are, however, two drawbacks to his version: that it is not a translation but a summary, and that he often uses terms which would be objected to by modern historians. There is too an occasional error in his reading of the text.

The date of the composition of the treatise, 1785, is important. This was the time the Bengal Revenue Council and (subsequently) the Board of Revenue were holding extensive and, not seldom heated, debates about the nature of land-tenure, landed property and land-revenue in Bengal. All the names associated with the formulation of the Decennial Settlement and, later, the Permanent Settlement—Philip

Francis, James Grant, Sir John Shore etc.—virtually flooded the Council with detailed minutes and counter-minutes on all these inter-related issues. The second volume of *The Fifth Report*, edited by Firminger, opens for us just a small window into these debates, while the social origins of the debates and their policy implications have been so movingly discussed by Ranajit Guha in his *A Rule of Property for Bengal*. Guha indeed establishes that *The Fifth Report* was merely the tip of the iceberg, while the base comprising a huge mass of information collected by the Co.'s officials, now available in its archives, awaits a thorough analysis. The debates led to a search for 'indigenous' sources of a form of property whose complexities were quite beyond the Co.'s comprehension as revenue authority in its early phase. Hence, *qānūngos* were sought out and interviewed in great detail and their opinions were minutely recorded and appended to the proceedings of the Revenue Council. The *Risāla* fits into this genre perfectly. It is a treatise written at the behest of a *sāhib* and seeks to explicate the welter of cross-cutting rights, interests and agencies involved in the agrarian surplus, operating at the level of the village—the complex web called revenue administration in pre-British Bengal. James Graham was closely associated with the early revenue experiments of the Co. in Bengal. It is probable that Murray, an otherwise obscure official, was assigned by Graham the task of getting a *mutasaddī* to give details of his version of the working of the system, though Murray seems keen to corner the entire credit for himself for the treatise. That the author was a *mutasaddī* seems fairly certain, going by the emphasis he places on his central role in the system.

The title of the text (*Risalā-i Zirā't* or 'A Treatise on Agriculture') is somewhat misleading, for its discussion of agriculture is rather meagre, except for purely descriptive notes on soil, crops and seasons. It has precious little on agricultural techniques and practices, implements and devices, soil-use, etc.etc. Its strength lies in its description of the actual working of the revenue administration with precision and admirable amount of detail, and this is what the Co. was primarily interested in in the 1780s. One then understands Murray's concerns and his excitement with the Treatise.

The translation that follows in the pages below is the first complete English rendering of the *Risāla*. Annotation and references have been kept to the bare minimum, partly at least for reasons of space. In making this translation I have tried to keep as close to the text as possible; I have also tried to make minimal use of modern English equivalents of medieval Persian technical terms, preferring the use of the original and explaining the meaning.

TRANSLATION

In the Name of God, Compassionate and Merciful

From trustworthy books of history it will become evident to the most exalted [English] gentlemen [*sāhibān-i ālīshān*] that in the past rulers of India often appointed illustrious princes as Governors to carry out the responsibility of administering the provinces. As they were sent out to the provinces, knowledgeable and experienced *mutasaddīs*[6] were nominated to accompany them so as gradually to familiarize them with the proceedings of governance and the actual assessment and collection (of revenues) of all those provinces. As a result, territories would prosper and subjects would attain comfortable circumstance, increased revenues would reach the government's coffers and no one could commit oppression[7] of any kind on another. Besides, for keeping themselves informed of matters relating to administration in every province and every *chaklā*[8] they (the rulers) appointed *wāqiā-nigārs* and *sawānih-nigārs*[9] who were to bring to the emperor's notice the events and affairs of all his territories without themselves exercising any discretion.

The intention of the great sultans in putting this arrangement into effect was that when, with the passage of time, the mighty princes ascended the imperial throne, they should be able to guard themselves against anyone's wrong and selfish advice because of their familiarity with all the affairs of state and governance, and that in arriving at minute judgments and in the management of matters of state, big and small, they should be guided by their own sense of discrimination; being familiar with matters inside out, they would not be dependent on others. However, owing to certain circumstances and in consideration of certain exigencies, the observance of this arrangement has of late been disturbed and the exalted princes have done no more than embellishing the imperial palace. Hence, no sooner would they ascend the throne than they would become dependent on others' advice on all matters and thus at one stroke hand over the reins of governance to the self-same others. The affairs of the empire of India then reached a stage of which the less said and the less written the better.

In these circumstances it becomes necessary that the lord of the realm should acquire some familiarity with the management of affairs and obtain information regarding all important matters so that in the governance of his territories and collection of revenues, he should not need to lean on others for advice, but, in propriety, should grasp for himself matters exactly as they stand and in their entirety so as to ensure prosperity to the country and its people as well as a continual increase in the revenues.

Although the unearthing of the entire range of tricks of the *mutasaddīs'* trade and recapturing all the shades of (his) knowledge and experience is beyond the realm of possibility, (this much is certain that) until a territory has a permanent administrator, prosperity will not in any way descend upon it. (Therefore) this miserable one amongst men, in accordance with the suggestion of a *Sāhib,* has recounted the affairs of the province of Bengal of his time, according to his own imperfect understanding, in nine Sections. He was impelled into this recounting by necessity, owing to the depression of his mood and dispersal of his energy caused by prolonged unemployment to the extent that he had not a piece of paper in his possession, nor a knowledgeable person around. He thus drew upon his own ability to recollect those affairs. It is a mere one person in a thousand who realises that the execution of such affairs largely depends upon competent *mutasaddīs.*

Section I : On a Brief Acquaintance with the Types of Land

Section II : On Agricultural Crops

Section III : On a Brief Acquaintance with the Categories of Cultivators
Section IV : The (Revenue) Officials of the *Mufassal*[10]
Section V : On the Methods of Collecting Revenue from the *Mufassal*
Section VI : On the Heads of Expenditure in the *Mufassal*
Section VII : On Certain Affairs of the *Mufassal*
Section VIII : On the Merits and Demerits of the System of Revenue-farming etc.
Section IX : On the Regulations implemented by the Past Governors in Administering their Territories.

He (the author) has the firm hope that if the ruler of the day pays careful attention to matters described here, he would not need to depend on the advice of others for the collection of revenue and management of administration. In case the description given in these few Sections meets with the approval of the most exalted gentlemen, the author has it in his deficient mind, for reasons of humility before them and for winning heart, to write another (work) on the management of revenue and administrative affairs in order that innovations in these matters in the *sadr* and the *mufassal* might be eliminated. God willing, he would write again in detail explicating these problems.

Section I
ON THE TYPES OF LAND

First, *Bāsā,* also called *Bastī,* is the place of the cultivator's residence;

second, *Audbāsā,* or courtyard or cowshed as well as the storehouse for threshed rice etc.;

third, *Lāl,* or the land under cultivation. The varieties and names of this type of land differ widely from one *pargana*[11] to another;

fourth, *Mat,* or plain tract which had never been brought under cultivation (though it was cultivable);

fifth, *Patit*, or land which was earlier under the plough but had been left untilled for the preceding two or three years;

sixth, *Banjar*, also called *Khil[a]*, or cultivable waste or *Jangal;*

seventh, wasteland that is desert, including ditches etc., which is unfit for cultivation.

Section II
ON AGRICULTURAL CROPS

In India there are two crop (seasons): one, *Rabī'*, and the other *Kharīf*. The latter extends from the beginning of the month of *Baisākh* (April-May) to the end of the month of *Āsin* (September-October); it is the season for the cultivation of paddy (*shāli*) in Bengal. This crop is also called *Bhadoi* (or the crop of *Bhādon,* (August-September). The other crop (season) is *Rabī* which begins in the month of *Kātik,* (October-November) and concludes in *Chait* (March-April). This is the season for the cultivation of wheat etc. In Bengal, the cultivation of paddy is predominant and that of wheat etc. is secondary. This crop is also called the *Aghni crop* (or the crop of *Agrāhan,* November-December). There are then supplementary 'crops' (*fasl-i dākhilī*): one, fruits such as mango and jack-fruit etc. (*phalkar*). Their season begins in *Māgh* (January-February) and ends in *Āsādh* (June-July); two, water products (*jalkar*) such as fish which is caught through the twelve months but the 'crop' is particularly good from the beginning of *Katik* (October-November) to the month of *Jeth* (May-June); three, forest-products (*bankar*) like grass and the cutting of wood which reach their end in the months of *Kātik* (October-November) and *Aghan* (November-December); four, betel-nut from the month of *Āsādh* (June-July) to the month of *Āsin* (September-October); five, sugarcane from *Chait* (March-April) to *Māgh* (January-February) and *Phāgun* (February-March); six, cotton from *Kātik* (October-November) to *Chait* (March-April); seven, tobacco from *Kātik* (October-November) to *Chait* (March-April); eight, mulberry which is produced in six yields (*bunds*) in twelve months; nine, salt from the month of *Āsin* (September-October) to *Baisākh* (April-May).

Section III
ON THE CATEGORIES OF CULTIVATORS

First, *muqarrarī* or *pattī* cultivator, or cultivator in possession of a *pattā*.[12] He paid revenue in every circumstance according to the document whether his crop was perfect or damaged;

second, *faslī*, also called *basatī* (resident)or *kḥud-kāsht* (self-cultivating) agriculturist; he secured a *pattā* every year in order to engage in cultivation and paid revenue on the land under actual cultivation. He resided in the *pargana* where he cultivated the land;

third, the *paikāsht* cultivators who resided in a village other than the one in which their field was located;

fourth, the *kaljanah* cultivator, or one who tilled land as a subordinate of another cultivator.

Section IV
THE (REVENUE) OFFICIALS

First, the *zamīndār;*

second, the *tā'lluqdār,*

third, the *shiqdār* who was in-charge of four or five villages;[13]

fourth, the *tarafdār,* also called *ihtimāmdār,* who looked after from one to four or five villages;

fifth, *patwārī* and *gumāshtā* to be found in each village; he is also known as *karmachārī;*[14]

sixth, *mandal,* head of five or six families of cultivators;

seventh, *hal shahna* also called *ath pahariyā,* a peon (*piyādah*) who was the watchman of the village and collected revenue from it;

eighth, *rasngīr* or the one who actually measured the land (for purposes of revenue collection).

Section V
ON THE METHODS OF REVENUE COLLECTION

First, the watchman would collect revenue from the cultivators according to the *patwārī's* demand order (*chitthī*) and bring it over to the *patwarī* and the *gumāshtā;*

second, the *patwarī* and the *gumāshtā* would collect the revenue of the village at one place and, after deducting the expense of the *mufassal* would remit the rest to the *tarafdār;*

third, the *tarafdār* would remit the revenue from one village or three or four village-settlements that fell within his jurisdiction to the *shiqdār* after deducting the expenses of the *mufassal;*

fourth, the *shiqdār* who looked after four or five villages passed on the revenues of the *mufassal* to the revenue-farmer (*mustajir*) or the *zamīndār* at the *sadr* after deducting the expenses;

fifth, the revenue-farmer or the *zamīndār* would prepare an invoice (*chālān*) of the *pargana* revenues after deducting the expenses of the *mufassal,* also called expenses of the *pargana,* of which details will be given below.

Section VI
ON THE EXPENSES OF THE *MUFASSAL*, ALSO CALLED EXPENSES OF THE *PARGANA*

These vary greatly from one *pargana* to another.

First, charges of the revenue-farmer in the form of monthly salaries etc. for the operatives;

second, charges on account of the *mufassal* or monthly salaries etc. for the operatives of the *zamīndār;*

third, expense on account of the village god (*deb kḥarch*), deities, charity etc;

fourth, local expense (*des kḥarch*), also called the expense on *chaklā* or the price of paper and ink, cost of repair of law-court, price of the carpet, oil, lamp etc. at the *sadr;*

fifth, expense incurred on travel (presumably of the officials);

sixth, presents, gifts (*nazūrāt* and *bhent*), offerings (*salāmī*) and gifts of fruits, sweets etc. (*dāli*);[15]

seventh, monthly salary of the *vakīl*[16] etc. (and other) officials at the *sadr;*

eighth, rent of the house in which the *vakīl* etc. at the *sadr* resided;

ninth, expense on the travel of the revenue-farmer and the *zamīndār* to and from the *sadr;*

tenth, expenses incurred on the Court;

eleventh, discount on currency and interest and the moneylender's discount.

Section VII
ON CERTAIN AFFAIRS OF THE MUFASSAL

Many *tā'lluqdārs* are themselves revenue-payers; in other words they are substitute *zamīndārs.* Many of the *tā'lluqdārs* share in the *zamīndārīs* by themselves paying the land revenue. In case a certain place has no *zamīndār*, an *ihtimāmdār* is appointed for the management of revenue collection. If the *pargana* is large, one *shiqdār* is appointed over the head of three or four *ihtimāmdārs.* Similarly, if the village-settlement is large, two persons, a *patwarī* and a *gumāshtā* are appointed to look after its affairs; otherwise only one *patwarī* manages it by himself. This depends on the amount of assessed revenue (*jama'*) of the *pargana.*

Second, in the *mufassal* the *pattadār* cultivators are treated leniently. If they hold the *pattā* for ten *bīghās,*[17] they actually cultivate fifteen, but pay revenue for the same ten *bīghās.* Consequently, they are well off. The *faslī* cultivators, on the other hand, pay annual revenue on the amount of land they actually cultivate, besides paying occasional imposts (*mathaut*).[18] For this reason they are utterly resourceless. The *paikāsht* cultivators, who have their residence at a different village (from the location of their fields) pay revenue according to the amount of land cultivated along with customary cesses (*mathaut-i mā'mūlī*) charged from them instead of other taxes (i.e. taxes other than land revenue, *abwāb*) etc.; they do not pay occasional imposts levied by the court or miscellaneous (non-customary) imposts (*mathaut-i nawādir*).

Third, on occasions in the *mufassal* when a revenue-farmer seizes the revenue free lands (*bāzē zamīn*) of *zamīndārs* owing to a shortfall in his income and promotes the cultivation of the cultivable waste in the *pargana,* the *zamīndār*, with a view to his own economy and that of the *pattādār* and the concession-holding cultivator, as well as for preempting publicisation of his own secrets, agrees to pay a cess to the extent of the revenue-farmer's deficit; upon which the revenue-farmer refrains from taking charge of the revenue-free lands. In such a circumstance the *pattādār* cultivator etc. who have long been used to leniency, perform their obligation in every way, but the *faslī* cultivators, who are poor to begin with, are brought to veritable ruin. In reality, the prosperity of village settlements and villages depends exclusively upon the *faslī* cultivators who are in a majority.

Fourth, in the *mufassal* the *patwarī* and *gumāshtā* measures the fields of the *faslī* cultivators every year according to custom. As he holds the rope in his hands, he would grab something or the other in offering (*salāmī*) from the cultivator and in turn give him a concession. Everytime the revenue-farmer, for reasons of preventing a shortfall in his income, desired to have the land in the *mufassal* measured or else to despatch an honest *amīn*[19] to the *mufassal* to measure the fields, the *patwarī* and the *gumāshtā* and the *rasngīr* would combine with the *zamīndār's* functionaries. If they discovered the *amīn* to be uninformed and inexperienced, they would cheat him through all manner of fraud and duplicity and would not allow the land to be measured fully. If (the revenue-farmer) made strict enquiries of the *amīn*, they would draw him too into the net of greed. In sum it is hard to complete the measurement of actual land and get hold of the (authentic) document.

Fifth, it is customary at many places in the *mufassal* that land which has been under cultivation one year should be left uncultivated the next year and be brought back under cultivation in the third year. Often, owing to poverty of the cultivators, land which had been tilled one year would subsequently be deserted and would remain uncultivated the next year. In these circumstances, it is extremely difficult to prepare permanent revenue accounts of *parganas* without allowing for discrepancies in consecutive years.

Sixth, the revenue-farmer and *zamīndār*, at the conclusion of every half-yearly crop season, would impose levies on the *mufassal* under such heads as worship (*pūjā kharchā*), expense incurred on peons and on the Court, interest and the moneylender's discount etc. in addition to the land revenue. In such a situation if the *mutasaddī* at the *sadr* be honest and competent and if he insisted only on what was proper and customary there would be no cause for distress to the cultivators; otherwise impoverishment of cultivators and desolation of the *pargana* would become manifest.

Seventh, a cultivator who fell into debt in the *mufassal* often did so owing to the exaction (of land revenue) and excessive new imposts; some contracted debts due to the death of their draught-oxen or else on account of a marriage or a death or unanticipated litigation.

Eighth, in the *mufassals* many of the *sanyāsī faqīrs* and a majority of the men from Buxar were engaged in the business of moneylending. They lent money at the interest of one and a half *ānnā*[20] for a rupee [on condition of its repayment in cash]; in addition they deducted something by way of offerings (*salāmī*) etc. They obtained a written undertaking (*tamassuk*) from the borrower promising to repay the loan within a period of two or three months. Of the money they handed over to the borrower, each rupee (coin) would be short of weight etc. by more than a *pie*;[21] but when the debtor repaid the loan, even though the coins would be of good quality, a *pie* per rupee would be deducted by way of discount. Thus the moneylenders collected more than two *annas* per rupee per month by way of interest and discount etc.[22] In case the debtor failed to repay the loan within the period stipulated in the undertaking, they would reconvert the loan so as to merge the principal and the interest into the new principal for which a fresh written undertaking was obtained (from the debtor). In this manner they would collect interest upon interest and in the process bring ruin upon the cultivators. If (a moneylender) lent money agreeing to its repayment in grain etc., he would first fix the price according to his will; at the time of repayment, if the grain weighed two maunds, he would set its weight at probably a maund and a half. The cultivators, of necessity, have to bear with all this.

Ninth, many of the *zamīndārs* are entitled to fixed allowances at the rate of ten per cent; such of them as do not get fixed allowances obtain their subsistence off former wasteland brought under cultivation by them (*khamār*), self-cultivated (*nij-jot*) or revenue-free lands. Most of the *zamīndārs* have apportioned lands to their brothers, kinsmen and near ones by way of shares (*mīrān*)[23] and for the maintenance of temples etc. and have issued documents (*sanads*) to that effect. But in fact they consume the incomes from these lands themselves. In this the allowance-holding *zamīndārs* are in league with them.

Tenth, of every rupee realised by the watchman in customary imposts in accordance with the *patwarī's* document and brought over to the *patwarī* and the *gumāshtā*, about an *ānnā* and a half goes to meet the expenses of the peons, levies of the law-court and presents etc., the details of which vary with each *pargana,* and the expenses of *patwarī* and the *tarafdār* etc., the other fourteen and-a-half-*ānnās* are despatched to the revenue-farmer or the *zamīndār* at the *sadr.* At the *sadr* expenses of the *pargana,* some brief details of which have been given above, amounting in all to five *ānnās* and a half get deducted and more or less nine *ānnās* are despatched to the (treasury at the) *sadr.* If the *mutasaddī* at the *sadr* be honest, the entire money mentioned in the invoice would be deposited in the treasury at the *sadr,* otherwise the *vakīl* at the *sadr* would send some of the money over to the *mutasaddī* and himself grab some, alter the invoice accordingly and deposit the rest in the treasury. Similarly, in the event of the *mutasaddī's* carelessness, the extent of increase in the *pargana's* expenses by way of corruption may well be visualised.

Eleventh, functionaries of the *khālisā* and the *nizāmat* and agents of the *qānūngos* etc.[24] in the past as well as at present would often buy land in villages in the name of someone else or in their own name, sometimes with the consent (of revenue officials) but mostly through fraud and manipulation. They would exclude their own lands from the payment of revenue. In the revenue-roll (*jama'-i tūmarī*) they prepared and presented to the officer (*hākim*) they showed a shortfall in the assessed revenue owing to desertion and diminution in the revenue paying capacity of (land in) the area. They would then make up this shortfall by devising new imposts for the rest of the *pargana*. In this manner they brought ruin to the *pargana*, keeping for themselves the entire advantage from this manipulation. A majority of such persons would detach their own *tā'lluqā* from one *pargana* while preparing its revenue-roll and attach (the revenue due from it) to another *pargana*. They would collect the revenue thus detached from the first *pargana* and indicate corresponding loss in the revenue of the second (and keep the amount with themselves). Besides, they would grant a concession in the rates (of revenue) to the cultivators of their own *tā'lluqā* and thus maintain its prosperity; on the other hand, other *parganas* would be ruined by excessive demands of arrears of revenue and other levies. Thus, for example, in the province of Azimabad (Bihar) the territory of the *jāgīrdārs* is flourishing due to concessional rates, but the territory under *nizāmat* stands ruined on account of excessive demand.

Twelfth, in the *mufassal* assessment of revenue takes place on two counts: one, land revenue (*māl*) and two, other taxes (*sāir*). Whatever is collected from the produce of agriculture is called *māl* and *sāir* is that which is collected in (other) articles from every village.

Thirteenth, in the reign of Jalal al-din Muhammad Akbar Badshah-i Ghazi Raja Todar Mal had fixed the revenue assessment of all the *mahals*[25] in the provinces of the empire very differentially according to the custom in each *pargana* and in keeping with the views of men in each locality; this assessment was brought to the notice of the emperor and it still stands as valid. This assessment was given the title of revenue-roll (*jama'-i tūmārī*). However, after him there was no able administrator and accomplished *mutasaddī* who would make fresh survey of the all *mahals* and once again determine the revenue assessment (*tashkḥis*). These days men paid (revenue) on the basis of the same revenue-roll but collected it on the basis of the current assessment of the revenue paying capacity of the land and its actual produce. At present the situation in the said revenue-roll is such that the actual assessment is a multiple many times over of the revenue-roll, and at very few places they are at par. There is scarcely a place in Bengal where the actually assessed revenue is less than the revenue-roll.

Section VIII
ON THE MERITS AND DEMERITS OF THE SYSTEM OF REVENUE FARMING ETC.

First, often a revenue-farmer would, before taking the contract, make enquiries in the *mufassal* regarding the situation of comparative revenue-roll (*hast-o-būd*)[26] and would then submit his application to the government seeking (the rights of) revenue-farming (of that area) by offering an increase in the amount of revenue for one year or for consecutive years; he would thus obtain charge. If he was competent and knowledgeable in the job and otherwise upright and honest, after taking charge at the *sadr* he would proceed to the *mufassal* and obtain the document pertaining to the comparative revenue-roll of the *pargana* for the preceding three years. On the basis of this roll he would make an estimate of the land revenue and the various expenses of the *mufassal* and expenses incurred on the Court etc. In this way he would proceed from the old to the new settlement (of revenue). In pursuit of his own profit, he would make enquiries about the newly settled land and would inform himself (in this regard) through various queries addressed to the *patwārī* and the *gumāshtā*. Else, upon examination of the *khasrā*[27] document of the village settlements, he would earmark a certain profit for himself. Besides, he would collect money in some other forms under the heads of fines etc. (but) would not impose new levies. In these conditions land would prosper and cultivators would feel grateful (to the revenue-farmer). But revenue-farmers of this kind are rare in this age.

Second, the revenue-farmer of the present age, even when he is possessed of competence in revenue administration, would make a bid without information about the comparative revenue-roll on the advice of selfish persons, on the basis of his own guess or else on account of competition with rivals. Thus, if one of them offered to increase the revenue by five thousand rupees, another would top it by an extra thousand and raise the offer to six thousand and thereby obtain the (right of) revenue-farming. Since the *mutasaddīs* of today did not bother much about preventing the accumulation of arrears of the settled amount and did not realise the impossibility of this matter (the impossibility of realising the enhanced amount), merely for showing themselves off and for earning the good opinion of their superiors, who would be pleased at the sight of the paper showing an increase in the revenue, they would present the application of the revenue-farmer to the officer, obtain his approval and make a settlement of revenue-farming. Just as they handed over the document (*sanad*) and the order (*parwānā*) to the revenue-farmer they would demand the first instalment of the stipulated amount. The said revenue-farmer would perforce borrow money from the moneylender and pay the dues to the government. In great haste and anxiety he would head for the *mufassal*. On arriving there he would examine the document of the comparative revenue-roll for the preceding three or four years and as he realised the loss he was going to suffer his senses would desert him. Not caring at all for the prosperity or ruination of the *pargana*, he would take resort to various kinds of oppression and innovation one after another—from measuring and attaching the revenue-free lands of the *zamīndār* to levying imposts. With the sole aim of exacting money, he would, in every way he could, execute his contract for the collection of the principal amount and meeting the expenses (of the *mufassal*). Placed in this situation where could he find the time for extending cultivation? On account of the harshness of (revenue) collection, levying of new imposts and excessive interest and discount of the moneylender, the cultivator would flee (his land), the *pargana* would become desolate and the *zamīndār* would be ruined. This would result in a shortfall in revenue; in the end (the revenue-farm) would be put to auction.

Third, there are inexperienced persons of the kind that have no knowledge of conditions prevailing in the *mufassal;* being misled by selfish advisers, they contract a desire for revenue-farming and obtain it by raising the bid. The *zamīndārs,* realising the revenue-farmer to be an ignoramus, join hands with his subordinates and, drawing them into the net of greed, ruin their *mufassal* with their own hands. Of the money they make they give a share to the revenue-farmer's men and the rest they keep with themselves. They would then complain to their superiors about the revenue-farmer's oppression and innovations and would thus reduce justice to injustice. They would demand a reduction in next year ('s revenue), blaming the revenue-farmer for the decline. The revenue-farmer on one hand suffers a loss in the contracted amount and on the other gets the blame before the officers for causing ruination of the *pargana.*

Account of conditions when the settlement (of revenue) is undertaken by the *zamīndār* himself:

First, the settlement with the *zamīndār* obtained by him on producing a moneylender's surety. To begin with, the *zamīndār* has all intention of realising the amount according to his settlement, but in the end this system proves harmful. It ensures gain only for the moneylender, for, in compliance with official injunction regarding the provision of surety, the *zamīndār* would approach the moneylender and, besides the five per cent commission that is officially sanctioned for such security, would in addition agree to part with something or the other by way of offering (*salāmī*) etc.; he would give an undertaking to deposit the gross income (*āmdanī-i kḥām*) at the said moneylender's headquarters (*kothi,* literally bungalow) and thus by entreating and imploring him the *zamīndār* would persuade him to stand surety. Often the moneylender would nominate his own agent to act as the treasurer of the *pargana* and would direct him to accompany the *zamīndār*. Again, they would often get hold of the gross receipts at the *chaklā* headquarters and for reason of having stood surety for the *zamīndār* would bring him under (their) control. They would secure from the *zamīndār* excessive profit by way of interest, discount and offerings and by changing the terms of the *zamīndār's* undertaking. They would in any case receive their due on account of the customary commission for standing surety. In these circumstances the *zamīndārs* would combine all these customary dues of surety and interest and discount etc. and turn them into new imposts which were then collected from the *pargana.* In consequence, the impoverished cultivator would take to flight. Whenever the collection of revenue fell into arrears in a *pargana,* the moneylender would never pay off from his own funds the amount for which he had stood surety. However, he would advance loan to the *zamīndār* over two or three years so that on the basis of his claim for the recovery of the loan he would be able to have the *zamīndāri* auctioned. If the *zamīndār* did not give his assent to the auction for repayment of the loan, the moneylender would prefer his claim before the Court quite forgetting that the amount he had already collected by way of interest and discount etc. equalled the principal. In this situation, the appointment of a moneylender as surety yields profit only to him. It is believed that some amongst the moneylenders apparently engage in the business of moneylending with the ulterior motive of purchasing *zamīndārīs* by standing surety for *zamīndārs* and, pending the realisation of this objective, earn large profits by way of the surety's customary perquisites, and interest and discount etc. And the ignorant *zamīndār,* being oblivious of this turn of things, ruins himself as well as the land.

Second, many of the *zamīndārs* of Bengal are completely ignorant (of the affairs of *zamīndārī*), and such amongst them as do possess the necessary skill are absorbed in luxurious living, carelessness and extravagance. In such a circumstance, acting entirely on their own, they would make the settlement and return home to devote themselves to extravagance and a life of luxury and indiscriminate expenditure. They would hand over the charge of the actual assessment and collection (of revenue) and extension of agriculture to the *nāib* and the *dīwān.*[28] Since the latter are not the real masters of the *pargana,* instead of devoting themselves to the promotion of its welfare, they exert themselves towards an even harsher collection (of revenue) than the revenue-farmer did and would care only for their own gain. After submitting the principal amount of land revenue, they would present another bit to the *zamīndār* as if this were an addition; this they did in order to impress the *zamīndār* with their efficiency. Since the said *zamīndār* would be ignorant of his own affairs, receipt of one additional bit would appeal to him as an unforeseen gain; he would thus regard the *nāib* and the *dīwān* as very efficient and as his well wishers and would give them even greater freedom than hitherto. But then, in the second or third year there would be a steep fall in the principal amount of land revenue and the said *zamīndār* would, of necessity, borrow from the moneylender to meet the government's demand. He would at this time change the *nāib* and the *dīwān*. In sum, within a period of three or four years, whenever he was unable to get hold of a loan, the *zamīndār* would come under the government's bondage, the land would be deserted and would be excluded from the revenue assessment. At this stage, the *zamīndār*, subjected to repeated reminders from the officers, would be left with little option except to put the *zamīndārī* up for auction. If a creditable buyer appears at this moment and buys the *zamīndārī* and makes up the deficit of the *pargana* from his own funds and devotes himself to resettling it, it can recover again within a period of two or three years; otherwise it has been noticed that where such a buyer does not materialise the government is left with no choice but to allow a reduction (in the land revenue).

Third, the boundaries of all the *zamīndārīs* are mixed up with one another. On occasions when their territories are devoid of a strong governor or his men, the business of the small *zamīndār's* lands is ruined by the tyrraneous hand of the bigger *zamīndār* and complaints keep being constantly lodged with the government on this score. Those amongst the *zamīndārs* who are at par with each other take to arms for settling their boundary disputes; in the process they bring ruin upon the cultivators and desolation to the *pargana*. To begin with, out of stubbornness and anger they would pay no heed to the desertion of land and the complaints being lodged with the government; ultimately, the tyranny of junior functionaries on both sides manifests itself to the extent that Court officials are hardly left with time even to breathe. In the end even this circumstance becomes a cause of the desertion of the *pargana* and decline of the government's revenue.

Fourth, many *zamīndārs* have a share of twenty or twenty-five per cent in a *zamīndāri.* In the circumstance of their own management (of the *zamīndārī*), disputes would arise and they would take resort to violent conflict with one another; they would all lodge complaints with the Court, keep the payment of government's dues in arrears and ruin the land.

Description of settlement (*muta'hudī*) where the obligation to pay a definite amount to the government is accepted by the *zamīndār* and on this declaration the signature of the contractor is obtained.

In the past this settlement was much favoured by the governors. In this settlement, if the contracting person be inefficient or dishonest, deficiencies of a different order make their appearance. The difference between the systems of revenue-farming and that of the formal contract (*muta'hudi*) is in that the deed of revenue farming carries no qualifications and no exceptions so that the revenue-farmer is himself responsible for his gains and losses. Ultimately no excuse by him is entertained with regard to the payment of the sum agreed to. The substance of the deed of formal contract is as follows: on the document of the acceptance of obligation (*qabūliat*) signed by the *zamīndār,* the contractor puts on record that he will deposit with the government the sum stipulated therein after collecting it from the *pargana* through the *zamīndār*. It is incumbent upon the contractor that if the revenue paying capacity (*jāidād*)[29] of the *mufassal* exceeds that mentioned in the principal settlement, he should inform the *hākim,* and if, God forbid, some terrestrial or celestial calamity befall the land, this too he should report (to the *hākim*) who is autonomous in this regard. If he so desires, placing his faith in the report of the contractor, he could send a proposal to the *amīn* to the effect that for the prosperity of the region if an appropriate remission of revenue is required due to damage caused, revenue be remitted accordingly; otherwise he could direct the contractor to make up the loss through imposition of levies upon the cultivators. In such a circumstance, if the contractor be competent and upright, the reality of the comparative revenue-roll in the *mufassal* comes clearly into light and the *zamīndār* is unable to raise the hand of oppression over the cultivators through the imposition of new levies etc.; nor can he grab the money collected from the *pargana* for payment of revenue to the government. In this way it (the system of formal contract) helps in making land more prosperous. This then in short is the system of formal contract and it is understandable that the appointment of a government official[30] as contractor might be more economical than revenue-farming or the system of the *zamīndār's* self-management in which he is obliged to pay for the surety's perquisites. This system is also efficacious in settling large tracts, in the appointment of (English?) men of sound disposition who are familiar with the language and who are accompanied by honest and competent *mutasaddīs*, in the submission of appropriate proposals to the officers of the district (*sāhibān-i zila'*) regarding (the appointment of) reliable contractors in the mufassal (to act) in concurrence with the aforesaid *mutasaddīs* and collecting information about the *mufassals* where the cultivators are greatly burdened with various innovations that are illegitimately imposed upon them and in eliminating these; through proper checks the excessive expenses in the *pargana* can also be minimized.

Description of the *amāni* system and the method of (revenue) collection (*hasb-i wusūlī*):

It is singularly known that attending to the settling of tracts in the *mufassal* by way of government's direct responsibility (*batarīq-i amānat*) falls to the charge of reliable *'āmils*. The said *'āmil* proceeds to the *mufassal*, undertakes appropriate actions to bring the *mahals* under complete settlement and despatches revenue to the treasury month by month. If the (total) sum despatched exceeds the preceding year's or the *pargana* grows in prosperity and the repose of the cultivators becomes firm thanks to the efforts of the *mutasaddī* of the *khālisā*, the next year too the said *'āmil* would remain in position to earn renown for his virtuousness and honesty. If the situation be different, he would be transferred and an account would be taken from him and whatever amount of graft could be traced to him would be seized. In the future he would be known to the *mutasaddī* for his incompetence and dishonesty. The past governors often assigned this kind of responsibility to their own kinsmen and near ones, and, relying upon their testimony, would not subject them to the taking of account.

Section IX
ON THE REGULATIONS IMPLEMENTED BY PAST GOVERNORS IN ADMINISTERING TERRITORIES

First, governors in the past would never appoint one person to the management of a task pertaining to two areas. For a man has just one heart and whenever his affairs went awry, he would lose control of his senses. In such a situation of loss of senses, ruination of both areas can be easily visualised. In particular, he would fail to collect information relevant to his responsibilities.

Second, although in the empire of India, owing to the need for proper precautions in the issue of *sanads* in revenue matters as well as in other matters relating to administration, certain signs and symbols have been earmarked for the use of officials—into the details of which there is no merit in going at this place except merely to prolong the discourse—governors in the past and the *mutasaddīs* that have gone by considered two departments as the most important among all departments of administration: one, the department of *dīwānī*, and the other the department of *amānat* which were both run as a check upon each other. Whenever an invoice of revenue from the *mufassal* was received it was in two parts; one part of it was entered in the *dīwānī* register and the other in the *amānat* register. No expense could be incurred without the seal of the office of *amānat*. Consequently, no discrepancy in accounts arose.

Third, past governors exercised utmost caution and placed a great deal of importance on the appointment of *mutasaddīs* in the *khālisā*, for the administration of territories and implementation of regulations lies in their (the *mutasaddīs'*) hands. They would appoint a person from amongst old employees who had proved his competence and honesty in the crucible of trial; or else, they would look out for a *mutasaddī* in an eminent family whose elders were known for virtuousness, integrity and loyalty and who was himself capable of handling the affairs of administration. Having located one such, they would honour him with entrusting the responsibilities of administration. It was thus that the late Nawab Mahabat Jung, who was a wise man of his age, after the death of Rai Rayan Bhairon Dutt, brought over Maharaja Kirat Chand, descendant of Rai Rayan Alam Chand, from Banaras and honoured him with the responsibility of the *dīwānī* of *khālisā-i sharīfā,*[31] despite the presence of other *mutasaddīs* such as Maharaja Mahendra, Durlabh Ram Bahadur, Raj Ballabh and Raja Sakat Singh etc.

Fourth, the *mutasaddīs* of the *khālisā-i sharīfā* subsist entirely off the *jāgīr* assigned to them by the government and do not obtain for themselves the various customary offerings and presents etc.; nor do they possess any *tā'lluqā* or *zamīndārī*. The past governors were particularly cautious about entrusting the responsibility of the office of the *mutasaddī* of the *khālisā* to anyone who was also in possession of *tā'lluqā* or villages, for it is unwise to set up the thief as the watchman. In fact they would exercise caution in appointing Bengalis to this office for many of them are relations or near ones of the *zamīndārs* and many would pass off barley in the garb of wheat.

Fifth, whenever a *mutasaddī* of the *khālisā* takes a bribe from the official of the *mufassal,* he falls completely into their grip and, out of embarrassment for taking the bribe, he is unable to take any punitive action on any count against them for such of their deeds as are unworthy of officials and functionaries of the *mufassal*. The moment these officials are able to ensnare the *mutasaddī* of the *khālisā* into the net of greed, they proceed to the *mufassal* unrestrained and, raising the hand of oppression, they make collections from the cultivator under the heads of such imposts as Court expenses etc. at their will. Of every rupee they collect, they hand over eight *ānnās* to the *mutasaddī* of the *khālisā* and the other eight *ānnās* they consign to their own pockets. As a result the land gets deserted and arrears in the payment of revenue get accumulated. For this reason, governors in the past used to exercise great discrimination in the appointment of *mutasaddīs* of the *khālisā*.

Sixth, past administrators (*hākims*) weighed officials in the balance of judgment. Whenever a person was found to be spending more than what would be his income as a government servant, an enquiry would be conducted. If the said official's dishonesty and corruption were proved, he received commensurate punishment. In case extravagance on his part came to light, he was not entrusted with superior jobs in the future, for they (the *hākims*) would remark that one who could not keep his own income and expenditure under check could hardly exercise economy when it came to others.

Seventh, such were the governors in the past that they would frequently transfer officials; they regarded the advantage of this policy in such a wise that with every transfer the person's honesty, integrity and competence would be tested and every official, high or low, would become fully conversant with the system of accounting; this would restrain him from giving-in to the temptation of corruption. Always keeping in mind the day of reckoning of accounts, they (the officials) would refrain from what is forbidden. Besides, even if one was inclined (towards corruption), the risk of dismissal would keep one's foot from transgressing the path of caution. The unemployed would also not lose heart and go astray, for they could hope for securing office and distinction. However, a person who had proved his perseverence in the path of honesty and virtue through repeated tests was exempted from transfer.

Eighth, if the incompetence of one amongst the officials regarding administrative responsibility came to the knowledge of governors in the past, or else if someone from amongst the officials brought to their notice a case of corruption on the part of a colleague, the latter was suspended from his office forthwith and was subjected to account-checking and through inquiries the facts of the case were ascertained. In case his incompetence was proved, he was demoted from a high position and entrusted with lowly responsibilities; if the charges of corruption were established, he was awarded punishment commensurate with his crime so that other officials would take lesson from it. On the other hand, if no discrepancy (in his accounts) appeared, he was rewarded with a higher honour than earlier and was given a corresponding office and the complainant, who had lodged the report out of animosity, or evil disposition, was similarly punished so that no one would dare indulge in speaking an untruth and creating fissures in the administration in the future.

Ninth, during the regime of the past governors, whenever someone applied for revenue-farming in one of the *mahals* by raising the bid, the *dīwān* of the *khālisā* did not have the courage to forward his application to the governor immediately. Only after he had satisfied himself fully did he forward it to the governor and explained the attendant circumstances. If the governor approved of it, he would place his signature on it and award the settlement to the said revenue-farmer from whom a written bond was obtained that he would not impose levies on the *mufassal* on account of the enhanced bid and that he would take appropriate steps to increase population, extend cultivation and effect a raise in the government's revenue. The *mutasaddī* of the *khālisā* too always kept himself informed of the working of revenue officials so that no one imposed new levies etc. on the *pargana* without the government's permission as these often became the cause of distress to the cultivator and desertion of land. If, God forbid, in spite of all this precaution, innovations of a different nature devised by an official appeared in the *mufassal,* a report about these was made to the governor and the official was immediately given the punishment he deserved so that an example was set before others. Yet, on occasion, when a part of the revenue remained unpaid in the *mahals* under the system of revenue-farming or else innovations devised by some came to the notice of the governors and were confirmed through investigations, (it became apparent that) the *mutasaddī* had lost his grip over the affairs and the time had arrived for his transfer. Similarly, the sharing of administrative authority is the cause of frittering away of the administration. Keeping this in view, the emperors that have gone by, while appointing governors in the provinces, always gave the reins of authority in its totality in the hands of those who would exercise it entirely by themselves in the management of the administration. However, for keeping himself informed of the virtues and shortcomings and of the omissions and commissions of the said governors, *wāqia-nigārs* and *sawānih-nigārs* were appointed in every province by the resplendent presence (the emperor) and they were unfailingly to despach a narrative of all the events and occurrences to the exalted presence.

Tenth, the practice of the governors in the past was such that besides the officials, they would retain one or two other persons in their service who had actual knowledge of the administration and who were wise, competent and honourable but no specific territorial jurisdiction was earmarked to them. For their subsistence, and by way of encouragement they were allotted a part (of the revenue) as an allowance, lest, at some stage, they might be faced with need in some form and they might soil their reputation in trying to meet it. An undertaking was obtained from them that they would pay no heed to the selfish words of any of the concerned persons, nor ever bring such words to their lips; that they would report without loss of time such actual news or hearsay that they came across; that they would answer every query regarding administration that is addressed to them exactly and clearly according to their understanding and would not allow their own interest to stand in any manner in the way of performing their duty. In retaining such men, the *hākims* of the past had at their heart the feeling that persons with territorial assignments sought to pursue their own selfish ends at the time of elaboration of the prevailing conditions by declaring the good to be bad and supporting it with sophisticated arguments. In such a circumstance, a person with no selfish motives, on being asked, would speak clearly and tender good advice. In this way correct news of the happenings in every corner would reach (them). It was thus that the *hākims* considered all precautions against untruthful persons in good order.

REFERENCES

1. E.U.L. Persian MS. no. 144.
2. *The Agrarian System of Mughal India*, Bombay, 1963, p. 413.
3. 'Agrarian Structure of Bengal at the Beginning of British Conquest', *Proceedings of the Indian History Congress*, 1974, p. 179.
4. A term commonly used for European men in authority in India; see H.H. Wilson, *Glossary of Judicial and Revenue Terms*, London, 1855, Indian edn., Delhi, 1968, s.v. Sahib.
5. Home Misc. Series MS. 68, OIOC, p. 711.
6. A clerk, a writer, also used as a generic term which includes very high revenue officials as well. In this document itself persons of the order of Maharaja Mahendra Vallabh and Raja Sakat Singh have been referred to as *mutasaddīs*.
7. Literally, 'innovation' [*bida't*]. Innovation of any tax or impost, apart from the customary dues, was seen as additional burden, hence oppressive. The term also has a religious nuance in Islam, for any innovation or departure from the path shown by Muhammad is perceived as heresy and therefore sinful.
8. A large, but unstandard, territorial unit carved out from mid-17th century for fiscal administration.
9. Both the terms literally mean 'inspector of events'. The former, more correctly *waqāi' nigār*, reported transactions relating to revenue in the provinces to his superior in rank at the court; the latter generally reported news of happenings in his territory to the ruler.
10. Lit. separate or distinct; contextually, country as opposed, as well as subordinate to town, big or small, the *sadr*, headquarters or the principal seat.
11. An administrative and revenue unit smaller than a district, but the size varies considerably.
12. *Pattā* is usually rendered as lease. I have preferred document, for lease would imply State ownership of land on which the cultivator held the lease, hardly a viable proposition among historians today.
13. Village, a somewhat more vague unit than *mauza'* which conforms more closely to the revenue unit properly identified in revenue records, though the two terms are often, as in this document, used interchangeably. However, in this translation *deh* has been rendered as village and *mauza'* as village-settlement, if only to indicate the term used in the text.

14. *Patwarī:* A village level functionary who kept records of all village lands, their produce, assessments, etc. *Gumāshtā:* An agent. The *Risāla* often uses the two terms to refer to one person.
15. Presents, gifts and offerings have each a different significance though all put together comprise things given by persons to their superiors. Thus they have as much a social function of reinforcing hierarchy as economic, i.e. transfer of resources from the lower to the upper strata. Professor Z.U. Malik reads *dālī* as *dānī* and translates it as 'alms-giving', op.cit., p. 183. If the word were indeed *dānī,* it would be translated as alms giver rather than alms-giving and would thus be a complete misfit in the Section on Expenses. Murray makes no mistake and reads it as *'Dally'* and translates it as 'garden stuff', op.cit., p. 732. See also Wilson, op.cit., s.v. *dali.*
16. Under the Sultans of Delhi, a high official of state; later merely a representative.
17. The *bīghā* was a measure of land; in Bengal it amounted to a third of an acre. Murray unfortunately reads two *bīghās* for ten, op.cit., p. 733.
18. Occasional cess or impost collected from the cultivators for some special purpose or under some incidental pretext either by the state or the *zamīndār;* see Wilson, op.cit., s.v. Murray renders it as 'additional assessment', op.cit., p. 733.
19. The assessor of revenue.
20. *Ānnā:* one-sixteenth of a rupee. Malik has made it a mere half *ānnā* per rupee, op.cit., p. 185.
21. A fourth of the *ānnā* or 1/64h part of a rupee.
22. I.e. 150 per cent per annum.
23. *Mīrān* is a share paid to one's superiors out of what one receives as fees or perquisites. Malik reads the term as *maisrān* but does not explain it, op.cit., p. 185. Indeed, to the best of my knowledge there is no such word in the Persian language.
24. *Khālisā:* those lands the revenue from which was deposited directly in the imperial treasury instead of being assigned away in *jāgīr* etc. *Nizāmat:* Office of the Chief of Police and Administrator of criminal law. *Qānūngo:* Keeper of land and revenue records in the village; also 'assisted in the measurement and survey of lands reporting deaths and successions of revenue-payers'; see Wilson, op.cit., s.v. Kanungo.
25. A varying unit of territory defined as revenue unit.
26. A comparative revenue-roll of dues collected from each cultivator in the past up to the current year.

27. A document which identifies each field by a number, details of its size, layout, the quality of its soil, the name of its owner etc.
28. *Nāib:* Lit. deputy; often, as here, deputy collector of the revenue. *Dīwān:* Originally the name for any high office, but gradually came to refer to the chief of the department of finance each at the imperial and the provincial levels.
29. *Jāidād* literally is property, used here in a slightly different sense. The use of the term is somewhat rare in revenue documents of the pre-18th century but appears to have become common in the 18th century when it refers to different kinds of land revenue-paying holdings. At times the term is used for the revenue assigned to mercenary troopers, especially Europeans; at others it serves as a substitute for the *jāgīr*. I owe this insight to Muzaffar Alam.
30. Actually *sihbandī,* a kind of irregular militia employed for collecting revenue; see Wilson, op.cit., s.v. Sibandi.
31. The lands from which the revenue is excusively reserved for the imperial Court.

TECHNOLOGY

13

Agricultural Technology in Medieval North India*

I

High fertility of Indian soils is a feature that has been noticed throughout the centuries of India's written history with a rare degree of unanimity amongst the country's own as well as foreign observers. This fertility was attested in two ways: positively by the number of crops the soils bore each year, and negatively by the virtual absence of fallowing from the cycle of agricultural production.

The earliest written evidence for the cultivation of two crops in a year comes from the Vedic text, *Taittiriya Samhita*.[1] Continuous corroboration of this evidence follows in Megasthenes' account (close of the fourth century B.C.),[2] Kautilya's *Arthasastra*,[3] and the *Brhatsamhita* of the Gupta period.[4] Ibn Battuta in the early fourteenth century A.D. makes the unambiguous statement that 'the Indians sow twice a year'[5] and of course by the end of the sixteenth century all recorded revenue rates of Akbar's empire pertained to the spring and

---

* Revised version of paper submitted to Seminar on 'Technology in pre-colonial India' organised by the Birla Industrial and Technological Museum, Calcutta, in September 1984. The paper was published in a badly mauled form by Sundeep Parkashan, Delhi, in A. Roy and S.K. Bagchi, eds., *Technology in Ancient and Medieval India*, 1986. It is hard to come across such atrocious publishing. Since then, however, it has been reproduced in several anthologies.

autumn harvests.[6] At the end of the eighteenth century or the turn of the nineteenth, Rev. William Tennant, no great admirer of Indian agriculture, could not help noting that '...here, the same field in the common culture, yields several crops, two and often three within the year.'[7]

The fact that the Indian soils yielded two crops a year is, of course, true merely as a general statement; understandably, there would be considerable regional variation in the degree of soil fertility. Thus, if some regions were capable of yielding three[8] or four crops[9] a year, others evened out nature's largesse by producing more or less one crop and perhaps an insignificant second in the year.[10] Indeed, such variation was noticed even in neighbouring regions at the end of the eighteenth century when Major Beatson toured the 'Calaitri, Neucataghire, Nellore and Ongole countries' and found them under continuous cultivation and lush green' even though 'there had not been a drop of rain for four months' but 'Guntur Circar exhibited a miserable contrast....'[11]

If we get an almost unbroken chain of evidence suggesting continuous cultivation of land which thus yielded two, or more, crops a year, this should by itself imply the virtual absence of the practice of fallowing from agricultural operations. But then there is the term *khila* or *khila-ksetra* used in several of our sources and generally translated as 'the fallow' by modern historians. This is an unhappy translation, for it lumps all categories of uncultivated lands under a single head, overlooking the distinction between a land which is virgin, and one which has been abandoned after an earlier bout of tilling and still a third from which the plough has been all-too-temporarily withdrawn.[12] Unlike the virgin and the abandoned lands, fallow is an integral part of the cycle of cultivation and often requires more intensive ploughing than the one sown, for its clods must be repeatedly smashed in order to spread out the soil and its weeds must be ploughed back or burnt down to be turned into green manure or potash. Clearly then the fallow could not be just any land which was not under cultivation. Indeed, at the beginning of the nineteenth century British observers made a clear distinction between the fallow and the lay (or the lea), both under the cycle of cultivation. Thus speaking of Bengal agriculture, William Tennant noted: '... the Indian allows it (the land) a lea, but never a fallow,'[13] a remark also made by Colebrooke.[14] The lay is the respite given to a field by leaving it temporarily untilled, thereby allowing it to recover its lost fertility on its own. The category of *parauti* land, among the four categories listed in the *Ain*[15] is the one that comes closest to the lay linguistically as much as an agricultural practice. It is worthwhile remembering that *parauti* was gradually to be brought over to the category of the continuously cultivated *polaj* land. Surely then, fallowing was a rigorous exercise and made considerable demands on human as well as animal labour. Fallowing also points to a soil that is quickly exhausted. The lay, or a brief withdrawal of the plough from the field on the other hand, would indicate a soil with a greater capacity to recoup its exhausted fertility without human intervention. Thus the indifferent translation of *khila* as the fallow can hardly be of much use for a reconstruction of the history of ancient and medieval agriculture. Indeed, such of our sources as deal with agriculture exclusively or in part are conspicuously silent on the practice of fallowing.[16]

The significance of obtaining at least two crops a year generally from most Indians fields, without the interruption of the fallow should stand in higher relief when compared with west European agriculture. Over the early medieval centuries to the end of the first millennium A.D., a half of western Europe's arable land lay fallow under the regime of the two-field rotation.[17] And the seed: yield ratio stood at 1:1.6 or at best 1:2.5.[18] It is only by the thirteenth century that the three-field rotation became common especially in southern Europe; this allowed two-thirds of the arable land to be sown within the year and raised the seed:yield ratio to 1:4.[19] Quite an impressive achievement, and yet a third of the cultivated lands still yielded nothing over the year. Compared with the almost continuous cultivation of most Indian fields, each yielding two crops a year at the theoretical seed:yield ratio of 1:12 for each crop,[20] this was yet a dismal level of productivity. It was only in the eighteenth century that western Europe was able to eliminate the fallow through rotation of crops and obtain one crop every year from each field; this was the 'agricultural revolution' which made the eighteenth century the threshold of progress in Europe.[21]

But then, if India had produced an average of two crops every year in each field, with practically no fallowing, what explains such high fertility of its soil? Surely, some part of this fertility must get exhausted with each harvest and, unless renewed, land just cannot go on yielding crops.

The renewal of soil fertility took place either naturally, thanks to the climate and the deposit of fertile silt in the river valley with each annual inundation, or through artificial manuring or through an admixture of both.

Climatically, the sizzling heat of the summer months, followed by the moisture of the monsoons, greatly facilitated the quick decomposition of organic matter and turned it into fertile humus at the soil's surface itself. When the enormous annual deposits of silt in the valleys of the great rivers in India are added to it, the high density of cultivated lands, and of rural population in those valleys become intelligible. The Indus and the Ganga alone are estimated to carry around a million tons each of suspended matter daily.[22] The average annual hydraulic discharge of Indus at Sukkur is over 5 million cubic feet and the silt it carries amounts to nearly 10 million cubic feet. In twenty-nine years between 1902 and 1930 the silt deposit between Sukkur and Kotri was estimated to have amounted to about 1300 sq. miles of land surface.[23] The Indus soils are on the whole coarser than the silt in the Ganga basin, for, the 'Indus rivers losing water, tend to drop their detritus early (while) those of the Ganga, continually reinforced by many large tributaries, carry their loads much further',[24] thus grinding the detritus down to very fine, and very fertile, silt. And yet, even in the less fertile Indus region the cultivation of foodgrains required no manure and 'involves an absolute minimum of skill, labour and aid of implements.'[25] It is therefore understandable that the more fertile Gangaic plains should be one of the most cultivated in India, with well over half the total area of some 40,000,000-45,000,000 acres cultivated and double cropping adds 20-25% to this figure.[26] It was in appreciation of this highly fertile property of the Ganga water that the eminent hydraulic engineer, Sir William Willcocks, argued so strongly in favour of shallow canals that would ensure 'overflow irrigation' carrying muddy river water into the fields.[27]

All these data set out above refer to modern practice. If we then consider that under the Mughals the area of land under cultivation amounted to between one-fifth and three-fourths in different regions compared to the early twentieth century,[28] it would be reasonable to assume that cultivation was then confined to the most fertile of these generally fertile plains. This should partly explain the decline in average agricultural productivity from the Mughal to the British period,[29] when the relatively less fertile lands were brought under the plough.

There is, besides, manure to consider. Manure was applied in two different ways; either solutions were prepared with mixtures of different fertilising agents and applied to the seeds prior to sowing and this was thought to ensure better germination; or else, manure was applied to the field at the time of sowing the seeds or when seedlings had been formed. The *Arthasastra* recommends the use of a mixture of honey, clarified butter, the fat of hogs and cow-dung for plastering the cut end of the seeds of sugarcane 'and the like'; seeds of bulbous roots were to be treated to cow-dung and the manure of the bones and dung of cows was to be given to the trees. The sprouts were to be manured with a fresh haul of minute fishes and irrigated with the milk of *snuhi* (*Euphorbia Antiquorum*).[30]

While the *Arthasastra* recongnises 'the fertilising qualities of cow-dung, cow-bones and fish'[31] these elements were still perhaps applied in the raw rather than as compost. Also that their application was still mainly confined to the seeds and only in one case (of cotton) to the sprouts; the manure had not yet been brought to the field itself except in the case of trees. Recommendation for the treatment of seeds with similar mixtures continued to be made in the following centuries.[32] The first clear reference to the actual application of cow-dung to the fields is to be found in the *Harsacharita* of Bana. Bana describes a cultivator driving bullock-carts filled with cow-dung and other refuse to the fields to restore their fertility.[33] It is the *Krsi-Parasara* that clearly refers to the preparation of compost from cow-dung to be used in the field at the time of sowing, though its use is limited to the cultivation of paddy.[34] The later texts make very scant mention of animal manure; but then its abundance itself could have been the reason for its omission from the records. If, as we have seen above, the Mughal age witnessed the breaking-in of no more than a fifth to three-fourths of the most fertile of Indian lands compared to the early part of the twentieth century, clearly the abounding forests and pastures would have supported a far more numerous cattle population then. Indeed, the *Ain* considers the peasants who owned four oxen, two cows and one buffalo for every plough too poor to be taxed.[35] Moreover, besides the forests which had been spared the aggression of the plough, pastures should have provided considerable sustenance to cattle. The care that was bestowed upon pastures is suggestive of the recognition of its significance. The *Arthasastra* instructs the king to earmark parts of a village for pasturage.[36] It refers to the office of the superintendent of pasture lands[37] and enjoins upon the village accountant to set up boundaries of the pasture grounds, among others.[38] Obstruction of approach to the pasture was to be punished with the highest amount of fine of 1000 *panas*.[39] Later sources continue to emphasize the significance of pastures and we even have an occasional reference to the officer specifically appointed to look after them,[40] much in the tradition of the *Arthasastra*. In the seventeenth century Manrique saw 'enormous herds' of animals grazing in pastures in Bengal even though the region was otherwise very densely cultivated.[41] It is interesting to note that among our sources there is hardly any mention of the cultivation of any fodder, much as oats was cultivated in Europe. Clearly, forests and pastures and, of course, the stubble left in the field after the crop had been harvested were adequate to maintain a large enough cattle population.[42]

If it be true that 'In most parts of the country, though not everywhere, there was more wasteland available for grazing, and it is reasonable to infer that cattle would be obtained more cheaply and easily than is now possible',[43] the religious ban on the slaughter of cows must also have helped. It might therefore be reasonable to derive two inferences from this: that manure in the form of animal droppings was far from being scarce and that such and other manures should have helped to restore the fertility of fields deprived of annual silt deposit to a greater extent than the ones where rivers themselves renewed the soil.[44] By the first half of the nineteenth century the scarcity of manure had come to be felt rather acutely so that its application came to be confined to particular crops, such as sugarcane, maize, jowar, cotton and tobacco, 'which cannot be brought to any perfection without manure'.[45]

II

If high fertility of soil was one feature of agricultural ecology of ancient and medieval India, the necessity of retaining moisture for proper germination of seeds and growth of plants was another. This in turn determined the shape of the primary agricultural implement, the plough. If the much maligned Indian plough merely scratched the soil rather than dig deep into it,[46] this was to preserve the moisture underneath, for, upturning the deeper soil would expose it to the harsh sun and thereby run it dry. Thus any deep ploughing could only reduce, instead of enhancing, soil fertility. Lt.-Col. G.B. Tremenheere had perceived this more than a century and a quarter ago and had stated thus: 'Many a disparaging remark has been made on the native plough, its simplicity and lightness and its merely "scratching the ground", but a little reflection will show that, under the peculiar circumstances of climate and soil, it is probably the best. In England, the object is to break up the hard masses of mould or stiff clay, and to get rid of superfluous moisture while here, in light and tractable soil, scarcely a clod can be seen, and to preserve, in the subsoil, the rain and moisture it imbibes at certain periods (is) the cultivator's greatest care. It is evident therefore that deep ploughing would be unsuited to such conditions. If the surface is loosened so as to allow the delicate fibers of the roots to penetrate and to secure free access of air, it will be sufficient; to turn up the soil from below, and to expose it to a hot sun and drying wind, would be most injurious.'[47] If the plough was therefore light and simple, it was not awfully deficient for being devoid of iron. It has been argued that the high price of iron put it beyond the reach of medieval Indian peasantry, rendered utterly resourceless by the State, since the bulk of agrarian surplus had been appropriated from it in the form of revenue.[48] The assumption underlying this argument is that iron plough would surely have proved more productive if only it could be afforded. This emphasis on the use of iron appears to have originated in the increasing use of it in west European plough from circa eleventh century; but evidently such emphasis is somewhat misplaced in the Indian ecological context.

It is of course not as if no iron was used in the Indian plough, or other agricultural implements. Indeed, the antiquity of such usage is quite impressive. D.P. Agarwal suggests that iron was used in making the plough in circa 800 B.C.,[49] and it appears fairly certain that Panini, who lived in the NBP phase, actually refers to iron ploughshare.[50] Several other agricultural implements made of iron have been recovered from excavations at Atranjikhera at PGW levels[51] and at Taxila from the period 300 B.C. to 100 A.D.[52] Brahaspati (early Gupta age) recommends that 'iron twelve *palas* in weight should be formed into what is called a ploughshare. It should be eight *angulas* long and four *angulas* broad'.[53] It would therefore be hard to believe that in the following centuries the price of iron had risen so high as to place even a scrap of it required for sheathing or making ploughshare beyond all strata of the highly stratified medieval Indian peasantry. If the price of iron in terms of wheat at the end of the sixteenth century was thrice what it was in 1914, as W.H. Moreland has shown,[54] that surely should be constructed as an argument in favour of, rather than against, the use of just a trifle of iron in the medieval plough, given its durability and its assumed high productivity.[55]

So far we have spoken of the Indian plough in the singular.

Such, however, was not the case, for there were considerable regional and temporal variations in the shape and size of this crucial instrument, and these variations too have great antiquity behind them. The *Rig Vedic* plough (*sira, langala* and not the *hala*) was apparently a simple and light apparatus, for the geographical vision of the *Rig Veda* was confined to the light soil of the Indus-Punjab region. By the time of the *Atharva Veda,* however, heavy ploughs, drawn by 6 to 8 oxen had come into the vogue perhaps for breaking hard virgin soil. The *Kathaka Samhita* refers to the yoking of as many as 12 and even 24 oxen. Later still, Panini mentions two types of the big plough *hali* and *jitya*.[56] The big plough of Panini was perhaps identical with the *brhaddhala* mentioned in the stone inscription of Chahamana Vigraharaja dated A.D. 973. Such a plough should have been useful in the Ajmer Jaipur region.[57] The celebrated early medieval treatise on agriculture, the *Krsi-Parasara* recommends the normal yoking of 8 oxen to the plough and 6 'for ordinary use.' The yoking of 4 oxen amounted to cruelty and of 2 to actual cow-killing.[58] Unfortunately, it is not clear whether the *Krsi-Parasara* is speaking of yoking all the oxen together to one plough or doing it by turns to relieve the animals.

N.G. Mukherji had noted the variation in the weight of the plough in different regions of India in the early twentieth century. The Bengal plough, drawn by puny bullocks and required merely to scrape the extremely fertile surface, weighed a maund and a quarter; and the one in the hardy Bundelkhand soil came to three and a half maunds.[59] Surely, these variations were unlikely to have been of a recent origin. Baden-Powell also recorded two different sets of plough in Punjab itself: the heavier *munna* and the lighter *hal,* each drawn by different species of oxen.[60] There were two different kinds of plough for different purposes. While the light ploughs were adequate for routine furrowing of light, slightly moist soil, a heavier one with an iron sheath would be used on the ground that had to be broken or had become hard and weedy, and required deeper ploughing.[61]

Recommendations regarding the number of times the field

ought to be or was actually ploughed differ from one authority to another, though all of them suggest multiple plouhing. Panini says that the field was at times ploughed twice and at others thrice; Patanjali makes it five times.[62] The *Arthasastra* recommends three ploughings for a certain good harvest.[63] The *Amarkosa* similarly suggests ploughing the field twice or thrice[64] and the *Krsi-Parasara* would have the field done anywhere between once and five times, the larger the number the better.[65] The number of times a field ought to be ploughed before sowing was evidently related to the crop being sown but unfortunately our sources are silent on this aspect. We know from later practice that the soil was ploughed five times to prepare it for receiving the seed.[66] In case of sugarcane the field was sometimes continually ploughed for as long as eight months and this practice came to be known after it as *athmas*.[67]

The seed was often, though perhaps not always, sown with the seed drill which had evoked so much of admiration in Henry Elliot.[68] Luckily we have two drawings of the drill done by Lockwood Kipling in Khangaum in March 1872. One of these depicts a drill with three channels joined at the top of a single, round, cup-like receptacle; the other depicts two channels each separated from the other but both joining a common platform at the bottom. Each is drawn by a pair of giant oxen.[69] Apparently each channel dropped one seed at a time at regular intervals into evenly distanced furrows so that each seedling would have the same amount of soil area in which it could spread its roots and from which it was to draw its nourishment. The drill appears to have spread to most parts of India, for its usage is reported, apart from Maharashtra where Kipling made his drawing, from South India,[70] Bihar,[71] and, of course, the North-West.[72]

Sowing of the field was immediately followed by leveling the soil so as to cover the seeds with it. This would be done either with a manually operated stick[73]—clearly a laborious process and workable only in small fields—or by running a plank over the soil drawn by a pair of oxen. The ox-driver would himself stand on the plank, legs drawn apart, to put even pressure.[74] The *Tuhfat-i Panjab* calls this instrument *Sohaga* and mentions among its functions the covering of seed with soil and breaking of clods, thereby facilitating the even spread of moisture.[75] This was moved transversely over the soil.[76]

We are somewhat less certain of the use of the harrow in antiquity. The term *kotisa* occurring in the *Amarkosa* has indeed been translated as the harrow,[77] but this could well be an arbitrary rendering. A later observer of the agricultural scene, John Capper, does speak of the use of the harrow but in rather contemptuous terms: 'Their harrows consist of a mere board pierced with rough pegs, or more frequently of the bough of a tree, on which one or two children will be seated to give it the necessary pressure'.[78] On the other hand, the *Tuhfat-i Panjab* mentions an instrument named *dandal* comprising a very heavy plank with teeth at one end, drawn by four oxen and pressed by two men. This was used for paddy cultivation and appears to be a highly sophisticated harrow.[79] It is possible that this was a late introduction to Panjab and remained confined there.

Seeds were sown in a variety of ways, the use of seed drill being one of these. Broadcasting the seeds was perhaps the simplest method.[80] Once seedlings had been formed, transplantation in the case of paddy was carefully done.[81] A prudent recommendation was made in the seventeenth century perhaps reflecting an old prevailing practice that seeds be sown in three stages: some of the seeds be sown at an early stage, some more a little later and the last bit at a still later stage so that if some of these should fail, others would nevertheless greminate.[82]

After germination had taken place and seedlings had erupted, the process of weeding and loosening the soil around the plants for letting air into their roots began. Both these processes took place simultaneously and the same instrument, the hoe, was used for them.[83] The *Krsi-Parasara* recommends the weeding of paddy twice.[84] The *Amarkosa* also mentions an implement named *khanitra* which has been indifferently translated as the hoe or the spade.[85] The mid-nineteenth century *Report* on the Panjab by Tremenheere, however, noted the hoeing and weeding of a few crops only, such as sugarcane, maize and the larger kind of millet and that in the early stages of their growth.[86] The hoe was a small instrument with a narrow iron blade and a short handle and was used by cultivators in a sitting position, much as is done today.

The amount and frequency of irrigation that each plant required would clearly differ from other plants. Unfortunately, our sources tell us nothing on this all-important question. Irrigation was of critical significance to Indian agriculture historically, as manure was to Europe. Understandably, therefore, Indian society through its history, has an impressive record on this score. In an effort to provide irrigation the state, the community and the individual peasant initiatives made substantial contribution and led to considerable technological and economic development.

The very scale of state effort was sufficient to ensure its recording by history; we therefore have a fairly clear idea of such effort. The Sudarshan lake in south Gujarat, constructed by Maurya rulers in the fourth century B.C. and repaired by a Saka king in the second century A.D., was to irrigate the fields for eight long centuries. The Nandas too had undertaken construction of a canal in Orissa and this too served the purposes of irrigation for the next five centuries. Its maintenance was looked after by the local ruler. Several imperial and provincial dynasties are known to have constructed or maintained reservoirs or canals for irrigation in various regions in early India; in Panjab, Rajasthan, Uttar Pradesh, Bihar, Bengal, in eastern Deccan, Kashmir and in the Kaveri delta.[87] The considerable number of canals built by Firuzshah Tughlaq in the fourteenth century and Shah Jahan in the seventeenth have also been well documented.[88]

No less substantial is the contribution of individual peasant initiative, however humble, in this effort. Apart from a simple method of carrying water for irrigation on one's shoulders which the *Arthasastra* mentions[89], as a device the *dhenkli* was perhaps the simplest. A sixteenth century manuscript of *Mrigavat*, illustrated in Uttar Pradesh sometime between 1525 and 1570 and now located at the Bharat Kala Bhavan at Banaras Hindu University, depicts this device[90] and the late seventeenth century traveller, Fryer, also gives a description of it.[91] This device consisted of a post buried into the ground at the edge of a shallow well at one end and shaped like a fork at the other; a long pole was fixed mid-way into this fork on the lever principle, with a rope hanging on to the pole holding bucket at the well end and a weight of stone at the other. One man could operate this contraption by pulling the rope down into the well and releasing it to let the pole lift the water-filled bucket and then upturning the bucket to let the water flow into a channel which would take the water into the field. This device was labour intensive and capable of being used only in shallow water; hence it would do only for small fields, not far from the well. One the other hand, its low capital and running costs should have brought it within the reach of very small peasants.

Chadas, of which Babur has given a detailed, though very derogatory description,[92] was both more capital and labour intensive; it required the labour of two men and one or two oxen. It also occupied far more land surface than the *dhenkli.* A pulley was attached to a forked pole through an axle over-looking a well. A large leather bucket, called *chadas,* was lowered into the well over the pulley; when filled, the oxen would carry the rope some distance and thus pull the bucket up which would be emptied into a channel by one of the two men; the second, at the other end, would guide the oxen back to the well to lower the bucket again for filling. Babur was horrified at the filth that the rope would carry back into the well, being soiled with dung and urine of the beasts. But then, it could operate in a much deeper well than the *dhenkli* and could therefore be used even in areas of relatively low water table. The amount of water lifted by this device was also considerably larger than that of *dhenkli* and thus it could irrigate comparatively larger fields.

Babur also adds that for some crops men and women carry water pitchers by repeated effort[93]—was this the practice the *Arthasastra* had referred to?

However, the most significant development in the field of irrigation in North India took place from the early medieval period onwards, a development which had until very recently supported agricultural production in several parts of our region. This was the three-stage evolution of the waterwheels.

In 1969 Irfan Habib had pointed out the difference between the *arghatta* (noria) and the *saqiya* or the Persian wheel.[94] The *arghatta* was a rim to which pots were attached; it was operated with human energy and it collected water from the surface of a pond or a stream. Its irrigation potential would thus be severely limited to the fields adjacent to the couple of ponds in a village or to the river passing through one. The Persian wheel, on the other hand, with a bucket chain and pin-drum gear could draw water from a well and was moved by bullocks. This increased irrigation potential substantially, especially in medium water table areas, so that whoever could afford to invest in a masonry well and a Persian wheel could be sure of irrigating his fields at will; the bullocks also spared human energy to be used for other agricultural activity. This device, according to Irfan Habib, had been brought to India from West Asia with the Turkish conquest and in subsequent centuries.[95]

Since this essay was written, research has conclusively shown that the progress of waterwheels in India had a three- rather than a two-stage history, that between the *arghatta* and the *saqiya* there stood an apparatus that had the bucket chain but did not have the gear.[96] This was the *ghatiyantra* of our sources.

The installation of the Persian wheel in a masonry well was understandably a costly affair and one would expect that only a small number of wells in a village would be equipped with it.[97] Indeed, even the making of a bricklined well, though in use since the Kushana days,[98] still entailed considerable expense, so that as late as the second half of the seventeenth century only 41out of 528 wells in 18 villages of *pargana* Dausa in eastern Rajasthan were bricklined.[99]

The construction of wells, however, should induce both extension as well as a more intensive cultivation of land; it would also initiate a greater systemisation of agricultural production for the amount of irrigation water could be regulated, and over-irrigation of crops prevented.[100] The capital investment, especially in the bricklined wells and the ones with the Persian wheel, would also suggest a shift to higher value crops. All these constitute not an inconsiderable record of agricultural progress. The *Report of the Royal Commission on Agriculture* had realised the great significance of the smaller irrigation works and urged the Government to pay more attention to them.[101]

Of the other agricultural implements the true spade has been recovered from Taxila.[102] The sickle has been referred to several times in *Rig Veda*[103] and a few sickle blades have been recovered from Taxila.[104] They continue to be mentioned in later works. There were, besides, the winnowing basket and the sieve to which early medieval sources refer.[105] An instrument used to scrape the black cotton soil in the Madhya Pradesh region in circa A.D.200 is located in the Sanchi Museum; this is the *bhakhar* that is still in use in that region.[106] The Persian language treatise, *Dar Fann-i Falahat,* also recommends the use of the auger for making holes in apple trees for the purpose of grafting.[107]

Of agricultural practices, apart from ploughing, weeding transplantation etc., which we have noted above, *Dar Fann-i Falahat* goes into quite some detail of system of grafting.[108] Apparently, the concept of the female and male parts of plants had either been developed, or had reached here by the early decades of the seventeenth century, for, this treatise uses the terms *maadah* and *nar* (female and male) for these plants.[109] And, although our texts make no reference to the system of crop rotation, the fact that two crops were grown every year in most fields should itself imply its practice. At any rate, the tables of *rabi* (spring) and *kharif* (autumn) crops in the *Ain* must mean crop rotation.[110]

We have referred above to agricultural progress following the spread of irrigation facilities, among other things. Meagre though our information is, it might still be possible to indicate some trajectories of this progress. That early medieval India witnessed some remarkable agricultural expansion is attested by several sources.[111] In the thirteenth and fourteenth centuries large tracts of the Gangaic plains still supported dense forests; by the end of the sixteenth century the forests had greatly lost out to the arable.[112] The march of the arable probably reached its high point early in the twentieth century.[113]

Perhaps an even more significant indicator of agricultural progress in this period is the growing number of new crops and an increasing number of varieties of old crops. The Harappa culture had depended on the cultivation of rice in the Kathiawad region, wheat, barley, sesamum and peas, apart from cotton.[114] The *Rig Veda* refers to barley, sesamum (both black and the white seeded varieties), cucumber, bottle-gourd and sugarcane. There is no mention in it of wheat, rice or cotton,[115] though of course it is possible that the term for barley, namely *yava*, was used as a generic term and included wheat. The later Vedic texts, such as the *Atharva Veda* and the *Taittiriya Samhita* do however mention rice; barley and wheat are mentioned in the *Atharva Veda*, and beans and sesamum, in the *Taittiriya Samhita*.[116] The millet called *bajra* was perhaps introduced in India from Africa in the PGW phase.[117] The *Arthasastra* mentions 17 kinds of crops of which some 10 are foodgrains (counting two varieties of rice as one).[118] By the twelfth century A.D. 24 to 25 kinds of food crops, including fruits and vegetables, were being cultivated.[119] These numbers do not take into account the several varieties of a crop such as rice. A medieval text, the *Sunya Purana*, informs us that more than 50 varieties of rice were grown in Bengal[120] and the *Ain* makes the same point more poetically: 'If a single grain of each (variety) were collected, they would fill a large vase.'[121] By the end of the sixteenth century the number of crops had risen to over 40, though there was considerable regional variation.[122] This was also the number of crops grown in the 1920s.[123] If some crops, such as *aal*, (shrub that yielded the red dye) had disappeared since Akbar's days, some other important crops such as tea, coffee, potato, tobacco, groundnuts, sweet-potato, oats and maize had been added to the list since.[124]

III

By any stretch this is an impressive record of progress both in its technical as well as economic aspects. It demonstrates an extent of dynamism seldom associated with the Indian peasantry by historians until very recent decades. And yet we would be hard put to describe it at any stage as a basic transformation in the mode of production. The long time span of this progress evened out its pace, so that one could hardly speak of any marked cluster of changes concentrated in a relatively brief period that would transform the structure of the economy. The stages of development in Indian economic history are not as clearly marked as they are in Europe's.

The outline of medieval Indian agricultural production was formed in the early medieval centuries, and this outline had three basic features: high fertility of the soil, low subsistence level of the peasant and peasants' control over their process of production.[125]

We have recounted above the evidence and the argument for assuming high fertility of Indian soil. The low subsistence level, permitted by the climate, was effected by the state which collected a large amount of agrarian surplus.[126] However, it is the last feature, the peasants' control over their process of production,[127] that concerns us here.

In the middle centuries of the first millennium B.C., we come across references in the Buddhist literature to large farms, sometimes, tilled by as many as 500 ploughs employing a gang of wage-labourers.[128] The *Arthasastra* also speaks of state farms, worked by 'slaves labourers and prisoners'.[129] In the post-Maurya period sharecropping and debt-bondage appear to have grown in importance as the basic form of labour.[130] References to large farms whether state-owned or private, practically cease in the Gupta and the post-Gupta period; on the other hand, the *sudras* at this time were being transformed into petty producers, so that by the first half of the seventh century, most, if not all, *sudras* had become peasants.[131]

The consolidation of petty peasant production in the midst of a highly stratified rural society provides the social context of the technological and economic progress that we have discussed above. For, this production system was based principally on the use of family labour.[132] On the farms of big land-owners the use of hired labour has been attested by several of our sources.[133] This labour both on the peasants' fields and on larger farms was supplemented by labour of the menial castes who were paid extremely meagre share of the produce in return.[134] In a specifically Indian form of social organisation, namely collective control over lower castes' labour exercised by the entire community of cultivators, irrespective of its own stratification, the problem of meeting labour needs of the production system had been solved. At some time in the course of the evolution of Indian economy, the caste system began to exclude menial castes from the right to own and cultivate land for themselves, even as land lay in great abundance. The utilisation of forced labour of the peasants themselves, as in feudal Europe, was dispensable in India. In Europe agricultural operations had to be concentrated over the few weeks of dry weather; in India they could be spread out over time. It is therefore capital investment in the form of irrigation devices and high value crops, rather than increasing the intensity of labour use, that would raise the value of one's output from land.[135] And we have seen above that early medieval centuries onwards is the period of impressive, though gradual, agricultural progress in terms of irrigation facilities, expansion of the arable and cultivation of a substantial number of new crops. Could the consolidation of petty peasant production and this agricultural progress at adjoining periods of time be a mere coincidence? Surely, 'the increasing impoverishment, subjection and dependence' of the Indian peasantry under the regime of 'Indian feudalism' would hardly coalesce with the attempt of all strata of peasants to move a little ahead by participating in this agricultural progress with however differential capital investment and very differential benefits.[136]

The consolidation of petty peasant production, subsisting with a high degree of rural stratification, significantly altered the form of exploitation of medieval Indian peasantry. From now on, while the peasants' process of production, including their labour, was free from extraneous control, they had to part with their surplus produce in the form of revenue paid to the state. Once the relationship of exploitation between the peasant and the state had come to be based upon the appropriation of the surplus produce, conflicts between them would inevitably arise on the quantum of the surplus so appropriated; these conflicts left the process of production untouched.[137]

Consequently, unlike in medieval western Europe, where social conflict inhered in the very process of production and transformed the production system by redistributing the means of production,[138] the social conflict in India pertained to the distribution and redistribution of the peasants' surplus produce. Even grave crises, such as the collapse of the Mughal empire in early eighteenth century, were neither caused by, nor resulted in the emergence of any new property forms; what did emerge was the resurgent class of zamindars everywhere, which was surely a millennium old property form.

The peasant production in medieval India, then, on one hand ensured a degree of slow and gradual, though considerable, progress in agriculture through the enterprise of individual peasants at various levels; on the other, it generated social conflict of a nature that was unlikely to have transformed the mode of production, whether or not colonialism had intervened.

REFERENCES

1. P.C. Jain, *Labour in Ancient India,* New Delhi, 1971, pp. 35-36; D.M. Bose et.al. eds., *A Concise History of Science in India,* New Delhi, 1971, pp. 353, 377-78.
2. Ramchandra Jain, *McCrindle's Ancient India as Described by Megasthenes and Arrian,* New Delhi, 1972, p. 31.
3. *Arthasastra,* tr. R. Samasastry, 8th edn., Mysore, 1967, pp. 131-32.
4. D.M. Bose et.al. eds., *Concise History,* p. 361.
5. Ibn Battuta, *The Travels of Ibn Battuta,* A.D. 1325-1354, ed. H.R.A. Gibb, vol. II, Cambridge, pp. 609-10.
6. Abul Fazl, *Ain-i Akbari,* ed. Blochmann, vol. I (text), pp. 304-36; tr. Jarrett, vol. II, pp. 76-122.
7. W. Tennant, *Indian Recreations: Consisting of strictures on the Domestic and Rural Economy of the Mahomedans and Hindoos,* vol. II, Edinburgh, 1804, p. 6.
8. Abul Fazl, *Ain,* vol. I (text) p. 513 and tr. Jarett, vol. II, p. 283 where Delhi *suba* is credited with three crops.

9. Bhimsen, a late seventeenth century chronicler, speaking of Tanjore, mentions four crops produced in that region each year; see his *Nuskha-i Dilkusha,* Eng. tr. Jadu Nath Sarkar, Bombay, 1972, pp. 193-94.
10. Abul Fazl, *Ain,* vol. I (text) p. 513, tr. vol. II, p. 273. The reference here is to the Ajmer *suba.*
11. Major Beatson, 'Report on the Watering of that part of the country between the Kistna & Godavary by means of those Rivers in June 1798', Mackenzie Collection no. 59, OIOC, p. 166.
12. Thus D.C. Sircar renders *khila* as 'uncultivated land, fallow land' without noticing any difference between the two, in his *Indian Epigraphical Glossary,* Delhi, 1966, p. 157. At another place he heads a section of a chapter as 'Reclamation of Fallow Land' again treating the fallow as virgin; see his *Landlordism and Tenancy in Ancient and Medieval India,* Lucknow 1969, p.4; R.S. Sharma also treats virgin land as fallow in *Indian Feudalism,* Calcutta, 1965, p. 36, as indeed do several other historians: Puspa Niyogi, *Contributions to the Economic History of Northern India,* Calcutta, 1962, p. 1; B.P. Mazumdar, *The Socio-Economic History of Northern India (1030-1194 A.D.),* Calcutta, 1960, p. 175: A.K. Chaudhuri, *Early Medieval Village in North Eastern India (A.D. 600-1200),* Calcutta, 1971, p. 52.
13. *Indian Recreations,* vol. II, p. 16.
14. H.T. Colebrooke, *Remarks on the Husbandry and Internal Commerce of Bengal,* Calcutta, 1804, p. 39: 'The Indian allows it a lay but never a tilled fallow'.
15. *Ain,* vol. I (text) p. 297, tr. vol. II, p. 68. The *Risāla-i Zirā't,* a late eighteenth century treatise dealing partly with agriculture in Bengal, also attests to the practice of the lay; Persian MS. no. 144, Edinburgh University Library, ff. 6b-7a. Eng. tr. in this vol.
16. Thus the *Arthasastra,* which devotes a chapter, 'The Superintendent of Agriculture', to giving detailed instructions on agricultural operations makes no mention of the fallow, nor indeed do such texts on agriculture as the *Krsi-Prasara* (ed. and tr. G.P. Majumdar and S.C. Banerji, Calcutta, 1960) and *Upvana Vinoda* (ed. and tr. G.P. Majumdar, Calcutta, 1936). The seventeenth century Persian language text, *Dar Fann-i Falahat* ('On the Art of Agriculture') which goes into great detail of horticultural and agricultural operations similarly omits any reference to the fallow, OIOC Persian MS., Ethe 2791. Even secondary works, which discuss in considerable detail the entire range of agricultural operations in ancient and medieval India,

fail to mention the fallow; see, for example, B.N.S. Yadava, *Society and Culture in Northern India during the Twelfth Century*, Allahabad, 1973, pp.256-62; M.S. Randhawa, *A History of Agriculture in India*, vols. I & II, New Delhi, 1980 and 1982; Irfan Habib, 'The System of Agricultural Production: Mughal India' in T. Raychaudhuri and I. Habib, eds., *The Cambridge Economic History of India*, vol. I, Cambridge 1982, pp. 214-25. The nearest any of our sources comes to the true fallow is the Urdu work, the *Tuhfat-i Panjab* by Maulavi Sirajuddin and Pandit Ajudhia Prasad, compiled at the request of the District Collector of Lahore, Major George MacGregor, sometime during the second half of the nineteenth century. The MS. is now located at the OIOC, Ethe 2528. It says: 'The land which has been ploughed but remains unsown is called *bahan...*', f.465b.

17. Georges Duby, *Rural Economy and Country Life in the Medieval West*, tr. Cynthia Postan, London, 1968, pp.90-99; Lynn White Jr., *Medieval Technology and Social Change*, London, 1973, pp. 72-76; C.Parain, 'The Evolution of Agricultural Technique', in M.M. Postan, ed., *The Cambridge Economic History of Europe*, vol. I, Cambridge, 1966, pp. 133-39.
18. G. Duby, *Rural Economy*, pp.25-27, 103; C. Parain, in *Cambridge Economic History*, p. 125; Lord Beveridge, 'The Yield and Price of Corn in the Middle Ages', in Carus-Wilson, ed., *Essays in Economic History*, vol. I, London, 1966, pp. 15-16.
19. G. Duby, *Rural Economy*, pp. 99-102.
20. Madhavacharya, writing a commentary on the text of Parasara in the fourteenth century assumes 1:12 as the general seed:yield ratio; see T.V. Mahalingam, *Administration and Social Life Under Vijayanagara*, part II, Madras, 1975, p. 102.
21. Paul Bairoch, 'Agricultural and Industrial Revolution, 1700-1914', in Carlo. M. Cipolla, ed., *The Fontana Economic History of Europe*, vol. II, London, 1973, pp. 452-506.
22. O.H.K. Spate and A.T.A. Learmonth, *India and Pakistan: A General and Regional Geography*, 3rd edn. Suffolk, 1967, p. 43.
23. Ibid, pp. 504-05.
24. Ibid, p. 43.
25. H.T. Lambrick, *Sind: A General Introduction*, Hyderabad (Sind), 1964, p. 76.
26. Spate and Learmonth, *India and Pakistan*, p. 550.
27. William Willcocks, *Lectures on the Ancient System of Irrigation in Bengal*, University of Calcutta, 1930, pp. 32-36.
28. W.H. Moreland, *India at the Death of Akbar*, Delhi, 1974, (reprint of the original 1920 edn.), pp.118-24.

29. T. Raychaudhuri, 'A Reinterpretation of the Nineteenth Century Economic History?', *Indian Economic and Social History Review*, vol. V, no. 1, 1968, p. 83.
30. *Arthasastra*, p. 132.
31. Lallanji Gopal, *Aspects of the History of Agriculture in Ancient India*, Varanasi, 1980, p. 99.
32. For the evidence of the *Brhat Samhita* and the *Agni Purana* see B.N.S. Yadava, *Society and Culture*, p. 257 and Bose et. al., *Concise History*, pp. 358-60; *Upavana Vinoda*, pp. 81-83.
33. L. Gopal, *History of Agriculture*, p. 99.
34. *Krsi-Parasara*, Verse 109: 'Having worshipped the heap of cowdung in *Magha* (January-February), one, with reverence, should lift it with spades on an auspicious day and *naksatra* (auspicious conjunction of starts)'; Verse 110: 'Having powdered all that and drying it up in the sun, throw the manure into a pit in every field in *Phalguna* (February-March)', Verse 111: 'Then at the time of sowing take out the manures; without manures paddy plants grow up bereft of fruit', p. 74.
35. Abul Fazl, *Ain*, vol. I (text), p. 287; tr., vol. II, p. 49.
36. *Arthasastra*, p. 48.
37. Ibid, p. 160.
38. Ibid, pp. 161-62.
39. Ibid, pp. 196-97.
40. P.C. Jain, *Socio-Economic Explorations of Medieval India*, Delhi, 1976, pp. 135-36.
41. Manrique, *Travels, 1629-43*, tr. C.E. Luard, vol. II, London, 1927. p. 123.
42. A Mughal miniature of 1595, illustrating a story in the *Khamsa*, beautifully depicts goats and cattle being led by their herds into the harvested fields for feeding on the stubble; see British Museum MS. no. Or. 12208, miniature no.24, f.195a. The nineteenth century text, *Tuhfat-i Panjab*, also refers to this practice: 'After the crop is harvested, the fields are open to the village poor who collect such grains as get left behind. The owners of the fields do not stop anyone from scrounging. After that the animals are let loose into the fields', 452b-454a.
43. W.H. Moreland, *India at the Death of Akbar*, p. 106.
44. There were besides other forms of fertilizers. We have already noted above the mention in the *Arthásastra* of small fish used as fertilizers. *Dar Fann-i Falahat* strongly recommends the cultivation of Egyptian beans *(tarmus)* in one year 'after which whatever is grown comes off well', ff.2b-3a. Evidently, the roots

of the Egyptian bean, like all other legumes, fertilize the soil with nitrogen even as the plant grows and this quality of the plant had been recognised.

45. G.B. Tremenheere, *Report on the Present State of Agriculture in the Punjab,* Lahore, 1853, pp. 199-200. The *Report* goes on: 'It (the manure) is not available in sufficient quantities to fertilize the general face of the country; so that for wheat and barley it is very sparingly used, and generally not at all for these, and other, crops over any considerable extent of land', ibid. Similar was the observation of W. Tennant in Bengal a half century earlier: '...the use of this article (cattle-dung) as a manure is restricted to sugarcane, mulberry, tobacco and poppy: and in these crops it is applied from necessity because few lands, without this stimulus, are sufficiently rich to raise these productions'; see *Indian Recreations,* vol. II, pp. 16-17.
46. Tennant, *Indian Recreations.* vol. II, pp. 77-78; John Capper, *The Three Presidencies of India,* London, 1853, p. 317.
47. *Report etc. in the Punjab*, p. 197.
48. Irfan Habib, 'Technology and Barriers to Technological Change in Mughal India', *The Indian Historical Review,* vol. V, nos. 1-2, July 1978-January 1979, p. 158. The high cost of iron was also Moreland's reasons for 'the economy of iron in agricultural implements in India', *India at the Death of Akbar,* p. 106.
49. Agrawal, *The Copper Bronze Age in India,* New Delhi, 1971, p. 107.
50. B.P. Mazumdar, *Continuity and Change in Technology in Ancient and Early Medieval India (c.2300 B.C. -1200 A.D.),* (in press) pp. 12, 44-45 (of the MS).
51. L. Gopal, 'Beginnings of Agriculture in India', in K.K.A. Venkatachari, ed., *Technology in India (Ancient and Medieval Period),* Bombay, 1984, p. 95.
52. M .S. Randhawa, *History of Agriculture,* vol. I, p. 393.
53. P.C. Jain, *Labour in Ancient India,* p. 60.
54. *India at the Death of the Akbar,* p. 150.
55. In 1963 Irfan Habib was also inclined towards this view; see his *Agrarian System of Mughal India,* Bombay, 1963, p. 25. Apparently some time later he changed his mind and decided to go along with Moreland without telling his readers why! For a critique of this notion see Harbans Mukhia's review of *The Combridge Economical History of India,* vol. I, in *The Indian Economic and Social History Review,* vol. XXI, no. 1, pp. 116-20.
56. B.P. Mazumdar, *Continuity and Change,* p. 11.

57. Ibid, p. 44.
58. *Krsi-Parasara,* p. 73.
59. N.G. Mukherji, *Handbook of Indian Agriculture,* Calcutta, 1915, pp. 93 and 95.
60. B.H. Baden-Powell, *Handbook of the Manufactures and Arts of the Punjab,* Lahore, 1872, p. 314.
61. John Capper, *The Three Presidencies,* p. 317.
62. P.C. Jain, *Labour in Ancient India,* p. 49.
63. *Arthasastra,* p. 130. It also suggests ploughing the field 'often'.
64. P.C. Jain, *Labour in Ancient India,* pp. 60-61.
65. *Krsi-Parasara,* p. 77.
66. George A. Grierson, *Bihar Peasant Life,* 2nd edn., Patna, 1926 p. 172.
67. Henry Elliot, *Memoirs of the History, Folklore and Distribution of the Races of the North Western Provinces of India,* ed., revised and rearranged by John Beames, vol. II, London, 1869, p. 223.
68. Ibid, pp. 314-42. Elliot says that the drill had been used in India since 'time immemorial'. Unfortunately it is not easy to trace its history in India. The pre-historic Sumer civilization is credited with a tube attachment to the plough through which seed was dropped; see M.S. Randhawa, *History of Agriculture,* vol. I, p. 114.
69. L. Kipling drawing nos. 0930-1 & 2, Victoria and Albert Museum, London.
70. Lt.-Col. Mark Wilks, *Historical Sketches of the South of India,* vol. I, London, 1810, p. 209.
71. Grierson, *Bihar Peasant Life,* pp. 4-5.
72. By H. Elliot cited in n. 68 above.
73. This too has been depicted in miniature illustration of the *Khamsa* about 1595; B.M. MS. Or. 12208, miniature no.3, f.19a.
74. Several agricultural operations, including levelling, have been depicted in a Mughal miniature illustration of the *Tarikh-i Alfi,* c.1590; see B.M. miniature no.1934-1-13-01a.
75. Folio 540a. Also Tremenheere, *Report etc. in the Punjab,* p. 197.
76. Satpal Sangwan, 'Level of Agricultural Technology in India, 1757-1858', *Proceedings of the Indian History Congress,* 43rd (Kurukshetra) Session, 1982, p. 467.
77. S.P. Raychaudhuri et.al., in Bose et.al., eds, *Concise History,* p. 360.
78. *The Three Presidencies,* p. 317.
79. Ff.451a-b.
80. Tremenheere, *Report etc. in the Punjab,* p. 197.
81. *Krsi-Parasara,* pp. 80-81.

82. *Dar Fann-i Falahat,* f.3a.
83. A number of hoes have been excavated from the Bhir mound at Taxila and these belong to the B.C.300-A.D.100 period; see plates in Randhawa, *History of Agriculture,* vol. I, p. 393.
84. *Krsi-Parasara,* p. 82.
85. S.P. Raychaudhuri et.al., in Bose et.al., eds., *Concise History,* p. 390.
86. P.197.
87. Nand Kishore Kumar, 'Hydraulic Agriculture in Peninsular India (c.300 B.C. to A.D. 1300),' *Proceedings of the Indian History Congress,* 40th (Waltair) Session, 1979, pp. 211-14.
88. T. Raychaudhuri and Irfan Habib eds., *The Cambridge Economic History of India,* vol. I, pp. 49. and 216.
89. P. 131.
90. Karl Khandalvala and Moti Chandra, *New Document of Indian Painting—a Reappraisal,* Bombay, 1969, plate 179.
91. John Fryer, *A New Account of East India and Persia, 1672-81,* ed., W. Crooke, vol. II, Hakluyt Society, 1912, p. 94.
92. *Babur Nama,* tr. A.S. Beveridge, Delhi 1970, (reprint of the 1922 original), p. 487.
93. Ibid, p. 153.
94. 'Presidential Address', Medieval India Section, *Proceedings of the Indian History Congress,* 31st (Varanasi) Session, 1969, pp. 149-51.
95. Ibid, p. 153.
96. B.D. Chattopadhyaya pointed this out in his essay 'Irrigation in Early Medieval Rajasthan', *Journal of Economic and Social History of the Orient,* vol. XVI, parts ii-iii, 1973, p. 304n. In doing so Chattopadhyaya questioned the readings of M.C. Joshi, R. Nath and R.C. Agarwal which treated all waterwheels with bucket chain as the Persian wheel. A three-stage history was also postulated in Harbans Mukhia, 'Was There Feudalism in Indian History?', *The Journal of Peasant Studies,* vol. VIII, no. 3, April, 1981, p. 309, n.214 and subsequently by Irfan Habib in *The Cambridge Economic History of India,* vol. I, p. 49.

    The first reference to the gearless bucket-chained wheel, the *ghatiyantra,* occurs in a Mandasore inscription of 532 A.D. and it was brought to light by M.C. Joshi in 'An Early Inscriptional Reference to the Persian Wheel', *Professor K.A. Nilkantha Sastri 80th Birthday Felicitation Volume,* pp. 214-17. The Introduction of the Persian wheel some six centuries or so later did not entirely eliminate the use of *ghatiyantra.* A beautiful painting done at Lucknow in 1770 depicts such a wheel in operation, though it has inevitably been described in the Library catalogue as a Persian wheel; see painting no. J.10-6, titled 'Ladies at a well with a Persian wheel', OIOC. The publication of Chattopadhyay's essay as far back as 1973 has not prevented Lallanji Gopal from still equating the gearless *ghatiyantra* with the geared Persian wheel in his 'Arghatta—the Persian Wheel', *Aspects of the History of Agriculture in Ancient India,* pp. 114-68. He appears hellbent upon proving Indian origin of Persian wheel, at least the one used in India, which he seeks to do by treating all bucket-chained wheels as geared Persian wheels, the existence of gears being implied by the uniformity of the wheels' motion. One piece of literary evidence, which refers to a pack of 16 oxen standing next to a *ghatiyantra,* is all the evidence he has been able to command for the yoking of oxen to the machine. One wonders whether Professor Gopal, or anyone else, has ever seen a water-wheel being moved by 16 oxen even if one grants that the oxen could stand next to the well for no other purposes than to operate the water-wheel—a difficult proposition by itself. As for the uniform motion of the wheel, the giant wheel (*hindola*) in small town fairs moved either manually or by human feet gives us a superb demonstration of uniform circular motion without gears; surely, waterwheels too could be similarly operated.

The fact is that gearing for some reason has remained alien to India's ancient and medieval past. It is this fact which strongly suggests the introduction of the Persian wheel from West Asia where (as also in the Roman Empire and China) gears had been in use for long. However, the earlier wheels, the *arghatta* and the *ghatiyantra,* appear to have been indigenously developed. The use of the gear does not seem to have spread even after several centuries of familiarity with the pin drum gear of the Persian wheel. The sketch of a gear reproduced by Abul Fazl in the *Ain,* whereby eight gun-barrels could be cleaned simultaneously, is quite an unworkable contraption, although it does depict the principle of the transfer of motion quite faithfully; see *Ain,* vol. I (tr.), plate XV. Indeed, even this unworkable contraption was the handiwork of a Persian gentleman in Akbar's court, Fathullah Shirazi; see M.A. Alvi and A. Rahman, *Fathullah Shirazi: a Sixteenth Century Indian Scientist,* New Delhi, 1968, pp. 4-7. In fact as late as the 1780s simple cog wheels, which moved Italian filatures that the East India Co. had introduced in Bengal, often broke down at the hands of Indian workmen who would mesh cog-wheels with unmeshable number of cogs; see *General Letters etc.*, Govt. of Bengal, 1765-1854, vol. I, West Bengal State Archives, Calcutta, Extract from General Letter from the Court of the Governor-General in Council, 12 July 1782. Clearly the workmen were still unused to these mechanisms.

97. B. Bhadani's estimate is that of all the wells in pargana Merta in western Rajasthan in the 17th century, 1.7 per cent had Persian wheels and these were made of wood; 'Economic Conditions in Pargana Metra (Rajasthan) (c.A.D. 1658-63)', *Proceedings of the Indian History Congress*, 36th (Aligarh) Session, 1975, pp. 216-17.
98. M.S. Randhawa, *History of Agriculture*, vol. I, p. 401.
99. That amounts to 7.76 per cent. Information kindly given by Dr. Dilbagh Singh.
100. A.V. Williamson, 'Indigenous Irrigation Works in Peninsular India', *The Geographical Review*, vol. XXI, no. 4, Oct. 1931, p. 621.
101. *Report*, London, 1928, pp. 338-39.
102. See fig. 185 in M.S. Randhawa, *History of Agriculture*, vol. I, p. 393. The spade might have been used for breaking the clods along with, or soon after, ploughing. It was certainly used for shovelling, for we have the *Krsi-Parasara* recommending its use for lifting cow-dung manure, p. 74. In a painting of Jahangir's period, a peasant is shown working in the field with a spade; its blade is of iron and the handle wooden; see Karl Khandalwala and Moti Chandra, *Miniatures and Sculptures from the Collection of the late Sir Cowasji Jahangir*, Bombay, 1965, plate 14.
103. M.S. Randhawa, *History of Agriculture*, vol. I, p. 299.
104. Ibid, fig, 185 p. 393.
105. D.M. Bose et. al., *Concise History*, p. 360.
106. M.S. Randhawa, *History of Agriculture*, vol. I, pp. 396, 399, 402.
107. Ff.6b-7a.
108. Ff.6a-7b.
109. F.9b.
110. Abul Fazl, *Ain*, vol. I (text), pp. 304-36; tr. vol. II, pp. 76-122.
111. R.S. Sharma, 'How Feudal Was Indian Feudalism?', in the special issue of *The Journal of Peasant Studies* on 'Feudalism and Non-European Societies', vol. XII, nos. 2-3, 1985, p. 36: 'This period was undoubtedly an age of larger yield and a great agrarian expansion.'
112. *The Cambridge Economic History of India*, vol. I, p. 48.
113. Irfan Habib, *Agrarian System*, p. 21.

114. R.S. Sharma, *Light on Early Indian Society and Economy*, Bombay, 1966, p. 53.
115. M.S. Randhawa, *History of Agriculture*, vol. I, pp. 299-300.
116. Ibid. p. 318.
117. Ibid, pp. 318-21.
118. *Arthasastra*, p. 131.
119. Puspa Niyogi, *Contributions*, pp. 23-24.
120. B.N.S. Yadava, *Society and Culture*, p. 258.
121. Abul Fazl, *Ain*, vol. I (text), p. 389; tr. vol. II, p. 134.
122. Ibid, vol. I (text) pp. 304-36; tr. vol. II, pp. 76-122.
123. W.H. Moreland, *India at the Death of Akbar*, pp. 102-103.
124. Ibid, p. 103.
125. Harbans Mukhia, 'Was There Feudalism in Indian History?' p. 286.
126. Long before the establishment of the Delhi Sultanate, various states in northern India collected taxes under a large number of heads and these have been documented by B.N.S: Yadava in *Society and Culture*, pp. 288-301 and D.C. Sircar in *Landlordism and Tenancy*, pp. 66-79. The sources these historians have used are mostly inscriptions, which always reflect the reality far more faithfully than court chronicles. At the end of the enumeration, Yadava comes to the conclusion that 'mostly the peasants appear to have been left with a bare margin of subsistence'. This tradition of collecting the bulk of peasants' surplus was continued and further systematised by the Delhi Sultanate and the Mughal Empire.
127. It is in this sense, rather than in terms of the legal freedom of mobility that the medieval Indian peasant has been defined as a 'free peasant'; see Harbans Mukhia, 'Was There Feudalism in Indian History?', pp. 275, 290-91 and 'Peasant Production and Medieval Indian Society', *The Journal of Peasant Studies*, special issue on 'Feudalism and Non-European Societies', pp. 241-47.
128. P.C. Jain, *Labour in Ancient India*, pp. 44-45.
129. P. 129.
130. Uma Chakravarti, 'Slavery and Bondage in Ancient India' (forthcoming), pp. 38-39, 45-46 (typescript).
131. R.S. Sharma, *Indian Feudalism*, pp. 61-63.
132. Ibid, p. 75: 'On the whole while a great part of the time and energy of European peasants was consumed by their work on their master's fields, the peasantry in India gave most of their time to their own fields, of the produce of which a considerable share went to the holders of the grants and other intermediaries; on the contrary, the number of free peasantry seems to have

been far greater.' Also B.N.S. Yadava, *Society and Culture,* p. 171.

133. Buddhist literature mentions the employment of wage labour on huge farms; P.C. Jain, *Labour in Ancient India,*p. 44-45; *Arthasastra* seeks to regulate wage payment to agricultural workers and artisans for part of the work or completed in whole by their substitutes, p. 213; law-givers of the Gupta age also sought to regulate payment of wages to agricultural labour; P.C. Jain, *Labour in Ancient India,* pp. 236-39. For later evidence, D. Singh, 'Tenants, Sharecroppers and Agricultural Labour in Eighteenth Century Eastern Rajasthan', *Studies in History,* vol. I, no. 1, 1979, p. 39.
134. In two rare documents of 1752 and 1766 pertaining to eastern Rajasthan their share is stated to have been 0.6 and 0.9 per cent respectively of the produce; see Dilbagh Singh, 'Local and Land Revenue Administration of the State of Jaipur, c.1750-1800', unpublished Ph.D. thesis, J.N.U., p. 53.
135. Harbans Mukhia, 'Marx on Pre-colonial India: An Evaluation' in Diptendra Banerji, ed., *Marxian Theory and the Third World,* New Delhi 1985, pp. 175-78.
136. The notion of 'Indian feudalism' is the subject of dispute among several historians in the special issue of *The Journal of Peasant Studies* on 'Feudalism and Non-European Societies', vol. XII, nos. 2-3, 1985 and subseqquent issues. See H. Mukhia, ed., *The Feudalism Debate,* New Delhi, 2000.
137. Indeed, it is rare to come across peasants' protest in any form on an issue other than the quantum of revenue demand throughout early medieval and medieval India. Even the restriction imposed on the peasant's mobility by the state was motivated entirely by its anxiety to avoid loss of revenue. This was the reason why the *Arthasastra* would not permit free migration to tax paying peasants to settle in a village not inhabited by tax payers, p. 197. The *Arthasastra* advises the state to compel peasants to grow an extra crop on their fields if its financial needs so required, p. 273. Manu prescribes the imposition of a fine on a cultivator who does not cultivate his field in proper time nor guard the crop against animals; see Mazumdar, *Socio-Economic History of Northern India,* p. 171. This has however been brought out most graphically in a document of the second half of fourteenth century when the peasants of one assigned village migrated to another and the assignee insisted on the return on the ground that the claim was not on the 'ownership of their persons' but on the right to collect the

assigned taxes from them; see *The Cambridge Economic History of India,* vol. I, p. 54. Clearly, so long as taxes were paid, which the peasants could not avoid paying even by not cultivating their lands, they could not be subjected to any other restrictions. At any rate, we need not take the legal restrictions on peasant mobility excessively seriously, for Babur does remind us that 'In Hindustan hamlets and villages—even towns—are depopulated and set up in a moment' and Irfan Habib reasonably explains this as being possible 'because of the large areas of virgin land available in most regions during the sixteenth and seventeenth centuries', *The Cambridge Economic History of India,* vol. I, p. 218. Surely even larger areas of virgin lands would have been available in the preceding centuries and therefore the possibility of peasant migration should have been even greater.

138. Harbans Mukhia, 'Maurice Dobb's Explanation of the Decline of Feudalism in Western Europe—A Critique, *The Indian Historical Revenue,* vol. VI, nos. 1-2, pp. 154-84.

14

Social Resistance to Superior Technology: The Filature in Eighteenth-Century Bengal*

Although Bengal silk did not figure high in the first two decades of the seventeenth century among the items of trade that had lured the English East India Company to India, it was nevertheless soon to acquire an exceeding and durable importance, if only because of the Company's failure to keep its more favourite sources of supply going. *The Calendar of State Papers* for the years 1617-21 makes repeated references to silk as an item of the Company's trade and indicates its preference

---

* Archival research for this paper was done in the West Bengal State Archives and the National Library, Calcutta, in 1981 as part of Homi Bhabha Fellowship. For field observation I visited Murshidabad and Maldah in April 1982. On the outskirts of Maldah, the filature is still used commercially for winding silk yarn and I was fortunate to witness a late eighteenth century device still in operation. I am very grateful to the School of Social Sciences, Jawaharlal Nehru University, for financing that visit. Mr. Gautam Bhadra was kind enough to accompany me on the trip; it is rare to come across his kind of generosity. I also recall with gratitude a long conversation at Maldah with Shri B.B. Roy, retired Deputy Director, Indian Silk Board. The essential hypothesis of this paper was first presented at a seminar at the Centre for Studies in Social Sciences, Calcutta. The excellent discussion at the seminar has helped me greatly in filling out the skeleton argument.

for the Chinese, Japanese and, above all, Persian silk.[1] During 1617-18 Sir Thomas Roe had tried hard to persuade the 'Sophy' of Persia to grant to the English Company the monopoly of trade in Persian silk; it was the failure of his efforts that turned the Company's attention to Bengal silk.[2] A beginning was made with the setting up of a 'factory' at Patna in 1621.[3] Soon after the middle of the century the English, along with other European traders, were reported to have established themselves at Kasimbazar,[4] Bengal's major centre of silk production. Tavernier credits Kasimbazar with the production of 2,200,000 lbs. avoirdupois of silk somewhere about the mid-seventeenth century[5]—a figure perhaps more appropriate for the 1760s and after; at any rate it does suggest the town's pre-eminence in the silk scenario of Bengal.

With the assumption of Bengal's *diwani* by the Company in 1765 the question of the form of remittance of revenues back to England presented itself to the Company's officials. The simplest form would of course have been money or bullion. However, if money collected in revenue could be invested in the purchase of Bengal's silk yarn (referred to in the Company's records as 'raw silk') and this in turn sold in the English and the Continental markets at considerable profit, the net amount remitted in revenues could be substantially increased. This was the meaning the Company's usage of the term investment came to acquire after 1765; understandably the call of the Company's Court of Directors in London to its officials in Bengal to raise the amount of 'investment' in raw silk became more and more strident.[6]

There was, however a problem with the raw silk of Bengal: the rude manner of its winding and reeling made its quality rather coarse. 'It was common to find part single, part double, treble and in many instances even quadruple The mode of assortment was also much neglected...'[7]

Even before the assumption of *diwani* the Company had been aware of this defect and had made attempts to rectify it. In 1757 Richard Wilder, 'an eminent expert', was posted at Kasimbazar to improve the existing method of silk winding; he died in 1761. In 1765-66, just after the take-over of *diwani*,

Joseph Pouchon was appointed to succeed Wilder and continue his work; he was soon joined by one John Chamier. However, even though the Court of Directors lauded the services of the latter gentlemen,[8] it does not appear that 'any considerable quantity of silk, wound by the improved method, was exported.'[9]

It was in 1770 that a major step was taken to eliminate the defects of winding and reeling. In that year a team of Italians led by James Wiss of Piedmont was appointed to oversee the introduction of Italian filature system, then the most advanced in methods of silk winding, in Bengal; they were charged with the responsibility of training Indian winders in 'raising and improving the produce of the worms and in spinning and drawing the silk from the cocoons in the perfect manner in which the same is done in Italy and other parts of Europe....'[10]

In essence the filature reeling made the silk yarn much finer, and nearly perfectly even, than the one produced by indigenous method which now came to be derogatorily referred to as the 'country wound silk', or simply as the 'Bengal wound.' Filature reeling involved the construction of a concrete and spacious building, a concrete furnace for each basin and the installation of cog-wheeled apparatus which would draw the yarn from cocoons and reel it at one go. The cocoons were to be carefully selected for their quality and 4 to 6 cocoons were to be used for winding the yarn. The threads drawn from the cocoons for winding of the yarn were to be crossed several times to give the yarn a roundness, and evenness, valued so highly in the market. The thread passed through loops to guide-pegs in an oscillating bar, whence to the reel turned by the cog-wheeled apparatus which was operated by a small boy rotating its crank handle. The oscillating bar facilitated the even spread of the yearn along the breadth of the reel.[11]

Filature winding and reeling was about the only improvement made by the East India Company in the sphere of silk production.[12] Initially, the cog-wheels were made of wood.[13] However, partly owing to the cracking up of the English wood in Bengal's humid environment and the strong sun[14] and in part because of the lack of familiarity with any gearing mechanism which led Bengal winders to mesh wheels with 25 and 35 cogs instead of the ones with 22 and 25, resulting in their collapse,[15] the wooden structures were soon replaced by the hardier brass, and afterwards steel contraptions, though the Court of Directors never failed to emphasize that the working of the mechanism remained unaffected by the material.[16] Even these machines did not function quite as smoothly as the Court of Directors had imagined so that greatly reinforced new apparatuses were dispatched from England; the Court of Directors hoped that these would 'last as long as 20 years'.[17]

Besides the general unfamiliarity with the new machine and its working principle, the filature also involved a different mode of the use of labour. If silk production centering on the 'country wound silk' was nearly a household activity, in which cocoon-rearing, winding, reeling, etc., were done in and around the domestic verandah and in which the entire household participated in varying degrees, filature reeling implied a different work culture altogether. The filatures were located in a separate concrete building presumably at some distance from the residential parts of the town; the winding was done there by adult males, with some help from young boys, under the supervision of alien eyes, with a strict time schedule. The new work culture itself generated tension, often released by sly deception of supervisors by winders: they would do a careful job of winding even silk in the lower reaches of the reel, loosen up a bit and let some coarse yarn get into the middle reaches and be very particular about the higher reaches that were most open to inspection.[18]

Even as the introduction of a new machine and a new work process encountered initial difficulties, the Italian experts found the Indian winders eager learners. A bare two years after the filature had been introduced in Bengal, Indian winders were being hailed as 'sufficiently expert in acquiring the European manner of reeling', the 'many Obstacles to its immediate Success' notwithstanding.[19] Slightly over a decade later James Wiss recommended to the Court of Directors that the Italian experts he had brought with him be dispensed with, for there was nothing more that Indian winders could learn from them. 'No Italian spinners', he wrote, 'are wanted in Bengal', for 'I have not the least doubt that the Natives in every station will be sufficiently instructed and capable to make good silk if it is their Inclination to do so...'[20] Although the Company's government in Bengal was slightly less enthusiastic about the dispensability of Italian experts, for 'the practice of filature reeling had not yet become general',[21] the Court of Directors decided to accept Wiss's 'representation' and offered the Italians the option of either returning to England at Company's expense or remaining in India on their own.[22]

The Court's wisdom in taking that decision could hardly be questioned, for several years earlier it had found to its satisfaction that the 'Samples of Filature Silks received' were 'deemed good marketable Silk and Approach near to the Italian.'[23] James Wiss, on whom the Court of Directors depended so much for sound judgment, also reiterated the sentiment and found 'the Bengal Italian wound silks... almost as perfect in their kind of any that come from Italy.'[24] Evidence of the better quality of silk also comes from the impressive increase in the quantity of its import from Bengal. From 1772 to 1775 the average annual import of raw silk, which included the filature assortments, did not exceed 1,87,494 lbs. A sea change occurred in the decade following the wider spread of the filature mode of winding by 1775. Between 1776 and 1785 the import of all kinds of silk from Bengal averaged 5,60,283 lbs. annually while the import of silk from 'Italy, Turkey &c.', figured around 2,82,304 lbs.[25] Yet the Company's officials at various levels felt let down, apparently because the targets they had set for themselves were way ahead of the ones they had achieved. They assumed that the targets could be approximated more closely if only persons in charge of 'investments' could exert themselves a little more vigorously. Thus the Board of Trade, while considering a letter of the Resident at Radhanagar, resolved that 'He would be strenuously urged to effect an additional provision of the Filature assortment and told that tho' the Board admit for the present the Estimate he has sent, they cannot forego the expectation of seeing the proportion of that assortment enlarged.'[26] The Board also found to its dismay a decline in production of filature silk and a corresponding rise in that of the 'country wound raw silk'[27]. Uncomfortable as the Board already was with the 'practice' of filature silk not having become 'general', the further embarrassment of a decline in its production levels, and a rise in those of its rival, compelled the Company's officials to seek an explanation. It should have been a disconcerting realization for the British that having so eagerly learnt the decidedly superior technique of filature silk winding, the Indians were so reluctant to use it. The explanation that ultimately gave them satisfaction was a psychological one: the innate conservatism of the Indian artisan. As early as 1772 the Board of Trade, while hailing the Indian winders for the expertise they had acquired in the use of the filature, nevertheless visualized 'many Obstacles to its Success altho' such are naturally to be expected upon the Introduction of any sudden change, especially in a Country where the people are attached with so much Bigotry to ancient Customs.'[28] The stereotyped explanation seldom failed to satisfy either the Company's officials[29] or later commentators.[30] All of then kept periodically reproducing it with a monotonous regularity.

In a recent paper Sabyasachi Bhattacharya challenged this explanation and posited an alternative one: the new technology brought in its train extraneous control over the artisan's process of production and the consequent loss of his mastery over his labour process; it was this loss that he was resisting in refusing to take to the filature whose 'superior technical efficiency... was indisputable.'[31]

This was a stimulating argument. And yet its basic premise was not very different from the one it had sought to challenge, in that it too held up artisans' psychology as the factor inhibiting the rapid diffusion of a superior technological device, though of course psychology was differently interpreted in the two versions. In both versions the economic logic of the filature technology *versus* 'country wound silk' had been overlooked; for after all, the paradox of the situation was that the Indian artisans had tried hard to master that superior technology, presumably in the hope of improving their lot, and having mastered it they showed reluctance to use it. They discovered that given the particular context in which the filature had been introduced, the more they used that technology the more they lost out.

It is to this context that we turn for a possible third explanation.

We have noted above that after the assumption of *diwani* in 1765 the Company remitted the revenues home partly in the form of silk yarn which was then sold in the market. Clearly then its quality and its price must be competitive vis-a-vis the products of other regions in the market, the chief rival being the Italian silk. The Company sought to bring the quality of Bengal Silk at par with the Italian by using the services of Italian silk winders; the price could be kept under control by using the Company's new found authority under the *diwani;* at any rate, by virtue of being the bulk purchaser of filature silk for overseas market, the Company anyway had a monopsonic control over its purchase in Bengal and could therefor dictate its price. It was thus that the introduction of the filature coincided with administrative intervention to prevent the market from determining the price of its product.[32] Its price in Bengal had been predetermined by prices in the European market through the administrative mediation of the Company.

If the Company's Court of Directors in London constantly admonished its officials in Bengal to keep the price of filature silk low and screamed at any rise in it,[33] the officials were not loath to making some private gain either through private trade of their own in filature silk or through getting a cut while fixing the price.[34] Indeed, greatly concerned that the price of Bengal (filature) silk had, despite cheapness of labour, surpassed that of Italian silk, the Court of Directors ordered the Board of Trade to conduct an inquiry into the matter along detailed terms of reference.[35] The Board of Trade first 'misunderstood' the terms and, these having again been clarified, fell into deep silence. It had good reasons to, for as the Court of Directors discovered through its own investigations over the next three years, members of the Board of Trade itself indulged in widespread corruption leading to rise in prices. The Court of Directors' sense of outrage at its discovery need not surprise us. 'In short', it concluded, 'we have strong reasons for believing that scandalous and corrupt practices have prevailed in the provision of this branch of our investment (and which also leads us to suspect that like in every other branch)....'[36] The Company was thus faced with a dilemma: any rise in price, for whatever reason, would make Bengal filature silk uncompetitive in the market for which it was intended; and any lowering of it would drive the Indian artisans into winding country silk. Let me elaborate this argument.

Admittedly, owing to its superior quality the price of filature silk was higher than that of the 'country wound silk' in any one year as well as throughout the period for which data are available. However, compared to the country silk, the productivity of filature silk was much lower per unit of labour, as also per weight unit of cocoons. If a person could wind 4 skeins of silk off the filature in a day, he could do 12 of the country variety, or *khamru* silk.[37] Besides, a maund of cocoons yielded between 2.5 and 3.5 *seers* of *khamru* silk and a half *seer* less when wound off the filature. And then there was the 'waste silk' as a bye-product, useless for the buyers of filature silk but, weighing 2 to 3 *seers* for a maund of cocoons, its sale itself could meet the cost of winding *khamru* silk, leaving a wide margin of profit off the sale of 'country wound silk'.[38]

If the productivity differential between the 'country wound silk' and filature silk was in the ratio of 3 : 1, the price differential was on an average in the ratio of 1 : 1.25 as would be evident from the following table.

If this was the average price differential over ten years, for which data are available to us, in any particular year the ratio does not seem to have exceeded 1:1.5. When other 'side benefits' of winding country silk are added on to the higher productivity of labour, it should not have taken the artisan long to realize that the very success of the Company in limiting or lowering the price of filature silk would make the winding of country

TABLE

Year	*Country Silk* (*Rs. as ps per seer*)	*Filature Silk* (*Rs. as ps per seer*)
1774	9 to 10	14
1775	8-8 to 10-15	12-8 to 13-8
1776	8-8 to 10-10	Not available
1777	8-8 to 10-8	10-8 to 13-8
1778	8 to 10-8	11-6 to 12 (Yellow variety) and 13 (white variety)
1779	8	11-10 to 12
1780	8-6 to 11-2	11-10 to 12
1781	8-12-6 to 11-2	11-10 to 12
1782	7-12	8-12
1783	7-12	8-12
1784	7-12	8-12
Average	8-14-1	11-13-1

Note: The averages have been arrived at by taking the mean price of each variety for each year, adding all up and dividing them by the total number of years, that is 10, leaving the year 1776 out.

Source: Extract of letter from Secret Committee of the Court of Directors to the Governor-General in Council, dated April 1786, *General Letters,* vol. II.

silk far more attractive for him. The logic of this situation did not escape the Board of Trade. It noted with concern that 'In some places the manufacture of the Filature assortment has much decreased, whilst Bengal wound is procured in abundance and with less trouble in the provision than the other gives'.[39] More forthrightly, in a letter to the Resident of Radhanagar, it observed: 'The Board have seen with much concern the great decline of the Filature assortment of this Aurang. They cannot conceive the cause to be necessary and unavoidable but rather to have been in part as least the equal profit and grater facility of furnishing Bengal wound'.[40]

Theoretically two options were open to the Company—one economic, the other administrative. First was to promote the production of filature silk to the desired level by making its price attractive enough for the artisan to compensate him for the relative advantages of winding *khamru* silk. This, however, was ruled out by the compulsions of a highly competitive European market where the silk was ultimately to be sold. The other was to foreclose the market for *khamru* silk by administrative intervention. This, too, was quite impracticable, for while the company's jurisdiction was limited to Bengal in our period, the country wound silk had an all India market.[41] As it happens, the Company chose to make administrative intervention in exercise of the first option, namely determining the price of filature silk, without being in a position to control the economy of silk production as a whole. In resisting the general spread of a technology which they had done so much to learn the artisans were in fact resisting an attempt at their forced impoverishment in a situation that had not yet turned against them.

REFERENCES

1. J. Geoghegan, *Some Account of Silk in India Especially of the Various Attempts to Encourage and Extend Sericulture in that Country* Calcutta, 1872, p. 1.
2. Ibid.
3. W. Foster, ed., *The English Factories in India, 1618-21*, Oxford, 1906, p. 198.
4. F. Bernier, *Travels in the Mogul Empire*, tr. A. Constable, reprint New Delhi, 1972, p. 440.
5. J.B. Tavernier, *Travels in India*, vol. II, tr., V. Ball, ed, W. Crooke, reprint, New Delhi, 1977, p. 2.
6. Letter form Court of Directors, 16 March 1768: 'It is in the encrease of this Article of our investment that we chiefly depend for bringing home our Revenues, the Importation being a national benefit and the Consumption more unlimited than that of Manufactured Goods. You must therefore continue to bestow your greatest attention to it', *Fort William—India House Correspondence*, vol. V, 1767-1769. ed., N.K. Sinha, New Delhi, 1949.
7. Geoghegan, op.cit., p. 2.
8. Letter from Court of Directors, 17 March 1769, *Fort William—India House Correspondence*, vol. V.

9. Geoghegan, op.cit., p. 2; Letter from court of Directors, 17 March 1769, *Fort William—India House Correspondence*, vol. V.
10. General Letter, 31 January 1770, in *General Letters to and from the Court of Directors etc.*, 1765-1854, vol. I, West Bengal State Archives, Calcutta.
11. Detailed instructions were recorded by James Wiss with the Court of Directors and the Court of Directors in turn directed its Board of Trade 'not to fail to have them carried into execution', copy of General Letter from Court of Directors, 14 April 1779, *General Letters*, vol. I. Description of the filature is also given in N.G. Mukerji, *A Monograph on the Silk Fabrics of Bengal*, published in *Art in Industry Through the Ages*, vol. I, New Delhi, 1976, p. 33; H. Maxwell-Lefroy, *Report on an Inquiry into the Silk Industry in India*, vol. I, Calcutta, 1917, p. 17.
12. N.G. Mukerji, *A Monograph*, p. 15.
13. Extract of General letter from Court of Directors, 14 July 1779, *General Letters*, vol. I.
14. Ibid.
15. Extract of General Letter from Court of Directors, 11 April 1785, *General Letters*, vol. I.
16. Extract of General Letter from Court of Directors, 12 May 1780, *General Letters*, vol. I; Extract of General Letter from Court of Directors, 12 July 1782, *General Letters*, vol. I; extract of General Letters from Court of Directors, 11 April 1785, *General Letters*, vol. I.
17. Extract of General Letter from Court of Directors, 8 July 1785, *General Letters*, vol. I.
18. James Wiss in his instructions on reeling warns the Overseers to be very vigilant on this count, copy of General Letter from Court of Directors, 14 April 1779, *General Letters*, vol. I; also Extract of General Letter from Court of Directors, 12 May 1780, *General Letters*, vol. I, which bemoaned: 'The first reeling and Outside Coat of the Skein is good silk, but the middle which forms large part of the whole is found to be little better than rubbish'.
19. Extract of Postscript of Letter to Court of Directors, 27 March 1772, *General Letters*, vol. I.
20. Copy of Letter of Mr. Wiss to Court of Directors, 22 September 1783, *General Letters*, vol. I.
21. *Reports and Documents Connected with the Proceedings of the East Indian Company in regard to the Culture and Manufacture of Cotton-wool, Raw Silk and Indigo in India*, printed by Order of the East India Company, London, 21 December 1836, p. xiii.

22. Extract of General Letter from Court of Directors, 21 July 1786, *General Letters*, vol. II.
23. Extract of General Letter from Court of Directors, 24 May 1779, *General Letters*, vol. I.
24. Copy of letter from Mr. Wiss to Court of Directors, 26 February, 1784, *General Letters*, vol. I.
25. *Reports and Documents*, p. xxiv.
26. Minute of *Proceedings of the Board of Trade (Commercial)*, 6 December 1788, vol. 74, West Bengal State Archives, Calcutta.
27. *Proceedings of the Board of Trade (Commercial)*, 5 December 1788, vol. 74.
28. Extract of Postscript of Letter to Court of Directors, 27 March 1772, *General Letters*, vol. I.
29. *Reports and Documents*, pp. xiii, 62.
30. Geoghegan, op.cit., pp. 2-7, where the author has discussed in detail the efforts made by the Company, on acquisition of the *diwani*, to extend sericulture and improve silk reeling through the introduction of the filature. There is, too, an equally detailed discussion of the apathy and resistance to the Company's efforts on the part of cultivators and winders. This latter discussion is marked by Geoghegan's and other European commentators' explanation of resistance in terms of Indians' lethargy, superstition, ignorance, etc.
31. Sabyasachi Bhattacharya, 'Cultural and Social Constraints on Technological Innovation and Economic Development: Some Case Studies', *The Indian Economic and Social History Review*, vol. III, no. 3, September 1966, pp. 240-67.
32. The Company made several experiments from establishing its monopoly over the purchase of silk to promoting 'free trade' and re-establishing monopoly (this time termed 'exclusive right'), giving up and then reviving the *'dadni'* system, instituting the 'Agency' system, entering alternately into long-term and annual contracts with suppliers of silk, etc. See a Letter to Court of Directors, 15 March 1774, *Fort William-Indian House Correspondence*, 1773-1776, vol. VII, ed, R.P. Patwardhan (New Delhi, 1971); Letter to Court of Directors, 17 October 1774, Ibid; Extract of General Letter from Court of Directors, 11 April 1785, *General Letters*, vol. I; Extract of General Letter, 10 April 1771, *General Letters*, vol. I; Extract of Postscript of General Letter to Court of Directors, 27 march 1772, *General Letters*, vol. I; Extract of General Letter from Court of Directors, 8 April 1789, *General Letters*, vol. II; Extract of General Letter from Court of Directors,

5 July 1780, *General Letters*, vol. I, N.K. Sinha has usefully summarized the Company's 'Investment' policy experiments in the *The Economic History of Bengal*, vol. I, Calcutta, 1965, pp. 6-34.

33. Letter from Court of Directors, 2 February 1774, *Fort William-India House Correspondence*, vol. VII; Extract of General Letter from Court of Directors, 24 September 1783, *General Letters*, vol. I; letter from Court of Directors 11 April 1785, *Fort William-India House Correspondence*, 1782-1785, vol. IX, ed, B.A. Saletore, New Delhi, 1959.
34. Letter from Court of Directors, 7 April 1773, *Generral Letters*, vol. I; N.K. Sinha, *The Economic History of Bengal*, vol. I, pp. 89-90.
35. Extract of General Letter from Court of Directors, 24, September 1783, *General Letters*, vol. I.
36. Extract of General Letter from Court of Directors, 21 July 1786, *General Letters*, vol. II.
37. N.G. Mukerji, A *Monograph*, p. 30.
38. Ibid, p.29; Maxwell-Lefroy, *Silk Industry in India*, p. 19.
39. Minute of *Proceedings of the Board of Trade* (*Commercial*), 5 December 1788, vol. 74.
40. Minute of *Proceedings of the Board of Trade* (*Commercial*), 6 December 1788, vol. 74.
41. In 1789 one Sadanand Bandopadhyaya testified to the all-India network of Bengal's silk trade, *Proceedings of the Board of Trade* (*Commercial*) 13 March 1789, vol. 75. There is, besides, constant lament recorded in the *Proceedings* over the inadequate, and at times actual decline in the quantity of filature silk relative to 'the abundance' of 'Bengal wound'; see Letter of Resident at Kasimbazar, 14 November 1788, read on 4 December, *Proceedings*, vol. 74; Letter of Resident at Kumarkhali, 24 November 1788, read on 5 December, *Proceedings*, vol. 74; *Proceedings*, Minute of 5 December 1788, vol. 74; Letter of Resident at Radhanagar, Minute of 6 December 1788, *Proceedings*, vol. 74. The all-India market for Bengal's *khamru* silk was still operative in the second decade of the twentieth century, see N.G. Mukerji, *A Monograph*, pp. 27-28.